Clinical Sociology
An Agenda for Action

John G. Bruhn
Pennsylvania State University / Harrisburg
Middletown, Pennsylvania

and

Howard M. Rebach
University of Maryland, Eastern Shore
Princess Anne, Maryland

Plenum Press • New York and London

Library of Congress Cataloging-in-Publication Data

On file

ISBN 0-306-45448-3

© 1996 Plenum Press, New York
A Division of Plenum Publishing Corporation
233 Spring Street, New York, N. Y. 10013

Printed in the United States of America

To my mentors Paul Meadows, Jerome K. Myers,
and August B. Hollingshead

—JGB

To Katherine, and to my students

—HMR

Compassion's Edge

Compassion's Edge

Fellow-Feeling and Its Limits
in Early Modern France

Katherine Ibbett

UNIVERSITY OF PENNSYLVANIA PRESS

PHILADELPHIA

A volume in the Haney Foundation Series, established in 1961 with the generous support of Dr. John Louis Haney.

Published by
University of Pennsylvania Press
Philadelphia, Pennsylvania 19104-4112
www.upenn.edu/pennpress

Printed in the United States of America on acid-free paper
1 3 5 7 9 10 8 6 4 2

Library of Congress Cataloging-in-Publication Data
Names: Ibbett, Katherine, author.
Title: Compassion's edge : fellow-feeling and its limits in early modern France / Katherine Ibbett.
Other titles: Haney Foundation series.
Description: 1st edition. | Philadelphia : University of Pennsylvania Press, [2018] | Series: Haney Foundation series | Includes bibliographical references and index.
Identifiers: LCCN 2017033939 | ISBN 978-0-8122-4970-5 (hardcover : alk. paper)
Subjects: LCSH: French literature—16th century—History and criticism. | French literature—17th century—History and criticism. | Compassion in literature. | France—History—Wars of the Huguenots, 1562–1598. | Religion and politics—France—History—17th century.
Classification: LCC PQ239 .I23 2018 | DDC 840.9/353—dc23
LC record available at https://lccn.loc.gov/2017033939

For Éric

Contents

Introduction

Compassion's Edge

A man fixes his gaze resolutely on something beyond the edge of the page, his eyebrows drawn together in concentration, his eyes a little downcast, his mouth slightly open, somewhere between apprehension and alarm (fig. 1). This is a sketch in black chalk by Charles Le Brun, Louis XIV's favored painter, gathered in a collection used to teach other painters the proper representation of the passions. The drawing was not included in Le Brun's original lecture in 1668, but by 1727 it had been bundled into a volume with those that were and coupled with a text narrating it as "compassion," a label many subsequent critics have resisted on the grounds of the subject's fierce and unyielding aspect. And indeed, the head is very distant from our imaginings of the compassionate, especially the compassionate as framed for us by the sympathetic and sentimental eighteenth century.[1] Yet within its seventeenth-century context, the man's unyielding aspect is easier to understand: the drawing represents the austere masculine compassion central to discussions of the emotion in the seventeenth century, far from our current understandings of the term. In *Compassion's Edge*, I restore the severe face of early modern compassion, and suggest what we lose if we turn away from its historical significance.

This book pursues the varied inflections of the language of fellow-feeling—pity, compassion, charitable care—that flourished in France in the period from the Edict of Nantes in 1598, which established some degree of religious toleration, to the official breakdown of that toleration in 1685 with that edict's revocation. But this is not a story about compassion overcoming difference; rather, it's about compassion reinforcing divides. Where an eighteenth-century literature of sympathy is often imagined to usher in newly communal concerns, in earlier texts the language of fellow-feeling marks or

Figure 1. Charles Le Brun. Compassion: man's head in profile, facing left, 1690.
White paper, black stone, 20.6 cm × 20.2 cm. INV28324-recto-folio34.
Musée du Louvre, Paris, France. © RMN-Grand Palais / Art Resource, NY.

even brings about isolation. Instead of being a precursor to eighteenth-century
sensibility, early modern compassion stands as evidence of the persistently
painful residues from France's sixteenth-century wars. This emotional legacy
continues to shape the way we think about difference and our emotional response to it today.

Compassion's overarching affective grammar structures relations between the object of compassion and its subject, the compassionater. Yet this
clear grammar of suffering and response could also pivot: the early modern
adjectives *piteux* and *pitoyable* indicated both someone likely to show pity

but also someone who should be shown it.[2] Compassion's clarity is easily troubled by the fear that we might find ourselves no longer merely compassionate but rather the object of the compassion of others. Accordingly, much early modern writing about compassion attends anxiously to the proper disposition of the compassionate self, rather than to the suffering abounding in the period.[3]

For seventeenth-century writers, the categorization of the passions was central to moral and political discourse. Many texts, especially from the middle of the century, devoted themselves to the repetitive but compelling task of defining and distinguishing the passions, determining their origin, their manifestation, and the best way to control them.[4] But compassion was often not seen as passion in the way the seventeenth century understood that term, as something one undergoes despite one's judgment or will. Compassion is also a technology that governs social relations, bringing out the structural affiliations of affect. Its surprising cognitive coolness reminds us that Aristotle considered emotions to entail a form of evaluation, and early modern writings about compassion often evaluate the social status of those who are, as the expression of the time has it, "worthy" of compassion, "digne de compassion."[5]

In distinguishing between the deserving rather than the undeserving, the seventeenth century—perhaps as we do today—assessed suffering within a differentiating and distancing structure. If compassion appears ideally able to broker a bond, to serve as what John Staines has called for seventeenth-century England "one model for public politics," it also insistently returned its feeler—the compassionater—to a sealed-off space of reserve; its publicness served chiefly to reinforce already existing categories rather than to broker any new settlement.[6] Far from reaching out to the others for whom it feels, compassion often kept the other at arm's length. This is what I call compassion's edge.

In mapping both compassion's edge and its hinterlands, I range over a number of different genres, contexts, and geographies. Most of the forms of writing I describe were produced and read chiefly by a relatively small and elite circle, but they all represent ways of describing and responding to social or religious difference, and they suggest that very different groups—Jesuits, tragedians, nurses—all drew on the language of compassion to describe something particular about their group identity. In the texts discussed here we will see that emotional communities, to use Barbara Rosenwein's term, repeatedly define themselves as much by what others do not feel as what they themselves do; the figure of the pitiless is as important to this material as the pitier him-self.[7] These texts name and perform compassion in varied ways, across differ-ent genres; in some places they account or ask for compassion, in others they feature an economy in which it can be glimpsed. But for the most part they show compassion to be a sifting mechanism, operating on a spectrum of in-clusion and exclusion, and they suggest that outside the bounds of Catholic compassion lies the unassimilable Protestant, and more broadly the unassimi-lated remainders of the Wars of Religion. In *Compassion's Edge*, we hear from the Catholics who determine the official structure of toleration in this period, but we will also step past the edge to hear the Protestant response.

Early modern compassion's concern for the self nonetheless often en-tailed a surprising evacuation of the first person. The emotion historian Wil-liam Reddy makes a particular model of "first person, present-tense emotion claims," what he calls "emotives," central to the eighteenth century's emo-tional and political changes; in turn, this concept has become central to much work in the field.[8] In contrast, very few of the texts I describe ask for or otherwise voice compassion in the first person; instead, they describe, elicit, or reject it in the third person by making a set of structural generaliza-tions, with the compassionater as judge or appraiser. The second half of the book, however, shows a range of first-person requests for compassion, both fictional and painfully factual: novels, requests for religious tolerance, and transatlantic demands for assistance. If the first part of the book insists on compassion's rigorous grammar, the tough apportioning out of emotion from subject to object, the second suggests that movement to new genres and to new places might sometimes shift some of compassion's rigidity, restoring something of its unsettling promise. In these final chapters, beyond compas-sion's edge, compassion sometimes enables some form of change, be it aes-thetic or social.

"What is pity," asks Augustine in the *City of God*, "except a kind of fellow-feeling in our own hearts for the sufferings of others *that in fact impels us to come to their aid as far as our ability allows?*" (emphasis mine).[9] Versions of the opening of this question can be found anywhere in the early modern period; yet the second part, on our impelled movement to help, is often absent in seventeenth-century accounts.[10] Many of my texts show the compassionate as an observer from the sidelines, unable to intervene. Sometimes, instead, the compassionate action is shown to fail, or to have misunderstood the suffering it seeks to relieve. What can we make of this compassionate inaction or misfire?

The classicist Elizabeth Belfiore notes that "*Eleein* in Homer, unlike the English 'to pity,' is primarily to do an action rather than to feel a certain way. For example, to pity a friend fallen in war is to seek revenge."[11] Those of us less given to heroic valor may ruefully recognize themselves more in the regretful tone of the seventeenth-century French military man Henri de Campion, who says that seeing a war crime gave rise to "une pitié que je ne puis exprimer, mais l'on ne pouvait rien empêcher" ["a pity that I cannot express, but we couldn't do anything to stop it happening"].[12] In Campion's observation compassion sidelines us; that is, it makes us spectators, as in Samuel Beckett's *Not I* of 1972, in which Beckett calls for an onstage auditor, hooded, who makes a repeated movement which "consists in simple sideways raising of arms from sides and their falling back, in a gesture of helpless compassion. It lessens with each recurrence till scarcely perceptible at third."[13] These scarcely perceptible gestures are also operative in many of the texts I read here. Yet if in the seventeenth century it could be said that to move someone is also an action, then equally to be moved is sometimes, at some historical moments, all the action of which one is capable.[14] If initially I looked at early modern inaction in a slightly chiding way, feeling shamefacedly that compassion then and now should do more, I've come to be interested in the productive aesthetics of that helpless compassion and the sort of media it shapes, as well as in the scarcely perceptible spaces for gestures of fellow-feeling carved out behind compassion's edge.

Compassion's Reformations

The new language of compassion took shape in a post-chivalric, post-Reformation France; out of the horror of the Wars of Religion came new discursive strategies for imagining difference. Most scholarly work on compassion begins in the eighteenth century. Yet the particularity of compassion after the wars tells us something not only about the early modern period but also about the way we think about emotion and toleration today. *Compassion's Edge* tracks not the political history of toleration but its affective undertow, and in so doing suggests a different way to read the history of our own time.[15]

My focus is not on what happened during the Wars of Religion or at the level of political negotiation, but rather on the ways in which the wars and their aftermath figured affectively in time of (relative) peace throughout the seventeenth century.[16] For a long time scholars of the French seventeenth century seemed to have swallowed the monarchical propaganda of the period, according to which the Edict of Nantes signaled a new peace and prosperity for France, a period in which France could begin again. In the last decade or so, things have shifted; scholars have increasingly begun to weigh the difficult legacy of the wars and to push against this historical fiction of the tolerant tabula rasa. Jacques Berchtold and Marie-Madeleine Fragonard's volume on the memory and memoirs of the Wars of Religion painstakingly traced the ways in which the wars returned in subsequent historiography; Hélène Merlin-Kajman has argued that the classical tragedy, paradoxically a literary form associated with the seventeenth century's modernity, drags around with it the unburied body of the wars; Andrea Frisch has shown how seventeenth-century historiography and dramatic theory are, despite the injunctions of the Edict of Nantes, unable to forget the crisis of the sixteenth century.[17]

The language of pity and compassion certainly marks the traces of the wars and their divisions.[18] But in attending to early modern compassion I want to do more than sketch the history of a concept. In thinking through compassion, I look back to the degree zero of the wars: the distinctions painfully established and sometimes eroded between one side and the other. If the language of compassion takes shape amid the rubble of the religious wars, it does so because it is necessarily attached not just to a partisan theology but also more broadly to the nature of partisanship itself.

Compassion's restrictions help us trace another limited ideal of the period: tolerance as attitude, and toleration as policy. The toleration of religious difference was not, in early modern understandings, a positive policy, even if we have been encouraged by Whiggish narratives centered on toleration's intellectual heroes to think of it as such.[19] We think of tolerance as an absolute virtue, but early modern France reminds us that no such absolute obtains. For early moderns, to tolerate meant to suffer or endure, to put up with something but also to allow; it marked the acceptance of an unacceptable loss of Christian unity. Until the end of the sixteenth century the term "tolerer," to tolerate, signified the ability to bear one's own pain, and the modern notion of an acceptance of a belief other than one's own separates only slowly from that first meaning.[20] In 1690 the French lexicographer Antoine Furetière puts it that tolerance is a "patience par laquelle on souffre, on dissimule quelque chose" ["patience with which one suffers and dissimulates something"], while the verb "to tolerate" marks a nonaction toward the other alongside whom one lives: "Souffrir quelque chose, ne s'en pas plaindre, n'en pas faire la punition. Il faut *tolerer* les defauts de ceux avec qui nous avons à vivre." ["To suffer something, not to complain about it, not to punish it. We must tolerate the faults of those with whom we have to live."][21] We can see such suffering at work in the *procureur* Omer Talon's infamous note of 1634: "Les Réformés ne sont soufferts que par tolérance et dissimulation, comme on souffre une chose qu'on voudrait bien qui ne fût pas." ["The Protestants are suffered only through tolerance and dissimulation, as one suffers something one would rather did not exist."][22] Furetière's declaration that in tolerance we must suffer those with whom we have to live is remarkably like his definition of "compatir," to compassionate, whose primary meaning he puts not as the positive virtue of sensitivity to suffering, but rather the capacity to "demeurer ensemble . . . sans se détruire l'un l'autre . . . Vivre bien avec quelqu'un" ["remain together . . . without destroying one another . . . to live well with someone"].[23] Both verbs, to tolerate and to compassionate, describe a base-level putting up with another's difference, a dealing with difference that might be understood on a national or a domestic scale; both might be heard in today's French formulations about the importance of the value of "vivre-ensemble," recently invoked in the court case *S.A.S. v. France* (2014) as a reason for Muslim women not to cover their faces.[24] Living together does not always mean to let live.

In the last twenty years historians have increasingly turned from high-minded narratives of toleration's virtue to attend instead to the "vivre-ensemble" of early modern civic life, looking at the pragmatic ways in which Catholics and Protestants got on with the task of living alongside one another, sometimes painfully: putting up with differences, observing the necessary distance for coexistence.[25] This book provides an account of the affective echoes of such civic projects. Both compassion and toleration were arm's-length pursuits, dispositions toward difference that leaned on much structural underpinning, and both defined from their edge. In early modern England, Ethan Shagan describes, "toleration was constituted precisely by normalising and naturalising its limitations."[26] Both toleration and compassion looked not to overcome gaps between selves but rather to observe a necessary distance, to mind the gap.

In looking at compassion's limits as an indicator of the limits of tolerance, I follow recent critiques of tolerance itself in trying to listen to different voices, rather than just according them a space apart from the norm. Kirstie McClure picks apart tolerance's significance in the history of liberalism by drawing in part on the tools of feminist critique, remembering Audre Lorde, who asked that her existence be more than just tolerated.[27] After 9/11, diagnosing

"something of a global renaissance in tolerance talk," Wendy Brown has argued that tolerance manifests "as a strand of depoliticization in liberal democ-
racies . . . construing inequality, subordination, marginalization, and social
conflict."[28] Brown's observation holds in both the United States and the
United Kingdom, although thinking about difference is mapped differently in
each tradition; in recent years the praise of tolerance has become a default response to fundamentalist separatism, much as an automatized "compassion
talk" has often surrounded the dismantling of state responses to social difference. The liberal tolerance Brown describes is often imagined to have been
established in response to early modern Europe's violent religious wars.[29] In
tracing the significance of compassion talk for the understanding of religious
and social difference in France after those wars, I point to an alternative genealogy for thinking through the affective promise of liberal narratives.

Compassion's Lexicon

You might already find my mingled use of the words "pity" or "compassion"
hard to tolerate. I began this project with just such an irritation, noting that
the seventeenth-century reception of Aristotle's *Poetics* translated the *eleos* of
the famous formulation *phobos* and *eleos*, fear and pity, sometimes as "pitié,"
sometimes as "compassion." In a first reading of those texts, seventeenth-
century usage seemingly did not engage what I took to be a common distinction today, where pity implies a hierarchical relationship and compassion a
more companionable sort of fellow-feeling (I return to that distinction in
Chapter 2).

Much of this book's work around lexical shifts arises from close readings
of genres that attend to compassion: dramatic and moral theory, religious
writing, the novel, pamphlet literature. But France's seventeenth century is
also a boom period for lexicography, and many of the dictionary definitions of
emotion were appropriating and recycling material from a range of genres,
making them something akin to commonplace books. Dictionary entries for
the terms of fellow-feeling show considerably more range and slippage than
we would give those terms today, making few firm distinctions: pity is described as compassion and vice versa, allowing for the emphatic hendiadys of
"pity and compassion" seen everywhere in this period. Furetière has compassion as a "mouvement de l'ame qui nous porte à avoir quelque pitié, quelque
douleur en voyant souffrir un autre" ["movement of the soul which brings us

to have some pity, some pain in seeing another suffer"]. Some lexicologists were keen to tip definitions immediately into solid theories, as in Richelet's 1680 entry for compassion, which gives a paragraph resembling the careful Aristotelian boundaries we will encounter in Chapter 2. For Richelet, compassion is an

> afliction qu'on a pour un mal qui semble menacer quelqu'un de sa perte, ou du moins de le faire beaucoup soufrir, quoi qu'il ne mérite nullement qu'un tel malheur lui arrive, à condition toutefois que celui qui a de la compassion se trouve en un tel état que lui-même apréhende qu'il ne lui en arrive autant, ou à quelqu'un des siens.

> [affliction one has for some trial which seems to pose a mortal threat to another, or at least to make them suffer greatly, even though they do not deserve such suffering; on the condition that he who feels compassion is in such a situation that he understands such a thing could happen to him, or to one of his own.]

In avoiding reducing compassion to any such singular and tightly defined story, my lexically eclectic gathering takes a lead instead from the definition of Cotgrave, who puts pitié as "Pitie, ruth, compassion, commiseration; charitie, kindnesse, or tendernesse of disposition; also, grace, clemencie, mercifulnesse." In English and in French in this period, compassion is a synonymically sticky cluster of terms.

These word choices work differently in different vernaculars. Marjorie Garber has shown how, in early modern English, compassion can imply a sharing of suffering or a feeling for the sufferer; only later, she suggests, did compassion take on the hierarchical feeling that I described above as pity, whereas sympathy retains fellow-feeling's affinity or likeness.[30] Compassion's history is inseparable from a history of translation. Béatrice Delaurenti describes how medieval medical accounts drawing on Aristotle turned to the vocabulary of *compassio* rather than *sympathia* to describe an almost contagious physical response to the movements of another, so that subsequent scholastic inquiry drew together the terms of antiquity and Christian resonances.[31] In Delaurenti's account, medieval compassion is a response something more like what seventeenth-century France would term sympathy. In French, sympathy seems to retain its corporeal, material sense longer than it does in English. During the seventeenth century it refers chiefly to the complementary properties of two objects, before a further exploration in the eighteenth century sets it on a more familiar philosophical path.

If in early modern French the use of these terms—pity, compassion, commiseration, mercy, and so on—is often mixed, we can nonetheless distinguish between something like what I would call a pity function and a compassion function: a narrow and hierarchical response or a broader, more generous one. I use the terms "pity" and "compassion" interchangeably throughout this book, insisting on one term when it seems to me (as it will in Chapters 2 and 5) that there is something at stake for early moderns in the way they use it; by the end of the century, for example, in part owing to the texts I describe in Chapter 5, pity (and "pitoyable" along with it) has taken on the language of scornful hierarchy, along the lines of Mr. T's famous "I pity the fool." Compassion talk also has complicated bodily origins which sometimes signify politically. Early moderns spoke of the bowels of compassion, "les entrailles" from the Greek *splagchnizomai*, to be moved to one's bowels, thought to be the seat of love; yet John Staines suggests that in England Protestants tended to avoid the term, indicating "the growing distrust of the visceral notion of compassion" that accompanied the rejection of Catholic Eucharistic forms. (In French, however, Protestants were seemingly less squeamish: the Bible de Genève gives "entrailles de compassion.")[32] If compassion itself is, in its best iterations, a form of translation—a movement across difference—it seems important to look both to its terminological particularity and its range across several conceptual positions.[33]

Some thinkers have depended on fierce distinctions between compassion and pity. Hannah Arendt, for example, distinguished between them, arguing that in attending to the singular or particular case, compassion is not generalizable, whereas pity reaches for a wider remit. In Arendt's reading, stemming from an engagement with Rousseau, compassion "abolishes the distance, the in-between which always exists in human intercourse," and this proximity erodes its ability to act politically: "Because compassion abolishes the distance, the worldly space between men where political matters, the whole realm of human affairs, are located, it remains, politically speaking, irrelevant and without consequence."[34] Compassion is "to be stricken with the suffering of someone else as though it were contagious" (75); pity, in contrast, shuns such touch, "keeps its sentimental distance" (79), and "can reach out to the multitude," though Arendt contrasts pity chiefly with a solidarity able to establish a more effective "community of interest." Arendt separates solidarity, compassion, and pity as different categories: "Terminologically speaking, solidarity is a principle that can inspire and guide action, compassion is one of the passions, and pity is a sentiment" (79).

Arendt's distinctions have inspired many. They are central, for instance, to the arguments made by Luc Boltanski, who, drawing on eighteenth-century discussions of pity, inquires into the ethical implications of seeing suffering at a distance, on-screen, without the possibility of direct action.[35] And something like Arendt's contagious compassion—but this time more eagerly embraced—returns in Jean-Luc Nancy's preface to his essay "Being Singular Plural," where he makes a plea for compassion as a social force, specifying "but not compassion as a pity that feels sorry for itself and feeds on itself. Com-passion is the contagion, the contact of being with one another in this turmoil. Compassion is not altruism, nor is it identification; it is the disturbance of violent relatedness."[36] For Nancy, compassion's contagion makes it a powerful force for rethinking the social; his scorn for pity, on the other hand, looks something like the long-standing Stoic rebuff of such an emotion.[37] Nancy's sacramental language makes of compassion a kind of political theology.[38]

Compassion's Histories

Of course, the philosophical battle over pity's scope and value has a long history.[39] Plato's scorn for pity can be countered with Aristotle's careful protection of its status by virtue of catharsis's regulatory machinery.[40] The Stoics dismissed pity's femininity and its attachment to external effects. In *De clementia* Seneca contrasted pity, an emotion to be rejected, and clemency, a rational and helpful one: "Misericordia non causam, sed fortunam spectat; clementia rationi accedit." ["Pity regards the plight, not the cause of it; mercy is combined with reason."][41] As Staines notes, this distinction between looking at (*spectat*) and rationally considering is significant, for the history of compassion is entangled with concerns about spectatorship.[42] Seneca further recommends that the merciful Stoic can relieve another's tears but not add his own to them. This concern over spectatorship, alongside the dismissal of a gendered pity, became central to seventeenth-century debates, which put the Stoic rejection of pity in fraught relation with Christianity's exhortation to charity.

The eighteenth century continued this anxious consideration of spectatorship, but a defense of pity became central to philosophical debate about the social bond.[43] Increasingly in eighteenth-century usage the term "sympathy" gains ground; if compassion referred to a shared suffering of pain, this model of sympathy could involve the sharing of any kind of emotion. David Hume's *Treatise on Human Nature* (1739–40) thinks through a fellow-feeling built on affinity and relation: "We have a lively idea of everything related to us."[44] Hume's exploration of sympathy's structure is not limited to the sharing of one emotion but addresses rather the communicative contagion that takes place between different selves, asking how the contagion praised by Nancy and feared by Arendt comes about. Hume also introduces a nuance that takes us closer to the hierarchy we hear in the language of pity today, addressing a kind of pity close to dislike. Rousseau's stance is mixed. Whereas in his *Discourse on Inequality* (1755) the naturalness of pity underwrites every social good, thus moderating our tendency to self-love, in his antitheatrical *Letter to D'Alembert* (1758) he fears that the pity felt by a theater audience might forestall any emotion leading to a real-world response to suffering.[45] In the *Theory of Moral Sentiments* (1759), Adam Smith praised compassion, placing the emotion as a crucial building block of what he calls the "immense machine" of human society. In Smith's usage, pity and compassion are broadly interchangeable terms, whereas sympathy indicates the sharing of any emotion. Kant distinguished between an admirably free and rational sympathy, to be considered as a duty, and a less admirable communicable or contagious compassion, which he saw as potentially "an insulting kind of beneficence, since it expresses the kind of benevolence one has toward someone unworthy, called *pity*."[46] Not every subsequent reader welcomed the Enlightenment embrace of fellow-feeling. Nietzsche, no friend to Rousseau, brushed aside this exploration of pity's social benefits, castigating pity (and his teacher Schopenhauer in so doing) as "the most sinister symptom of a European culture that had itself become sinister."[47]

Despite Nietzsche's best efforts, though, many theoretical discussions of emotion today draw squarely on eighteenth-century vocabularies and histories. The critical predominance of a secular eighteenth-century sympathy and sentimentalism, as well as a later and looser vocabulary of empathy, has obscured the particularity of seventeenth-century fellow-feeling and its religious battles.[48] Accounts of humanitarianism, for example, often trace a secular and Enlightenment origin for such debates, with Jean-Jacques Rousseau and Adam Smith as their tutelary figures.[49] Yet the religious battles of the Reformation and Counter-Reformation provide an alternative if unhopeful genealogy for our own concerns about a response to suffering. In early modern theological debate about compassion, a tentative theory of global justice begins to make itself felt. Early modern Jesuits, launching their missionary projects even as they worried about the state of their order in Europe, inquired into the nature and extent of our obligations to others whether they be the proximate poor or the distant needy (Chapter 3). We could say that global justice theory is a secularized theological concept.[50]

Likewise, the language of the *human* and of *humanity* arises out of bitterly sectarian battles. To speak of "humanity" suggests that one abandons any claim to particularity or partisanship, but like the term "compassion" the language of the human often crops up just at the moment that its potential fails. For some of my writers, the human is held up as an ideal against the animal, the beastly, or the stony; for others, it is contrasted with a machine-like calculation.[51] For a rare few (the dramatic theorist André Dacier in Chapter 2, for example), the "human" refers to the contingencies of lived lives; for many, it is hailed as an easy universal even as it pushes away the suffering of actual humans. Yet for those in imperiled circumstances, like the Protestant refugees of the late seventeenth century (Chapter 5), the language of the human provided an urgently needed vocabulary that broke sovereign stalemate and made international intervention possible.

Samuel Moyn has recently suggested that the language of human rights stems from a 1930s Christian Democratic insistence on the language of human dignity. "No one interested in where human rights came from can afford to ignore Christianity," he writes.[52] Moyn offers a powerfully disruptive model that suggests terms arising from theological doxa can reappear or be reappropriated in surprisingly different contexts. In offering sectarian genealogies for the way we today worry about the relative distance or proximity of suffering or the vexed language of humanity, I do not propose to source an unbroken intellectual history but rather to show how such languages can be swiftly appropriated and reworked for surprisingly varied political ends. In "compassion talk" (like that which Moyn identifies as a language of international politics in the 1990s), we must learn to hear a negative heritage of exclusion and restriction. The language of the human, like the language of compassion, is always polemical; we should eye it with care.

Compassion's Judgment

Calls to compassion often look to an emergency heroism, an immediate affective response, yet the discourse of compassion also builds a slow and enduringly rigid structure of appraisal.[53] Like other social mechanisms of the period, early modern compassion was dependent on a keen sense of timing, for compassionate and compassionable alike. For Saint-Evremond, even the solicitation of courtly pity depended on a particular temporality; he notes that a woman will take pity on her lover's punctual and discreet expressions of pain but will mock him if he moans too long.[54] Some writers presented compassion as an immediate affective reaction to suffering, akin to a passion that one undergoes. The Dominican Nicolas Coeffeteau thought of it as a reaction to suffering immediately present: "Il faudroit avoir renoncé à tous les sentimens de l'humanité pour n'avoir point l'ame attendrie de douleur quand l'image s'en presente à nos yeux." ["One would have to have had renounced all human feeling to not have the soul touched with pain when the image presents itself to our eyes."][55] Others imagined it as a mental exercise capable of a more careful and considered temporal reflection. Eustache de Refuge's *Traité de la cour* imagined compassion as a possible response to past, present, and future events: "Mais non seulement le mal present, mais aussi l'advenir s'il est proche nous esmeüt à pitié: comme semblablement le passé, s'il n'est trop esloigné de temps, ou que la souvenance en soit encore fraiche." ["Not only present suffering, but also the future if it is close moves us to pity; as does the past, if it is not too distant, or if the memory of it is still fresh."][56] For many writers, to label an action compassionate was chiefly to mark it as a heroic event, a one-off, like the incident of the Good Samaritan, around which many such discussions turned; compassion tends to be figured as an incident rather than a more general and steady disposition to be compassionate. It appears more often as noun than as adjective or verb. The quotidian labor of care carried out by women, for instance, something I take up in the final chapter, too often fell under the radar of the compassion label; it simply went unseen.[57]

In the early modern period as now, compassion is a judgment which, as Lee Edelman puts it, "commits us to a calculus, a quantification of the good."[58] Admirers of compassion often allow for compassion's appraising nature—even its narrowness—but they see that as part of compassion's skill and power. The philosopher Martha Nussbaum's account, for example, celebrates compassion as "a reasonably reliable guide to the presence of real value. And this appears to be so ubiquitously, and without elaborate prior training."[59] Nussbaum acknowledges that we need to be cautious about compassion, since as the Stoics argued our judgments show partiality and are "narrow and uneven" (386), and she imagines an ideal and properly instructed compassion that would not be subject to such conditions: "Compassion will be a valuable social motive only if it is equipped with an adequate theory of the worth of basic goods, only if it is equipped with an adequate understanding of agency and fault, and only if it is equipped with a suitably broad account of the people who should be the object of an agent's concern, distant as well as close" (399). Nussbaum reads the altruism available through a properly trained and properly deployed compassion in the light of a Rawlsian understanding of justice, and she concludes that "compassion makes thought attend to certain human facts" but suggests that to do more than this it must take on a larger theory of "desert and responsibility" (342). The seventeenth-century compassionate judge or careful appraiser—always a man—who figures throughout my chapters would certainly like to imagine himself in these terms, even if his improvisational and contingent judgments often remind us of compassion's partiality.

Nussbaum's normative distinction between weaker (more immediate) and more valuable (reflective) compassions pursues the same urge to distinguish that characterizes the debate about compassion from Aristotle on. In contrast, I want not to make normative claims about compassion itself, but rather to suspend judgement about its virtues even as I trace what its limitations can tell us about early modern France.[60]

Compassion's Gender

Most seventeenth-century instances of the compassionate subject describe men, although before that point compassion is often a female virtue, associated especially with devotion to Christ. But in the wars of religion, compassion is wrenched away from that private devotional context to become a masculine and public emotion, brokering a public religious compromise. This regendering of compassion is central to my story.

In late medieval Europe, compassionate devotion to Christ was chiefly marked as women's work.[61] Sixteenth-century compassion, too, is insistently feminine, whether within a devotional or a Petrarchan context in which women are asked to take pity on their lover's sufferings, a scene stitched throughout Renaissance love lyrics and reimagined in Marguerite de Navarre's *La Coche*, which both represents and elicits a mutual pity between women, with the queen herself promising three weeping women that she will suffer "grant compassion" ["great compassion"] with them.[62] In these instances, compassion is women's domain: embodied and forming a particular form of Christian or courtly community.

In the early seventeenth century, this embodied feminine compassion is still central to the writing of Pierre de Bérulle, founder of the Oratorians and a key figure in postwar French repositionings of state and religion in the role of confessor to the newly converted king, Henri IV.[63] In a meditation entitled "Des souffrances de la Vierge compatissante à son Fils," probably from around 1615, he suggests the particular role female compassion might be imagined to play in the theological mystery of the Incarnation. Bérulle posits that the flesh of Jesus is also and quite literally the flesh of his mother, specifying that the two do not share the same flesh "selon l'animation" ["in life"] but rather "selon l'affection" ["in emotion"].[64] This maternal version of the corporate communion makes the mother the essential compassionate because of her embodiment, and makes the primal mothering scene into one of emotional labor: because of Jesus, after Jesus, she gives birth only to pain.[65] It suggests that emotions come about through a physically embodied sharing, an understanding also key to the work of Nicolas Malebranche, an Oratorian philosopher active half a century later.[66] Since Bérulle's works circulated in manuscript form among Oratorians, Malebranche might well have been thinking of his incarnate maternal compassion when he declares that the greatest of all human unions is that between the mother and the child in utero. But Malebranche's pivot from maternal compassion to other forms of emotion also tells us something about the regendering of compassion in seventeenth-century discourse.

Like many seventeenth-century thinkers, Malebranche was insistent that the emotions and experiences of pregnant women affected their unborn children.[67] These theories of maternal impression were understood to form part of what contemporary scientists termed "les principes mécaniques de compassion" ["the mechanical principles of compassion"].[68] Although Malebranche begins his discussion of compassion with this maternal body, he then branches off to consider compassion as a larger moral concern. For Malebranche, compassion is always an incarnate suffering which begins in the body. If we see someone hurt, we might also feel a twinge—especially, of course, if we are one of those "personnes delicates, qui ont l'imagination vive, et les chairs fort tendres et fort molles" ["delicate people, with a lively imagination, and very tender and soft flesh"].[69] And where the body leads, the emotions follow: "Cette compassion dans les corps produit la compassion dans les esprits." ["This compassion in the body produces compassion in the mind."][70]

In distinguishing between types of compassionate, Malebranche, like other writers of the period, suggests that women and children will be especially prone to such delicacy, such that they will "machinalement" ["mechanically"] respond to sights of brutality, even when exercised only against animals, which in turn are "que des machines" ["only machines"] (281). (Think of Agnès in Molière's *L'École des femmes*, whose compassion even to animals marks out her vulnerability; she can't see a chicken die without weeping, she says, so when a man tells her he suffers for want of her love she is dead meat.)[71] On the one hand, Malebranche's attentive praise of the unique bond between mother and child, worthy of the praise of God and man, proclaims women to be central to compassion; on the other (and in keeping with Stoic tradition, though he was usually opposed to it) he distinguishes between masculine and feminine experiences of compassion.[72]

Here, as elsewhere in the period, women's animality places them outside of the reason that the seventeenth century saw as central to the proper procedures of compassion. In early modern French discussions of compassion, the compassionates are mostly men, even if sometimes maternal figures both despised and praised recur as a motif in their theories.[73] In the descriptions of the proper sort of compassion that feature in the first half of this book, the body disappears, and with it women's significance.

Women as objects of compassion feature frequently as literary topoi throughout the materials I explore. More than one of my austere compassionates will remember Dido with tears in his eyes, recalling Augustine's reading of Virgil in so doing. (In contrast, Heather James argues that in early modern England Dido becomes a figure for compassionate response to suffering, and that such a response was, in English texts, gendered female.)[74] Leah Whittington describes how boys in humanist classrooms were often invited to take on the characters of suffering women from antiquity, suggesting, "The humanist schoolroom . . . was a laboratory for compassion."[75] Yet those who exercise or, as in Whittington's example, learn to perform compassion are gendered male. Where eighteenth-century compassion will, via the new language of *sensibilité* and sentimentalism, return to the domain of women and move back into the female body, made visible by a woman's tears, the male compassionates I study here might well have nodded at Bérulle's maternal incarnation, but they set their own emotional practices resolutely apart from the bodily compromise it suggests.

In the final chapter, however, I suggest that away from theoretical discussion, away from metropolitan France, and away from what has come to be our canon of the period, women's writing on their own compassionate practices sometimes spoke of a less restrictive compassion, one able to bind people together instead of hold them apart. In proffering this difference I mean not to cling to an essentialized gendering of emotion but to complicate the rigors of compassion's edge by approaching it from a different perspective and via a very different territory.

One woman central to the writing of emotion in this period makes only a fleeting appearance in this book: Madeleine de Scudéry, briefly discussed in Chapter 2. Yet Scudéry, the great architect of civility, and her salon women set the terms for many of the emotional concepts of the period, most famously in the *Carte de Tendre*, or map of the land of tenderness, which features in her beloved midcentury novel *Clélie, histoire romaine* and which mapped emotional vocabulary for women and men for decades to come. Scudéry's key term is "tendresse." To arrive at that tenderness, we learn from our heroine Clélie's map, we must pass through certain named practices: show "petits soins" ["small cares"], send a "billet doux" ["love letter"], demand "exactitude" ["exactness"], or demonstrate "constante amitié" ["constant friendship"].[76] Tenderness might seem akin to compassion, and indeed Eric Langley's reading of Shakespeare shows that in English the two concepts are elastically intertwined, *tendering* a new vision of the self.[77] Scudéry's French tenderness, however, is a practice of civility built through outward performance rather than by interior movement. Scudéry's civil practice suggests itself at various moments in this book. For some figures I discuss, especially Pierre Nicole (Chapter 2), a true inner compassion is importantly nourished out of worldly civility. But figures like Nicole remain attached to an anxious theological dialectic between inner emotional fidelity and outward show, whereas Scudéry's graceful secular gestures do not dwell on such a fear. Since I (like many other new friends of the period) first learned to think about emotion in the seventeenth century from Scudéry, I hope that the admirable Clélie will understand me when I say that compassion's edge and its troubled hinterlands are scarcely set out in her map, even if I hope to show the routes between them on another occasion.

Compassion's Present Time

In 1640s Paris, Thomas Hobbes set out a classification of different sorts of grief: "griefe for the calamity of another is Pitty, and ariseth from the imagination that the like calamity may befall himselfe, and there fore is called compassion, and in the phrase of this present-time a fellow-feeling."[78] Hobbes's observation that a response to another's suffering stems from a fear for the self is common to the period; it stems from Aristotle's reflections on pity in both the *Rhetoric* and the *Poetics*, and I discuss its implications in Chapter 2. Hobbes tells us that the phrase "fellow-feeling" is "of this present-time," and he is etymologically correct in that: the term was a seventeenth-century neologism.[79] But we could also say that compassion's anxious recourse to the self is also always a reflection on our own present time, wherever we find ourselves. Lauren Berlant writes that scholarly work on compassion is necessarily a history of the present because "the word *compassion* carries the weight of ongoing debates about the ethics of privilege."[80] Each present time—and perhaps our own time is in particular connection to that of Hobbes—produces a form of compassion adapted to its own moment.

In today's present time, compassion is certainly familiar currency. A University of California research project, for example, has devoted itself to "the deep roots of human goodness," fusing cognitive research with a social task by sharing "inspiring stories of compassion in action."[81] A MOOC (massive open online course) at Wesleyan asks students worldwide to perform a day of compassion as their final assignment, with a prize at the end, thus blending virtue and strategy in a way that would have appealed to the seventeenth century.[82] This affective optimism spills over into popular work like Jeremy Rifkin's *The Empathic Civilization*, which asks breathlessly, "Can we reach global empathy in time to avoid the collapse of civilization and save the Earth?"[83] Rifkin's staging of a temporal drama alerts us to the centrality of heroic moments in studies that are pro-compassion, and suggests how easily such work can be exploited by those in power. The rhetoric of compassion is equivalent to the dangerous rhetoric of the "necessary" in its capacity to spur immediate political action in whatever sense the orator feels it should be directed.

Compassion is also big business. A Charter for Compassion, started by Karen Armstrong, with the Dalai Lama as mascot, rubber-stamps various institutions and companies as compassionate.[84] The charter's website provides a range of case studies as part of a "business compassion reader," showcasing figures such as John Mackey, CEO of Whole Foods, who promotes executive sleepovers as a bonding experience. There's a burgeoning field of therapeutic self-compassion, too. Paul Gilbert's 2009 *The Compassionate Mind* draws on a liberal narrative of progress, calling for "the start of a compassionate awakening."[85] Self-compassion's emphasis on doing things for oneself, on the self-training of what two practitioners call "portable therapy," is entangled with the swiftly instrumentalized languages of cognitive behavioral therapy and mindfulness; it speaks of a moment at which larger social structures are failing many in need, where mental health is something one does, entrepreneurially, for oneself.[86]

This self-reliance recalls the language of American compassionate conservatism in the 1980s, when the influential evangelical Marvin Olasky set out the relations between compassion and enterprise. Effective compassion, Olasky argued, needs forms of nonpublic affiliation. Families work best when they help themselves, and compassion works best when women don't take paid jobs but can organize soup kitchens instead.[87] Such language, writes Berlant, "resituates who the subject of compassionate action ought to be," turning that much-touted hardworking family into the focus of our care.[88] This entrepreneurial compassion was revived by George W. Bush and has become standardized across party lines. Twenty years after Olasky, Barack Obama declared the United States to be competitive and compassionate, and in 2011 the UK's David Cameron called for a "modern compassionate conservatism."[89] This neoliberal compassion is always quantifiable. Cameron even suggested that nurses should be promoted on the basis of their relative compassionate capacity (an early version of this quantification of care appears in Chapter 6).[90] If compassion is meant to rally political sentiment in positive ways, pity—or its lack—is used today in a way that recalls the partisan rhetoric of the Wars of Religion. The day after the November 2015 attacks in Paris, then president François Hollande called for an "impitoyable" ["pitiless"] response to the terrorists, making an absolute affective division between two sides. The language of fellow-feeling, and its threatened lack, is central to contemporary modalities of political life that seek to create and maintain partisan divides to political and military ends.

How have scholars responded to this present time's insistent language of compassion? If the Enlightenment probed compassion's place in a rather abstracted social bond, in recent years scholars working on the underside of normative national cultures have proffered more specific critiques of contemporary compassion. Where a 1990s interest in trauma sought to operate or provoke compassion, more recent work seeks to study its effects.[91] In these scouring readings of the contemporary, compassion blinds us to larger asymmetrical relations and to historically embedded structures of power. For both French and American critics of compassion, compassion is an antipolitics which focuses on particular cases of need instead of establishing wider political responses to inequality or suffering, but the difference in their approach tells us something of how difference itself is conceived in each national tradition.

In readings of French situations, an attention to compassion's particularity allows us to see the frays in the apparently seamless universalism of the republican ideal. Through a compelling analysis of governmental and journalistic discourse, the anthropologist Didier Fassin explores the tensions between compassion and repression in immigration and asylum policy, reading immigration law as an oscillation "between a politics of pity and policies of control."[92] Miriam Ticktin pursues these insights by focusing on the French "illness clause," a humanitarian exception in France's 1998 immigration laws allowing suffering undocumented migrants to be granted immigration rights as a compassionate response to their particular need.[93] Ticktin argues that compassion is "inherently exclusionary" since in determining the morally legitimate suffering body the possibility of larger and more collective forms of change is reduced. The body for whom the state feels compassion is, as Ticktin puts it, a victim without a perpetrator.[94] Ticktin argues persuasively that this does not mean we should abandon care and compassion but that we must think about how "we might care differently."[95]

In contrast, during and after the Bush years, U.S. scholars like Lauren Berlant and Lee Edelman have traced what Berlant memorably calls "compassion's withholding" in recent American history.[96] For Berlant, "reparative compassion"[97] has been central to liberalism's attempts to grapple with the racial violence of American history: "Compassionate liberalism is, at best, a kind of sandpaper on the surface of the racist monument whose structural and economic solidity endures."[98] In a similar vein, Lee Edelman has explored "compassion's compulsory disavowal of its own intrinsic callousness"; Edelman gives as an example the Catholic Church's proffering of compassion to homosexuals only if they deny their sexuality.[99] U.S. critiques of compassion often interrogate uninflected whiteness or heteronormativity, showing compassion to be a move that seeks to silence difference.[100] "What if," Berlant asks, "it turns out that compassion and coldness are not opposite at all but are two sides of a bargain that the subjects of modernity have struck with structural inequality?"[101]

Compassion is a key site for scholars who, like Berlant, cluster around what might loosely be called affect studies. If an emotion is understood to belong to an individual, to usher out from an interior core, then affect work has a rather different configuration, unattached to the self or the subject that might produce one of Reddy's first-person emotives, instead emerging socially, extra-individually, often bodily.[102] Thinking about affect enables us to read feeling within larger transpersonal or social networks and relations; it erodes our notion of what Elspeth Probyn, writing on Deleuzian affect, calls "the boundedness of bodies."[103] And compassion, of course, is a feeling dependent on sociality—it takes place because of a being-in-relation with another—even though it does not always signify a fellow-feeling or feeling together as much as a feeling about another or even a judgment on another's feeling.

Affect work has tended to focus on contemporary cultures, and it is no accident that it has burgeoned in the United States since 2001, drawing on our own (often negative) emotions in relation to larger political situations. But the term has an important early modern heritage, derived loosely from Baruch Spinoza via Gilles Deleuze; it offers an occasion to put the early and late modern in a necessary and charged relation to one another. The early modern, read through the lens of affect studies, is not the birthplace of rationalist subjectivity as much as a moment when various assumptions about the relation of emotion to reason, or to body, or to self, had not yet hardened into familiarity.[104] Where older models of emotion history imagined rationality to be set firmly against feeling—perhaps most of all in seventeenth-century France, the imagined home of a rigidly overdrawn Cartesianism—more recent work has eroded this distinction, which does not hold in many early modern texts.[105] Recent work on the seventeenth century suggests that early moderns thought of what we now call the emotions as having a more social, more bodily, and more cognitively significant status than that rigorous divide would suggest.[106] Reclaiming the early modernity of affect prompts a very different history both of early modern France and of critical theories of emotion.

Compassion's Forms

Compassion is itself a medium, reaching for common ground between two parties. This book traces not so much the experience of compassion's historical phenomenology (to use the term of Bruce Smith) but rather the way we know compassion through particular media, and in particular through the medium of the printed book and its various expositional devices.[107] How do early modern texts in their various genres and material forms—books, pamphlets, staged plays—represent and construct compassion? The compassion I dissect here lives textually, but it frequently draws on books about "live" rhetorical persuasion, our oldest models for reflecting on the emotions, and that relation between performed gestures and the textual tradition is central to the weighing of the relation between inward emotion and its outward show in many of the texts I discuss.[108] Textual compassion strives to indicate movements of the body or modulations of the voice, and to do so it will often look to new forms of writing.

Compassion's forms also prompt us to look into the relation between reading and emotional response. There's a powerful and popular narrative about reading and compassion, which has it that we can learn to feel for others through reading itself. Martha Nussbaum's recent work on compassion, for example, glimpses compassion's breadth at work in art forms that bring us the experiences of people for whom we might not otherwise feel. Nussbaum calls us to build a "public culture of compassion" by building "a *bridge* from the vividly imagined single case to the impartial principle by challenging the imagination."[109] Nussbaum is not attached to works from any single place or period (though she has a preference for the nation-building nineteenth century), but other such narratives about reading have centered themselves on versions of the early modern, around the development of prose fiction.

In one such narrative about the eighteenth-century novel, the sentimental novel is a force for social good. Heroines swoon, are betrayed, die; readers weep, learn, and come together in so doing. This novel teaches its readers to feel, and through feeling to know themselves in relation to countless others. Through sentiment, through *sensibilité*, through sympathy, communities are formed; the reader becomes sensitive to a shared kinship, a gathering together of like-minded readers, a humming, caring hive of emotion which stands ready to be co-opted into all sorts of new social formations. This is a particularly hopeful narrative of the novel's progress, or rather of the novel's relation to social progress. In this story, readers cry over novels, but they learn from their tears and are able to imagine forms of social union hitherto unexpressed. This is the case for the novel made by Lynn Hunt in work on the invention of human rights.[110]

The psychologist Steven Pinker notes that literary scholars often resist such notions: "They see the idea as too middlebrow, too therapeutic, too kitsch, too sentimental, too Oprah."[111] I count myself firmly among the resisters such as Suzanne Keen, who in a study of readers has shown how empathetic reading tends only to reaffirm in-groups and out-groups.[112] Not all resisters of the Nussbaum/Hunt model are literary scholars. The historian Thomas Laqueur, for example, cautions that "sad and sentimental narratives can raise just as readily as lower the alterity threshold. The divide between who is in and who is out, between neighbor and stranger, is terrifyingly vulnerable and is secured by exactly the same means as it is breached in the name of humanity."[113] Again, the term "human" prompts us to read with caution.

Keen's and Laqueur's resistance draws on reception, real and imagined, but we can also resist the therapeutic model by attending to formal devices and structures. Insisting on the importance of "structures of identification," Lynn Festa's trenchant response to the sentimentalization of sentimentalism argues that eighteenth-century tropes and figures work to differentiate as much as to consolidate diverse groups.[114] Festa reads sentimentalism as "affective piracy," a system which usurps the voices of sufferers to insist upon "the humanity of the feeling subject"; she insists that "sentimental form institutes *restrictive* communities. Sentimental tropes . . . create the *semblance* of likeness while upholding forms of national, cultural, and economic difference."[115] Reading sentimentally reinforces difference rather than overcoming it.

How does early modern compassion function as form? In French writing a varied set of structures of compassion—modes of address, rhetorical set pieces, spatializations of affect—are built out of the techniques and aftereffects of the writing of the Wars of Religion. In Chapter 1, for example, we will see the way in which texts frame events as pitiful spectacles; that tableau of affectively fraught spectatorship will also structure the genre of the novel, which I discuss in Chapter 4. The structures of compassion are a *dispositif*, a set of formal contrivances for bringing a spectator into relation with an instance or idea of suffering; but that *dispositif* also shapes a disposition, a way of feeling. Where *sensibilité* lingers on the object, compassion constructs our relation to it.[116]

Throughout this book I suggest that a certain compassionate mode—not sentimental or contagious, but rather reserved and reflective—is figured by a particular way of reading and interpreting. In many of the texts discussed here, compassion is mediated through images or through other texts; characters frame their encounters with suffering as a spectacle, or philosophers distinguish a compassion elicited by tragedy from a feeling retained from the reading of a poem. These aesthetic experiences are not the contagious and community-building scenes imagined by the readers of sentimentalism. The compassionate mode of reception is not a form of fervent identification. Its readers mark an affective relation with what they read but keep it at a distance.

In *Compassion's Edge*, fictional representations of and theoretical discourse about compassion mingle, both participating in the construction of compassion's exclusions. The history of emotions has tended to disregard literary texts as sources.[117] Yet my aim in bringing these different forms of writing together is not to insist on literature's privileged perspective on the emotions; indeed, very few of the texts I read here come from what are usually understood to be literary genres. Instead, I want to insist that fictive representations and theoretical discussions of compassion in this period alike reflect on the emotional and ethical engagements of our modes of reading. Sometimes this reading-for-compassion is explicit, as it is in the multiple texts where theorists of compassion reflect on scenes of reading or spectating, on novels or on tragedy. More broadly, both kinds of texts suggest that compassion is a way of reading the other, of appraising and responding to signs of suffering that are imagined to figure a narrative. And if I read nonliterary texts with the perspective of my own literary training, sometimes pushing them out of their more usual places in an intellectual history, that serves to remind us that reading, like the compassion I describe here, is a contingent and partisan way of apprehending the world even as it reaches out to draw others in.

Compassion's Chapters

The first three chapters of this book establish the structures of early modern compassion as they unfold in early modern France, exploring compassion's edge and looking at the drawing of partisan distinctions and the theoretical structures generated by such distinctions. In the final three chapters, I suggest that those rigid structures are reworked in varied forms of early modern writing which speak from the sometimes more nuanced territory beyond the edge, looking at fiction, at writing about religious difference and transnationalism, and at writing from New France. In these liminal zones, I suggest that compassion's edge is still fiercely observed but also sometimes recuperated, even if only briefly. In some of this material, the compassionate gesture reaches across difference, although often with troubling results.

In the first chapter, "Pitiful Sights: Reading the Wars of Religion," I explore the topos of the pitiful spectacle that punctuates writing from the period of the wars on both the Catholic and Protestant sides. This pitiful spectacle became a key weapon in the affective policing of a divided France, across a range of genres and sectarian divides: from Ronsard to Montaigne, via Agrippa d'Aubigné. The pitiful spectacle functioned as an apparatus for the apportioning and directing of pity, underscoring the increasing partisanship of the wars. It also established response to spectacle as something central to the political life of the troubled nation. Through that figure, which returns throughout the book, the Wars of Religion make themselves felt repeatedly and affectively throughout the seventeenth century; the language of pity and compassion shapes the way the French negotiated both the wars and the difficult experiment with toleration that followed them.

In the second chapter, "The Compassion Machine: Theories of Fellow-Feeling, 1570–1692," I pursue the secular structures of compassion as they were explored by writers of moral and dramatic theory from the late sixteenth to the late seventeenth century: La Taille, Montaigne, Charron, Descartes, La Rochefoucauld, Esprit, Nicole, La Mesnardière, Corneille, Rapin, and Dacier. These very different writers all return to the structure of fellow-feeling set out in Aristotle's account of pity and terror in the *Rhetoric* and *Poetics*: we pity another's suffering and, in pitying, fear that the same might happen to ourselves. For some this structure makes pity into a narrow response to suffering, whereas for others the ritual observation of the same pairing leads to a broader reflection on human vulnerability. In tracking the variant breadth of pity over these theorizations, I trace the sharply structured constructions of compassion's edge.

In Chapter 3, "Caritas, Compassion, and Religious Difference," I ask how religious difference disrupted structures of proximity and distance, looking at Catholic and Protestant understandings of *caritas*, the bond of universal love. I describe the reach to universalism sketched out in the compassion theories of the Jesuits Jean-Baptiste Saint-Jure and Pierre Le Moyne, and the Capuchin Yves de Paris, but set them against writers who insisted that compassion was importantly differential: the Jansenist Blaise Pascal, the midcentury

Protestant theologian Moïse Amyraut, and the refugee minister Pierre Jurieu. How did such different early moderns imagine the "us" of their community to which a "them" stood in opposition? This theological gerrymandering of fellow-feeling—the re-ascription of sameness and difference—allows us to see something central to compassion's mechanisms. Even as compassion aspired to the universal, it betrayed its limits, and those limits eventually gave rise to another edge: the modern distinction between compassion and pity.

The final three chapters turn to varied textual instances of compassion, considering how generic or rhetorical structures (the novel, drama, journals) explore the hinterland behind compassion's edge. In the fourth chapter, "Pitiful States: Marital Miscompassion and the Historical Novel," I turn to the problem of misreading in seventeenth-century historical fiction, exploring Lafayette's careful experiments with the motif of failed compassion between husband and wife in the novellas *La Princesse de Montpensier* and *La Comtesse de Tende* and the longer novel *La Princesse de Clèves*. In moments of misplaced compassion or what I call "miscompassion" in the novellas, Lafayette draws on the tableau of the "pitiful spectacle," recalling the figure of Chapter 1; in so doing, she points her reader to a larger historical inquiry about coexistence in France after the Edict of Nantes. In the longer novel, she also builds a new aesthetic out of failed compassion.

Chapter 5, "Affective Absolutism and the Problem of Religious Difference," continues the dialogue between Catholic and Protestant writing seen in Chapter 3. The Revocation of the Edict of Nantes—which denied freedom of worship to Protestants and constrained them to convert—deployed a language of nonconsensual compassion, and I explore the ways in which the Protestants responded to this absolutist affect. The chapter begins with pro-Revocation material and then turns to Protestant accounts of the Revocation: Élie Benoist's *History of the Revocation*, Protestant pamphlet literature, and pastoral writings from Jurieu and Pierre Bayle. Lastly, in counterpoint to those polarized positions, I read the affective language of Jean Racine's play *Esther*, first performed for the king four years after the Revocation, and centrally concerned with supplication and religious difference. In moving between these shifting emotional rhetorics, we get a more complex picture of what I term affective absolutism.

My final chapter, "Compassionate Labor in Seventeenth-Century Montreal," crosses the Atlantic and turns to women's labor in texts addressed to women from the Hôtel Dieu, Montreal's first hospital. For the nuns that served as nurses, compassion was not the glancing product of a singular encounter but rather something that had to be reproduced in accordance with an institutional routine. I examine rule books sent from the nursing order's original French home, set against a journal (Marie Morin's *Histoire simple et véritable*) and letters produced in Montreal. Morin's settler story unsettles the textual rules of metropolitan compassion, and the consideration of care that arises from the Montreal material allows me to frame an epilogue about our own practices as readers of both the past and the present time. The austere compassion I trace throughout the book affords us a different understanding of early modern differences and how they still signify for us today. It also lets us think anew about what a compassionate poetics might mean for our ways of reading.

Chapter 1

Pitiful Sights

Reading the Wars of Religion

On dit prov. *Guerre et pitié ne s'accordent pas ensemble,* pour dire,
qu'Ordinairement à la guerre on n'est pas fort touché de pitié, et que
mesme il est quelquefois dangereux de l'estre.

[One says proverbially *War and pity do not go well together,* to mean
that ordinarily in war one is not much moved by pity, and that
sometimes it is even dangerous to be so moved.]

So a 1694 dictionary tells us.[1] In this opening chapter, though, and more
broadly throughout the book that follows, I investigate the ways in which war
and pity were necessarily connected in early modern France. I turn first to one
particular and powerfully formative intertwining of war and pity: the topos of
the "pitoyable spectacle" or "pitiful spectacle" that punctuates writing from
the period of the Wars of Religion on both the Catholic and Protestant sides.
This topos functioned as an apparatus for the apportioning and directing of
pity, underscoring the increasing partisanship of the wars. What did it mean
for history on both sides to be told with such repetitive recourse to the pitiful
spectacle?

The insistence on spectacle was a strange feature of printed texts about
and from the Wars of Religion, especially those by Protestants. These texts
often insisted on the verbal quality of their message, the senseless noise of
battle translated into words that could be carried like a militant gospel to
those ready to hear it. In the capture of one French town, wrote the Protestant

historian Simon Goulart, the streets resounded with sighs, with lamentations, yells and miserable groans, all mixed up together as a confused noise and strange *tintamarre* heard throughout the town. In short, Goulart concluded, "it was a *pitoyable spectacle*, a pitiful sight."[2] In Goulart's very typical formulation, noise becomes spectacle and spectacle in turn becomes words. The pitiful spectacle depends on the transubstantiation of the printed page. It is a thing witnessed by those present that through the medium of print becomes something readers, too, can look upon. (It is worth noting that Goulart wasn't there, either; he relied on others for his accounts.) But the reader's eye does not merely glance back to what is recounted; in painting such a sight, the author imagines a future for the scene of sorrow. The discourse of the pitiful spectacle imagines emotional spectators and readers, crafting a future in which the pain of the past will make itself insistently seen and heard and in the process will become central to the history of the wars on both deeply contested sides. In this chapter, I sift through the pitiful spectacle's appearance on the Catholic side (Pierre Ronsard, the genre of the *histoire tragique*, Loys de Perussiis, and Pierre de l'Estoile), before turning to the principal Protestant spectacle-shapers, Jean de Léry and Agrippa d'Aubigné, and then considering a rather different iteration of the topos in the *Essais* of the moderate Michel de Montaigne.[3] But before we hear from the partisans, I will try to give a less impassioned account of events.

It is hard to settle on any single account of the Wars of Religion, whose historiography has from the beginning been fragmentary and partial.[4] The writing of the wars involved conflicting and competing genres and voices, building to a cacophony of confused noise. The colloquy of Poissy in 1561, at which Catholics agreed to give the "parti protestant" or Huguenots a hearing, sought to establish some shared ground on forms of worship but was unable to do so. In 1562 Catherine de Médici's regency government introduced the Edict of Saint-Germain, which allowed a very limited freedom of worship for Protestants and encouraged tolerant relations between the two communities. Yet in March of that same year members of the ultra-Catholic Guise family household attacked a Protestant service and a massacre followed, opening what would be almost four decades of violence.

Historians sometimes distinguish between a series of wars—usually eight in total—each brought to a close by an edict or treaty, initially making concessions or granting amnesty to the Protestants and insisting on the forgetting of what had come before.[5] On each occasion the suppression of Protestant freedoms started up again soon afterward. In between the promised pauses, violence was widespread across most regions of France and across ranks, with hugely damaging effect on the noncombatants dragged in its wake. A particularly bloody turning point was the St. Bartholomew's Day massacre of August 1572, in which Protestant leaders and nobles gathered in Paris for a wedding between the king's Catholic sister and the Protestant Henri de Navarre were slaughtered by the Guise faction; approximately two thousand died in Paris and three thousand in the provinces.[6] The death and mutilation of the Protestant leader Coligny, a key event of the massacre, figured in Protestant martyrologies and Catholic celebrations for decades thereafter; the tortured body of Coligny frequently figured as a spectacle at the center of accounts of the wars from both sides, becoming what a contemporary described as a "spectacle à tout le peuple" ["spectacle for all the people"].[7] Huguenot strength was seriously diminished after the massacre, but the rancor and revenge stirred up by the events would prove central to Huguenot organization in the coming decades. In response to the increasing partisan violence on both sides, the years after Saint-Barthélémy also saw the development of a more moderate Catholic grouping who came to be known as the *politiques*; figures such as Michel de l'Hôpital and Jean Bodin began to look toward a secular state that would not be driven by religious factionalism.[8]

By the late 1570s the Catholic League, led by the Guise and now supported by Spain, opposed all concessions to Protestants and set themselves against the moderate king Henri III. In the subsequent impassioned battles between the League and the king, Henri was assassinated, as were the Guise; in 1589 the Protestant Henri de Navarre became king, to reign as Henri IV. The new king faced lengthy battles to win back his kingdom and his capital from the League supporters. Paris succumbed only after Henri's conversion to Catholicism; some provinces took longer, but by 1598 the Peace of Vervins marked an official ending of the wars.[9]

Henri's much-lauded Edict of Nantes of 1598 ushered in a series of concessions to the Protestant minority. Nantes was not the most generous of the wartime edicts, but it was the one that held at least for a while, for reasons of expedient timing perhaps as much as firm belief. It allowed for limited freedom of worship and the establishment for a series of years only of a number of Protestant enclaves known as safe cities. From that point on, Catholics and the Protestant minority were bound to share their differences, to live alongside each other and observe their distinctions instead of trying to overwhelm them. Yet in its spatialized model of forbearance, the working toleration established by Nantes also reified religious difference; what the French shared

was the observation of a lived rift. Toleration was an uneasy settlement between commonality and absolute difference. Together, everyone lived its differences, although some more brutally than others.

The pitiful spectacle, too, bound Catholics and Protestants apart. It was a
key weapon in the affective policing of a divided France, but it was also a
shared language that suggested the cultural common ground between the two
sides. Of course, Catholics and Protestants parsed the pitiful spectacle differently according to their differing views of the conflict. Yet for both sides pity
demarcated their political stand, allowing writers to shape their position in
relation to the conflict and to the community they imagined as their audience. In delineating the pitier (both represented in the text and looked for as
the reader), the pitied, and the pitiless, this language figured the larger factionalism of the wars and in so doing established fellow-feeling as something
central to the political life of the troubled nation.

Reading Spectacle

The political plaintiveness of the pitiful spectacle makes it an obvious ancestor
of the scenes relayed to the modern viewer by documentary photography or
reportage, popularly considered to be great motivators of humanitarian action. A critical discourse on documentary photography has raised questions
about the stakes and legitimacy of photographs of suffering and the way in
which they create or forestall community making. After 9/11 Susan Sontag
(following Virginia Woolf) asked to whom photographs of suffering are addressed: Who is the "we" targeted by such images?[10] Yet the sixteenth-century
discourse reminds us that images do not only draw on an assumed community; they also anxiously make and remake their community in a necessarily
continual process.

Sontag's essay also raises concerns about what she terms the instability of
compassion that arises on looking at suffering: "It needs to be translated into
action, or it withers."[11] The sociologist Luc Boltanski's work on the televised
spectacle of suffering takes a more flexible perspective on affective spectatorship, suggesting that the distinction between spectating and acting may not
be as straightforward as that envisioned by Sontag. For Boltanski, the spectator "can point towards" action when she is prepared to report what she has
seen; the sight of suffering, he suggests, demands that one speak about it.[12] Far
from the atomized compassionate response critiqued by Hannah Arendt,

Boltanski's model looks very much like early modern, and particularly Protestant, imaginings of the relation between seeing and doing, in which one singular report can rapidly be disseminated with great effect. In the insistently repetitive writings of the sixteenth century, emotion does not wither; it is ceaselessly renewable.

One might even imagine, Boltanski suggests, that emotion is in itself a form of report or commentary, a kind of action.[13] Likewise, sixteenth-century texts ask whether to be moved is also a form of action. The texts I read in this chapter worry over the relation between pity and action in different ways, and in so doing they set up a particular problem about readership. Is the reader called to action, or is a call to feeling enough of a response? What is it we do when we read, and can we imagine reading's compassion as an action in itself?

The question of reading is important: the pitiful spectacle calls us to look and read all at once. Sontag and Boltanski draw on visual models: photos or television. But in the Wars of Religion, spectacle is dependent on the word.[14] The spectacles conjured by Protestant and Catholic writers are tightly wrought texts that engage with visual material but also with a long tradition of rhetorical arts and the literary sources that displayed them. Writers drew on ancient models for envisaging the very notion of civil war. The Catholic Joachim Blanchon writes of "cette guerre Civille ou aultrement commune misère: Laquelle je compare et me semble fraterniser, ou encores estre plus cruelle, que celle dont a traicté Appian" ["this civil war or common misery, which I compare to and seems to resemble or be even more cruel than that which Appian described"].[15] Protestants were more likely to draw on Lucan's *Pharsalia*, the epic of choice for those on a losing side.[16] But both sides shared a deep familiarity with rhetoric as a training in the deployment of emotions, seeking to bring about a particular effect. Renaissance rhetorical texts and editions of classical rhetoric directed an increasing amount of attention to the emotions, setting out a series of protocols for arousing pity. Sometimes, the Roman rhetor Quintilian writes, an accuser might weep tears of pity for the guilty party he condemns, in order to provoke the judge's response, but this is a risky practice he warns us against.[17] At other moments the orator must adopt a persona in order to bring about pity in his listener, for Quintilian notes that first-person narrations are most apt to bring about emotion. But trying to evoke pity is a delicate task: the moment of compassion cannot last too long nor be too overplayed, and its timing is important.[18] Quintilian suggests that the proper punctuation of emotion will often depend on the careful use of visuals: the showing of a wound, the appearance of the client, and so on. The care in the proper distribution of these managed moments of pity is certainly key to the texts of the Wars of Religion, in which words recall bodily actions or gestures that denote emotion. But whereas Quintilian discusses how to deploy pity in the conclusion or epilogue of a trial, sixteenth-century writers distribute such moments throughout their texts, frequently repeating and re-cycling scenes from other writers even as they proclaim each scene they de-scribe to be superlative in the suffering it shows. In the arousal of pity, repetition is crucial.

Catholics: From Ronsard to the League

In Catholic writing, the arousal of pity tells us a great deal about Catholic understandings of their position relative to the fortunes of the nation. Al-though Catholic forces were frequently besieged, especially in the south, their political position was preeminent and they imagined themselves not as a party but rather as representatives of the whole; the Catholic voice imagines itself to be objective where the Protestant knows it can never be. In the first years of the wars, Catholic usage of the topos illuminates these Catholic assumptions about the national imaginary. In Ronsard's first of the *Discours des Miseres de ce temps* of 1562, written for the queen regent Catherine de Médicis in the first year of the conflict, France's ship of state has become a "piteux naufrage" (44) ["pitiful shipwreck"], and Ronsard bemoans that the situation of France is so dire that even her unfriendly neighbors "a nostre nation en ont mesmes pitié" (90) ["even have pity for our nation"].[19] To open the following poem, the *Continuation*, Ronsard invokes the affective horror of the wars by figuring the horror of he who could ignore them:

> Ma Dame, je serois ou de plomb ou du bois,
> Si moy que la Nature a fait naistre François,
> Aux siècles à venir je ne contois la peine
> Et l'extreme Malheur dont nostre France est pleine. (1–4)

> [My lady, I would be made of lead or of wood,
> If I, whom Nature made born a Frenchman,
> Did not, to the centuries to come, recount the suffering
> And the extreme unhappiness with which our France is beset.]

In the first poem France herself, the whole nation, is the object of pity because of her internal divisions; in the second, factionalism makes a conditional unpitier imaginable. This distinction between the sensitive pitier and the unpitying other will later come to full fruition in the partisan Protestant epic of Ronsard's great reader Agrippa d'Aubigné.

Yet if pity's grammar was shared on both sides, Catholic emotive language bemoaning the civil wars often looks rather more like courtly tropes than it does the epic models on which Protestants draw. Where Ronsard's love poetry, decades earlier, had drawn on Petrarchan tropes of the pitiless woman spurning her lover, now Ronsard set out the binaries of pitiful and pitiless in a martial context.[20] Wartime texts like the poem "Complainte sur les miseres de la guerre civile" set into Jacques Yver's *Le Printemps* of 1570, in which six nobles gather together to spin tales taking their mind off the war, consistently recycle the figure of the spurned lover, this time voiced by a distressed France: "Jamais de mon piteux œil / Ne se tarit la fontaine" ["Never shall my pitiful eye / See its fountain run dry"].[21] This is language that provides a familiar literary framework through which to understand France's crisis; it seeks not to shock but to console.

The Catholic language of pity also draws on a more generalized sensationalism stemming from the genre known as the *histoire tragique*, in which accounts of the wars blend in with other sorts of horror. In these stories pity marks the stakes of a story in which it is important to take sides. The *histoire tragique* displays horrors so that readers might be directed to the right— Catholic—path, and the represented and elicited pity displays the proper feelings we must show. The collections of *Histoires tragiques* (1559–60) by Pierre Boaistuau and François de Belleforest established the topoi of the genre just before the outbreak of the wars; as the wars evolved, so did the genre.[22] These stories often ended with a pitiful spectacle, a body over which readers were asked both to mourn and to reflect on their own Christian comportment. One figures a woman about to be executed who calls on her children to fear God "et que souvent ils eussent à se rémemorer ce piteux spectacle" ["and that often they might recall this pitiful spectacle"].[23] The genre was rapidly widespread and instantly recognizable, with each production vying for superlatives. A *Complainte pitoyable d'une damoyselle angloise qui a heu la teste tranchée* [*Pitiful complaint of an English maiden who had her head cut off*] published in La Rochelle in 1600 notes, "Entre les calamités plus pitoyables, qui sont arrivés en ce siecle au sexe feminin: Cestuy-ci me semble tres digne d'estre remarqué." ["Between the most pitiful calamities which have happened to women in this present time, this one seems to me very worthy of comment."] Like the versions forty years before, this story too ends with the family weeping over a body, and the insistence that "chacun avoit pitié et horreur d'un si piteux spectacle" ["everyone felt pity and horror at such a pitiful spectacle"]. This pairing of pity with horror draws loosely on Aristotle's pairing in the *Poetics*, in which the pity we feel for a sufferer is accompanied by a fear that a similar suffering may befall us (this pairing returns in the following chapter). It points to the beginnings of the language of tragic response that will structure seventeenth-century discussions of compassion, even if later French readers would likely have been familiar with the pairing as much from the *histoire tragique* as from more formal discourses on tragedy.[24]

In its insistence on the horrors of "this time," the story of the executed *Anglaise* is typical of the *histoire tragique*'s mingled methodology, in which ubiquity and horrific particularity are simultaneously underlined. The wars make themselves felt in such stories as both outlying horror and ever-present backdrop for "ce siècle," this present time. The Parisian Catholic Christophe de Bordeaux wrote chiefly about the wars, but in a *Discours lamentable et pitoy-able sur la calamité, cherté et necessité du temps present* [*Lamentable and pitiful discourse on the calamities, scarcities and necessities of the present time*] (1586) he offers a story that is both about the wars and yet displaces their details from their specific emplotments.[25] Christophe's account of the "temps present" moves through a number of famine stories from the Bible to Léry ending with the story of a woman who strangles her children because she has nothing to feed them. The Catholic Christophe even borrows the most horrific point of his story—a cannibal mother—from the Protestant writer Jean de Léry's ac- count of the siege of Sancerre, to which I will return later. Pushing Ronsard's more stately allegorical language into the realm of *faits divers*, Christophe piles up the language of fellow-feeling in a rush of hendiadys: he tells us a story "plaine de commiseration et pitié" ["full of commiseration and pity"].[26] The starving widow was refused "pitié et commiseration" (c3) ["pity and commiser- ation"] by others, and so, as frequent authorial nudges remind us, it will fall to the readers to supply the necessary emotion. A family who stitch themselves into their sheets and wait to die are "*chose si pitoyable* que je ne sache cueur si dyamantin qui ne fust rompu voyant une telle pitié" (a4) ["*something so pitiful* that I know no heart hard enough that it was not broken on seeing such a pity"]. Such language asks the readers to lean in to see the scene and test their hearts. The story denounces the hardheartedness of present-day France but also allows its readers—or spectators—a ghoulish thrill along the way.

The pitiful spectacle's many invitations to its readers suggest the extent to which this genre seeks to shape an ideal readerly community. The topos frames our viewing of particular sights: it builds careful sight lines along which our sentiment can be properly organized. Like many texts of the late sixteenth century, Christophe begins his account by addressing "lecteurs mes amis."[27] The ideal reader is the friend, a person on side with the writer. These texts build both ideal community and ideal reader at the same time and as necessary conditions of each other. With the reflowering of the *histoires tragiques* in the early seventeenth century, pitiful scenes are increasingly directed to our attention not by the characters but by the narrator. In François de Rosset's *Histoires mémorables et tragiques de ce temps* (1619) the narrator pauses to exclaim, "Démons de la douleur, génies effroyables, prêtez-moi vos plaintes lamentables, afin que je puisse dignement décrire cette pitoyable aventure!" ["Demons of pain, terrifying sprites, lend me your lamentable plaints so that I may properly describe this pitiful adventure!"][28] In Pierre Boitel's *Le théâtre tragique* of 1622 the narrator begins quite straightforwardly, "C'est ici une histoire digne de compassion." ["This is a story worthy of compassion."][29] The *histoire tragique* chivvies its reader into the proper affective stance, deriving some of its authority from the wartime need to choose sides amidst the difficulties of the "present time."

The clunky narratorial interventions of this sensationalist genre go on to shape more refined forms of fiction throughout the seventeenth century. In Boaistuau and Belleforest's 1559 collection of *histoires tragiques*, which piles up the possible instances of pity, a woman imprisoned writes to her jailer in the hope of moving him to "quelque compassion et pitié" ["some compassion and pity"] as "l'objet d'un si piteux spectacle" ["the object of such a pitiful spectacle"].[30] When the jailer reads her letter he is "surpris de grand sursaut car haine et pitié, amour et dédain (ainsi que dedans la nuée le chaud et le froid avec plusieurs vents contraires) commencèrent à se débattre et contrarier en son cœur" ["surprised with a great start, for hatred and pity, love and disdain (as clouds mix together heat and cold with several contrary winds) started to battle and contradict themselves in his heart"].[31] Here, the flickering of pity and its eventual loss shapes both a sense of character and our readerly response to such figures. Similar scenes in which women ask for pity and men respond with mixed emotions will in more elegantly poised prose punctuate the late seventeenth-century *nouvelle historique* and early novel seen in Chapter 4.

The demarcation of readerly community was particularly fraught in the

early years of the war. The pitiful discourse seen in wartime accounts like that
of Loys de Perussiis published in 1563 makes clear that distinctions between
Catholic and Protestant were fairly recent and somewhat porous. Loys writes,
he says, wearily, "aiant veu et ouy dire que le filz soit allé contre le père, les
frères et cousins l'un contre l'autre, amis contre les siens plus intrinsèques.
Brief ce n'ha esté que une propre guerre civile, sanglante et sans mercy" ["having seen and heard say that sons went against their fathers, brothers and cousins against one another, friends against their most familiar friends. In short it
had been a real civil war, bloody and merciless"].[32] In describing the "pitoyables tragédies" (430) ["pitiful tragedies"] inflicted on southern Catholics by
the Protestant regional majority, Loys gives up, faced with "tant d'autres cru-
autés que les escrivant la force me default, pour la pitié que mon ame en sent"
(404) ["so many other cruelties that I have not the strength to write them, for
all the pity that my soul feels for them"].

These the distinctions between Protestant cruelty and Catholic suffering
are, for Loys, not always absolute. In one dreadful battle, some of the Protestants turn out to be kinder than might have been feared. On seeing a Catholic
dangling from a rock, "Ce voyant lesdictz adversaires (parmy lesquelz se
treuvent quelques pitoyables) le firent secourir, et la vie luy fut sauve" (453).
["Seeing this the said adversaries (amongst whom were some men of pity)
rescued him, and his life was saved."] In this period, the usage of "pitoyable"
wavers between "object of pity" and "feeler of pity," with most usage still relating to object rather than subject. Fittingly, here the usage switches to the subject, and the surprise that the Protestant other might show pity suggests how
easy it would be for subject and object to change sides in these early years of
the civil wars.

Yet the Protestant pitier's emotional exception is made only for one individual; the rest of the Catholics are killed and floated downstream to Avignon,
with horns on their head and a mocking note in their hand, to be received by
the Catholic prelate Fabrice de Serbellon: "Voyant Monseigneur Fabrice ce
piteux spectacle, meu de pitié et de compassion, ordonna qu'ilz fussent tous
inhumes et ensevellis et honnorablement en terre sacrée . . . usant de son ac-
coustumée grandeur et clémence" (454). ["When Monseigneur Fabrice saw
this pitiful spectacle, moved by pity and compassion, he ordered that they
were all disenhumed and buried honorably in sacred ground . . . with his
usual grandeur and clemency."] The priest's response to something he sees
("voyant") recalls that of the exceptional Protestant who spared a Catholic in
seeing his suffering ("ce voyant"), but Loys makes clear that the Protestant

action is parenthetical where the Catholic is usual. Loys's praise of Serbellon's accustomed compassion is key to the rebuilding of a Catholic community in the Protestant-dominated district, where the prelate had recently arrived; he dedicates his book to him, building his history around a compassionate response that is both exemplary and entirely to be expected.

In Loys's account, compassion between Protestants and Catholics is possible only in an exceptional and singular instance which does not alter the terrible flow of events. We are reminded that the rift is recent, and left in a state of shock that such neighborly or even familial closeness has been so rapidly polarized by the early events of the wars. Pity marks the flickering of something that reaches across those boundaries, but it never manages to make room for a lasting understanding or peace. Loys's observation of that passing pitiful instant speaks of a relatively moderate Catholic positioning that can still imagine a compassionate gesture from the other side, something akin to what would later be the position of the "politiques."

This Catholic language of pity would also become ripe for exploitation by more extremist voices. In his *Registre-journal* written during the reign of Henri III, the moderate *politique* Pierre de l'Estoile recounts an incident that took place in the summer of 1587. The extremist League, the Guisard faction, had placed a painting in a cemetery showing the anti-Catholic cruelties of England's Elizabeth I, in order to whip up the crowd against the Huguenots. L'Estoile writes that when the "sot peuple" ["stupid people"] of Paris saw it, they fell for the Guise logic and cried out for war: "Il s'esmouvoit, criant qu'il faloit exterminer tous ces meschans Politiques et Huguenos." ["They were moved, shouting that all the wicked Politiques and Huguenots should be exterminated"]. In early modern usage, "esmouvoir" and "esmoution" refer primarily to unrest; the affective meaning of emotion comes secondarily to the sense of civil disorder, and L'Estoile suggests that here the crowd is moved to passionate unrest. In order to prevent this misuse of spectacle by the Ligue, the king's more moderate forces then had to act without themselves causing a spectacle; the king orders that the painting be removed "mais le plus secrettement et modestement qu'ils pourroient, crainte d'esmotion" ["but the most secretly and modestly as possible, for fear of emotion/unrest"].[33] L'Estoile clearly means that the king seeks to order unrest; but his text also suggest that such an "esmotion" can arise from the exploitation of what we today call emotion in the form of the pitiful spectacle. The Ligue respond to the king's gesture by turning the missing painting into an emotional ekphrasis, placing sonnets all over town:

Laissez cette peinture, ô Renars politiques,
Laissez cette peinture, en laquelle on void peints
Les spectacles piteux et les corps de sang teints,
Sang, dy je, bien heureux des devots catholiques.

[Leave this painting, you *politique* foxes,
Leave this painting, in which we see painted
Pitiful spectacles and bodies drenched in blood,
The blessed blood, I say, of our devout Catholics.]

Here in the Ligue account, the pitiful spectacle functions as a set term in which the target audience knows indisputably who is the object of our pity and who is responsible for such a situation.[34] Pierre de l'Estoile's response insists that the pitiful spectacle is dangerous propaganda; it must be skirted around by moderates and controlled lest the ignorant masses be abused. The two meanings of emotion, feeling and unrest, are all too easily brought into dangerous relation with one another.

Catholic usage and wariness of this language tells us much about the shaping of attention and affect in prose and political life of the period. But it was Protestant writers who rendered the topos in the most compelling style, often drawing across the party line on Catholic inspiration. In Protestant writing, the pitiful spectacle becomes a reflection not merely of contemporary France but a meditation on how affective sight lines can build and maintain a political community.

Protestant Pity

In the first decade of the wars, a moderate Protestant invocation of pity was almost indistinguishable from the language employed by Ronsard, forming a category described by the literary historian Jacques Pineaux as "chants d'appel" ["appeal songs"].[35] Reformist writers of this period sing for peace. Estienne Valancier's *Complainte de la France* of 1568 calls on the French people to stop the war and silence "les chants piteux / Que tu orras ici chanter la France" ["the pitiful songs / That you hear France sing"].[36] Likewise the moderate Protestant historian La Popelinière's *Vraye et entiere histoire de ces derniers troubles* of 1571, dedicated to the nobility of France, features an end poem praising the compassion of the young king and calling for peace.[37] In both these invocations, it is France herself that is the object of pity, and writers speak to and sometimes for an imagined whole of France. After Saint Barthélemy, however, a more embattled form of pity makes itself heard; its language, central to Protestant polemic and to the making of a more martial literature, slices into that imagined whole.

It is not coincidental that the discourse of the pitiful spectacle is so prevalent in Protestant writing, and it is not so merely because Protestant forces suffered the greater blows during the wars. Protestant thinkers were already highly ambivalent about the status of the image. Stuart Clark describes the Protestant reformation as a "shock to early modern Europe's visual confidence" that made vision itself the "subject of fierce and unprecedented confessional dispute."[38]

Where Catholic tradition had insisted that the sight of suffering alone was enough to affect and convert the onlooker, Protestant martyrologies like Jean Crespin's *Livre des martyrs* gave rise instead to a great outpouring of words. Protestant histories customarily added appendices of names of the sufferers, recording those unspectacular deaths that would otherwise have gone unnoticed. This genre of history forged Protestantism; it allowed a wider audience to bear witness to Protestant suffering, although they were not present at the scene. For Théodore de Bèze, leader of the French Protestant movement, historical writing allows for an expansion in time and space: "L'histoire est le seul moyen par lequel . . . l'homme peut cognoistre ce qu'il n'a oncques veu ni ouy, voire sans aucun danger, et trop mieux, bien souvent, que si luymesme l'avoit ouy ou veu." ["History is the only way that man can know what he has never seen or heard, with no danger, and better, very often, than if he himself had heard or seen it."][39] Reading grants a privileged perspective on events, and that perspective forms the Protestant community.

The texts that make the Protestant reader make clear the position from which they speak. Andrea Frisch has shown how the premodern witness is not an isolated individual but always what she calls "dialogic"; the witness's account draws attention to its status as something "overtly constructed and made."[40] This means that the witness must establish himself as part of the same group as his readers; he is trusted not because of what he says but because of who he is.[41] Thus in Jean de Léry's *Histoire memorable de la ville de Sancerre*, the address to the reader carves out the author's right to speak and to be heard based on his identity as a Protestant: "Pource que je suis, et seray jusques à la fin de ma vie, moyennant la grace de Dieu, du nombre de ceux qui font profession de la Religion, pour laquelle la ville de Sancerre a este ainsi

rudiment et estrangement traictee que la presente Histoire le contient." ["Because I am, and if the grace of God allows will be until the end of my life, one
of those who profess the religion for which the town of Sancerre has been so
rudely and uncouthly treated, as the present story tells."][42] Léry hopes that
those who have been there will be able to "recongoistre" ["recognize"] what
they saw, but his desire is also to expand the audience beyond the immediate
witnesses: "Mais il y a une autre sorte de gens auquels je desire aussi de satis-
faire, afin que de cette Histoire ils puissant recueillir le fruit." ["But there is
another kind of person I would like to satisfy, so that they may harvest the
fruit of this story."][43] Written after the Saint Bartholomew's Day massacre at a
time of horror for Protestant France, Léry's preamble presorts writers and
readers so that the right sort of history will build the right sort of religious
community.

This careful construction work comes with detailed attention to sight
lines and spectatorship, an attention to who sees what, and how. Léry's history
posits insiders and outsiders very clearly; he even supplies diagrams of each
military position he describes. Sancerre was the site of a siege famous for its
famine, which pushed a couple to cannibalism after the death of their daughter; the scene returns in innumerable texts of the period, including Christophe de Bordeaux's *Discours lamentable*, described above, and Théodore-Agrippa
d'Aubigné's *Les Tragiques*. Léry insists on the particularity of this French
crime:

> Car combien que j'aye demeuré dix mois entre les Sauvages Ameri-
> quains en la terre du Bresil, leur ayant veu souvent manger de la
> chair humaine . . . si n'en ay-je jamais eu telle terreur que j'eu fray-
> eur de voir ce piteux spectacle, lequel n'avoit encores (comme je
> croy) jamais esté veu en ville assiegee en nostre France. (147)

> [For though I lived for ten months with the American savages in the
> land of Brazil, having often seen them eat human flesh . . . I have
> never been as terrified as I was frightened to see this pitiful specta-
> cle, which had not yet (or so I believe) ever been seen in a besieged
> town in our France.]

This scene is the baseline Protestant pitiful spectacle to which many others
make reference; like the *histoires tragiques* which sometimes draw on it, it pairs
pity and terror in Aristotelian style but brings its horror home to "nostre

France." The spectacle is superlative, and signaled as such, but also paradoxically reiterable; pages later, Léry asks of still another scene, "Qui a jamais ouy ni entendu chose plus pitoyable?" ["Who has ever heard or listened to such a pitiful thing?"][44] The aural hendiadys (ouy, entendu) intensifies the urgency with which we are asked to listen. In its piling up of examples and its insistent hendiadys in describing each case, the pitiful spectacle is compassion as *copia*, a profusion that asks us to look back to painful memories even as we attempt to build France's future.

Another scene from Léry's account of the siege of Sancerre makes the pitiful spectacle into a sorting mechanism that sifts the right sort of spectator or reader from the wrong. He tells the story of Protestant townspeople up against Catholic forces, all of whom were barricaded into the castle. The townspeople go to the castle and parade old people, women, and children in front of the opposing forces, "pensans esmouvoir à pitié ceux qui estoyent dans les Chasteau" ["thinking to move those inside the castle to pity"].[45] Pity is structured around an inside and outside, and here those outside the circle ask to be let in. But the townspeople's attempts to soften the hearts of their opponents does not work; far from being moved to pity, those inside the castle throw things at them. In the history of the French pitiful spectacle, this invention of the pitiless *spectator* is the key Protestant innovation.

Agrippa d'Aubigné

Both pitiful sight and pitiless spectator are central to the most ferociously partisan of Protestant texts, Agrippa d'Aubigné's *Les Tragiques*. First composed starting in 1577, as he lay injured after fighting at Casteljaloux, d'Aubigné's text was unpublished until 1616, although fragments seem to have circulated in manuscript well before. The text's dizzying temporality is thus able to conjure up the bitter period of intense battles between Catholics and Protestants as well as its eventual end; in the preface "Aux lecteurs" d'Aubigné even claims that Henri de Navarre had read and reread the text before he took the throne in 1589.[46] Its title draws on the genre of the *histoire tragique*, but d'Aubigné is busy recycling all sorts of references from all sides. He uses Léry's account of Sancerre in one of his most searing passages on a cannibalistic mother; reaching across the sectarian divide, he also calls up Ronsard, to whose work he was dedicated and whose allegorical maternal France, coupled with Léry's cannibal mother, reappears in ghoulish format in his text.[47]

Most strikingly, d'Aubigné's text revels in a series of ekphrases, turning ghastly sights into words; four of the seven books (III, *La Chambre dorée*; IV, *Feux*; V, *Fers*; VI, *Vengeances*) are structured as a series of visual tableaux, satirizing an unjust justice and recounting martyrdoms and massacres.[48] The presence of these tableaux might seem jarring given Calvinist rage against artifice and ornament.[49] Yet in the *Tragiques*, visuality is redeemed for the Protestant reader. Ekphrasis and *enargeia*—the process of making visible—were central to the training of classical orators, and they shape what Simon Goldhill calls "a viewing subject."[50] These exercises were central to d'Aubigné's rhetorical training and to the drive of his poetical projects. In insisting on the shaping of the viewing subject, d'Aubigné's *tableaux* and their imagined affective response prompt us to a reflection on perspective.[51] In the *Tragiques* it is pity or its absence that allows us to gauge the presence of suffering; we know the violence of the wars because we are continually provided with spectators' reactions to it. The sight of the suffering body matters less than the emotional reaction—or mourned absence of such a reaction—to it.

The importance of the imagined spectator might seem to sit uneasily with d'Aubigné's famous call to his readers to abandon any hope of distancing themselves from the events of the wars: "Vous n'estes spectateurs, vous estes personages" (I:170). ["You are not spectators, you are characters."][52] The text urges Protestant readers to think of themselves positioned within the battles but at the same time asks them to look on at scenes presented through images, or indeed to look upon those who look on, making them into a hybrid and displaced spectator-actor. David Quint has suggested the Stoic who shows constancy faced with death as the ideal figure of the *Tragiques*, exemplified by the figure of Coligny, who is described in terms which recall Lucan's Cato.[53] To be an actor in civil wars, one must show constancy. But d'Aubigné's text complicates this inheritance by inquiring into the proper affective stance of those who *are* spectators and will never be anything else. Though he urges or praises constancy from actors, he also drafts the urgent necessity of an affective response to the wars.[54]

It is not enough, of course, just to be roused to emotion in seeing; the Protestant suspicion of illusion means that the connections between looking and feeling and acting must be carefully delineated. The text presents a clear rift between those who see poorly and those who see right. Sometimes the evil thrive, d'Aubigné tells us, but we must not let ourselves be fooled by thinking that such earthly success is all. In *Les Feux* the narrator drives away worldly illusions:

Si la prosperité dont le meschant jouit
Vous trompe et vous esmeut, vostre sens s'esblouit
Comme l'œil d'un enfant, qui en la tragédie,
Void un coquin pour roy . . . (IV:819–22)

[If the prosperity the wicked man enjoys
Tricks you and moves you, your senses are dazzled
Like the eye of a child, who in a tragedy
Takes a wretch for a king . . .]

This theatrical illusion is the model for bad seeing, in which we are fooled and
moved. In contrast, d'Aubigné proffers exemplars who see correctly. A son
whose weeping father has been condemned to die tells him:

Mon amour est esmeu, l'ame n'est pas esmeuë,
Le sang non pas le sens se trouble à vostre veuê:
Vostre blanche vieillesse a tiré de mes yeux
De l'eau, mais mon esprit est un fourneau de feux. (IV:937–40)

[My love is moved, but my soul is not moved,
My blood but not my judgment is troubled at your sight:
Your gray-haired age has pulled water
From my eyes, but my mind is a fiery furnace.]

This correct vision makes room for emotion—the response of love—but does
not trouble rationality; blood can boil and eyes can weep, but the seer is not
fooled and remains untroubled. This austere and distanced appraisal is the
model Protestant emotional response. Like that model son, even when they
suffered losses Protestants were so certain of their position as God's elect that
they could imagine themselves to have won a heavenly victory if not an earthly
one.[55] Against a background of such radical indifference to earthly outcomes,
Protestants rewrite the relation between affect and action. It is more important to *feel* properly than to have brought about earthly victory. D'Aubigné's
take on pity asks not only what sort of emotion might be the best response to
suffering but also what kind of an action emotion might be. Might that affective response alone be enough to guarantee the future of the Protestant
Church?

In d'Aubigné's telling the true distinction of the Wars of Religion is less theological then emotional. From his opening address to readers, d'Aubigné stakes his claim to wrangle with the emotions of his audience. People are bored of books that teach, he writes, and they clamor for something else, for the writer to "esmouvoir" ["move"] (Au Lecteur:13) them, even if seeking to move others might suggest "la passion partizane" ["partisan passion"] (AL:167), a label d'Aubigné takes on with gusto.[56] As it is for other writers of the wars, the pitiful spectacle is d'Aubigné's prime way to move readers. The first book *Miseres* is described as a "tableau piteux du royaume en general" ["pitiful painting of the whole kingdom"] (AL:134), and it opens the way for long sequences of tableaux which encapsulate the bloody action of the religious wars: allegories, portraits, dreams, and so on. Throughout these scenes, d'Aubigné forms the reader's properly directed emotion by labeling events with their affective force: readers are urged to look upon "Le massacre piteux de noz petits enfans" ["the pitiful massacre of our little children"] (I:408), or more generally on "l'estat piteux de nos calamitez" ["the pitiful state of our calamities"] (I:1207). This adjectival usage is compulsively partisan, and in its forceful repetitions it underlines the partisan structure of pity itself. In one telling couplet—"Quand esperdu je voy les honteuses pitiez / Et d'un corps divisé les funebres moitiez" ["When lost I see the shameful pity / Of a divided body the deadly moiety"] (I:131–32)—the rhyme words, pity and moiety, underline the affective distinctions and divisions at work. To pity is to observe a distinction between sufferer and observer; and to write about pity, as d'Aubigné does so insistently, is also to observe a distinction between those who pity and those who do not.

One key passage in *Les Feux*, detailing the execution of the English Protestant Anne Askew, sets out the clear structure of this affective otherness. When presented with the scene of her torture, this extraordinary exemplar takes pity on those who inflict pain on her: "On presente à ses yeux l'espouventable gehenne, / Et elle avoit pitié en souffrant de la peine / De ces faux justiciers." ["They present to her eyes the dreadful rack / And she took pity on them, feeling grief / For the false justice of her jailers"] (IV:161–63). In contrast, her jailers' anger blinds them to such generous emotion: "la passion desrobbe / La pitié de leurs yeux" ["passion steals / pity from their eyes" (IV:174–75). D'Aubigné presents us with a scene that ought to bring about pity but that instead underscores only the emotional gulf between Catholic and Protestant, in which one passion, an anger so great as not to need a specific name, drives out the more precise response of pity. In these pages, we know Askew is a martyr because of her eyes on heaven; we know the judge is a tyrant because of his pitiless response. As if to underwrite the correct way to look, we learn that God himself responds to the sight of the English martyrs with pity, seeing "deux precieux tableaux, / Deux spectacles piteux" ["two precious tableaux, two pitiful spectacles"] (IV:151–52). In looking without pity, the Catholic cuts himself off from God.

This identifying unpity structures the ethical world of the *Tragiques*. We recognize the enemy other by their lack of emotion faced with scenes that *ought* to bring about pity, scenes in which the ordinary affect of human intimacy is denied: "ces proches inhumains / Dessus ces tendres corps impiteux s'endurcirent" ["these inhuman neighbors / grew hardhearted and pitiless over these tender bodies"] (IV:1016–17); in battle the Catholics sound the noisy alarm "de peur que les voix tremblantes, lamentables, / Ne tirent la pitié des cœurs impitoyables" ["lest the trembling, lamentable voices / Pull pity from pitiless hearts"] (IV:569–70). It is not just historically identifiable characters who are marked out by their pitilessness; in *La Chambre dorée*, d'Aubigné sketches a series of pitiless allegorical figures: Cruelty, with a portrait of pity thrown at her feet (III:379); pitiless Stupidity (352); Ignorance, lacking pity (365); Ire, veiled "De peur que la pitié ne volle dans le cœur / Par les portes des yeux" ["Lest pity fly into her heart / Through the doors of her eyes"] (303–4). All of these figures refuse sight and in so doing refuse pity.[57] D'Aubigné places modern Protestant suffering as part of a long history of the elect; even the massacre of the Innocents "ne sonnoient la pitié dans les cœurs impiteux" ["could not sound pity from the depths of pitiless hearts"] (VI:468). Pitilessness places the enemy beyond the transhistorical bounds of humanity: "ce cœur sans Oreille, et ce sein endurcy / Que l'humaine pitié, que la tendre mercy / N'avoient sceu transpercer" ["this unlistening heart, this hardened breast unpierced / by human pity and tender mercy"] (VI:475–77). D'Aubigné wields the label of humanity not as a universalizing gesture but as another rhetorical weapon allowing him to distinguish between sides: on one side humans, on the other horror. He holds out the hope that pity will bring the other side round, that it may serve as a weapon of proselytization—"La je vis estonnez les cœurs impitoyables" ["There I saw pitiless hearts amazed"] (I:433), he writes of one moment of proper response—but such moments are always isolated. The pitiful spectacle allows us to distinguish between sides; it is a contrivance for the proper direction of attention, the apportioning and distribution of affect, and for the immediate identification of those who ally themselves against the true faith whether throughout history or in the present day.[58]

One particular pitiless figure in the *Tragiques*, whose presence reverberates throughout the text, is of particular historical significance for the French early modern configuration of pity: the pitiless mother. D'Aubigné returns to this figure again and again. In the opening pages of *Miseres*, he sets up France as mother. Later in *Miseres*, that maternal figure reappears in viciously deranged guise as the cannibal mother who eats her own child during a siege, and in order to act so dreadfully she must deny all pity even as she invites it:

> La mere deffaisant pitoyable et farouche,
> Les liens de pitié avec ceux de sa couche,
> Les entrailles d'amour, les filets de son flanc,
> Les intestins bruslans, par les tressauts du sang,
> Le sens, l'humanité, le cœur esmeu qui tremble,
> Tout cela se destord, et se desmesle ensemble. (I:505–10)

> [The mother, pitiful and wild, undoing
> The bonds of pity and those of family,
> The bowels of love, the filiation of her flanks,
> Her burning guts, through the leaping of her blood,
> The sense, the humanity, the moved heart which trembles,
> All that is tangled and untangled together.]

Yet here the pitiless mother, undoing the bonds of pity and the bowels of love (recalling the biblical bowels of compassion) is herself worthy of pity, "pitoyable et farouche." Even as her wildness places her beyond the bounds of humanity, she is still somehow within the reach of our emotion. D'Aubigné plays here on the twin valence of *pitoyable*, to be full of pity or to be worthy of pity, and lets us feel the painful balance between the two possibilities. This mother is not like the pitiless figures above; she undoes her pity from necessity. It is not the mother but an allegorized and agency-bearing hunger that is without pity:

> Cette main s'emploioit pour la vie autrefois,
> Maintenant à la mort elle emploie ses doigts,
> La mort, qui d'un costé se presente effroyable,
> La faim de l'autre bout bourrelle impitoyable:

La mere ayant long-temps combatu dans son cœur,
Le feu de la pitié, de la faim la fureur . . . (I:515–20)

[This hand was once used for life,
Now for death it uses its fingers,
On one side dreadful death,
But hunger on the other side torments without pity:
The mother having long fought in her heart
Against pity's fire and hunger's rage . . .]

The mother is herself divided, between love and the drive to survive, between the sweetly nostalgic sigh for the sustaining "autrefois" and her dreadful future. Unlike the allegorical pitiless women elsewhere in the text—Stupidity with her dead complexion (III:350–51)—this mother is still fleshly, still human even as she trembles on the border of humanity. This is a touched and touching figure, despite her horrific action. And where d'Aubigné's usual assignation of pity or unpity marks the absolute divide between Protestant and Catholic, here the mother's troubled unpity is a sign of her own internal divisions: she is both sufferer and causer of suffering, a Protestant who has lost her natural pity through no fault of her own. As d'Aubigné puts it, "C'est en ces sieges lents, ces sieges sans pitié, / Que des seins plus aymants, s'envole l'amitié" ["It is in these slow sieges, these pitiless sieges / That love flees from the most loving breasts"] (I:499–500). It is the times that are without pity, not the poor pitiful mothers. The sorting mechanism of pity fails for a moment as it encounters the troubled figure of the mother.

This version of the pitiless mother is, I contend, a historically significant figure. It recalls, of course, the figure of Catherine de Médicis, the queen mother reviled as pitiless by the Protestants. But more significantly it bitterly revises the allegorical figure of France as mother. D'Aubigné's dreadful imagining of this most inhuman and yet pitiable figure seems to mark a limit case that cannot be repeated. In sketching the mother who cannot show pity, d'Aubigné draws on seemingly unshakable gender norms to imagine the horrors of what history had wrought. In Léry's account of the siege of Sancerre, from which d'Aubigné draws this scene, it is a couple who eat their child. Here, d'Aubigné focuses on the woman alone in order to shock his readership more effectively. As Sarah McNamer has shown, late medieval and early Renaissance reckonings of pity and compassion drafted such emotions as the ultimate feminine virtue, stemming from a tradition of Marian worship.[59]

Such figures are frequent in France in the sixteenth century, too, but seventeenth-century compassion is largely a masculine preserve. Of course, theological battles between Catholic and Protestant had made the Marian figure more controversial. But I suggest that the compassionate as mother disappears chiefly because of wartime accounts such as that of Léry, and d'Aubigné's extraordinary pitiful rendering of them. After the cannibal mother, the representation of female compassion becomes impossible. To what new figure does d'Aubigné point in her place?

Another maternal scene suggests the new affective exemplar after the displacement of the compassionate mother. A mother divided against her maternity returns in different form with d'Aubigné's ekphrasis of the judgment of Salomon, where two mothers dispute their claim on one child:

> On void l'enfant en l'air par deux soldats suspendre,
> L'affamé coutelas, qui brille pour le fendre:
> Des deux meres le front, l'un pasle et sans pitié,
> L'autre la larme à l'œil tout en feu d'amitié. (III:725–28)

> [We see the child suspended in the air by two soldiers,
> The hungry sword, which shines ready to cut him in two:
> The faces of the two mothers, one pale and pitiless,
> The other, tears in her eyes and burning with love.]

The emotional rift between these two mothers recalls the divisions of France: on the one side pity and on the other the absence of affect. Both mothers are looking at the same thing, but they respond to what they see differently, figuring once again the absolute distinction between pity and unpity stitched throughout this text. Yet ultimately their emotional response is of less import than the careful response of Salomon the judge. Salomon judges not the mothers' actions but their affective response; in turn, d'Aubigné asks his readers to reflect on which kind of looking and which kind of emotional response entails that we will, at the Last Judgment, be judged to be right. In this settlement, as elsewhere in the period, the ideal compassionate is not the maternal nurturer but rather the cool-headed male judge who apportions affective resources; each side figures themselves as a Salomon, a judge able to respond to the emotion of others to good effect.

In these necessarily partisan accounts, the pitiful spectacle is always related to a structure of judgment.[60] It posits a binary of spectatorship—the good and the bad, the inside and the outside—and it polices the borders of that binary. But other moderate or *politique* writers imagined a different affective relation to the spectacle of the wars. In the next section I turn away from the pitiful spectacle that cries out for judgment to the account of the pitiful spectacle given by a retired judge: Michel de Montaigne. Montaigne's version of this language establishes a less partisan way of seeing and reading.

Pity and Reading: Montaigne

In "De la physionomie" (III, 12), an essay centrally concerned with the wars, the essayist Michel de Montaigne writes,

> Comme je ne ly guere és histoires ces confusions des autres estats que je n'aye regret de ne les avoir peu mieux considerer présent, ainsi faict ma curiosité que je m'aggrée aucunement de veoir de mes yeux ce notable spectacle de nostre mort publique, ses symptomes et sa forme. Et puis que je ne la puis retarder, suis content d'estre destiné à y assister et m'en instruire.
>
> Si cherchons nous avidement de recognoistre en ombre mesme et en la fable des Theatres la montre des jeux tragiques de l'humaine fortune.
>
> Ce n'est pas sans compassion de ce que nous oyons, mais nous nous plaisons d'esveiller nostre desplaisir par la rareté de ces pitoyables evenemens.[61]

> [As I seldom read in histories of such commotions in other states without regretting that I could not be present to consider them better, so my curiosity makes me feel some satisfaction at seeing with my own eyes this notable spectacle of our public death, its symptoms and its form. And since I cannot retard it, I am glad to be destined to be able to watch it and learn from it.
>
> Thus do we eagerly seek to recognize, even in shadow and in the fiction of the theatres, the representation of the tragic play of human fortune.
>
> Not that we lack compassion for what we hear; but the exceptional nature of these pathetic (*pitoyables*) events arouses a pain that gives us pleasure.][62]

Montaigne's discussion of spectacle distinguishes between reading accounts of change and *seeing* them with his own eyes; to this extent he stays within the rhetoric of the eyewitness so important to much writing of the religious wars. But his positioning as reader or witness is very different from that posited by partisan writers. Both reading and seeing allow him to exercise his curiosity, a notion that sets him apart from the partisan spectator. As Neil Kenny describes, early modern curiosity is not only the desire for knowledge; the term also marks a diligence or care (the terms are related) for the object of curiosity. In the sixteenth century it was frowned upon by Catholic and Calvinist orthodoxy alike.[63] Montaigne's curiosity to look upon the spectacle of the wars makes him an observer who is not disinterested, but neither is he blindly driven by affect. His reappraisal of the arousal of pity makes room for an entirely different sort of reading.

Montaigne continues with a statement of some embarrassment at how little these public misfortunes have cost him as a moderate sheltered from the effects of partisan opinion, concluding: "Aussi qu'en matiere d'interests publiques, à mesure que mon affection est plus universellement espandue, elle en est plus foible." ["Also, in the matter of public calamities, the more universally my sympathy is dispersed, the weaker it is."][64] Montaigne's pitiful spectacle allows for a less ferociously partisan response and affords its onlooker something almost pleasurable. Where the wartime rhetoric sought to direct and focus affective response, here Montaigne speaks of diffused affections. In this model, one can feel—pitifully, pleasurably—in response to what one sees, but this feeling does not compel communitarian identification nor partisan action. The *Essais* draft a new model of political spectatorship, moving away from the exemplary toward an imagining of things invisible to the public eye. In "De la gloire" (II, 16) Montaigne inquires into the status of deeds unwitnessed but not unwasted: "Combien de belles action particulières s'ensevelissent dans la foule d'une bataille?" ["How many fine individual actions are buried in the press of a battle!"][65] Where Protestant writers build a pitiful spectacle and imagine that the right sort of audience will come, Montaigne is uncertain that any spectacle can give rise to a predictable outcome. How many pitiful sights disappear without anyone being moved at all?

This hesitation about the legitimacy of the pitiful spectacle structures the extraordinary opening essay of Montaigne's *Essais*, "Par divers moyens on arrive à pareille fin," probably written in 1578 and first published as the opening to the first edition of 1580.[66] Montaigne begins the essay and his book by first explaining a military strategy and then complicating the notion that a strategy can be explained at all:

> La plus commune façon d'amollir les cœurs de ceux qu'on a offensez, lors qu'ayant la vengeance en main, ils nous tiennent à leur mercy, c'est de les esmouvoir par submission à commiseration et à pitié. Toutesfois la braverie, et la constance, moyens tous contraires, ont quelquefois servi à ce mesme effect.[67]

> [The commonest way of softening the hearts of those we have offended, when, vengeance in hand, they hold us at their mercy, is by submission to move them to commiseration and pity. However, audacity and steadfastness, entirely contrary means, have sometimes served to produce the same effect.][68]

Montaigne's exploration of how to soften a victor's heart is, David Quint suggests, a refraction of his thinking about and through the Wars of Religion.[69] But unlike the other accounts of pity we have seen stemming from those wars, Montaigne's essay does not let us rest with an easy distinction between subject and object of pity, pitier and pitied. And unlike most writers discussed throughout this book, he does not deliberate on how or when to grant compassion but rather on how to get it. Montaigne draws on the familiar language of writing the wars but also in this first essay of his book sets a deliberately new tone as thinker, writer, and perhaps most of all reader. "Par divers moyens" sets up reading as a form of response to the wars.

Montaigne's essay is in part, of course, a reading of and meditation on Seneca, whose essay "De clementia" ["On Mercy"] written for Emperor Nero famously distinguishes between mercy and pity in order to dismiss the latter.[70] In granting clemency, writes Seneca, we gain security and thus exercise a reasoned mercy; but in pity we lose that rationality and lose our security, too. Seneca's distinctions between different categories of emotion, attitude, and effect also structure Montaigne's essay, but where Seneca uses those distinctions to push some categories of emoters aside—notably those who respond to suffering but not its cause—Montaigne lets no distinction remains secure for long. He begins with the example of Edward, prince of Wales, hailed for his greatness, who responded not to supplications but only to the bold resistance of three gentlemen whose "notable vertu" ["remarkable valor"] eventually causes him to "faire misericorde à tous les autres habitans de la ville" ["show mercy to all the inhabitants of the city"].[71] Here greatness responds to the greatness it recognizes in others; compassion, in this instance, responds by following similarity.

The following example gives us the prince Scanderberg, who on the point of killing a soldier is struck by the "resolution" of his foe and desists. Here great nobility reaches across difference and responds to the great virtue of a common man; Montaigne notes that Scanderberg's refusal to act might be read differently by those "qui n'auront leu" ["who have not read"] (8, 3) the strength and valor of the prince, who might imagine his inaction to be a sign of weakness. In this phrasing, what we see is bolstered by reading; the text hesitates between imagining that we might read the person or have read *about* the person (Donald Frame translates the line in full as "who have not read about"). Montaigne puts the two practices—reading texts and reading people—in necessary relation with one another.

Earlier in this chapter we saw how compassion proceeds through and constructs rigorous social structures. In "Par divers moyens," Montaigne moves carefully through a range of such structures, trying out each variation in turn. Already in his first examples of mercy in response to audacity, we see the structural underpinning of supplication and response. In responding to another, we respond across or behind a mesh of similarities and differences: rank, gender, courage. In his third example Montaigne worries at the gendered distinctions between male virtue and womanly softness that are so important to the Stoic tradition: the "cœur magnanime" (8) of the noble women who "great-heartedly" (3) carry their duke and their households on their shoulders so impressed Emperor Conrad that his hatred for the duke is lost and he begins to treat them "humainement" ["humanely"] (8, 4).[72] Here the emperor responds across a gender distinction but within the circle of nobles. His human treatment is of humans who are, in some way, like him. In this example, you get a better result from your valor if you are the right sort of person to start with. Although Montaigne began by announcing that he would study "the commonest way," up to this point it looks as though the common way depends almost exclusively on being born noble.

From these historical examples Montaigne falls back upon himself, in what Quint has described as "from an ethical standpoint, the single most important contribution to the self-portrait that will be a major project of his book."[73] We swing from one perspective to another. Leaving behind the position of the vanquished, Montaigne notes that either supplication or Stoicism would undo him were he the victor, "car j'ay une merveilleuse lascheté vers la misericorde et la mansuetude. Tant y a qu'à mon advis je serois pour me rendre plus naturellement à la compassion qu'à l'estimation" (8). ["I am wonderfully lax in the direction of mercy and gentleness. As a matter of fact, I believe I should be likely to surrender more naturally to compassion than to esteem"] (4). This attitude is indeed something we see played out throughout the *Essais*, in his response to animal suffering in "De la cruauté" (II, 11), or in "De l'expérience" (III, 13) where he speaks of a "naturelle compassion, qui peut infiniement en moy" (1100) ["natural compassion, which has infinite power over me"] (1028) for those he sees suffering in war. This preferential option for pity is, he acknowledges, something that sets him apart from the Stoics, who "veulent qu'on secoure les affligez, mais non pas qu'on flechisse et compatisse avec eux" (8) [want us to succor the afflicted, but not to unbend and sympathize with them"] (4), and as he goes on to note it is "des femmes, des enfans, et du vulgaire" (8) ["women, children, and the common herd"] (4) who are most prone to it. He continues by turning to "ames moins genereuses," "less lofty souls", the "peuple" who might be imagined in Stoic terms to be prone to pity. Yet in the example of the Theban people, they too yield to valor rather than supplication: they respond sympathetically to difference rather than sameness, as does Montaigne.

What can we make of this aside on the self which surges up in the midst of the essay's strange dialectical proceedings? Montaigne's procedure in this essay is based on Renaissance rhetorical training.[74] Peter Mack suggests he takes his cue from the Renaissance rhetorician Agricola, who asks in *De inventione dialectica* "For if we are more likely to pity gladiators the less they beg for life, how much more will a very brave man who despises danger move us?"[75] But Montaigne's method also and more importantly suggests a particular disposition of the self. Quint argues that it is not only through commiseration that Montaigne eagerly takes up the "mollesse" or softness criticized by the Stoics, but also through his continual practice of seeing more than one side, practicing "mollesse" as what Quint calls an ethical pliancy.[76] Montaigne's acknowledgment of his own pity, and perhaps of his womanliness or vulgarity, is the pivot point of the essay: we pirouette from imagining the position of the pitied to that of the pitier and back again. Where the pitiful spectacles seen earlier in this chapter allowed for only one proper perspective, Montaigne allows himself to try out all positions in response, asking himself: Am I like this historical example, or unlike?

The sifting of similarity and difference that structures the essay's examples is also crucial as a structuring pattern within each individual example. Montaigne tries out the same but different story again and again in order to establish some sort of common rule for finding commiseration, the emotion which brings people together in common emotion. Distinctions of rank and gender are crucial to the careful choreography of sameness and difference in this essay. Sometimes the great are moved by great virtue (sameness), sometimes the people are (difference); sometimes the greatest, Alexander, is not moved by the valor of Betis for in his greatness he cannot see how uncommon it is: "Seroit-ce que la hardiesse luy fut si commune que, pour ne l'admirer point, il la respectast moins?" (9–10). ["Could it be that hardihood was so common to Alexander that, not marveling at it, he respected it the less?"] (5).[77] In moving through these examples, Montaigne essays the distinctions between pity and valor, victor and vanquished, noble and common, men and women. From this play of sameness and difference, we see the trickiness of finding a common ground from which one can acknowledge difference. Montaigne tries out different ways to make bonds signify something, looking at the connections between diverse historical examples or between diverse human positions and experiences. Where Seneca (and the Stoic tradition in general) dismissed compassion as a character problem, Montaigne reads it as a structural one. His essay explores not the intention of emotion but rather the edges of its complicated organizational patterns.[78]

Montaigne eventually rereads and revises one essay into another as he adds a palimpsest of objections to his original premise. In parsing these examples, Montaigne gropes his way toward finding a pattern of similarities, examples that can be followed or understood, only to break that pattern in later revisions of the essay by proffering up differences: in the B text (the revision of 1588), the great Alexander who shows cruelty to the obstinate Betis; in the C text (the revision of 1595), Dionysius the Elder who drowns the valorous Phyto because although he, as a great man, is unmoved by Phyto's valor he fears that the rank and file might admire it. (Dionysius, like Montaigne, fears what will come from spectacle, even if his reaction to that—to kill Phyto away from view—is not necessarily what Montaigne, whose vulgar "mollesse" makes him more akin to the soldiers, would admire.) In a final addition to the essay, Dionysius is moved to act against Phyto because he is a reader, this time reading not the foe but rather the emotions of his soldiers (i.e., reading their reading of the enemy):

Dionysius, lisant dans les yeux de la commune [la foule] de son
armée qu'au lieu de s'animer des bravades de cet ennemy vaincu, au

mespris de leur chef et de son triomphe, elle alloit s'amolissant par l'estonnement d'une si rare vertu. (9)

[Dionysius, reading in the eyes of the rank and file of his army that, disregarding their leader and his triumph, they were softened by astonishment at such rare valor.][79]

Reading, then, is necessarily a form of interpretation and judgment of events: a method that can lead to widely diverse ends, since we can never be sure what will stem from such readings.[80] In the example of Dionysius, it is a way of responding to "la commune" and acting against them; but it is also, contradictorily, a way of establishing some sort of commonality. If Montaigne's essay reads and rehearses the structures of compassion, it also reaches across them to imagine the sort of common ground between different sorts of text and between writer and reader that can be shared in the process of essaying and reading.[81] Montaigne's opening shot of the *Essais* functions as something like a rhetorical *captatio benevolentiae* to garner the goodwill of his audience. By setting out his own vulnerability, he also asks the reader to take mercy on his book.

Montaigne returns to this link between reading and compassion in an essay that has often been read in a pair with "Par divers moyens": "Divers evenemens de mesme conseil" (I, 24).[82] He begins with the story of François duc de Guise, the notoriously unmerciful leader of the Catholic extremist faction, and describes his clemency to someone who has plotted against his life, noting without further comment on Guise's reputation that this did not save him from another and this time successful attempt on his life. This story becomes part of a larger meditation on fortune, a question brewing in "Par divers moyens" but brought to explicit articulation here. Montaigne notes that fortune has a large part in both writing—which escapes from the author's intention—and in military enterprises. But in both, he counters that the capacity to read—to sift and to judge—is something more within our own control. Thus, "Un suffisant lecteur descouvre souvant és ecrits d'autruy des perfections autres que celles que l'autheur y a mises et apperceües, et y preste des sens et des visages plus riches" (127). ["An able reader often discovers in other men's writings perfections beyond those that the author put in or perceived, and lends them richer meanings and aspects"] (112). The "visage" or face (Frame has it as "aspect") that we discover in reading is significant, for when Guise speaks to the plotter he knows he is guilty from reading his face:

"votre visage le montre" (124) ["your face shows it"] (109). Skillful reading does not save Guise, but it helps him understand what he faces.

In "De la diversion" (III, 4) Montaigne returns again to this question of clemency, recounting how he counseled a young prince (probably Henri de Navarre) away from revenge by diverting him with the idea of "clemence et bonté" (835) ["clemency and kindness"] (769) not solely by praising these virtues but by suggesting what he might gain in them: "Je le destournay à l'ambition" (835). ["I diverted him to ambition"].[83] Montaigne nips at the relation between emotion and belief. Just as Henri might not believe in clemency but believes it might stand him in good stead (like Guise), so readers can be moved by fictional regrets even when they do not believe them: "Ainsi nous troublent l'âme les plaintes de fables; et les regrets de Didon et d'Ariadné passionnent ceux mesmes qi ne les croyent point en Virgile et en Catulle" (837). ["Thus the laments in fiction trouble our souls, and in Virgil and Catullus the regrets of Dido and Ariadne impassion even those who do not believe in them"] (771). (We will see the power of these same fictional regrets return in Chapter 2.) Montaigne is untroubled by the fictiveness of these regrets and the nonbelief of the ensuing emotion; he suggests that hired mourners are sometimes carried away by true grief, and recounts Quintilian's observation that he was sometimes overcome by emotions he sought only to arouse in others (838, 772). He offers the example of local mountain women who both praise and dismiss their husbands in mourning them, "comme pour entrer d'elles mesmes en quelque compensation et se diverter de la pitié au desdain" (838) ["as if to bring themselves to some sort of balance and to turn themselves aside from pity to disdain"] (772). Montaigne praises this "bien meilleure grace" (838) ["much better grace"] (772) which breaks the usual habit of speaking only well of the dead. The women's emotion-diversion—from pity to disdain and back again—is a mark not of the fickleness of women (as one can imagine it might be elsewhere in this period) but stands in the text as an example of flexibility, and Montaigne gives a name to their activity: they are doing "le prestre martin" (838) ["play the part of Prester Martin"] (772), that is, following a proverbial priest who gave both call and responses as he said the Mass.

The mourning women could be almost comic, but Montaigne is serious about their grace. In their diversions they do better than a pairing of philosophers he had set against each other in another essay also centrally concerned with judgment, "De Democritus et Heraclitus" (I, 50). Contemplating the human condition, Democritus is always laughing; Heraclitus always hangs his head with "pitié et compassion" (303) ["pity and compassion"] (268). In this instance Montaigne plumps for Democritus's disdain rather than the "estimation" compassion traces for its object. But in the essay on diversion, the mourning women move more flexibly, making an agile flip-flop between each affect or attitude.

The graceful switch of the mountain women returns us to Montaigne's attempt in "Par divers moyens" to try out the positions of both vanquisher and vanquished. Though judgment is a question central to Montaigne's *Essais*, it is a judgment that partakes of both curiosity and compassion; it is capable of inhabiting a range of positions. Where in partisan accounts the pitiful spectacle draws a community together and defines that community from a tightly drawn perspective, Montaigne's revision of the topos tries out differing kinds of response, imagining and inhabiting different perspectives. Most importantly, Montaigne makes room for a particular model of bystander, emoter, and reader, who can observe with shared sympathy and whose lack of partisan action is a form of "bien meilleure grace."

In what follows I ask how the seventeenth century, seemingly past the worst of the wars, will frame and respond to the legacy of the sixteenth century's pitiful spectacle in different ways. Montaigne's readerly vulnerability with regards to compassion—and especially the regrets of Dido—will recur at sometimes surprising points in this material; but, more often, seventeenth-century writers will draw their circle of compassion narrowly and carve out instead a sovereign scorn for those who ask for mercy. France's political communities continued to look out for pity long after the end of the wars, but more often took their cue from the partisans than the *politiques*.

Chapter 2

The Compassion Machine

Theories of Fellow-Feeling, 1570–1692

How do we imagine the relation between political life and poetic representation? In Jean de La Taille's "Art de la tragédie," written between 1570 and 1572, the Huguenot playwright notes that the French court is surrounded by horror "si pitoiable" ["so pitiful"] that tragedy risks being too much after "les piteux desastres advenus nagueres en la France par nos guerres civiles" ["the pitiful disasters which came about of late in France because of our civil wars"].[1] La Taille's essay, reprinted three times before the end of the wars, insisted that tragedy's goal is to move its audience through emotion for the "piteuses ruines des grands seigneurs" (226) ["pitiful ruins of great lords"] but that what we see on stage must be distanced from us, depicting someone else's suffering instead. La Taille's observations make brief reference to Aristotle and Horace, but he assures his dedicatee Henriette de Clèves that he is suiting his discourse to her ears and not those of the erudite alone. This is a domesticated discourse; it proposes a new commonsense language for writing about tragedy, and it is also bound up in France's domestic piteousness even as it seeks to distance it. This careful affective distancing will be central to the French stage in the century to follow.

Yet La Taille did not succeed in distancing the memory of the wars, and he did not succeed in distancing Aristotle either.[2] In this chapter I trace a seventeenth-century story about tragedy, ethics, and pity, showing how a particular Aristotelian formulation about pity comes to structure a century's reflection on both tragedy and moral life. In the *Rhetoric* Aristotle maintains that pity is "a certain pain occasioned by an apparently destructive evil or pain's occurring to one who does not deserve it, which the pitier might expect to suffer himself or that one of his own would."[3] These terms suggesting that pity is a form of fear for ourselves, along with the insistence that the sufferer must not deserve their suffering, are repeated in the *Poetics*, whose passages on the question provoked vigorous debate in France (even before the text itself was translated into French later in the century). Some early moderns insisted that theatrical pity and terror purged all passions, others that they addressed only the smaller and more precise emotional machinery pertaining to pity and terror themselves.[4] Yet the Aristotelian formulation was to be found on both sides of that argument and throughout a very broad range of reflections on tragedy or ethics. The standard seventeenth-century reading of pity sees it as never entirely disinterested since the pity one feels for another stems from a fear for one's own interests, and in describing this position early moderns pulled on one or the other of the Aristotelian source texts, as their interests or professional obligations dictated. The seventeenth century's reflections on Aristotle sought to theorize suffering in the context of a particular classical tradition and perhaps to hold its horror at bay in so doing.

In this chapter I draw together moral and dramatic theory, two different sorts of accounts that draw on Aristotle's conception of pity. (I take up more explicitly theological discussions of compassion in Chapter 3; these categories overlap to some extent, but the texts of this chapter draw on a classical as well as a Christian vocabulary and direct themselves more to civility than theology, even if they sometimes imagine the two hand in hand.) In the first section of the chapter I read a series of essayists and moralists in dialog with Aristotle, with slantingly different relations to him; in the second, I ask how dramatic theorists elucidated the Aristotelian formula differently and consider what sort of moral theory they propose. Many of these writers are reading each other. To try and bring out that reading and reflection, I have staged the series chronologically, although they do not form a progression as much as a continual oscillation around two affective positions.

Both moral and dramatic theory often revolved around the affective draw of literary forms. In dramatic theory, of course, the imagined emotional relation between stage and spectator is central to any argument. Moral theory frequently references a staged scene but also calls on a different sort of scene of reading, in which a relation to a literary text brings about a different relation to compassion. In both cases, these reflections on the emotions of aesthetic response gesture to new imaginings of civility and sociality. How does this ideal literary response, either reading or spectating, shape the structures of compassion?

Compassion and the Self: Michel de Montaigne,
Pierre Charron

For some commentators of the period, the observation that pity indicates a concern with the self suggested that pity could be only a narrow and almost mean response to suffering, prompted by the self-love so key to the thinking of seventeenth-century moralists. For others, the ritual observation of this same pairing leads to a broader reflection on pity that understands the connection to mark a human vulnerability that cannot be dismissed as mere weakness. Some writers move across this affective spectrum and even mock it. Montaigne clearly draws on the familiar pairing of pity and fear when he notes lightly of his kidney stones that his mind tells him, "La crainte et pitié que le peuple a de ce mal te sert de matiere de gloire." ["The fear and pity that people feel for this illness is a subject of vainglory for you."][5] Elsewhere he comments on this desire to turn the pitiful self into a spectacle for others, something he describes as "cette humeur puerile et inhumaine, qui faict que nous desirons d'esmouvoir par nos maux la compassion et le deuil en nos amis" ["that childish and inhuman humor that makes us want to arouse compassion and mourning in our friends by our misfortunes"].[6] Montaigne's insides are not just pained by kidney stones, for even in the generous movements of compassion, he notes the sharp interior turn of a less pleasing and less definable emotion: "Au milieu de la compassion, nous sentons au dedans je ne sçay quelle aigre-douce poincte de volupté maligne à voir souffrir autruy." ["In the midst of compassion we feel within us I know not what bittersweet pricking of malicious pleasure in seeing other suffer."][7] Yet Montaigne puts his bittersweet interior into necessary consideration with the wider world. Jean Starobinski argues of "Des coches" that "it is Montaigne's initial attention to his own bodily discomfort that prepares and makes possible the lively sympathy he feels with the suffering endured by other men, inhabitants of a remote corner of the earth."[8] Despite his sharp attention to the self, or rather because of it, Montaigne essays the space for a more supple and generous compassion, as we also saw in the previous chapter.

In contrast, seventeenth-century responses tend to demarcate more sharply the borders between responses to self and others. In the *Tusculan Disputations*, Cicero suggests that some people are prone to pity as others might have a proclivity to infirmity; seventeenth-century accounts eagerly subdivide and catalog the various causes of such proclivities, often attributing them to different social types or to different genders.[9] The neo-Stoic Pierre Charron, usually a keen recycler of Montaigne, sets out these social variants neatly in one small chapter of *De la sagesse* which seems to draw on Aristotle and Cicero rather than Montaigne as reader of them:

> Nous souspirons avec les affligez, compatissons à leur mal, ou pource que par un secret consentement nous participons au mal des uns des autres, ou bien que nous craignions en nous mesmes ce qui arrive aux autres.
>
> Mais cecy se fait doublement, dont y a double misericorde: l'une fort bonne, qui est de volonté, et par effect secourir les affligez sans se troubler ou affliger soy-mesme, et sans se ramollir ou relascher de la Justice ou de la Divinité. C'est la vertu tant recommandée en la Religion, qui se trouve aux Saincts et aux Sages: l'autre est une passion d'ame foible, une sotte et feminine pitié qui vient de mollesse, trouble d'esprit, loge volontiers aux femmes, enfans.[10]

[We sigh with the afflicted and compassionate with their suffering either because through a secret consent we participate in the sufferings of others, or because we fear for ourselves what is happening to others.

But this is done doubly, so there is a double kind of mercy: one very good, which is willed, and assists the afflicted without being troubled or afflicted oneself, and without being softened or letting justice or divinity slide. This is the virtue so recommended in religion, which is found in saints and the wise; the other is the passion of the feeble soul, a foolish and feminine pity which comes from softness, a trouble of the mind, and easily resides in women and children.]

Compassion can be the sign of a willed (and secret) choice, or of a weak and womanly pliancy; this gendered distinction will be central to many subsequent separations of good from bad compassion. The Stoic response to compassion teaches us that we can assist but not "flechir et compatir" ["bend and compassionate"]; instead, like a doctor with his patient or a lawyer with his client we must show "diligence et industrie" ["diligence and industry"] without accepting the pain of the other. If woman is the rebuffed negative exemplar of

compassion, the troubled weakling who responds too fully, the proper unfurl-
ing of compassion is defined through its masculine professionalism.[11]

Compassion's Regulations: René Descartes

Descartes's version of the Aristotelian formula for the relation between pity
and fear is the most sustained of the period. In drawing on the theater as an
example for discussions of moral life, he exemplifies the tightly bound relation
between moral and dramatic theory. Descartes begins his account of pity in
Les passions de l'âme by describing its status as a mingling of other passions
that arises only in certain circumscribed situations: "La pitié est une espèce de
tristesse mêlée d'amour ou de bonne volonté envers ceux à qui nous voyons
souffrir quelque mal duquel nous les estimons indignes." ["Pity is a sort of
sadness mingled with love or good will towards those that we see suffer an ill
of which we judge them unworthy."][12] To Aristotle's precision on judgment,
Descartes adds the carefully parsed relation of each passion to another. Since
pity is what he terms a mixed emotion, he divides out his articles in *Les passions* as if to parse out its varied possibilities. In the following article, Descartes
draws on Aristotle to note that pity's intrinsic fear for the self means that the
emotion is a mark of weakness:

> Ceux qui se sentent fort faibles et fort sujets aux adversités de la for-
> tune semblent être plus enclins à cette passion que les autres, à cause
> qu'il se représentent le mal d'autrui comme leur pouvant arriver; et
> ainsi ils sont émus à la pitié plutôt par l'amour qu'il se portent à
> eux-mêmes que par celle qu'ils ont pour les autres.[13]

> [Those who feel weak and subject to the adversities of fortune seem
> more inclined to this passion than others, since they imagine the
> sufferings of another as something that could happen to themselves;
> and they are thus moved to pity more through self-love than though
> love for others.]

With a modicum less disdain but also following Aristotle, the Christianizing
Cartesian Nicolas Malebranche makes the same consignment of compassion to
the weak (this time distinguishing women as likely compassionaters) in *De la
recherche de la vérité*, as I discussed in the introduction. For Malebranche and

his very bodily philosophy, feeling for a suffering other has most effect "dans les fibres d'un corps délicat" ["in the fibers of a delicate body"].[14] This broadly Stoic position on pity imagines the emotion as a mark of moral or physical weakness, regarding an oversensibility to suffering as a block to rational reflection. For both Descartes and Malebranche, the problematic example of pity is part of a larger system of reflection on the place of the passions within rationality. In forming his general system, however, Descartes distinguishes between different forms of pity allowed to different social or moral types.

In the following article, Descartes goes on to propose a more redemptive vision of pity, for he distinguishes between two kinds of feeling or rather two kinds of *feelers*: whereas for the weak pity marks a fear for the self, stronger minds will feel for others in a more admirable way.

> Mais néanmoins ceux qui sont les plus généreux et qui ont l'esprit le plus fort, en sorte qu'ils ne craignent aucun mal pour eux et se tiennent au-delà du pouvoir de la fortune, ne sont pas exempts de compassion lorsqu'ils voient l'infirmité des autres hommes et qu'ils entendent leurs plaintes. Car c'est une partie de la genérosité que d'avoir de la bonne volonté pour un chacun.[15]

> [But nonetheless those who are the most noble (generous) and who have the strongest mind, so that they fear nothing for themselves and imagine themselves to be out of reach of fortune, are not exempt from compassion when they see the infirmity of other men and hear their woes. For it is a part of generosity to have good will for all.]

Descartes's use of the term "généreux" allows for a particular social inflection of the structures of fellow-feeling. The "généreux," in seventeenth-century French, is noble: he who acts without self-interest and without expectation of return, in a display of expenditure.[16] For Descartes, only such a noble figure can imagine himself beyond fortune and thus take pleasure in a benevolent compassion. To describe the particularity of such pleasure, Descartes draws upon a literary structure, describing the way a spectator feels for the tragic events seen on stage:

> Mais la tristesse de cette pitié n'est pas amère; et, comme celle que causent les actions funestes qu'on voit représenter sur un théâtre,

elle est plus dans l'extérieur et dans le sens que dans l'intérieur de
l'âme, laquelle a cependant la satisfaction de penser qu'elle fait ce
qui est de son devoir, en ce qu'elle compatit avec des affligés. Et il y
a en cela de la différence, qu'au lieu que le vulgaire a compassion de
ceux qui se plaignent . . . le principal objet de la pitié des plus
grands hommes est la faiblesse de ceux qu'ils voient à se plaindre.
(art. 187, 233–34)

[But the sadness of this pity is not bitter; and, like that brought
about by the tragic actions we see on stage, it remains more in the
exterior and in the senses than in the inside of the soul, which however has the satisfaction of thinking that it does its duty in feeling
compassion for the afflicted. And therein lies the difference, that
whereas the vulgar have compassion for those who bewail their sufferings, the principal object of the pity of the greatest men is the
weakness of those whom they see thus complaining .]

Theater is the model for a better-regulated fellow-feeling, in which the
"généreux" feels for the other with a certain degree of distance but never
stoops to imagining a similarity between them.[17] In drawing on this example,
Descartes seems to rewrite Augustine, who in the *Confessions* critiques the
pleasurable but illusory pity he felt in the theaters of his Carthaginian youth.[18]
In contrast, Descartes's theatrical pleasure observes and maintains the distinction between suffering and its spectator; pity is redeemed through a particular
model of the theater. The ideal compassion is not immediate but mediated
through distance and detachment; this model of theater, likewise, insists on
distance rather than on immediate likeness and emotional contagion.

Descartes sets out another example of such exteriorized pity in article 147,
where in discussing the interior emotions generated by the soul (as opposed to
the passions suffered) he suggests that the different movements of such emotions can become entangled, giving us the troubling example of a husband
who weeps at his wife's funeral even though he is glad she is dead: "Il se peut
faire que quelques restes d'amour ou de pitié qui se présentent à son imagination tirent de véritables larmes de ses yeux, nonobstant qu'il sente cependant
une joie secrète dans le plus intérieur de son âme." ["It can happen that some
remainder of love or pity which comes to his imagination pulls real tears from
his eyes, even though he feels a secret joy in the depths of his soul."][19]
We have seen something like this mingled emotion in the *histoires*

tragiques of Chapter 1, and we will see it again in the *nouvelles historiques* of Chapter 4. Descartes, though, turns to this snippet not as the seed of a narrative but as a way to account for intellectualized emotions, and the example he gives is again based on a literary structure, this time imagining someone both reading and seeing a play:

> Et lorsque nous lisons des aventures étranges dans un livre, ou que nous les voyons représenter sur un théâtre, cela excite quelquefois en nous la tristesse, quelquefois la joie, ou l'amour, ou la haine . . . mais avec cela nous avons du plaisir de les sentir exciter en nous, et ce plaisir est une joie intellectuelle qui peut aussi bien naître de la tristesse que de toutes les autres passions.

> [And when we read strange adventures in a book, or we see them represented on stage, sometimes that excites sadness in us, sometimes, joy, or love, or hatred . . . but along with that we are pleased to feel those passions excited in us, and this pleasure is an intellectual joy which can as well be born of sadness as of all the other passions.]

In this account, as Henry Phillips has suggested, there is no suggestion (as there will be from defenders of the theater) that drama could be a didactic force.[20] Rather, the story serves as an example of an emotional exteriority. What we see at the theater, and the way we respond to it, cannot (and should not) affect our interior and secret emotion.[21]

For Descartes, this distancing theater serves as a model for how we should experience the world: our response to events in general should be more like our literary or theatrical response. In a letter to Elisabeth of Bohemia (May 18, 1645), he tells her how "les plus grandes âmes" ["the greatest souls"] are able to consider the events of fortune "comme nous faisons ceux des comédies" ["as we do those of comedies"].[22] Watching "les histoires tristes et lamentables" ["sad and lamentable stories"] at the theater, Descartes notes, can make such people cry, but they also take satisfaction in them, just as seeing their friends suffer "elles compatissent à leur mal, et font tout leur possible pour les en délivrer" ["they compassionate with their suffering, and do all they can to alleviate it"].[23] The pleasure they take in carrying out their duty has more effect on them than the first affliction of compassion.

In our modern distinction between the two notions, we might term

Descartes's superior model a distanced *pity* rather than *compassion*, although the distinction between those two terms is not yet fully determined in this period.[24] Without venturing into such loaded descriptions, though, we can say that Descartes distinguishes between a narrow and a larger understanding of the emotion's scope. Descartes casts the "généreux" as a Stoic who feels not for the material difficulty of the afflicted but rather for the smallness of mind that allows the afflicted to think of material loss as suffering, since Stoic objections to compassion imagined softheartedness for material conditions to obfuscate more truly important claims.[25] This careful appraisal of and response to suffering displays a true mastery of the self.[26] Compassion is a chosen reaction, applied neatly and precisely to the suffering object without contaminating the feeling subject.

Descartes particularly valued the proper exercise and taming of passions, and in this model the theater becomes a privileged model for imagining the proper emotional life, a rational emotional life. But this is not the theater of the distracting and illusory emotion described by Augustine; rather, the theatrical pity Descartes imagines is almost juridical, both regular and capable of regulating its object. In casting theater as the model for a regulation of compassion, Descartes imagines theater as a compassion machine which sorts and disposes self and suffering other in the appropriate fashion, insisting on a firm distinction between suffering and the spectator, he who is the object of compassion and he who experiences it. In this model of theater, the ideal spectator must never imagine any similarity between what he sees on stage and his own life. Descartes's theatrical pity does not create a bond but rather works to police existing barriers.

Gender and Civility: Madeleine de Scudéry

Descartes does not gender his distinction between the *généreux* and the feeble compassionate in the way that Charron does when he assigns the latter role to women and children. The notion that women were easily and irrationally drawn to a feeble compassion was standard in contemporary writing on women. Du Bosc's *L'honnête femme* (1632–36) insisted on the naturalness of women's pity and suggests that their habitual leaning to "douceur," "clémence," or "tendresse" [sweetness, clemency, tenderness] stems from their weak nature.[27] In contrast, Descartes's scrupulous separation of the lofty from the ordinary allows for the existence of superior female virtues such as that of his correspondent Elisabeth of Bohemia.

Descartes's distinction, turning on social rank rather than gender, would be recycled by a writer who abandoned Du Bosc's understanding of *tendresse* as weakness to build instead one of her greatest texts around a new ethic of *tendresse* particularly available to women, though only certain women. In *Clélie*, Madeleine de Scudéry holds tenderness to be "une certaine sensibilité de cœur, qui ne se trouve presque jamais souverainement, qu'en des personnes qui ont l'âme noble, les inclinations vertueuses, et l'esprit bien tourné, et qui fait que, lorsqu'elles ont de l'amitié . . . elles sentent si vivement toutes les douleurs, et toutes les joies de ceux qu'elles aiment, qu'elles ne sentent pas tant leurs propres" ["a certain sensibility of the heart, which almost never rules except in persons with a noble soul, virtuous inclinations, and a well-turned wit, such that, when they are friends with someone, they feel all the pains and all the joys of those they love in so lively a fashion that they feel their own the less"].[28] Scudéry clings to the notion of a social refinement that shapes emotional capacity. It is Clélie's nobility, as well as her gender, that makes her exceptionally able to wield tenderness with the proper social competence, with "la civilité et l'exactitude" (117) ["the civility and exactitude"] demanded. The social homogeneity of the characters in *Clélie* means that compassion as a response to difference counts less than civility, an emotional capacity played out in exteriorized social acts. Like seventeenth-century compassion, civility implies a gesture toward others even as it remains bound by a rigidly hierarchal structure. But where discussions of compassion in this period figure it chiefly as the response to a particular instance of suffering, Scudéry's ethic of tenderness describes a more diffused and less event-responsive emotional disposition dependent on the rhetoric of friendship. If compassion presents itself as a response dependent on distinctions, in *Clélie* Scudéry instead sets out a new language more akin to empathy, entering into the other's emotional experience, but only another with whom one shares similarities and who does not step out of the bounds of civility. By 1680, Scudéry would have a character mock the kinds of people "dont toute la Conversation n'est que de longs Recits pitoyables & funestes, extremement ennuyeux" ["whose whole conversation is only long pitiful and mournful tales, extremely boring"]; in civil conversation, the sorts of stories that might generate compassion quickly move outside the social norm.[29]

Rhetorical Reworkings: François de La Rochefoucauld

Another midcentury commentator on civility set out a troublingly untender vision of compassion which delighted in playing with earlier writings in the tradition. In 1659, La Rochefoucauld published an anonymous self-portrait, suggesting that he sought to be the sort of ideally distanced compassionate extolled by Descartes:

> Je suis peu sensible à la pitié et je voudrais ne l'y être point du tout.
> Cependant, il n'est rien que je ne fisse pour le soulagement d'une
> personne affligée et je crois effectivement que l'on doit tout faire,
> jusques à lui témoigner même beaucoup de compassion de son mal,
> car les misérables sont si sots que cela leur fait le plus grand bien du
> monde, mais je tiens aussi qu'il faut se contenter d'en témoigner et
> se garder soigneusement d'en avoir. C'est une passion qui n'est
> bonne à rien au-dedans d'une âme bien faite, qui ne sert qu'à affaib-
> lir le cœur et qu'on doit laisser au peuple qui, n'executant jamais
> rien par raison, a besoin de passions pour le porter à faire des
> choses.[30]

> [I am not easily touched by pity, and wish I were not at all, al-
> though there is nothing I would not do to comfort people in afflic-
> tion, and indeed I believe that one should do everything, even to
> the point of showing great compassion for their sufferings, for mis-
> ery makes people so stupid that such pity does them all the good in
> the world. But I also hold that one should not go beyond showing
> pity, and take the greatest care not to feel it oneself. This passion
> should have no place in a noble soul, for it only makes one soft-
> hearted, and it should be left to the common people, for they never
> do anything because of reason and have to be moved to action by
> their emotions.][31]

La Rochefoucauld's rejection of pity, like that of Descartes, sets out a distinction between greater souls and the vulgar. He indicates his profound civility
but also his concomitant desire to keep himself at a distance; he goes on to say
that he likes his friends, although he does not show it in "caresses." This is a

Stoic rejection of pity, made all the more compelling for being told in the first person with an account of that person's struggles; here, the theories of antiquity are turned into a very seventeenth-century self-portrait.

What happens when that moral world of the portrait becomes concentrated in the form of the maxim? La Rochefoucauld's carefully poised barbs stay familiarly in the territory set out by Descartes, and also turn around the Aristotelian linking of pity with fear, but his characteristic renaming of virtue lends the familiar material a virtuosic rhetorical turn: "Ce qu'on nomme libéralité n'est le plus souvent que la vanité de donner, que nous aimons mieux que ce que nous donnons."[32] ["What is called generosity is most often just the vanity of giving, which we like more than what we give"] (72). This critique of generous emotions and actions participates in the important tradition of paradiastole, in which one redescribes something so that it may be seen in a different light than usual, a trope central to the moralist project. The famous maxim "Nos *vertus* ne sont, le plus souvent, que des *vices* déguisés" ["Our virtues are usually only vices in disguise"] (37), which La Rochefoucauld sets as the epigram of his 1678 edition, is a baseline example of the trope, central to early modern political writing.[33] In La Rochefoucauld's reformulation of the Aristotelian-Cartesian position, the maxim's pithiness and its presence among other paradiastolic zingers makes it seem as though he is reversing a standard position rather than simply repeating a very old insight. The sense of effort apparent in the self-portrait disappears, and in its place comes a generalized position. In maxim 264, we find an edited reworking of the familiar formula:

La pitié est souvent un sentiment de nos propres maux dans les maux d'autrui; c'est une habile prévoyance des malheurs où nous pouvons tomber; nous donnons du secours aux autres, pour les engager à nous en donner en des semblables occasions, et ces services que nous leur rendons sont, à proprement parler, des biens que nous nous faisons à nous-mêmes par avance.[34]

[Pity is often feeling our own sufferings in those of others, a shrewd precaution against misfortunes that may befall us. We give help to others so that they have to do the same for us on similar occasions, and these kindnesses we do them are, to put it plainly, gifts we bestow on ourselves in advance.] (72)

The mimetic power of the maxim means that already by Richelet's dictionary of 1680 La Rochefoucauld's iteration is given as the first usage under the definition of "pitié":

> Compassion. Douleur qu'on a du mal d'autrui. (La *pitié* est souvent un sentiment de nos propres maux dans les maux d'autrui. C'est une habile prévoiance des maux où nous pouvons tomber. *Mémoires de Monsieur le Duc de la Roche-Foucaut.*)[35]

> [Compassion, A pain one has for the suffering of another. (Pity is often feeling our own sufferings in those of others. It is a shrewd precaution against misfortunes that may befall us. *Memoirs of Monsieur le Duc de la Roche-Foucaut.*)]

Richelet's speedy recycling of La Rochefoucauld sets the moralist up on the same standing as Aristotle, whose *Rhetoric* is the first text cited under his definition of "compassion." If Descartes considers Aristotle within the terms of a seventeenth-century philosophy of the passions, it is La Rochefoucauld's spin on that conversation which fixes and Frenchifies the pity-fear dyad within the terms of worldly observation. This is not the redemption of pity that Descartes sees in the disinterest of the "généreux"; rather, it is a canny accrual of compassion points. In La Rochefoucauld's rhetorically deft handling of the question, the economically inflected language of the moralist tradition allows him almost to mock pity as a form of anxious savings policy. This economic language will be taken up not only by the Richelet dictionary but also by other devoted readers.

Christian Emotional Economies: Jacques Esprit

For Jacques Esprit, a Jansenist collaborator of La Rochefoucauld, pity is a force which regulates all social transactions.[36] In *La fausseté des vertus humaines* (1678) Esprit describes a complicated collaboration between Providence and personal intervention that attenuates human suffering:

> La vie de l'homme est sujette à tant de sortes de maux, d'infortunes et de traverses, qu'il seroit presque toûjours consumé d'ennuis et de déplaisirs, si personne n'étoit sensible à ses peines et ne prenoit soin

de les adoucir: Mais la Providence a pourvû à son soulagement
d'une manière admirable par les différentes liaisons qu'elle a établies
entre les hommes; car ces liaisons les engagent à s'intéresser à ce qui
les touché, et à s'assister mutuellement.[37]

[The life of men is subject to so many kinds of ills, infortunes and
setbacks, that they would be almost always consumed by sorrow or
displeasure, if no one were aware of our sufferings and took no care
to soften them. But the foresight of Providence has provided relief
in an admirable way through establishing various relations between
men; for these relations bring them to be interested in what touches
them, and to help each other mutually.]

Providence provides not just family but also a larger sense of shared
humanity:

Mais comme la proximité du sang ne s'étend qu'à un petit nombre
de personnes, et que l'amitié est encore plus limitée, la pluspart des
miserables seroient abandonnés, si la même Providence n'eût trouvé
le secret de les joindre aux plus heureux par la nature qui leur est
commune. (368)

[But since the proximity of blood extends only to a small number of
persons, and since friendship is even more limited, most sufferers
would be abandoned had not this same Providence found the secret
to join them to the happiest through their common nature.]

In this case, pity is a contrivance that brings together divine and human assistance. Those who feel pity provide a sort of social service for those without
friends or family; they "tendent les mains aux personnes qui leur sont le plus
indifférentes" (368) ["reach out their hands to those with whom they have no
connection"]. For Esprit, our self-love certainly underwrites such an emotion;
when we see people who help the poor, he notes that

quoy que leurs actions nous persuadent qu'ils ont une veritable
compassion des afflictions et des miseres de leur prochain, ce sont
des gens qui n'ont pitié que d'eux-mêmes, qui se servent, s'assistent
et se soulagent en la personne des autres. (371–72)

[although their actions persuade us that they have true compassion
for the sufferings and misery of their neighbor, these are people who
have pity only on themselves, who serve, assist and comfort themselves through the person of others.]

We are in familiar territory here. But this is not the immediate reaction to
suffering that we see described in Descartes's reading of the weak man's pity,
since for Descartes passion is above all a "live" reaction to what we see immediately around us. In contrast, Esprit's pity takes on a quite different temporality, looking more like an insurance policy: we take care of the sick so that
someone will take care of us in the future. Thus, explains Esprit in a deft recycling of La Rochefoucauld, "La pitié est un sentiment secrettement interessé;
c'est une prévoyance habile, et on peut l'appeller fort proprement la providence de l'amour propre." (373) ["Pity is a secretly interested emotion; it is a
shrewd precaution and we can rightly call it the providence of self-love."]
    Esprit's break from La Rochefoucauld's worldliness comes in this interest-
ing doubling of providential rhetoric. On the one hand, it is our own very
humanly interested forward planning that motivates us to respond to suffering. Yet, on the other hand, Providence is the divine agent that pushes us to
take care of each other. Esprit brings out the Jansenist undertow of La Rochefoucauld's dark visions and places the lengthy tradition of reflection on pity
squarely within a Christian framework.
    If Descartes takes his initial formula from Aristotle, Esprit too is clear
that the primary notion of pity on which he draws comes from the Rhetoric,
noting "Rhetor Cap 3" in the margins when he reminds his reader,

    L'idée que j'ay conçüe de la pitié est tout-à-fait conforme à la defini-
    tion qu'Aristote en a donnée: La pitié, dit-il, est une douleur que
    nous sentons des disgraces et des afflictions qui arrivent aux autres,
    dans la creance que nous avons qu'elles pourront quelque jour nous
    arriver à nous-mêmes. (374–75)

    [The idea that I have of pity conforms completely to the definition
    that Aristotle gave of it: pity, he says, is a pain we feel for the dis-
    grace and afflictions that happen to others, in our belief that they
    could one day happen to us.]

Esprit announces that (like La Rochefoucauld) he rejects pity and that this places him on Plato's side rather than that of Aristotle (376). But even as he rejects it, he makes room for it as a social mechanism and imagines especially that what he sees as the error of the Aristotelian model will be recuperated by Christianity. It is charity, *caritas*, that redeems the feebleness of pity:

> La charité rétablit le pouvoir de la raison dans l'homme; la pitié l'af-
> foiblit; la charité luy fait toujours sentir et soulager en la maniere
> qu'il peut les maux de tous les hommes, amis, ennemis, domes-
> tiques, étrangers, et même ceux qui sont absens; la pitié ne le porte
> à les assister qu'autant qu'il y est excité par les objets presens.
> (385–86)

> [Charity reestablishes men's power of reason; pity enfeebles it; charity
> makes him always feel the sufferings of all men, friends, enemies,
> servants, strangers, and even those who are absent, and assist them
> as he can; pity brings him to assist them only when he is stirred to it
> by what he sees in front of him.]

Where Descartes distinguishes between different sorts of virtuous selves, the weak or the more generous, Esprit Christianizes the better more generous self. His Christian charity improves on a compassion that responds only to what is in front of it—his phrasing, like that of Descartes, dismisses pity as a childish sort of immediate response—and instead enables both forethought and action to respond to suffering. Out of that comes a gesture toward a different mode of social enterprise. For Esprit, the proper emotion is the heart of something akin to a Christian *état-providence*, a welfare state.

Reading Charitably: Pierre Nicole

Jansenist Augustinian writers are often thought to rebuff fiction or rhetorical figures as a form of falseness indicating an attachment to exterior things. Pierre Nicole, to whom his fellow Jansenist Esprit had sent his text in man-uscript, might at first glance seem to exemplify that position.[38] Nicole was the coauthor, with Antoine Arnauld, of the famous *Logic* of Port Royal, and an assistant to Pascal on the *Provincial Letters*; he was to write the period's greatest diatribe against the theater, a *Traité de la comédie* of 1667, dismissing too the new genre of the novel and its heroes and heroines, who filled the mind, he complained, with idle ghosts. Yet in the 1660s Nicole had begun to publish a series titled *Essais de morale*, which went on to have a vast readership.[39] These essays propose a particularly Jansenist theory of affect, in which we are moved to feel correctly because of our knowledge of our place in relation to God. And somewhat surprisingly, Nicole's take on this affect often posits it as a *literary* sentiment brought about by our readerly relation to a text.

In his essay "De la connaissance de soi-même," it looks at first glance as though Nicole is merely repeating the Aristotelian-Cartesian orthodoxy on pity and fear:

> Car il y a, dans les sentiments de compassion que nous avons pour les autres, quelque réflexion secrète sur nous-mêmes, par laquelle nous nous regardons ou comme ayant souffert les mêmes maux, ou comme les pouvant souffrir.[40]

> [For there is, in the feelings of compassion that we have for others, some secret reflection on ourselves, by which we see ourselves as having suffered the same ills or being able to suffer them.]

But Nicole follows this up by moving to a very different reference which takes him away from theory and toward the literary imagination, from Aristotle to Virgil. He continues, "*Non ignara mali miseris succurrere disco*" (333) ["No stranger to misfortune, I am learning to offer help to the suffering"], using the line spoken by Virgil's Dido when she receives Aeneas with kindness (*Aeneid*, I, 630).[41] This Didonian insert tempers the original Aristotelian binary of pity and fear in an extraordinary way. Where that formula as understood by Descartes is a mark of weakness in contrast to the better emotion of the "généreux," here the Virgilian tag allows for a redemption of pity as an instance of imagination's power. (Montaigne, who noted in "De la diversion" that readers can be moved by fictional regrets like that of Dido even when they do not believe they really happened, might have liked this.) Nicole continues:

> Et c'est ce qui fait que les gens qui se croient au-dessus de tout, et qui s'imaginent que les maux dont les autres sont affligés ne sauraient venir jusqu'à eux, sont d'ordinaire impitoyables, parce qu'ils

ne font pas sur eux-mêmes ces sortes de réflexions qui attendrissent le cœur à la vue des maux d'autrui. (333)

[And this means that the people who believe themselves above everything, and who imagine that the ills with which others are afflicted cannot touch them, are ordinarily pitiless, because they do not reflect on themselves in the way that makes the heart grow tender when we see the sufferings of others.]

What sort of self-reflection does Nicole mean? Nicole's idea of reflection on suffering is readerly. In an earlier Latin text on beauty in literature (*Dissertatio de vera pulchritudine et adumbrate*, 1659) he had cited the same line from Virgil, explaining that Dido appears more human when she tells us this, so that a sentiment silently ("tacitusque") rises up in the reader: "Humanè Virgiliana Dido, cum ait. *Non ignara mali miseris succurrere disco*. Tacitusque in illam inde exoritur Lectorum favor."[42] This gesture to Dido appears at an extraordinary moment. Nicole has been arguing that wellborn people avoid teasing others for physical defects. Here is a 1698 French translation of the text:

> Les personnes bien nées ont encore une aversion naturelle pour toutes les railleries malignes et piquantes, sur tout lors qu'elles roulent sur les defauts du corps, les accidens de la fortune, ou quelqu'autre de ces disgraces dans lesquelles il n'entre point de la faute de celui à qui elles arrivent; car comme chacun connoît qu'il n'est pas exempt de pareils accidens, il ne voit qu'avec peine qu'on les tourne en ridicule dans les autres. Didon est plus humaine dans Virgile, lorsqu'elle dit, que les maux qu'elle a soufferts lui ont appris à prendre part à ceux des autres; un sentiment comme celui-là attire la bienveillance du lecteur.[43]

[Wellborn people still have a natural aversion for all malign and sharp-tongued jesting, especially when it is about bodily defects, accidents of fortune, or some other of these disgraces which are not the fault of those to whom they happen; for since everyone knows they are not exempt from such accidents, seeing them ridiculed in others causes pain. Dido is more humane in Virgil when she says that the pains she has suffered have taught her to share in those of others; a sentiment like that attracts the good will of the reader.]

Surprisingly, given this touching literary memory, Nicole then goes on to cite an epigram mocking someone's baldness.[44] The 1698 translation drops this jocular example; it is compassionately veiled, perhaps out of respect for Nicole's serious reputation.

It is certainly jarring to have potentially shared sufferings exemplified by the misery of baldness. In the *Essais*, some years later, Nicole leaves the suffering unspecified, as if cognizant that we might have more disparate and even larger causes for pain. But the two instances of acknowledging a shared human vulnerability are, importantly, stitched through by the reading of Virgil as an exercise in affect. For Nicole, it is through literature that we know the proper exercise of pity, that we see its representation and that we have such an emotion elicited in us.[45] Where theater had opened up the spectator to dangerous impulses, the Virgilian epic broadens the reader in better ways because it makes him aware of his own vulnerability. Nicole's reader is able to partake in an arm's-length compassionate reflection rather than having compassion forced upon him by the contagion of spectacle. And like Descartes's distinction between the ordinary and the noble feeler of compassion, Nicole's Virgilian exception relies on nobility: this time, not the nobility of the reader but that of the epic genre itself.

That compassion is recuperated via the figure of Dido is also significant. The Jansenists were of course committed to Augustine; but if we know a great deal about the Jansenists' Augustine, we also know a great deal about Augustine's Virgil.[46] In the first book of the *Confessions* (translated for the Jansenists by Robert Arnauld d'Andilly) Augustine bemoans his youthful compassion for the dying Dido in the fourth book of the Aeneid, on the grounds that it displaced the compassion he should have felt for his unsaved and dying self: "What, after all, is more pitiful than a pitiable person who does not look with pity on their own pitifulness—and who weeps for the death of Dido, which came about through her love for Aeneas; yet does not weep for their own death, which was coming about because they had no love for you, O God." (It is possible that this story of youthful reading was in itself a trope drawn from earlier texts.)[47] But where Augustine's tears for Dido take him further away from God, Nicole turns his feeling for Dido into the pathway to the divine. The scene that draws him to humanity is not Dido's death but Dido's welcome to the stranger, and her gesture to Aeneas draws us closer to God rather than taking us away from him. Where Augustine flinched from his compassion for a woman, Nicole is one of the rare seventeenth-century figures to suggest he learns from a woman's compassion.[48]

Nicole sets out his Virgilian revision of Aristotle in the context of an essay on knowing oneself. Our weakness or vulnerability, reviled by Descartes, is here redeemed as a source of strength: "la source de la douceur et de l'humilité envers le prochain" (332) ["the source of sweetness and humility toward our neighbor"]. Where knowing oneself in Descartes means distancing oneself from the weakness of others, for Nicole understanding the shared nature of that weakness brings about something more like what Martha Nussbaum means when she writes that pity requires "fellow feeling, the judgment that your possibilities are similar to those of the suffering object."[49] Nicole's compassion (and he tends to use this term) comes from the proper humility all Christian fellows should feel before God, and it is that humility which makes us "justes et équitables" (333) ["just and equitable"].

"All pity is in essence theatrical," writes Paul de Man; for Nicole, we might say that all morality is theatrical, or at least mimetic.[50] In a famous distinction between charity and self-love, Nicole explores the question of the authenticity or otherwise of emotion.[51] In his essay "De la charité et de l'amour-propre," Nicole suggests that proper civility—honnêteté, as seventeenth-century French puts it—must mimic caritas where one cannot supply it naturally. Nicole opens by setting an absolute distinction between "charité" ["charity"], which relates everything to God, and "amour-propre" ["self-love"], which understands everything in relation to the self. But he complicates this by suggesting that the effects of both are the same, since "l'amour-propre tende . . . à contrefaire la charité" (381) ["self-love tends to counterfeit charity"]. Nicole's essay probes the relation between affect and effect and between emotion and action in the world, and reminds us that unlike God we cannot judge the interior world but only the external acts that are shown in the world.

This distinction means that Nicole is not so much an analyst of emotions as of emotional behaviors. Compassion in this reading is not an essential virtue but rather a social practice. Nicole describes a bishop said to have different faces for different activities, one "doux et compatissant quand l'occasion le demandait" (83) ["sweet and compassionating when the occasion called for it"]. In another essay, drawing on a new vocabulary for the theory of compassion, Nicole terms this "civilité chrétienne" ["Christian civility"]. In an essay on the submission to the will of God, he writes:

Si c'est une occasion où il soit à propos d'être gai, il faut témoigner
de la gaieté. S'il est besoin d'être triste, il faut faire paraître de la
tristesse. Il y a des rencontres où il faut témoigner de la tendresse, de
la confiance, de la cordialité, de la compassion; et il faut tâcher d'en
exciter en soi les mouvements selon que la raison réglée par la volonté de Dieu nous dicte qu'il est juste et utile de les avoir. (82)

[If it is an occasion when it is appropriate to be gay, one must show
gaiety. If there's a need to be sad, one must make sadness show.
There are encounters where one must show tenderness, confidence,
cordiality, compassion; and one must try to excite in oneself these
movements as reason, regulated by the will of God, tells us that it is
right and useful to have them.]

Such guidance takes us close to the worldly writings of courtesy literature. But
although Nicole's advice might look like a social strategy, it is quite differently
motivated.[52] For Nicole, emotional behaviors can only be understood in the
context of a serious reflection on what human agency amounts to when set
against divine will. To say that we show compassion out of self-interest is, in
this analysis, not to take a gloomy view of human action but rather to give a
proper account of the function of God's grace. He continues with a vivid
image of our interior-exterior dialectic:

Que s'il ne nous est pas possible de les ressentir vivement, il faut au
moins qu'ils soient comme imprimés dans notre extérieur: et par ce
moyen il faut espérer que Dieu nous fera la grâce de régler nos mouvements intérieurs comme nous aurons réglé les extérieurs pour
l'amour de lui. (82)

[That if it is not possible for us to feel it vividly, it must at least be
as if it is imprinted in our exterior; and through this one must
hope that God will give us the grace to regulate our interior movements as we will have regulated the exterior, for the sake of his
love.]

The image of an imprinted feeling is common in the seventeenth century, but
it is usually printed in the *interior* of the self. Here Nicole makes a curious
turn on that figure, placing the feeling *in* our exterior, with the preposition

already indicating the oddness of this clash between surface and interior. We put on a feeling on the surface; God, in recognizing our appropriately disposed exterior habit, might then be able to set our interior, too. Nicole's twist makes emotion a practice that, given grace, will slowly dig itself into our intimate experience.

Nicole's insistence on the submission to God's will also reorganizes the Aristotelian social landscape in new ways. When we see another's suffering, Nicole writes, we can see that it is sometimes "juste," right. For Aristotle, this would mean that we do not pity the sufferer. But for Nicole, we must also acknowledge that man's wrongness comes from his "dérèglement" ["unruliness"] and distance from God. For Nicole, unlike other thinkers on compassion, it is not ultimately our judgment of the sufferer that is called into question but rather God's final judgment on us.

Nicole's "secret reflection" is not the self-interested fear for the self that Descartes diagnosed (nor the secret joy of his weeping husband) but a compassion that comes about precisely because of his awareness of the complex range of the self and the strange relations between exterior and interior. Where Descartes wanted the properly schooled compassion to remain an exterior emotion, as at the theater, Nicole rewrites the dialectic between self and other that is orchestrated in theories of compassion, redrafting it as the internal-external dialectic of the reader aspiring to an internally lived grace and in the meantime arranging what he can of his printed exterior.

Compassion in Translation: The *Poetics* and the Human

If Descartes's examples of the theater and Nicole's examples of reading both draw on a particular literary structure as a model for compassion, how then does the theater reflect on the morally significant affective structures which it creates? The second part of this chapter traces the resonance and evolution of Aristotle's pity and fear pairing in writing on the theater. In part, this story is a philological one. I have been using both the terms "pity" and "compassion" up to this point, and in the French seventeenth century these terms are mostly broadly interchangeable.[53] But in writing about the theater, a new sense of semantic distinction begins to appear.

In some instances, the term "compassion" appears to be mostly an easy synonym for "pity." Racine, in the preface to *Iphigénie*, writes that Euripides "savait merveilleusement exciter la compassion et la terreur" ["knew marvelously how to excite compassion and terror"], where in his scribbled marginalia to the *Poetics* he uses "pitié"; Norville's 1671 translation of the poetics puts Aristotle's pairing as "la crainte et la compassion" ["fear and compassion"].[54] In other instances, like those I described in the genre of the *histoire tragique*, the two words are paired in a hendiadys of affective intensification. But at still other moments, and in particular in dramatic theory, "compassion" sometimes seems to point to something new, to a different and broader understanding of a response to suffering.

The term "compassion" draws on a particularly Christian tradition. Where "pity" takes root in Roman *pietas*, which would enable but not compel a Christian inflection, *compassio* was first introduced into Latin by the Christian writer Tertullian.[55] Thinking about the term as early moderns used it is firstly a philological problem relating to the translation of Aristotle's *Poetics* into Latin and then into the Italian vernacular, from which it made its way into French. The instability of the translated term in French (as pity or as compassion) indicates the considerable leeway critics granted themselves in dealing with such a very unforthcoming text as the *Poetics*, and the different texts they brought to bear upon their understanding of its tradition. But that philological slippage ushers in a different model of imagining theatrical community; the introduction of "compassion" seems to allow for a broader interpretation of the Aristotelian heritage.

It was Lorenzo Valla's Latin translation of 1498 that established the terms which then filtered into the vernacular. Valla uses *miseratio/commiseratio* interchangeably, and in that shifting place of the "*co*" the slippage between the two terms creeps in.[56] Some translations, like Pazzi's of 1536, reprinted at least twelve times in the sixteenth century, used instead the theologically resonant "misericordiam" as the term for pity; these translations had considerable impact since they formed the basis for Maggi's famous commentaries on the *Poetics*.[57] (The Dutch commentator Heinsius also uses "misericordiam" in his 1611 text, eagerly read in France.) The Italian vernacular discussions of tragedy, meanwhile, seemed to favor "compassion." In 1524, Giovanni Giorgio Trissino, dedicating his *Sophonisba* to Leo X, describes how "la tragedia muove compassione" ["tragedy brings about compassion"].[58] Cintio's *Discorso* of 1553 describes how the poet must fill out the action with "cose terribili e compassionevoli" ["things terrible and worthy of compassion"].[59] Giraldi's translation notes "horrore e . . . compassione"[60] as the key terms, and Castelvetro's commentaries, the most important for the generation of French neoclassical critics, speak of "spavento e compassione."[61] In the Italian commentaries it is the term for fear that moves through a variety of expressions, whereas the term for fellow-feeling remains relatively stable.

The French seventeenth-century usage of the term "compassion" begins by presenting it merely as a synonym for "pity." Nicot's *Thresor de la langue française* of 1606 pairs the two words, "la pitié et la compassion qu'on a d'aucun, *commiseratio*)" ["the pity and compassion one has for the other, *commiseration*"].[62] Yet by the late eighteenth century, compassion implies what is "humain" [human] and its meaning is severed from that of pity.[63] In the seventeenth-century examples, we see how that separation of the term is enabled; in dramatic theory, compassion is no longer automatically paired with fear in the Aristotelian formulation, and it gains its own status quite apart from pity. Looking at the abbé d'Aubignac's usage in the *Pratique du théâtre*, written during the 1630s, we can see that he moves beyond the Aristotelian formulation and uses "compassion" to refer to our response to what we see on stage, and "pity" in a way that suggests it now implies a form of derision. D'Aubignac places compassion at the center of theatrical emotion: it is "le plus parfait sentiment qui règne au Théâtre" ["the most perfect sentiment which reigns in the Theater"], but pity has a quite different valence. Discussing a mediocre play, he draws on the humanist Joseph Scaliger's description of "la Comédie de ce Rhodophile, que Scaliger dit avoir été plus capable de faire pitié que de faire rire" ["the comedy of Rhodophilus that Scaliger says was more likely to bring about the audience's pity rather than their laughter"].[64]

This separation makes room for the association of compassion with a more broadly empathetic response stressing a shared humanity. Although this move might seem to mark a distancing of Aristotle's rigorous distinctions, it also represents a turn to a different Aristotelian inflection. In chapter 13 of the *Poetics*, Aristotle distinguished between pity and a broader sense of the human, *oute gar philanthropon*. This emotion is directed towards the bad man who, because he deserves his fall, cannot bring about pity or fear in the hearts of the spectator. But he can bring about a more generalized, human fellow-feeling; in Greek the term points to someone who is gentle and kind toward others.[65]

This question is explicitly addressed in Italian Renaissance channelings of the *Poetics*, as Adrien Walfard has described. For the humanist Francesco Robortello, the *philanthropon* was set in anxious relation to the question of pity. He imagines an interlocutor interrupting Aristotle to say he is wrong to imagine that the unhappiness of evil men does not awaken pity (given in the Latin as *commiseratio*); Aristotle responds that this kind of affection is not pity, *commiseratio*, but humanity, *humanitas*. It is both weaker and more general-ized than pity and comes about from our shared nature.[66] In another com-mentary, by Alessandro Piccolomini, this notion was translated in even more friendly fashion as "amicabilità . . . un certo quasi congiungimento di tutti gli huomini" ["friendliness . . . a certain connection of all men"]. Even when we see our worst enemy hurt we experience "un non so che di natural commovi-mento" ["some sort of natural agitation"].[67]

In Ciceronian discourse, the language of *philanthropon* is translated as "humanitas," and the humanness of this language will be crucial in French discussions of tragedy.[68] But the language also gestures to the fear of what is *not* human. Before coming to designate relations between humans, the term *philanthropon* indicated a domesticated animal, understood as a zone of tran-sition between human and animal.[69] It is fitting, then, that the seventeenth-century language of humanness seeks to tame the wild if venerated beast Aristotle, and to make him safe for modern audiences.

The new language of wary friendliness will be taken up by two key French theorists of the theater, first La Mesnardière and then even more explicitly by Pierre Corneille. Their tentative and weltered vocabulary of friendly fellow-feeling brings about a move beyond Aristotle, though it is originally brokered by the mishmash of translations of the *Poetics*. Theater allows for a new rela-tion between spectator and sufferer that shifts the terms of early modern com-passion.[70] But unlike Descartes's figure of the moved spectator who maintained a necessary distance between his situation and that of the sufferer, the new and more human model for theater begins to erode such distinctions.

Commiseration: Hippolyte-Jules Pilet de La Mesnardière

A first glimmer of the French softening toward theatrical compassion can be seen in La Mesnardière's *Poëtique* of 1640, commissioned before the writer's death by the chief minister Richelieu. La Mesnardière disconnects pity and terror from their Aristotelian intertwining, turning terror into a sort of horror chill rather than the fear that something we have seen happen to another might befall us, and looking instead to compassion and commiseration toward imperfect people as the touchstone of audience experience. Criminals are sometimes legitimate in tragedy, he admits, and that is how "les Edipes, les Orestes, les Alcméons, les Medées & les Thyestes" found their place on stage.[71] But he urges turning away from them:

Mais puis que nous epreuvons que la Commiseration est infiniment
plus douce, plus humaine & plus agréable que la terreur & l'effroy,
je conseille à nôtre Poëte d'introduire rarement de ces criminals
détestables, & de ne point servir d'une dommageable licence, dont
l'usage est plus nuisible qu'il ne peut estre avantageux. (19)

[But since we feel that commiseration is infinitely sweeter, more
human and more agreeable than terror and fear, I recommend our
poet to introduce these detestable criminals only rarely, and not to
use a regrettable license, whose use is more dangerous than it could
be advantageous.]

La Mesnardière is at pains to establish that he knows the Aristotelian tradition
but can urge a modest and docile departure from it:

Ce n'est pas que la Terreur ne soit utile sur la Scéne. Mais comme
elle est desagréable, & qu'elle ne doit regner que dans les Sujets hor-
ribles qui exposent le chastiment des parricides, des incestes, & des
crimes de cette espece, il vaut mieux que la Compassion, qui est un
sentiment plus doux, & qui naist des calamitez des personnes im-
parfaites, moins coupables que malheureuses, fasse impression sur
les esprits, & que mesme elle y domine jusques à tirer des larmes.
(22)

[It is not that Terror is not useful on Stage. But since it is disagree-
able, and that it reigns only in horrible subjects that set out the
punishment of parricides, incest and crimes of this nature, it is better that Compassion, which is a sweeter sentiment, and which is
born from the calamities of imperfect people who are less guilty
than unhappy, should make an impression on our minds, and even
dominate them such that tears come forth.]

In insisting on commiseration, La Mesnardière writes a new kind of French
poetics, which domesticates Aristotle and puts him into more agreeable terms.
This gentler Aristotle is indicative of a broader shift throughout the period, in
which Aristotle's concept of *philanthropon* gradually merges with the original
category of pity. La Mesnardière's gentle commiseration is a restrained version
of what will flourish in eighteenth-century poetics, such as Houdar de la

Motte's 1715 *Réflexions sur la critique*, in which terror is jettisoned and pity attenuated as *attendrissement*.[72] Like that later model, La Mesnardière allows for a weepy reaction to tragedy, but without entering into the full-bodied teariness of later years.[73] This is a teariness not unlike the distanced emotion felt by Descartes's ideal compassionate, and La Mesnardière writes for a new kind of idealized French stage, for a cleaned-up, regularized tragedy which relies on a structural distance between spectator and suffering. On this newly professionalized stage, modest compassion is ushered in by an actress who does not herself feel but knows how to lean on "endroits pitoyables" ["pitiful places"], and in so doing makes room for the proper response of the properly ordered man: "l'Auditeur honneste homme, et capable des bonnes choses, entre dans tous les sentimens de la Personne theatrale" (74). ["The *honnête homme* of the audience, capable of good things, enters into all the sentiments of the theatrical persona."] This modest proposal further insists upon the gendered structure of compassion: to the man to feel, to the woman to make him feel—but only because she draws on the authority of the author.

The Friendly Human: Pierre Corneille

The tragedian Pierre Corneille returns to the pairing of pity and terror in his essays on dramatic theory, but in circling around this familiar coupling he introduces a broader and more skeptical relation to the Aristotelian tradition, in keeping with his leanings to the "modern" side of the dispute between ancients and moderns.[74] Corneille, often tagged as a neo-Stoic, might be presumed to revile pity. But this stance is inflected by an abiding interest in the positions of those—especially women and other figures of remainders—whose affective positioning is very far from stoic. Ellen McClure argues that Corneille's Stoicism stems chiefly from a reading of Guillaume du Vair; she shows that du Vair does not condemn pity in his *De la constance et consolation ès calamitez publiques* (1589) but instead allows for the importance of tears.[75]

In his *Discours* of 1660, Corneille takes on the Aristotelian tradition with apparent suspicion, expressing his confusion as to what catharsis might involve beyond the repetition of the terms pity and fear. Corneille is straightforward about the difficulties of following the orthodox Aristotelian tradition as derived from Italian commentaries; at one point he goes as far as to say, "J'avoue donc avec franchise que je n'entends point l'application de cet exemple." ["I

frankly admit that I do not understand the point of this example."][76] He tries
to see how Aristotle's dicta apply to his own work, thinking through the movement of pity and fear as it might relate to the unhappiness of *Le Cid*'s Rodrigue
and Chimène, which, he admits "fait pitié" (146) ["makes us pity them"].

But how does this particular effect on the audience relate to the Aristotelian tradition? Corneille, who knows his theory, continues

> Cette pitié nous doit donner une crainte de tomber dans un pareil
> Malheur, et purger en nous ce trop d'amour qui cause leur infor-
> tune, et nous les fait plaindre; mais je ne sais si elle nous la donne,
> ni si elle le purge, et j'ai bien peur que le raisonnement d'Aristote
> sur ce point ne soit qu'une belle idée, qui n'ait jamais son effet dans
> la vérité. (146)

> [This pity must make us fear a fall into a similar unhappiness, and
> purge in us this surplus of love that causes their misfortune, and
> makes us pity them; but I do not know if it does that, or if it purges
> love, and I am rather afraid that Aristotle's reasonings on this point
> are just a nice idea, which never has any truth in reality.]

Corneille's insistence on the audience effect—a real and experienced emotion—
as a counterpoint to the *Poetics* points him toward a particular historicized
reading even of Aristotle, in which he suggests that Aristotle might insist on
the corrective effects of catharsis in order to defend tragedy against Plato. For
Corneille, then, pity is both contingent and necessarily instrumental.

Though Corneille's careful parsing out of the relation between pity and
terror stays close to that of Aristotle, his break for modernity also establishes
itself around this same issue. In particular, he pushes at the Aristotelian doxa
that pity must be based on an understanding of similarity. Through pity and
fear, Corneille understands that "semblables passions" ["similar passions"] are
purged, and that pity for another brings us to fear for ourselves: "La pitié d'un
malheur où nous voyons tomber nos semblables, nous porte à la crainte d'un
pareil pour nous" (143). ["The pity for the sufferings of those like us makes us
fear similar suffering for us."] But the notion of the "semblable," who is similar to us, is both eroded and expanded by his work. Corneille reminds us that
the finely calibrated puzzle of purging shifts when the community present on
stage and in the audience changes. He tries to explain Paolo Beni's assertion in

his 1613 commentary that the process of catharsis applies only to kings and princes:

> Peut-être par cette raison, que la tragédie ne peut nous faire craindre que les maux que nous voyons arriver à nos semblables, et que n'en faisant arriver qu'à des rois, et à des princes, cette crainte ne peut faire d'effet que sur des gens de leur condition. (143)

> [Perhaps for this reason, that tragedy makes us fear only the sufferings we see happen to people like us, and that since it happens only to kings and princes, this fear can have no effect except on people of their rank.]

There is some leeway in this formulation, and Corneille is drawn to it, going on to argue against this restrictive interpretation by suggesting

> Mais sans doute il a entendu trop littéralement ce mot de *nos semblables*, et n'a pas assez considéré qu'il n'y avait point de rois à Athènes, où se représentaient les poèmes dont Aristote tire ses exemples, et sur lesquels il forme ses règles . . . Il est vrai qu'on n'introduit d'ordinaire que des rois pour premiers acteurs dans la tragédie, et que les auditeurs n'ont point de sceptres par où leur ressembler, afin d'avoir lieu de craindre les malheurs qui leur arrivent: mais ces rois sont hommes comme les auditeurs, et tombent dans ces malheurs par l'emportement des passions dont les auditeurs sont capables. (143)

> [But doubtless he understood too literally these words "like us" and had not adequately considered that there were no kings in Athens, where the plays Aristotle gets his examples from where staged, and around which he forms his rules . . . It is true that ordinarily only kings are the heroes of tragedy, and that the audience has no scepter to resemble them, so that we might fear the sufferings that beset them; but these kings are men, like the audience, and fall into their sufferings by being carried away by passions of which the audience is capable.]

Corneille's own understanding of this process of purgation posits a form of fellow-feeling that relates the king on stage to the spectator, "lui qui n'est qu'un homme du commun" ["he who is only a common man"] who could end up in "un pareil malheur" (143) ["a similar unhappiness"]. What is important is not so much their status but that they all share a common (perhaps even homogeneous) humanity, like the audience. This audience is not extreme in composition and character, and from that comes a sort of common standard: "Notre auditoire n'est composé ni de méchants, ni de saints, mais de gens d'une probité commune" (144). ["Our audience is composed neither of wicked men nor of saints, but of men of common probity."] Corneille, the only seventeenth-century theorist to have a successful career as a playwright, has a keen sense of what happens in the theater, and the way in which the theater sees common experiences and shared work bear fruit in some new form. It is through this theatrical commonality that he expands the traditional sense of pity into a broader fellow-feeling.[77]

Corneille often uses the term "compassion" when he wants to double the focus of our emotional attention: "la pitié qu'on a pour ces fils généreux" (150) ["the pity we have for these noble sons"]. The *pity* we feel for certain figures, he notes, does not entirely push aside the feelings we have for others, such as the bad father, for whom we may still feel "quelque compassion d'eux-mêmes" (151) ["some compassion for them"]. In this case, compassion is merely a useful supplement to a vocabulary in need of flexibility as it moves beyond the judgments of Aristotle.[78] But Corneille's use of the term is also significant in the context of a larger understanding of his often very generous poetics, in the modern sense of the term. Like La Mesnardière, he introduces a third term, "commisération," as a synonym for pity (148), and this commiseration ushers in a suggestion of broader human relations. The term recalls Valla's "commiseratio" but also the usage of the Dutch dramatic theorist Daniel Heinsius, whose *De Tragediae constitutione* (1611) had a major impact in France. Heinsius's work sketches a fellow-feeling that is based on the shared humanity of Aristotle's *philanthropon*: "Men feel pity for men, indeed as men—the Philosopher calls that the sense of humanity, and that is what comes the closest to true commiseration."[79] This distinction points to a real-world compassion distinguished from that familiar from the precisions of the poetical tradition. Corneille's very human theorizing draws on this appraisal, moving him beyond the rigid pairing of pity and fear.[80]

This affective supplement changes the way we think of dramatic characters. In explaining that passion and familial duty may collide, as they do in his most famous tragedies, Corneille suggests that it is this feeling of kinship between characters that in turn brings about our own feelings of connection to them:

> Horace et Curiace ne seraient point à plaindre s'ils n'étaient point amis et beaux-frères, ni Rodrigue s'il était poursuivi par un autre que par sa maîtresse . . .
>
> C'est donc un grand avantage pour exciter la commisération que la proximité du sang, et les liaisons d'amour ou d'amitié entre le persécutant et le persécuté, le poursuivant et le poursuivi, celui qui fait souffrir et celui qui souffre. (151)

> [Horace and Curiace would not be pitiable if they were not friends and brothers-in-law, nor Rodrigue if he was pursued by someone other than his mistress.
>
> Blood proximity then makes it greatly easier to excite commiseration, and so do liaisons of love or friendship between the persecutor and the persecuted, the pursuer and the pursued, he who causes suffering and he who suffers.]

When the characters are friends, our friendly feelings for them—and for the plays in which they figure—are drawn out. Corneille tells how he altered the historical source and rearranged the ending of *Rodogune* so that Antiochus should not himself be guilty of poisoning his mother. This means, he argues, that "Antiochus ne perd rien de la compassion, et de l'amitié qu'on avait pour lui, qui redoublent plutôt qu'elles ne diminuent" (160). ["Antiochus loses none of the compassion and friendship that we had for him, that are doubled rather than diminished."] This beautifully domesticated language of compassion and friendship marks a real change in the notion of how we relate to a tragic figure, who is no longer an exemplar or a warning but our friend.[81] Rather than letting fellow-feeling trace a preexisting community, Corneille suggests that it might expand our ways of understanding "nos semblables." This is the French-style *philanthropon*: in Corneille's account of things, the friendly human displaces the powerful machines of pity and terror.

Natural Movements: René Rapin

Corneille's broader, friendlier imagining of fellow-feeling did not always make him friends. It was greeted with approval by fellow "modern" critics like Saint-Evremond, who welcomed the building of a new kind of pity accompanied by a very Cornelian admiration: "Nous la dépoüillons de toute sa foiblesse, et nous lui laissons tout ce qu'elle peut avoir de charitable et d'humain." ["We strip it of all its weakness, and leave it everything that is charitable and humane."][82] But the move to a less circumscribed fellow-feeling was met with skepticism by the Jesuit René Rapin, author of a series of 1674 *Réflexions* on Aristotle.[83] Rapin acknowledges compassion's invitational draw but also regrets the way in which it has swamped the French emotional landscape. For Rapin, tragedy should instead be a question of regulation. Its careful affective mechanisms stop the spectator from becoming too fearful or too full of pity ("trop pitoyable"), perhaps implying that he who feels pity is himself liable to become an object of it.[84] Tragedy schools us by showing us where our emotions should be directed, showing spectators how to

> ménager leurs compassions pour des sujets qui la méritent. Car il y a de l'injustice d'estre touché des malheurs de ceux qui méritent d'estre misérables. On doit voir sans pitié Clytemnestre tuée par son fils Oreste dans Eschyle: parce qu'elle avoit égorgé Agamemnon son mary: et l'on ne peut voir mourir Hippolyte par l'intrigue de Phedra sa belle-mère, dans Euripide, sans compassion: parce qu'il ne meurt que pour avoir esté chaste et vertueux. (98)

> [manage their compassion for worthy subjects. For there is injustice in being touched by the sufferings of those who deserve their misery. One must see without pity Clytemnestra killed by her son Oreste in Aeschylus, because she had killed Agamemnon her husband; and one cannot without compassion see Hippolytus die because of the intrigue of his stepmother Phaedra in Euripides, because he dies only because he was chaste and virtuous.]

Rapin, then, maintains the Aristotelian distinction between those who do and do not deserve a particular and poetically endorsed response to their suffering.

In observing the French scene as he sees it in 1674, however, Rapin suggests—without himself endorsing this shift—that French theater has now moved away from Aristotle and taken up precisely the broader and more generalized fellow-feeling that Corneille describes. Indeed, Boileau's *Art poétique* of the same year suggests that to succeed on stage one needs a "*Pitié* charmante" ["charming *Pity*"] and a "douce *Terreur*" ["sweet *Terror*"], with the italics and the softening modifiers suggesting how the new affective triggers were beginning to swamp the old formula.[85] Rapin's account suggests that the Aristotelian pairing of pity and fear has got lost in a mix of other, less organized emotions (one of which is compassion), a move he seems to regret:

> Ce n'est pas assez que la tragédie se serve de toutes les avantures les plus touchantes et les plus terribles, que l'histoire peut luy fournir, pour exciter dans les cœurs les mouvements qu'elle pretend, afin de guerir les esprits de ces vaines frayeurs, qui peuvent les troubler, et de ces sottes compassions qui peuvent les amollir: Il faut encore . . . que le poète mette en usage ces grands objets de terreur et de pitié comme les deux plus puissans ressors, qu'ait l'art, pour produire le plaisir, que peut donner la tragédie. (98–99)

> [It is not enough that tragedy draws on all the most touching and most terrible adventures that history can supply, to excite in our hearts the movements it claims to do, in order to cure us of these vain fears that can trouble us, and these foolish compassions that soften us. The poet must also put into use these great objects of terror and pity as the most powerful triggers that art has, to produce the pleasure that tragedy can give.]

Rapin imagines that some rational organization must counter the arousal of "foolish compassions," and the provider of order is the playwright, who should remember to cling to the more rigid terms of pity and terror. But instead he sees that the French theater is moving beyond Aristotle toward something supplementary and softer:

> La tragédie moderne roule sur d'autres principes: peut-estre que le genie de notre nation ne pourroit pas aisément soutenir une action sur le théâtre par le seul mouvement de la terreur et de la pitié. Ce sont des machines, qui ne peuvent se remuer comme il faut, que par

de grands sentimens et par de grandes expressions, dont nous ne
sommes pas tout à fait capables que les Grecs. (103)

[Modern tragedy moves according to different principles; perhaps
the genius of our nation could not easily support an action on stage
through the sole movement of terror and pity. They are machines,
which cannot be moved as they are needed, except through great
sentiments and noble expression, of which we are perhaps not as
capable as the Greeks.]

The *galanterie* of the French, claims Rapin, necessitates a new kind of tragedy:
"Nous sommes plus humains, la galanterie est davantage selon nos mœurs"
(103). ["We are more human, *galanterie* is more fitting for us."] He judges that
for the seventeenth-century French spectator the new pleasure of tragedy
comes about not in the exercise of emotions brought about in catharsis but
rather in a broader elision of identity that erodes the distinction between spectator and stage:

La tragédie ne devient agreeable au spectateur parce qu'il devient
luy-mesme sensible à tout ce qu'on luy represente, qu'il entre dans
tous les differens sentimens des acteurs, qu'il s'intéresse dans leurs
avantures, qu'il craint, et qu'il espère, qu'il s'afflige, et qu'il se réjouit
avec eux. (99)

[Tragedy becomes agreeable to the spectator because he himself becomes sensible to all that is represented to him, he enters into all the
different feelings of the actors, he is interested in their adventures,
he fears, he hopes, he suffers, and rejoices with them.]

Rapin's observations of the new-style French spectator's heart, "des mouve-
mens si naturels et si humains" (99) ["such natural and human movements"],
shows the distance France had traveled from the Aristotelian formula by the
1670s. The classicist David Konstan has argued that in Greek "the subject
and object of pity do not merge but rather maintain distinct emotions—that
of the pitier is precisely pity—and perspectives: the pitier is always to some
extent in the situation of an observer rather than a participant in the experience of the other, and views the suffering of the pitied from the outside."[86] In
Rapin's understanding, in contrast, feeling for and with the other dissolves

the boundaries of the self. This is *French* feeling: where the Greeks were able to apportion emotion along Aristotelian lines, French emotion is no longer penned in by such formal mechanisms. Instead it spills over into everything:

> C'est alors que le cœur s'abandonne à tous les objets qu'on lui propose, que toutes les images le frappent, qu'il épouse les sentimens de tous ceux qui parlent, et qu'il devient susceptible de toutes les passions qu'on luy montre: parce qu'il est ému. (99)

> [It is then that the heart abandons itself to all the objects proposed to it, that all images strike it, that it espouses the feelings of all those who speak, and that it becomes susceptible to all the passions displayed, because it is moved.]

What kind of theater is Rapin imagining when he describes such a reaction? The repetition of "tous/toutes" points to Racine's famous preface to *Bérénice*, four years earlier, in which the playwright claims a generalized emotion as the mark of tragedy, "que tout s'y ressente de cette tristesse majestueuse qui fait tout le plaisir de la Tragédie" ["that everything suggests this majestic sadness that is all the pleasure of tragedy"].[87] In this new imagining of tragedy, *everything* hurts, and that globalized and globalizing hurt is all the pleasure of it. The "tout"-ness of such tragic pleasure swamps the pity and terror machine and in its place puts only a nonspecified state of being overwhelmingly moved. Rapin's position on the question is mixed: he takes pleasure in describing it but reserves the right to worry.

Pity Versus the Human: André Dacier

Rapin was not alone in his concern about such changes. André Dacier, broadly on the side of the ancients, was resolute in his defense of tragedy's particularity, its purgative procedures, and the particular forms of affect to which theater gives rise: "Les memes sujets qui ont fait répandre tant de larmes dans le théâtre d'Athènes & dans celuy de Rome, en font encore verser aujourd'huy dans le nôtre" (20). ["The same subjects which made so many tears flow in the theaters of Athens and Rome still make them flow today in our own theater."] (He might be thinking here of Racine's preface to *Iphigénie*, where Racine, insisting on the intelligence of his audience's emotional reactions, asserts that his audience was moved by the same things that made the Greeks weep.) Where Saint-Evremond celebrated the humanity of Cornelian pity, Dacier criticized Corneille for distancing himself from the more rigorous notion of pity and catharsis of the poetics, and insisted that tragic pity must be different from a more generalized sense of humanity. For Dacier in his 1692 commentary on the *Poetics*, our human response to suffering is quite distinct from the particular ethical and poetic emplotments of pity:

> Les hommes sont naturellement faits de manière qu'ils ne sçauroient voir, ni des blessures ni des morts sans être touchez; mais ce sentiment ne vient que du mal même sans aucun raport à la personne qui le souffre; c'est plûtôt un sentiment d'humanité que de compassion. Or la compassion que doit exciter la Tragedie, ne naît pas seulement du mal même, mais de l'état où se trouvent, et des liaisons qu'ont entr'elles les personnes qui le souffrent, & celles qui le font souffrir.[88]

> [Men are naturally made so that they cannot see either injury or death without being touched; but this sentiment comes about only because of suffering, even where they have no relation to the person who suffers: it is a sentiment of humanity rather than of compassion. Yet the compassion which tragedy must excite is not born only of suffering but of the situation and relations of the sufferers, and of those who make them suffer.]

For Dacier, the human response to suffering is a quotidian emotion that does not depend on a larger aesthetic structure, whereas the pity that is proper to tragedy can come about only in the context of a particular poetic tradition. Dacier responds to Corneille's breadth of fellow-feeling by narrowing the occasions that demarcate a truly tragic compassion and by insisting once again on the boundaries between a circumscribed response to theater and the emotional turmoil of everyday human experience. Instead of allowing a broader sense of humanity as a tragic response, Dacier insists that tragic emotion stay within bounds; a properly tragic compassion emerges only from carefully defined structural relations between the sufferer and the cause of their suffering. For Dacier, these bounds stand as a defense against a more abstract, even baggy, ideal of humanity that risks eroding the particularity of tragedy's structures. Humanity is all very well outside the theater, but inside we must be held tightly by a rigorous relation to affective rule.

Structures of Feeling

Rapin's and Dacier's concerns about dramaturgical humanitarianism could not stop the tide. In the eighteenth century, the reserved pleasure of tears that Descartes describes found a fuller and more embodied realization in the burgeoning of new genres marked by *sensibilité* and no longer hemmed in by the fierce diktats of tragedy's theorists. Compassion's contagion was no longer to be resisted. In imagining a common humanity shared by kings on stage and the people in the audience, Corneille had asked his audience to make an imaginative leap over a rigid social hierarchy. That leap would be made more often in the eighteenth century. In depicting the contemporary life of ordinary persons, genres like the *drame bourgeois* made the feeling of friendship that Corneille posits for the stage more tangible. And despite Rapin's chastising of the "foolish compassions" of his compatriots, that sentimental story was not unique to France and would also become important elsewhere, most notably in Germany. Gotthold Lessing's 1767 *Hamburg Dramaturgy* insisted that pity responds to human beings and not their social status. Speaking for what is sometimes called bourgeois drama or domestic tragedy and for the presence of the "common person" in tragedy, Lessing ushers in what Julie Ann Carlson describes as "the standard of the common, the domestic, the egalitarian, the everyday."[89] Yet Lessing's development of this similar solidarity made clear how this seeming reaching out is also a closing down: as Carlson puts it ruefully, "Making-like to be like and likeable serves hierarchical difference." The figure of the human comes to be its own kind of machine.

Compassion's seventeenth-century theorists vary in their assessment of emotional capaciousness and in the vocabulary they deploy to determine its limits. Their compassionate structures may be tightly and narrowly drawn, or so broad as to appear almost absent, but they are always hemmed in by a necessary framing that polices the border between self and other. In pursuing the legacy of Aristotle's pity/fear binary throughout the period, we can of course trace the extent to which both moral and dramatic theorists disentangled themselves from an Aristotelian legacy, driven by particular theological dispositions or by the exigencies of contemporary dramatic practice. But we could also say that compassion's seventeenth-century theorization still largely resembles Aristotle's careful structural assessment. In tracking the variant breadth of pity over these theorizations, we see the sharply structural nature of seventeenth-century emotion come to the fore. Far from being an immediate affective reaction to suffering, seventeenth-century pity emerges as from a machine that properly configured the precise relation between judgment and emotional response. It turns its back on particular instances to consider generalities. Gone are the compulsively superlative spectacles of the sixteenth century, and in their place comes a considered abstraction of suffering. The pity and terror paired by Léry to account for the siege of Sancerre is displaced by a cooler framing of emotional relations, in the manner recommended by La Taille. Yet some of the bitterness of pity's wartime sorting mechanism still makes itself felt in the vigorous distinctions set out by seventeenth-century writers. Even as critics like Nicole and Corneille dispute and displace the boundaries between the self who compassionates and the sufferer he observes, they remain attached to the significance of boundary vocabularies. If they strike out for new emotional territories through reading and the imagination, they do so only while casting an anxious eye at compassion's edge.

Chapter 3

Caritas, Compassion, and Religious Difference

Among the many sufferers laying claim to the heartstrings of early modern Europeans, the Christian captives of the Ottoman Empire might seem to have had a special appeal to the imagination. And yet, their supporters complained, these captives had fallen victim not only to their captors but also to the indifference of their compatriots at home. One seventeenth-century Englishman, Charles Fitz-Geffry, duly urged the readers of a tract named "Compassion Towards Captives" to remember with "compassion and pity" the Britons taken prisoner by the Turks.[1] Fitz-Geffry asks that his readers "have a fellow-feeling with [the captives], as being members of the same body" and imagines the response from his unfeeling audience: "But they are strangers unto me, neither kiffe nor kin; I never saw their faces nor heard of their names. They have friends, acquaintance, kindred of their owne, let them relieve them" (24). Fitz-Geffry answers them insistently, angrily: "But they are of thine owne *religion*, thine own *nation*, thine own *nature:* And is not the least of these sufficient acquaintance when they are in misery?" (40, original emphasis). In this chapter I ask what "sufficient acquaintance" was required for early modern compassion and explore how religious difference disrupted such ties. In tracing questions of community near and far, this chapter pursues the structuring principles of early modern compassion seen in the previous chapter, in which compassion's reach ranged over a spectrum from broad to narrow, but this time does so with particular reference to theological questions. Out of the fierce differences tackled by religious thinkers, a differential theology of compassion emerges.

If commentators today sometimes claim that compassion is, as Terry

Eagleton puts it, "acknowledging that anyone whatsoever has a claim on you, regardless of their culture," early moderns in contrast were more ready to set out compassion's limits. Nicolas Coeffeteau in his 1620 account of the passions notes that we are most moved by people "comme présent à nos yeux" ["as if in front of our eyes"] and that prisoners in Algers and slaves in Tunisia— *pace* Fitz-Geffry—will thus not move us.[2] Yet different religious communities defined these questions in varied ways. Fitz-Geffry's anxiety that compassion be properly directed to those who are out of sight speaks to the worries of an era in which the understanding of neighborliness had radically shifted. Which element of religious faith, national identity, or natural humanity might be described, in his terms, as "the least of these," at a moment when the relation between all three elements had been put under extraordinary pressure in Europe by the Reformation and the subsequent religious wars, and further afield put under a different pressure again by European imperial ambitions? How did compassion negotiate and construct questions of proximity and distance, and did Catholics and Protestants draw those markers differently? How did Catholic writers map out the terrain of universal love, and how did Protestant (or marginalized Catholic writers like the Jansenists) point to the limits of that universalism?

For seventeenth-century French readers, Fitz-Geffry's questions would have had particular urgency as they navigated the new philosophical and spatial territory of toleration. As the newly centralizing nation came into being, it dragged with it the caveat that French identity was now fragmented and contested between Catholic and Protestant, a situation that as time went by was to prove increasingly untenable. Fitz-Geffry was neither French nor Catholic, but he drew on a language that all French readers, Catholic or Protestant, would have been able to recognize. His description of the captives as "members of the same body" stems from the apostle Paul's articulation of the Christian community in which Christians are imagined as multiple parts that form one body in Christ: "For as with the human body which is a unity although it has many parts—all the parts of the body, though many, still making up one single body—so it is with Christ."[3] Paul's elucidation of this early Christian community was central to the ways that early modern Christians, both Catholic and Protestant, imagined "fellow-feeling." The language of *caritas* or charity (the love between fellow humans) which is so central to Paul's text was one of the richest shared discourses of early modern Christianity; if Protestants and Catholics often had difficulty imagining themselves as one body together in Christ, they nonetheless shared the textual body of Paul's words.[4] Catholic and Protestant writers responded very differently to Paul's exhortation to *caritas*; the common text took on real social and stylistic suppleness as it was inflected by different sectarian positions or different ways of reading Christian tradition.

The chapter is divided into two parts. The first section takes in Catholic writers who understood compassion as a natural law and discussed it in terms of a human universalism: in chronological order, the Jesuit Pierre Le Moyne, the Capuchin Yves de Paris, and the Jesuit Jean-Baptiste Saint-Jure. (For shorthand, I call this group "mainstream Catholics.") The second section places one decidedly nonmainstream Catholic and two Protestants in polemical counterpoint: first the Jansenist Blaise Pascal and then the work of two Protestants writing at two strikingly different moments in the history of French Protestantism: the midcentury theologian Moïse Amyraut and, some decades later, the refugee minister Pierre Jurieu.[5] Protestant writing on compassion significantly redraws the lines of distance and proximity that animate so much Catholic writing on *caritas*; but Pascal, too, forces differentiations into the mainstream Catholic discourse of compassionate universalism. Pascal and the Protestants reappraise compassion according to increasingly urgent understandings of religious difference: for Pascal the difference between kinds of religious yearning, and for the Protestants the more partisan battles between the Catholic majority and the Protestant minority. Since early modern French writers tend to veer between the terms "charité," "compassion," and "miséricorde" I will follow suit, drawing attention only to those distinctions that point to substantial difference. More marginal writers, for example, begin to articulate distinctions between pity and compassion that make up our modern understanding of these questions.

Early modern theologians' divergent understandings of compassion often stemmed from a readings of a shared text which related the abstraction of *caritas* to compassionate scenarios in the world. Like Paul's epistles, Luke's story of the Good Samaritan, in which Christ asks his listener to identify the true neighbor, was central to the parsing of compassion. The illustrated Bible de Royaumont for children, dedicated to the Dauphin, described the Samaritan who comes to the rescue of the injured man as a religious outsider who was nonetheless "touché de compassion" ["touched by compassion"].[6] At the beginning of the period of state persecution against the Protestants, this suggestion that someone outside the religious fold might nonetheless show compassion seems to suggest a surprising hospitality or openness to those outside one's narrowly defined community. Yet even the translations through which

Catholics and Protestants knew this compassionate parable reinforced social and religious boundaries. In the Catholic Louvain translation of the Bible, the neighbor is "celuy qui a exercé la misericorde" ["he who has exercised mercy"], but in Protestant Bibles of the same period it is he who has "usé de misericorde" ["used mercy"].[7] The Catholic use of the verb "exercer" points to the labor demanded by compassion, in keeping with Catholic doctrinal insistence on the good works which earn salvation, whereas Protestant usage merely draws on an emotion that is already granted. This detail of translation speaks large; even as early modern compassion made gestures to the outsider, it betrayed doctrinal differences.

Catholic versions of the tale also went further in their insistence on the translation of feeling—"charité"—into an active compassionate engagement with the world. In these accounts, good works are not enough; we must also properly distinguish between the sorts of good works we are called to exercise, drawing hierarchical distinctions between different forms of compassionate action. The Bible de Royaumont's commentary scorned the inaction of the priest and the Levite who pass by the injured man without stopping:

> Ce Prestre et ce Lévite croyoient peut-estre avoir de fort bonnes raisons de passer sans s'arrester. Ils furent même apparemment attendris en voyant ce misérable. Mais cette compassion stérile n'empêcha pas qu'ils ne fussent cruels en manquant à un devoir si pressant de la charité. Le Samaritain ne raisonna pas tant qu'eux. Il agit plus simplement et plus charitablement. Il luy suffit de voir cet homme mourant pour se croire obligé de le secourir. C'est ainsi que nous devons faire, et nous serions bien peu disposez à secourir les maux de ceux qui sont éloignez de nous, lors que nous négligeons ceux dont nous sommes témoins nous-mesmes, et que nous voyons de nos propres yeux.[8]

> [This Priest and this Levite perhaps thought to have good reason to pass without stopping. They were even apparently made tender by seeing this unhappy man. But this sterile compassion did not stop them from being cruel in missing the pressing duty of charity. The Samaritan did not reason as much as they did. He acted more simply and more charitably. He only had to see the dying man to believe himself obliged to help him. We must act the same way, and we would be poorly disposed to help the suffering of those a long

way distant from us when we neglect the suffering we witness ourselves, which we see with our own eyes.]

This chiding distinction between feeling and action is relatively common to
confessional texts. The Jesuit Nicolas Caussin, director of conscience of Louis
XIII, advised his readers to "n'avoir point une charité oisive, et languissante,
qui soit seulement en idée; mais être officieux, cordial, obligeant, non pour ses
interests, mais par pure maxime de vertu" ["to renounce a lazy and languish-
ing charity, which is only abstract, and to be instead officious, cordial, oblig-
ing, not for one's own interests but through pure virtue"]; the theologian
Jean-Baptiste Thiers likewise argued, "Il est de l'essence de la charité du prochain, non seulement de luy vouloir du bien, mais aussi de luy en faire." ["It is
of the essence of loving one's neighbor not only to wish him well but also to do
him well."][9] But the Royaumont commentary also makes the crucial distinction between suffering near and far that Fitz-Geffry's *Compassion Towards Captives* attempts to override. Here charity does not merely begin at home; instead,
it supervises the limits of what we may call home and suggests that those limits
define how we understand our duties of hospitality and neighborliness.

   Fitz-Geffry urges us to feel for those far away (on whose behalf we can,
presumably, not act directly); the French texts I have cited above ask us, instead, to act rather on our feeling for those near at hand. Both vigorously spa-
tialize compassion's capacities and in so doing both construct compassion's
regulation of sameness and difference, carefully reapportioning who is like us
and who is set aside, policing the borders both of and between us and them,
the self and the other. This gerrymandering of fellow-feeling—the re-ascription
of sameness and difference—is central to the sectarian debate of the period.
Even as early modern compassion aspired to the universal, it betrayed its limits. In reading both Catholic and Protestant responses to compassion, this
chapter posits a quiet but contentious dialog between parties who rarely considered the other their neighbor.

The Catholic Science of Compassion
Pierre Le Moyne: Compassion's Natural Mechanisms

Le Moyne is a central figure in French Jesuit spirituality, and he wrote a number of works central to Counter-Reformation culture: the *Galerie des Femmes
fortes* (1647) and a vast work on the passions, *Les peintures morales* (1640–43),

in which passions are represented by pictures and by rhetorical figures. His most lengthy discussions of compassion come in *La dévotion aisée* of 1652, in which Le Moyne, influenced by François de Sales, shows how devotion can be sweetly accessible to those who wish to remain anchored in the pleasures of the world.

Le Moyne posits compassion as natural law, as something timeless set in vigorous contradiction of recent scientific debates. His Christian reading of emotion's sociality draws on a scholastic vocabulary in sharp conflict with more recent discoveries. *La dévotion aisée* appeared four years after a bitter debate between Pascal and the Jesuits on the nature of the vacuum. For the Jesuits, drawing on scholastic tradition, the notion of the horror of the vacuum figured a world naturally gathered together in unity, an inexorable human movement.[10] Jesuit scientific assertions underwrote Jesuit beliefs in the natural sociability of humans, a notion also fiercely opposed by Pascal. For the Jesuits, just as the natural bodies of physics were drawn together, so too were humans.[11] Le Moyne's reading of compassion stems from this Jesuit natural philosophy.

In accordance with this tradition, Le Moyne describes the love of one's neighbor as "natural," but he defines this natural neighborliness in a rather socially particular way:

> L'Amour du Prochain qui est une appurtenance et une suite, un écoulement et une reflexion de l'Amour de Dieu, ne sçauroit estre ny moins naturel ny moins facile. Et cela certes aussi seroit bien étrange, qu'il luy fallust de la contrainte et de la violence, pour descender par une pente que les Sens luy ont preparez; qu'il eust besoin de ressorts et de machines, pour aller où la ressemblance l'attire. De quelque condition que soit un homme, il ressemble à un autre homme: et la ressemblance est la matiere des inclinations et des sympathies, le nœud des cœurs et des Esprits, le lien des Couples et des Assemblées. Par la ressemblance un Sauvage est le familier de tous les Sauvages, un Lyon est privé pour tous les Lyons, un Tygre est l'amy naturel de tous les Tygres.[12]

> [The love of one's neighbor depends on and follows from, flows from, and reflects the love of God, and is as natural and as easy. And it would be very strange, if it needed constraint and violence to go down a slope that the senses had prepared; if it needed springs and

machines, to make it go where resemblance was drawing it. Whatever kind of man we have, he resembles another man; and resemblance is the stuff of inclinations and sympathies, the knot of hearts
and minds, the bond between couples and gatherings. Through resemblance a savage is the familiar of all savages, a lion is at home
with other lions, a tiger is the natural friend of all tigers.]

Le Moyne's exuberant insistence that we love one another is kept in check by
a strong sense of where the limits of the "we" might lie, and he insists on our
similarities as humans by insisting on our differences from animals. A man
resembles a man, a savage a savage, and a tiger a tiger, and it is similarity that
binds us; we cannot imagine other forms of neighborliness. The connection
between "man" and "savage" is not articulated and seemingly not imagined;
the savage is what separates man from the lions and tigers, and he is as different from them as are those beasts, whose habits are presumably gleaned from
travelers' tales, including those by Le Moyne's fellow Jesuits. The lion is "privé"
for all other lions, in the early modern sense that he is tame or domesticated
for lions but presumably still savage to other beasts; there is to be no crossing
of party lines in Le Moyne's structure of fellow-feeling. The natural both binds
together and rigorously separates. Le Moyne stumbles over the delineation of
difference that nonetheless relies on an analogical understanding: man's friend
is to man as tiger's friend is to tiger. Ontologically humans and tigers might
not be similar, but our bonds are of the same order. We love each other because we are made that way, but our maker made us in very particular and
separate ways.

    In an extraordinary hypothesis reflecting on similarity and sympathy, Le
Moyne continues:

> Des Statuës qui seroient l'ouvrage d'un mesme sculpteur, et seroient
> faites d'un mesme marbre et sur un mesme modèle, si elles avoient
> de l'esprit et du mouvement, bien loin de se heurter et de se détru-
> ire, se traitteroient de parentes et d'alliées, et chacune pour le moins
> aimeroit sa ressemblance en sa voisine, et y respecteroit l'art de leur
> commun Père. (253)

> [If statues made by the same sculptor, from the same marble and on
> the same model, were to have mind and movement, then far from

clashing and destroying each other they would call each other relatives and allies, and each would at least love his resemblance in his
neighbor, and would respect the art of their common father
therein.]

The image recalls Paul's metaphor of the Church as one body in Christ but
stages it through the chillier figuration of many bodies in marble. This elaborate example of the naturalness of compassion, staged through an artificial
analogy, suggests at once a boundless enthusiasm about compassion's power
and a recognition of its limits: it can overcome the borders between the artificial and the natural, if it cannot bridge gaps between lions and statues and
humans. Le Moyne arrays many different "naturals" alongside each other but
does not make clear how they might relate to one another.

     In his delineation of lions and statues and humans, Le Moyne holds
firmly to a Creator-centric understanding of the natural. But elsewhere his
language lets us glimpse the new Jesuit science. Le Moyne describes how

> le commerce des Bien-faits, qui est le propre commerce des Ames
> nobles, se fait de la plenitude qui est d'une part, et du vuide qui est
> de l'autre: il se fait de la compassion que donnent les pauvres et les
> affligez, et du soulagement que rendent les riches et les heureux. Or
> d'une part le vuide attire naturellement, et la misere donne naturel
> lement de la pitié; D'autre part aussi il est naturel à la plenitude de
> se répandre, et la plus naturelle felicité des heureux est le bien faire.
> (256–57)

> [The commerce of good deeds, which is the proper commerce of
> noble souls, is made of the plenitude which is on one side, and the
> vacuum that is on the other; it is made of the compassion that the
> poor and afflicted inspire, and the relief that the rich and happy give
> to them. For on one side the vacuum naturally draws us to it, and
> misery naturally gives rise to pity; on the other hand it is also natu
> ral for plenitude to spread, and the most natural happiness of the
> happy is the good deed.]

This passage, making heavy use of the notion of the natural, leans on the Jesuit science of sociability which brings physics to bear upon human bonds.

Where Le Moyne's earlier passages insisted on God as maker and regulator of difference and similitude, here charity obeys the impersonal laws of scholastic physics, moving goods and emotions in seamless and natural exchange, an exchange which builds a moral economy: the noble soul participates not in the usual bourgeois exchange of goods (*biens*) but rather good deeds (*bienfaits*). This scientific figuration of charity displaces individual judgment, the delicate judgment needed to properly identify and respond to suffering described by the partisan writers of the wars. In contrast, Le Moyne's naturalizing compassion mechanism systematizes charity and suggests that it happens even without our agency, flattening out our particularized reactions to a human other into a normalizing landscape of redistribution in which our will has no place:

> Les Rivieres qui sont pleines et contraintes, rompent leurs levées: les Fontaines qui regorgent et sont retenuës, crèvent leurs canaux; en nous mesmes la repletion fait les maladies; et generalement toute abondance qui n'a point de cours est ruineuse; et la felicité qui ne se communique point, est une felicité imparfaite et incommode. (25)

> [Rivers which are full and constrained break their levees; fountains which brim and are held back, burst their canals; in ourselves repletion brings about illness, and generally all abundance which has no outlet is ruinous, and happiness which is not communicated is an imperfect and awkward happiness.]

This passage lets the natural metaphor overflow its usefulness; as any seventeenth-century contemplator of the landscape knew, even natural forces must be regulated. The threat of Le Moyne's flooding emotional economy suggests that the natural must, after all, be carefully regulated.

Jesuit writing on compassion was also characterized by its concern for the proper arrangements of proximity and distance in compassion. The global projects of the new missionary order had radically restructured the traditional affective networks of the Church. Le Moyne's intervention in this debate comes close to the satirical anxiety Dickens will display over the figure of *Bleak House*'s Mrs. Jellyby, whose "telescopic philanthropy" pushes her to care for the missions overseas even as she neglects the needs of her own children.[13] Le Moyne criticizes a seventeenth-century Jellyby and worries about the consequences of her intemperate and distant charity:

Si elle prefere des charitez de surérogation, qui se font avecque
montre, à des charitez de justice qui se feroient en secret; si elle
porte à un Hospital éloigné, les soins et les assistances qu'elle doit à
un Hospital domestique; ne doit-elle pas craindre que . . . ses domestiques abandonnez luy reprochent devant Dieu ses aumosnes
profanes et ses charitez infidelles? (32)

[If she prefers acts of supererogation, which are made ostentatiously,
to charitable acts of justice made in secret; if she gives to a distant
hospital the care and assistance she owes to a domestic hospital,
must she not fear that her abandoned servants reproach her before
God for her profane offerings and her unfaithful charity?]

Once again Le Moyne's argument depends on a hypothetical example; perhaps his Madame Jellyby is, after all, as unlikely a creature as his living statue.
Le Moyne hyperbolizes his argument with terms that underline the gendered
nature of his caricature; he makes these charitable actions profane and unfaithful, violations of the domestic and familial. Where the Jesuit global
agenda was criticized for seeking missions overseas rather than attending to
domestic affairs, Le Moyne displaces that charge by trumping up the charges
against a Madame Jellyby rather than a Révérend Père. Once again, women's
compassion is figured as excessive or wrongly placed; compassion needs a
male compassionater if it is to be correct and corrective.

Le Moyne says that we do not need springs and machines to keep compassion flowing where the natural law of resemblance draws it, but in fact his
science of compassion is a mechanism that regulates our assessment of similarity and difference and that asks only—at least in front of the *domestiques*—
that nothing be allowed to stand out from that norm. It is natural to care for
each other, Le Moyne insists, but for him it would be easier if, like the statues,
we recognized and observed the artificial boundaries that police our understanding of that nature.

Yves de Paris and the Natural Theology of Compassion

Le Moyne's natural science of compassion is taken to exuberant ends by the
Capuchin Yves de Paris, a thinker indebted to the Salesian vein of devout
humanism who in his midseventies produced an extravagantly curious work
entitled *Les œuvres de miséricorde* (1661).[14] The works of mercy are, of course,

in orthodox Catholic practice a set of procedures by which one gains salvation: visiting the sick, burying the dead, and so on. But Yves's extraordinarily
all-encompassing understanding of mercy takes in a whole slew of other behaviors and affects, amounting to nothing less than a global vision of the
world and its workings. In Yves's work, the naturalization of compassion articulated by Le Moyne comes to its full fruition.

Deeply indebted to the scholasticism of Jesuit natural philosophy, Yves
revives the natural imagery at work in Le Moyne and makes it the basis for
what an earlier book of his calls natural theology, a global vision which traces
reciprocal "sympathies" drawing together all parts of the world.[15] Arguing for
the essential sociability of the human and the protection afforded to him by
society, Yves draws on long series of natural similes, in which comparison itself becomes a stylistically compassionate gesture, allowing for the yoking together of two unlikes to make a new whole:

> Comme la terre après un grand tremblement tire quelquefois de ses
> abymes, et fait couler de grands fleuves pour la commodité des
> Provinces; ainsi les personnes émeues de compassion ouvrent leurs
> thresors, et font de grandes largesses pour l'assistance des pauvres.[16]

> [As the earth, after a great quake, sometimes produces something
> from the abyss, and makes great rivers flow for the commodity of its
> provinces, so people moved by compassion open their treasures, and
> make great gifts to help the poor.]

This resembles Le Moyne's riverine charity turned into a more generous spring
of emotion. Yves's usage of the "Comme . . . ainsi . . ." formulation (recalling
that of François de Sales) often allows him to articulate a truly capacious compassion, even as he is aware of the limiting motivations of human behavior.
Like the moralists of the previous chapter, Yves is clear that compassion cannot be entirely separated from self-love: "La compassion est là par effet une
douleur qu'on a, non pas tant de la misère d'un autre que de la sienne propre,
et la foiblesse d'un esprit qui s'abat sous les coups de l'infortune" (33). ["Compassion is a pain one has not so much from the suffering of another as one's
own suffering, and the weakness of a will that bows under the blows of misfortune."] But this thriving vein of self-love can have real and important social
effects. Yves explains, for example, that the rich should be kind to their

servants not merely out of the goodness of their hearts but also out of the fear that when reduced to poverty their servants will flee them (this fear in itself suggesting something about social turmoil in the seventeenth century). When a rich man suffers, "[La souffrance] le reduit à la miséricorde de ses valets: Car s'ils n'ont des affections sincères pour luy, s'ils ne sont touchez de compassion, ils trouveront leurs libertez dans sa maladie, et leurs gages ne peuvent pas empecher que leur fidelité ne soit corrompüe par les presens de ses ennemis" (92–93). ["Suffering throws him to the mercy of his manservants: for if they do not have sincere affection for him, if they are not touched by compassion, they will find freedom in his illness, and their wages will not prevent their fidelity from being corrupted by the gifts of his enemies."] In this reading, being kind to the servants is a form of self-interested social insurance similar to that traced by Jacques Esprit.

Elsewhere, though, Yves suggests that to commit oneself to compassion is to go positively beyond the interests of the particular in search of a kind of commonality. Where the moralists tended to dismiss compassion as merely a variant on the bitter erosions of self-interest, Yves announces from the outset that to commit oneself to compassion is to make a new form of community. Mercy is "ce que l'on doit à la société civile, qui périroit bien-tost, si chacun n'avoit des soins et des industries pour soy-mesme" (21) ["what one owes to civil society, which would soon perish if people had care and industry only for themselves"]. This discourse restructures the relations between the private individual (the "particulier") and the public; because compassion reaches out to another, it must, Yves argues, be organized into more than a spasmodic immediate reaction of one person alone, and the immediate individual response should be encouraged to also explore the work of establishments and foundations, which can do things not possible for private individuals.[17] For Yves, *caritas* leads inexorably to charity; as the title of his book indicates, "charité" is an emotion which requires a practice in the world. But the needs of the public are not motivated by a selfless humanitarianism; rather, Yves argues that the state will thrive only when all its members have a minimum standard of welfare: "L'estat y trouvera ses profits, quand l'extreme pauvreté ne reduira pas ses sujets dans l'impuissance de l'action et du commerce" (8). ["The state will profit, when extreme poverty does not reduce its subjects into impotence of action and commerce."] *Caritas*, then, can also be a form of proto-Keynesian economic lubrication.

Yves's compassion also shifts the Jesuit calibrations of distance and proximity that end by calling for attention to those at home. Instead, he sets out a distinctly global justice, acknowledging that the bonds of humanity go beyond national borders. In a chapter on the need for hospitality to pilgrims, he insists, "L'éloignement du lieu ne rompt pas la proximité du sang, le pelerin est donc vostre frère, de quelques pays qu'il vienne, et quoy que sa personne vous soit inconnuë, il suffit qu'il porte le visage d'homme pour estre recue de vous, avec les tendresses que vous luy devez en qualité de vostre parent" (291). ["Distance does not break the blood bond, the pilgrim is thus your brother, from whatever country he comes, and even though he might be unknown to you, it is enough that he has the face of a man for him to be received by you, with the tenderness that you owe him as your relative."] Yves even suggests that global linguistic diversity was allowed by God because all we need is compassion: "Les larmes, les gemissemens, les yeux et les gestes sont des langues entendues de toutes les nations" (19). ["Tears, groans, eyes and gestures are languages understood by all the nations."] Though both Le Moyne and Saint-Jure investigate the claims of distant sufferers, Yves goes further than them in insisting on the global pull of emotion.

Yet closer to home one group finds itself excluded from the universal sigh as sign: "une malheureuse secte, qui ne subsiste que par un exces de tolerance" (402) ["an unhappy sect, which subsists only through an excess of tolerance"]. This sect, of course, is France's Protestants, clinging to existence thanks to the rather unexcessive terms of the Edict of Nantes, by 1660 on distinctly shaky ground. As Yves turns to write of the Protestants in a series of angry chapters that come late in the book, he draws on terms that recall his initial vision of world harmonic understanding only to repeat it in soured and eroded fashion. Thus Protestant children should be understood to be exempt from charges of heresy because they are "des âmes qui ne sont malades que par sympathie, et par la dépendance des autres" ["souls which are sick only through sympathy, and because of their dependence on others"], those terms of sympathy and dependence now appearing as a form of contagion rather than as something to be admired. Now that a universal Christianity has been split, that vision of sharing common goods and treating one's neighbor as oneself is lost. The neighbor, that is, can no longer be recognized as like oneself; what's more, he refuses to recognize us, too: "Les Huguenots ne souffrent pas les Catholiques dans les villes et les pays où ils sont les maistres" (394). ["The Huguenots do not suffer Catholics in the towns and countries where they are masters."] In this simple declaration, the failures of compassion and of toleration crash up against one another. We can feel for those who suffer, but we cannot feel for those who cannot suffer us. This is the voice of compassion reaching its limits.

Yves's lengthy diatribes on the Protestants reveal how Counter-Reformation compassion functions to regulate social difference. Though compassion can reach across differences, it also reifies them. In one arresting image, Yves suggests that emotion's instinct has a strange regulatory power, functioning as a sort of interior coup d'état: "la compassion, qui n'attend, ny le discours de la raison, ny le choix de la volonté; comme un Prince peut obliger ses sujets à ne tenir pas pour ennemis ny pour estrangers, ceux qu'il a recues dans son alliance" (27) ["compassion, which waits neither for the discourse of reason nor for the choice of will; like a Prince who can oblige his subjects to regard those in his alliance as neither enemies nor strangers"]. Moving away from the rolling lyricism of his comparisons between emotion and nature, here Yves makes fellow-feeling function as absolutist decree. We are ruled by our compassion, Yves suggests, but his metaphor also reminds us that, in seventeenth-century France, a prince was ultimately the regulator of compassion and of the place of religious difference within it.

Jean-Baptiste Saint-Jure: Home and Away

Le Moyne's concerns about the different obligations of proximity and distance are taken up somewhat differently by my final Jesuit, Jean-Baptiste Saint-Jure. Saint-Jure was at the center of a distinctly French movement of Catholic renewal. A follower of the cardinal de Bérulle, he was also spiritual director of a number of figures key to the changes at work in French Catholicism, like Jeanne des Anges, directed by Saint-Jure after her infamous possession and her work with his fellow Jesuit Joseph Surin.[18] More importantly for my focus, Saint-Jure was the confessor (and biographer) of Gaston de Renty, who directed the charitable Compagnie du Saint-Sacrement from 1639 to 1649, and also of Jeanne Mance, the woman who along with other devout lay adventurers formed the nucleus responsible for the first settlement of Montreal and the Hôtel-Dieu hospital in that city (I return to that hospital settlement in the final chapter). Saint-Jure's work as a spiritual director exemplifies a central feature of the French Catholic renewal: the burgeoning of lay networks of *dévots* and their engagement in active charitable enterprises in the sense that we understand the term "charity" today.[19] Though Saint-Jure did not himself engage in the sort of social organization coordinated by a figure like Vincent de Paul, his writings on charity are of interest because of his

alliances with those engaged in such practices; in his role as confessor to world
travelers, the discourse on proximity and distance takes on an urgent tone.
Saint-Jure suggests that compassion should also be understood as a professional bond, and he writes above all for fellow Jesuits about the emotion they
should share.

Saint-Jure sets out his theories of compassionate life in *L'homme religieux*
of 1663, a text that delineates a properly Jesuit sociability. This is a book
framed, as its title indicates, for those living in religious orders, and its second
volume, on how to live well in a community, addresses the proper attitude
required in such a life. For Saint-Jure, charity is the link which binds all Christian virtues. In an image that recurs throughout Catholic writing on charity,
Saint-Jure describes it as a band binding the faithful together and surpassing
all other bonds, "beaucoup plus de perfection, que ne fait ni le lien de la
parenté ou de l'alliance, ni celuy de la sympathie d'humeur ou de mesme âge,
ni celuy des mesmes employs ou de la mesme profession, ou de la mesme de-
meure, ou de la mesme nourriture, ni celuy de la participation mutuelle de
toutes les autres choses" ["much more perfect than kinship, or alliance, or
sympathy of humors or shared age, or the sharing of jobs or professions, or of
the same house or the same food, or the mutual participation in anything
else"].[20] Charity erases difference and, furthermore, surpasses all other forms
of union that might be imagined to do the same. It creates new understandings of community.

Like the other writers I address here, Saint-Jure's imagining of Christian
charity is deeply imbued with Pauline thought, drawing on the notion of the
body of the new Church in Christ. But here the familiarly Pauline body is sentimentalized. Where Paul merely sets out the relational structure of the members that form one body, Saint-Jure grants emotional capacity to each limb:

Les membres de nostre corps s'entr'aiment sans feintise, et pour
effet de cet amour, ils ne s'entrenuisent jamais, mais ils se font tout
le bien qu'ils peuvent, ils s'entr'aident, ils se soulagent, ils se defend-
ent, ils se compatissent, et ont de merveilleuses inclinations et tendresses les uns pour les autres. (94–95)

[The limbs of our body love each other mutually and without pre-
tense, and through an effect of this love, they never hurt each other;
on the contrary, they do each other all the good that they can do,
they help each other, they care for each other, they defend each

other, they have compassion for each other, and they have wonderful inclinations and tenderness for each other.]

Saint-Jure joins together Paul's description of the Church with his insistence on charitable love and embroiders upon it a more hyperbolic language of emotion. The unusual reflexive verb "se compatir" turns a verb that would usually be unidirectional (I compassionate with X) into a mutual and nonhierarchical emotionality ideal for fellow members of an order. Yet though Saint-Jure writes chiefly for an internal audience, he casts a wider net for the tools with which he addresses them, here drawing on the popular language of novelistic discourse (*inclination, tendresse*).

Saint-Jure shows a similar argumentative bricolage in venturing far afield with his illustrations of the naturalness of compassion; even the source of his examples, drawn from travelers' tales, speak of the new concerns with distant others. In one example, he tells the story of

un elephant aux Indes, transporté d'une passion si ardente pour un enfant qui estoit encore au maillot, qu'il n'en pouvoit souffrir l'absence, mais falloit qu'il le veist toûjours, et l'eust perpetuellement auprés de soy, et si parfois on le luy ostait, il en témoignoit de la tristesse, et ne pouvoit manger. C'est pourquoy quand sa nourrice l'avoit allaité, elle le mettoit dans son berceau prés de l'elephant, qui le regardoit avec une certaine complaisance: lors qu'il dormoit, il chassoit les mouches avec sa trompe; quand il crioit, il trouvoit bien le moyen avec la mesme trompe de le bercer, et taschoit de l'appaiser et de l'assoupir. (79)

[An elephant, in India, transported by so ardent a passion for a child still in swaddling clothes that he could not bear his absence, and had to see him constantly and have him continually near him; if sometimes he was taken away from him, he showed sadness and could not eat; that is why, when the wet nurse had fed him, she used to put him in his cradle near the elephant, who looked at him with a real kindness. When he slept, he would chase the flies with his trunk; when he cried, he found a way to cradle him with that same trunk, and tried to settle him and get him back to sleep.]

Saint-Jure's example of a caring elephant might have been familiar to early

modern readers of Pliny or of travel writing, but his elephant tells us something rather distinctive about fellow-feeling's capaciousness and its limits.[21]
First, this touching form of child care seems to suggest the ecumenical broad-
ness of Saint-Jure's understanding of the ways in which sympathies can bind
us (a broadly construed "us") together despite apparent differences. Compassion is *natural*, Saint-Jure argues, because it happens even between different
species. (Contrast his elephant with Le Moyne's lions, who stick resolutely to
their own kind.)

Saint-Jure's invocation of natural law also calls attention to some of the
displacements that this form of natural love imposes. The passage figures two
forms of child care: the elephant and the wet nurse. The elephant's cradling of
the baby springs from a surprising but natural love, whereas the wet nurse's
care of the child is an artificial reproduction of the natural, a paid labor that
replaces maternal care with a socially sanctioned substitute. Together, these
two iterations of naturalness serve to remind us of the surprising absence of
maternal affect from religious discussions of the naturalness of compassion
that draw on the tradition of natural law even as they appropriate surprising
anecdotes such as Saint-Jure's elephant. At a moment when the Catholic Reformation was particularly insistent on the value of Christian motherhood, its
figuration is largely absent from Catholic writings on compassion. Although
Catholic writers insist on the naturalness of emotion, they figure that nature
chiefly through the relation of limb to limb, man to landscape, or man to
animal. The early modern compassionate elephant could be read as an expansion of traditionally imagined forms of community, but it also trumpets other
forms of exclusion.

Saint-Jure's elephant asks us to imagine Christianity's universal love as a
socially surprising and capacious bond capable of pulling together the vast
and the tiny, but at other instances Saint-Jure endorses a narrower and particularized view of community that understands some fellow humans to be
closer to us than others. Thus he makes room for a specifically Jesuit form of
fellow-feeling, arguing:

> Tous les Religieux doivent pour ces raisons aimer leurs Freres plus
> particulierement que les autres, et leur rendre de grans témoignages
> d'une vraye et sincere charité, nous en nostre Compagnie, qui fais-
> ons une profession toute special d'aimer le prochain, et de travailler
> à son salut, le devons sans doute executer advantage: car ne seroit-ce
> pas une chose estrange, et que tout homme de jugement trouveroit

extravagante, que nous nous exposions à toutes sortes de danger par terre et par mer, et allions jusques au bout du monde chercher des personnes inconnuës pour les convertir, et exercer envers elles toutes les actions de la Charité Chrestienne, et que nous laissons icy des personnes qui pour plusieurs raisons nous doivent estre beaucoup plus considerables et plus cheres, et nos Freres, sans leur faire premierement et plus qu'aux autres sentir les tendresses de nos affections, et les effets de nostre zele? Que diroit-on d'un Medecin, qui abandonneroit chez soy son pere, sa mere, ses freres et ses sœurs malades, sans apporter pour leur guerison ce qui seroit de son art, et s'en iroit bien loin traiter de pauvres villageois, et les assister avec grand soin et grande assiduité dans leurs maladies? Certainement on seroit fort surpris d'un tel procedé, et on se regarderoit l'un l'autre par estonnement d'une telle folie, où tomberoient pourtant ceux d'entre nous, qui zelez du salut des estrangers, ne le seroient pas de celuy de nos Peres et de nos Freres, pour lequel à ce dessein il faut que tous les jours ils fassent quelque action particulière, quand ce ne seroit que quelque priere à Dieu. (153–54)

[If, for all these reasons, the Religious must love their brothers more particularly than others, and show them great evidence of a real and sincere charity, must not we who in our company have a very special profession to love our neighbor and to work for his salvation, have an even stronger reason to do this? Wouldn't it be strange, something that every man of good judgment would find extravagant, if, exposing ourselves to all kinds of dangers by sea and by land, by going to the ends of the world to find unknown people to convert and toward whom we exercise all the actions of Christian charity, we then left here near to us people who should be much dearer to us for various reasons, without making them feel principally and more than anyone else the tenderness of our affections and the effects of our zeal? What would we say of a doctor who left his father, his mother, his brothers, and his sick sisters at home, without doing anything that his art prescribes for their cure, going instead far away to care for poor villagers, to help them with great care in their illness? Assuredly we would be rather surprised by this, and we would look at one another with amazement at the sight of such madness. Yet it is into that madness that we would fall, those of us who, fired up for the salvation of strangers, ignore that of our fathers and brothers, for whom we must do something particular every day, even if it is only a prayer to God.]

The community is delineated less capaciously than in the story of the elephant: all humans and even some elephants deserve charity, but some deserve it more than others. In this lengthy defense, Saint-Jure argues for a community within the human community, for the ability to recognize a particular allegiance—here, that of the religious order—which compels a particular kind of charitable connection. The passage teems with the language of particularity, distinction, hierarchy, even as it touts the universal. Priests must love more particularly then others, for they have professionalized the Gospel's call, making "a very special profession to love our neighbor." Here "profession" primarily means, of course, "making an announcement, an intention," as in the term "profession de foi." But it also points to the ways in which religious communities formed a special emotional elite, a crack team of compassion, and in so forming themselves further endorsed hierarchies of those who were more or less worthy of such emotion. Here, those near are to be targeted "principally and more than anyone else." The image of the doctor (another caring professional) who shocks because he cares for distant others rather than looking after his own is particularly surprising given the Gospel stricture to leave one's family (Matthew 19:29). Saint-Jure argues instead that one should on the contrary care first for those near to us, that charity begins at home. But the borders of that home are hard to define. If on the one hand charity is a more perfect union than that of kinship, as Saint-Jure suggests in a passage I described earlier, but on the other the doctor is to be chided for leaving his sick mother at home (as Le Moyne's charitable Jellyby was mocked for her interest in overseas work), there seems to be some degree of fuzziness about its borders.

This account of Jesuit fellow-feeling is not just a description of a particular community; it also works to creates a community of like-minded sympathizers with Saint-Jure's view. The writer works to chivvy his reader into agreement, pushing us to affirm his case: "Wouldn't it be strange, something that every man of good judgment would find extravagant?" Likewise, at the view of the doctor who leaves his family behind we are invited to look at one another in amazement. The community of readers is carefully if cheerfully coerced into sympathizing with Saint-Jure's position: a gerrymandering of emotional communities. In its insistence on differentiating between the known and unknown in need of help, Saint-Jure's text seeks to shape a new kind of commonsense common knowledge about the proper procedures of compassionate action.

Saint-Jure's charity reflects on action in the world, but it is also insistently erudite, and in many cases its considerations of otherness are chiefly philological. A large portion of the text is devoted to careful readings of the New Testament and early Christianity, proclaiming it the only site of such emotion: "La Charité . . . est en terre la marque du Christianisme et la vertu particuliere des Chrestiens" (116) ["Charity . . . is on earth the mark of Christianity and the particular virtue of Christians"]. Where Paul described the new law of Christianity as marking the move from fear to love, Saint-Jure makes compassion the distinguishing feature of the new religion. He briefly conjures up a vision of the Church as a place of overwhelming sentiment, suggesting that the earliest priests always had a handkerchief handy because of their overwhelming compassion for their fellow men, a sentimentalizing of Paul's early Christians in the same way that his mutually tender limbs represent an emotional spin on Paul's original image.[22] But this insistence on a Christian monopoly soon drifts into a number of learned remarks that suggest, on the contrary, a willingness to recognize compassion on the part of other religions: "Mais je remarque que generalement tout homme de bien, en tout temps, et en tout lieu est misericordieux et sensible aux miseres d'autruy. Le mesme mot qui parmy les Hebreux, signifie bon, juste et saint, *chasid*, signifie encore misericordieux, tendre et compassif" (162). ["But I note that generally every good man, in every time and place, is merciful and sensitive to the sufferings of others. The same word which, in Hebrew, means good, just, and holy, *chasid*, also means merciful, tender, and compassionate."][23] Saint-Jure briefly abandons the particularizing dynamic describing Christianity's uniqueness, and embraces the universal: "tout homme . . . tout temps . . . tout lieu." He generously extends the right to compassion to other religions and other historical moments. All this marks an expansion of emotion: historically, geographically, socially.

For Saint-Jure, more than most commentators of the period, compassion must be both an internal emotion—a gut feeling—and an external practice:

Revestez-vous des entrailles de misericorde, dit saint Paul, qui par ces paroles veut que nous ayons exterieurement et interieurement cet esprit de pitié pour le prochain. *Induite*, revestez-vous, voilà pour l'exterieur, comme si l'Apostre disoit, revestez-vous de la

misericorde et de la compassion envers vostre prochain, comme
d'une belle robe que vous portiez par tout, et par laquelle vous soyez
reconnus vrais Chrestiens, enfans de Dieu, et distinguez des autres,
comme on reconnoist un Religieux à l'habit, et on le distingue d'un
seculier, et un homme d'une femme. *Viscera*, des entrailles, voilà
pour l'interieur. (156–57)

[Clothe yourselves in the bowels of mercy, says saint Paul, who by
this means that we should have both outside and within this spirit
of pity for our neighbor. *Induite*, clothe yourselves: that's the exterior. It is as if the Apostle were saying: clothe yourselves in mercy
and compassion toward your neighbor, like a beautiful dress that
you wear everywhere, and by which we can recognize true Christians, children of God, and distinguished from others, as one recognizes a monk by his habit, by which he can be distinguished from a
layman, or a man from a woman. *Viscera*, bowels, that is for the interior.]

In Saint-Jure's version of Paul, the Christian must both feel and show his charity, and both facets of the Christian self come into being together. Our interior emotion, the bowels, are set forth on external show; we bring the inside
out in our performance of our Christian selves. In Reformation England,
Kristine Steenbergh suggests, the rhetoric of compassionate bowels marks
both an opening, a softening to the exterior world, but also a closure, a control of the border between self and other.[24] Here, Saint-Jure's recall of the
Pauline bowels functions as just this sort of affective sphincter. The expansive
dynamic of the text, insisting on compassion's universalism, also hinges on
this concern about how to distinguish "true Christians" from something
else—for Paul, the old order of Jewishness; for Saint-Jure, the threat of Protestantism against which the new universalist Jesuit order fought. Properly
clothed in compassion, Saint Jure suggests, the true Christian will easily be
distinguished from others, although his certainty that a monk can be recognized by his habit seems to counter a French proverbial wisdom that was already current in the seventeenth century: the habit does not make the monk.[25]
Lurking behind the apparent generosity of his ecumenical compassion is the
excluded figure of the false Christian who is as different from the true Christian as is man from woman. And yet Saint-Jure's method suggests how hard it
might be to distinguish these parties, given that all Christians shared Paul's

vision of universal love and a universal Church even as they sought to reject each other from their vision of charity. The figure of the false Christian represents that which is distant and yet worryingly close at hand. Elephants yes, false Christians no; for Saint-Jure, Jesuit compassion must police the boundary between the body of the order and the outside world which threatens it.

Compassion and Difference
Blaise Pascal: Compassion's Differential Geometry

It is easy to think that in identifying these false Christians Saint-Jure might be referencing his Protestant neighbors, who look like true Christians but, from the Jesuit perspective, are quite other. Saint-Jure can imagine the compassion of the ancients, but his contemporaries are more proximately disturbing. Yet a midcentury Jesuit would have been at least as likely to critique another sort of Christian, a Catholic even closer to home: the Jansenist.

The battle between Jesuits and Jansenists was fierce, and none fought it more firmly than the Jansenist Blaise Pascal. Pascal's disregard for Jesuit reasoning (he had attacked Le Moyne, among others, in the *Lettres provinciales*) had often set him against them; here, we see that even his imagining of compassion will set him at odds with the Jesuit and Capuchin account of compassion's sociable universalism. In the *Pensées*, Pascal posits a form of compassion that is radically distinct from that examined in the first half of this chapter and that illuminates his larger understanding of salvation. For Pascal, asking for whom we should feel compassion is not a social differentiation but rather an assessment of differing approaches to our own potential salvation, and of salvation's necessary differentiation of souls.

Some of Pascal's observations on compassion sit squarely within the same Augustinian tradition that underwrites La Rochefoucauld's maxims, revealing the stakes of our self-interest even as we respond to the other's suffering: "Plaindre les malheureux n'est pas contre la concupiscence. Au contraire, on est bien aise d'avoir à rendre ce témoignage d'amitié et à s'attirer la reputation de tendresse sans rien donner" (S 541, LG 556). ["To pity the unfortunate is not contrary to concupiscence. On the contrary, we can quite well give such evidence of friendship and acquire the reputation of kindly feeling, without giving anything."][26] Where the writers I discussed in the first half of this chapter imagine the sociability of compassion to indicate its naturalness, Pascal points to the flaws of such a social understanding of emotion: "tendresse" in this scenario is a performance for the outside world rather than a signal of an inner virtue. For Pascal, following Augustine, our organization on behalf of others points not to true love but to concupiscence: "Grandeur de l'homme dans sa concupiscence même d'en avoir su tirer un règlement admirable et en avoir fait un tableau de la charité" (LG 109, S 150). ["The greatness of man even in his concupiscence, to have known how to extract from it a wonderful code, and to have drawn from it a picture of benevolence"] (128). As we saw in the previous chapter, Pascal's fellow Jansenist Pierre Nicole develops similar insights into a paradoxical defense of civility in the world. Pascal is not prepared to do that; in his formulation this human instinct is somehow admirable but remains only a "tableau," a picture.

Pascal's broader appraisal of compassion's possibilities is central to his whole project of Christian apology. The language of compassion, like everything else, turns around our confrontation with the truth of God's existence, on which depends our own salvation. In the lengthy fragment Philippe Sellier terms "Lettre pour porter à rechercher Dieu" (S 681, LG 398), key to the concerns of the *Pensées* as a whole, Pascal rails against those freethinkers who scorn God without making an effort to look for him: "Cette négligence n'est pas supportable." ["This negligence is insufferable"] (66). Making the effort is key. Pascal distinguishes between those who look for God and those who choose not to care: "une extreme différence de ceux qui travaillent de toutes leurs forces à s'en instruire, à ceux qui vivent sans s'en mettre en peine et sans y penser" ["a vast difference between those who strive with all their power to inform themselves, and those who live without troubling or thinking about it"]. For Pascal, the possibility of compassion itself stems from this differentiation: "Je ne puis avoir que de la compassion pour ceux qui gémissent sincèrement dans ce doute." ["I can have only compassion for those who sincerely bewail their doubt."] Compassion is allotted to those who strive to know God; but for those who choose to live the unexamined life, "je les considère d'une manière toute différente" ["I look upon them in a manner quite different"], and their blindness to God must exclude them from all compassion: "Cette negligence en une affaire où il s'agit d'eux-mêmes, de leur éternité, de leur tout, m'irrite plus qu'elle ne m'attendrit. Elle m'étonne et m'épouvante: c'est un monstre pour moi." ["This carelessness in a manner which concerns themselves, their eternity, their all, moves me more to anger than to pity; it astonishes and shocks me; it is to me monstrous."][27] In Pascal's rigorous account, compassion is far from the universalist natural law shared by our three previous writers. Instead, compassion always and necessarily differentiates because salvation is granted differentially; on that differentiation, all else depends. Compassion's sorting mechanism, whose secular workings we traced in the previous chapter, now figures the larger sorting of salvation.

Pascal's scouring account does, however, allow for affect to spur us to agency. If he himself cannot feel compassion for those who refuse God, he suggests that they might be able to "avoir pitié d'eux-mêmes et à faire au moins quelques pas pour tenter s'ils ne trouveront pas de lumières" ["to have pity upon themselves, and to take at least some steps in the endeavour to find light"] (71). Where we imagine self-pity as a form of luxurious self-regard, Pascal imagines it as the rock-bottom recognition of our misery, fragility, and sin; out of this devastating self-regard, even the most miserable might be spurred to climb. Self-pity can, paradoxically, lead to action.

Elsewhere Pascal suggests that pity or compassion (he seems to use the terms as equivalents) is internally differentiated: there are different kinds of pity, allocated to different kinds of sufferers. These different categories of pity hinge, as does all else, on the essential distinction between those who seek God and those who refuse to seek: "On doit avoir pitié des uns et des autres, mais on doit avoir pour les uns une pitié qui naît de tendresse, et pour les autres une pitié qui naît de mépris" (S 662, LG 403). ["We must have pity on the one kind and the other, but for one kind we must have a pity born from tenderness, and for the others a pity born from scorn."][28] Those without religion, considered as a general category, are certainly worthy of Pascal's pity, but that pity itself is torn in two: on the one hand, pity as an easily tender emotion for those who make an effort to know God but have not yet reached him; on the other, for those who do not look to know him, only pity that stems from scorn. If today we tend to distinguish between a caring and nonhierarchical compassion and a hierarchical and scornful pity, Pascal makes both those affective functions possible within the single term "pity."

Pascal's pity has an extraordinary affective range, and it rewards those sufferers who stretch to meet its challenge. Pascal's tenderness is not the tenderness of Madeleine de Scudéry's formalized social geography, which is a tenderness mapped by instances of civility; it marks out instead the person ready to tender themselves, to reach toward God.[29] The person who reaches can be met with tenderness, with human love or caritas. This desperate reach of the person seeking God, and the emotional response it occasions, are at the heart of Pascal's affective project.

Even the pity that stems from scorn does not stay there; it is recuperated by the stretchiness of Pascal's affective range. In the same fragment (S 662, LG

403), Pascal continues to consider those who resist religion, and notes that
their stubborn blindness is a sign of something larger at work that might
bring light to those less enlightened than Pascal himself:

> Mais ceux-là mêmes qui semblent les plus opposés à la gloire de la
> religion, nous en ferons le premier argument qu'il y a quelque chose
> de surnaturel. [Ils] n'y seront pas inutiles pour les autres. Car un
> aveuglement de cette sorte n'est pas une chose naturelle. Et si leur
> folie les rend si contraires à leur propre bien, elle servira à en garan-
> tir les autres par l'horreur d'un exemple si déplorable, et d'une folie
> si digne de compassion.

> [But even those who seem most opposed to the glory of religion,
> from them we will make the first argument that there is some form
> of supernatural. They will not be useless for others. For a blindness
> of this sort is not a natural thing. And if their madness makes them
> so opposed to their own good, it will also serve to keep others from
> the horror of so deplorable an example, and from a madness so wor-
> thy of compassion.][30]

The mad who turn their back on religion are so mad that they must figure as
the proof of the "surnaturel"; in their extreme opposition they prove the opposite of what they proclaim. Their madness is the proof of fallen nature, and
the horrific example they give to the world means that others will be restored
to the Christian fold because of them. In this way their exemplary and extreme status recuperates even such blind outsiders for compassion. In the earlier part of the fragment, they were worthy of Pascal's pity born from scorn;
here, it seems that the granting of their place (as negative exemplars) within a
larger scheme of salvation makes them potential recipients of compassion
from others, too. For in this passage Pascal seems to distinguish between different sorts of compassionaters. He himself is already on the side of God: he
has "pity on the one kind and the other," pity springing up for saved and sin-
ners alike. But "the others," those slower to see eternal truth, need to see the
supernatural blindness of those most opposed to religion in order to be roused
to compassion. Pascal's fragmentary and thorny theory of compassion attends
to all points of its differential geometry. He gives his attention to both the
object and subject of compassion, the sufferers and the seekers, the others
who do not look for God and those other others who will find God because of

them. All of these are able to enter somehow into the possibilities of the Christian affective promise.

Whichever way we parse them, these observations on pity and compassion are not marginal to Pascal's project. Where other theologians dwell on worldly suffering, Pascal's horror at those who refuse to acknowledge what is at stake in Christian salvation makes the skittering of affective variance—pity, irritation, tenderness, scorn, compassion—a way into the larger investigation of human misery and joy at the heart of the *Pensées*. Pascal thinks through these affective extremes. The *Pensées* are a polemical, angry text, and Pascalian pity and compassion are produced out of that anger; they are wielded as weapons in a battle with eternal consequences.

Though still a Catholic, albeit a marginalized one, Pascal's take on compassion puts him close to the two Protestant theologians I will explore in the rest of this chapter. Where Le Moyne, Yves, and Saint-Jure all imagine compassion as a natural universal, an easy reach (even as they indicate, sometimes against themselves, that there are limits to it), Pascal and the Protestants are clear from the start that such a unilateral universal is built around clearly defined limits, and that it spawns a series of distinctions. They articulate their compassion around a bitter awareness of boundaries. For these polemicists, beset by powerful antagonists—the Jesuits or state power—the language of compassion becomes an important tool for acknowledging difference: both theological difference, according to which salvation cannot be imagined to be possible for all, and political difference, in which some groups know themselves to be on losing ground. Compassion cannot be universal when such rigorous and significant separation is at stake.

Protestants in the second half of the century led a life structured by the pains of that separation. The increasing disregard for the terms of the Edict of Nantes and the fear of Protestant separatism led to *dragonnade* attacks on Protestant communities and eventually in 1685 to the Revocation's outlawing of Protestantism. The writers I address here bookend this period. Moïse Amyraut writes in a position of relative coexistence in midcentury, and Pierre Jurieu in the bloodily contentious years after the Revocation led many Huguenots to seek to leave France.

If Catholic writing on compassion inflects the commonalities imagined by natural philosophy with an anxiety about distance and proximity, Protestant writing takes up the question of *caritas* with a different relation to political formations. Catholics in religious orders, even contested ones like the Jesuits, set out a particular understanding of human sociability. Protestant writers, of course, had a very different take on human potential, and their reading of compassion insists on the gulf between God's mercy and human fault. But Protestants also set out a particularly political reading of human incapacity. It is not only God who relates to human suffering; in Protestant writing, we also see a gesture toward the political crisis of the confessional community, and eventually a call for a political intervention to resolve it.

Moïse Amyraut: Tender Humanity

The great Protestant theologian Moïse Amyraut, pastor and professor to the important Protestant church at Saumur in the first half of the seventeenth century, was widely known in his own time in part because of an incident at the synod of Charenton in 1631. Charged with submitting a document to king Louis XIII, the young Amyraut refused to kneel before the monarch, arguing that the requirement to kneel to the king was an infraction of the Edict of Nantes that guaranteed his Protestant freedom and insisting that he should be allowed to stand in the same way as Catholic churchmen at the same gathering.[31] (Eventually he persuaded Richelieu of this.) Throughout his career, Amyraut got along well with centralized Catholic power because of his insistence that subjects should obey the king (if not kneel to him), a doctrine he claimed with vigor even during the contentious years of the civil skirmishes known as the Fronde. Like Bayle and unlike most other senior Protestant figures, Amyraut called for a sort of freedom of conscience, rather than a defense of faith on narrower sectarian grounds.[32] He was involved with many intra-Protestant debates, but it was only in 1652 that he turned his attention to a major statement on Christian life, in *La morale chrestienne*, which appeared in six volumes over the course of the decade, and has been described as "the first major attempt within Reformed Protestantism to produce an ethical system."[33]

Protestant accounts of Amyraut celebrated him for his own practice of compassion to the poor, without regard for sectarian difference: Pierre Bayle notes that he gave freely to Catholics and Protestants alike.[34] Where Jesuits were often praised by their biographers for their kindness to the poor, Bayle's description of Amyraut's ecumenical charity makes clear that if Catholic writing often chose to ignore its Protestant other, Protestant culture did not have that luxury; its accounts of compassion were always embedded in sectarian difference even as they described attempts to overcome it.[35]

Amyraut's theological take on compassion, too, was distinctly different from that of Catholic writers who emphasized the potential of fellow-feeling even if they were unable to follow through on its promise. Where Catholic compassionates celebrated the human practice of compassion, Amyraut was sceptical about human feeling and looked instead to divine mercy. In an early sermon, he notes:

> Si nous regardons vers les hommes, nous n'y trouverons point de matiere de confiance ny de consolation non plus. Ou bien ils n'auront point de compassion de nostre calamite, parce qu'ils sont impitoyables et meschans: ou s'ils sont touchés de compassion pour nous, cela ne durera pas, parce qu'ils sont inconstans; ou s'ils sont capables de persister en cette disposition, ils sont incapables de nous secourir, à cause de leur impuissance.[36]

> [If we look to men, we will find neither cause for confidence nor consolation. Either they will have no compassion for our calamity, because they are pitiless and cruel; or if they are touched by compassion for us, that will not last, because they are inconstant; or if they should be capable of keeping on that way, they are then incapable of helping because of their lack of power.]

Amyraut's Protestant theology insists on the incapacity of man on either the level of emotion or action; our meager compassion traces only the inability of the human to match up to the divine.

Like many of the Catholic compassionates, Amyraut is opposed to Stoic critiques of pity, but on rather different grounds. The fourth volume of the *Morale chrestienne* sets out the terms of his difference with the Stoics: "Quand les Stoïciens ont dit qu'il falloit que le Sage fust insensible à la Pitié, et que neantmoins il fist toutes les choses louables auxquelles les autres sont portés par cette passion, ils se sont en quelque sorte figurés un Dieu, et non pas un homme." ["When the Stoics said that the wise man should be insensible to Pity, yet that nonetheless he should do all the praiseworthy things to which others are brought by that passion, they imagined some sort of God, and not a man."][37] Like the Stoics, Amyraut rates humans as essentially weak; unlike them, he cannot imagine a special sort of exceptional human, the wise man who might properly apply compassion (like the man Descartes figures as the "généreux"). To imagine such a man borders on idolatry, for it imagines someone with skills close to the divine. Referencing Aristotle's familiar pity/fear mechanism, he remarks:

Il faut donc d'un costé estre hors du peril de toute calamité, pour ne
sentir jamais cette sorte d'affliction; ce qui passe la condition de
l'humanité; et de l'autre, avoir la bonté de la Divinité, pour se voir
absolument au dessus des atteintes du malheur, et neantmoins ne
laisser pas de faire du bien aux miserables. (*Morale*, 559–60)

[So on the one hand we must be out of all fear of danger, to never
feel this kind of affliction, which is beyond our human condition;
and on the other, we must have the goodness of the Divine, to see
oneself as absolutely above misfortune and yet not neglect to do
good to the unfortunate.]

We must act, but we must not feel too much; in this scenario, only God is
capable of the proper balance that, for someone like Descartes, was attainable
by the right sort of noble human. Amyraut's take on compassion is structured
around his Calvinist understanding of the radical heterogeneity between God
and man. The ultimate compassion is that of God, and it is not just unattain-
able but also unknowable: God's forgiveness, he writes, goes beyond the
knowledge of men or of angels.[38] Where many seventeenth-century writers
called for men to deploy judgment in compassion or to let compassion serve
as a form of judgment, Amyraut gives up the task of judgment to God.

And yet despite this unknowable divine, Amyraut also argues for a deeply
sociable understanding of what he calls "our common humanity."[39] Unlike his
fellow Protestant d'Aubigné, for whom the term "humanity" pushes some
sorts of Frenchmen aside, Amyraut reaches for a broader meaning. He draws
on the familiar argument that for our fellow human, "nous les devons aimer
parce que ce sont des hommes, qui ont un estre semblable au nostre, et digne
de nos affections. Or il se trouve mesmes des bestes qui sont sensibles aux
maux qu'elles voyent endurer à celles de leur espece." (565) ["We must love
them because they are men, who have a being like our own, and are worthy of
our affections. For even animals are sensitive to the sufferings they see one of
their species enduring."] Going beyond Aristotle's mechanism and instead
drawing on a broader vocabulary of emotion he argues that we feel for others
not only out of self-interest but also because we love "tendrement" (566)
["tenderly"]. Amyraut's tender humanity suggests that the vaunted "tendresse"
of the 1650s was not just the preserve of the Scudéry circle. Protestant theology, too, was moving toward imagining an emotion that escaped the Aristotelian machines we saw at work in the previous chapter.

Amyraut's compassion is certainly structured around gaps and distinctions: not the distinctions between different groups of humans so dear to d'Aubigné and the Aristotelians, but the distinctions between feeling and action and between human and divine emotion. This allows him to draw more pointed attention to the difference between *caritas* and compassion, which the Catholic writers often elide:

> Car il y a de la ressemblance entre le sentiment general de la
> Charité, et le mouvement particulier de la Compassion, en ce qu'en
> l'un et en l'autre nous nous portons à faire à autruy ce que nous
> voudrions que l'on nous fist à nous-mesmes. Mais il ya aussi cette
> difference entre eux: c'est que dans le premier, l'idée de ce que nous
> voyons dans un autre, et dont nous faisons quelque application sur
> nous, est plus esloignée; dans le second, elle est beaucoup plus de-
> terminée, et considerée comme une chose proche de nous, ce qui
> fait qu'elle touche plus vivement, et qu'elle emeut beaucoup plus
> puissamment nos ames. (567)

> [For there is a resemblance between the general sentiment of char-
> ity, and the particular movement of compassion, in that in one and
> the other we do to others what we would like to be done unto us.
> But there is also this difference between them: in the first, the idea
> of what we see in another, which has some hold on us, is more dis-
> tant; in the second, it is much more determinate, and considered
> near to us, in that it touches us vividly, and moves our souls more
> powerfully.]

In the first part of this comparison, Amyraut describes *caritas* as feeling and compassion as action, providing a more precise vocabulary distinction than that used by the Catholic writers. In the second part, he localizes compassion. But this is not exactly the problematic of proximity and distance so troubling to the Jesuit writers, for the distance and closeness he describes refers to our interior world rather than our sphere of global influence. Rather, Amyraut's concern distinguishes a concept from something closer to political pragmatism. Where *caritas* is abstract, Amyraut suggests, compassion is necessarily localized in that it requires an encounter that could potentially elicit an action. Compassion is not just an abstract theory of the universal but an embedded practice.

What might such a practice look like for a mid-seventeenth-century Protestant? In a long analysis of who does and does not feel compassion, Amyraut argues that knowing things about politics and history make us compassionate, putting "mille choses devant les yeux qui ne sont point considerées par les ignorans" ["a thousand things in front of our eyes which are not considered by the ignorant"].[40] He might, of course, have had a particular history in mind. In an earlier volume of *La morale chrestienne*, Amyraut describes the recent history of Europe, setting out the patterns of divisions between Catholics and Protestants across several countries and weighing up the peculiar situation of tension and coexistence so central to the post-Nantes, post-Westphalian European order:

> Ainsi non seulement la différence de la religion ne leur a pas osté ce
> que tous les hommes ont de commun, mais ils sont demeurés pour
> la plus part habitans d'un mesme païs, citoyens d'un mesme Estat,
> sujets d'un mesme Prince, voisins dans une mesme ville, parens et
> crées d'un mesme sang, et hormis la religion, conjoints par les plus
> sacrés liens qui puissent estre entre les hommes. Et neantmoins cette
> diversité d'opinions en ce qui touché la Religion, semble bien sou-
> vent avoir tout à fait esteint en eux les sentimens de charité et d'hu-
> manité que toutes ces autres relations y devroyent produire.[41]

> [Thus not only religious difference did not take away from them
> what all men have in common, but they stayed for the most part
> inhabitants of one same country, citizens of one same State, subjects
> of one same Prince, neighbors in one same town, relatives made
> from one same blood, and, outside of religion, joined together by
> the most sacred bond that there can be between men. And yet this
> diversity of opinions about religion seems often to have completely
> extinguished in them the sentiments of charity and humanity that
> all these other relations should produce.]

Amyraut's listing of the ties that bind is complex and multilayered: country, state, prince, town, blood, all of which might be imagined in some complicated and overlapping relation to the other, creating a dense network of common ground. But all of these commonalities are destroyed by the absolute distinction of religion, which in sundering other ties sunders precisely that—charity—which should by both Catholic and Protestant accounts be a universal bond. In a rhetorically gracious mode, Amyraut demurs from listing anti-Protestant persecutions even as he manages to speak of them, but without entering into detail on Protestant suffering he nonetheless clearly expresses a particularly Protestant relation to compassion not only through his position on divine mercy but also in his understanding that charity and compassion are social practices that define and realign communities.[42] Already in 1652, Amyraut's deft unpacking of Protestant compassion in a Catholic France seems to adumbrate what lies in store for the Huguenot community.

Pierre Jurieu: Political Crisis and Pity's Scorn

My second Protestant, Pierre Jurieu, was to experience the horrors of what Amyraut could only fear, and in response he sets out a clearly Protestant take on compassion as a political emotion. Jurieu's explicitly sectarian reworking of *caritas* makes clear that the discourse of compassion is inextricably bound up with the question of religious intolerance. In this writing, compassion is combat: not the internal battles fought by Pascal but rather responses to a wounding political crisis.

Jurieu began his ministry in the Reformed Church in 1661, the same year that Louis XIV began to govern and that Yves published his great work on mercy. After his exile in 1681, he became a rallying figure for Protestants during the years of Revocation and refuge, although by the 1690s a bitter dispute with Pierre Bayle over the nature of tolerance led to his exclusion from the Protestant establishment.[43] The year 1681 was a turning point in the state persecution of Protestants. For the first time, organized and systematic state violence made itself felt against French Protestants, with troops of soldiers or "dragonnades" sent to Protestant settlements to forcibly convert inhabitants. From 1683, Protestant groups began to gather for open-air worship known as the "assemblées du Désert," though such resistance could be punished by with a period in the galleys. Since ministers were compelled to emigrate (unlike their congregations), Jurieu left France for Rotterdam after the suppression of the Académie de Sedan in 1681 and in that same year published his first major work, the *Politique du Clergé de France ou Entretiens curieux de deux Catholiques Romains*. This text called for a separation of civil and religious orders, and it triggered a great outpouring of texts, responses, and letters.

Characterized by a deeply entrenched sectarianism, Jurieu's writing on compassion throughout his career delineates the terms of pity and compassion with more fervor than Amyraut. For Jurieu, even more than for Amyraut,

compassion is the preserve of God alone, and to arrogate it to the human indicates the extent of Catholic conceit. In a book on papism from 1687, Jurieu
argues that the Catholic doctrine of the intercession of saints appropriates divine glory for humankind, praising the "créature" rather than the Creator.[44]
Jurieu argues that mercy comes from God alone and cannot be mediated by
figures like the Virgin:

> Rien n'est plus reserve à Dieu que l'exercice de la misericorde que le
> Prophete implore dans le Pseaume 51. *O Dieu aye pitié de moy selon
> ta misericorde* &c. Le Papisme renversant le Dieu souverain de des-
> sus le Thrône de grace, fait dire à son penitent: *Ayés pitié de moy ô
> nostre Dame, qui estes appellée mere de misericorde, et selon les en-
> trailles de vos compassions purgés moy de mes iniquités, épandés vostre
> grace sur moy et ne retirés pas de moy vostre clemence ordinaire.*[45]

> [Nothing is more reserved to God than the exercise of mercy for
> which the Prophet begs in Psalm 51. *O God have pity on me accord-
> ing to your mercy* etc. Papism throws the sovereign God from his
> Throne of grace, and makes its penitent say: *Have pity on me Our
> Lady, who art called mother of mercy, and according to the bowels of
> your compassion purge me from all iniquities, shed your grace on me
> and do not withdraw your clemency from me.*]

Where Catholic writers stress the importance of human judgment in the
proper application of compassion, Jurieu rebuffs the notion that judgment
belongs to any but God and that we will know anything of it until the Last
Judgment:

> Je ne nie pas que Dieu n'ait de la compassion et de la misericorde
> pour ceux qui errent de bonne foi; mais il y a de l'impieté à étendre
> cette misericorde à toutes les erreurs, et de la temerité à définir, elle
> s'étend precisément jusques-là. Nous ne saurons qu'au jour du juge-
> ment, jusqu'où Dieu poussera les severités de sa justice et les
> relâchemens de sa misericorde.[46]

> [I do not deny that God has compassion and mercy for those who
> err in good faith; but there is impiety in extending this mercy to all
> errors, and temerity in defining its exact dimensions. We will know

only on the Day of Judgment to where God will push the severity
of his justice and how he will shed his mercy.]

Like Amyraut, Jurieu underscores the absolute difference that obtains between
our human emotion and the dispositions of the divine.

Yet where Amyraut spoke of a tenderly shared humanity, for Jurieu as for
d'Aubigné compassion between humans is a sectarian sorting mechanism.
His deployment of the vocabulary of fellow-feeling does not confine itself to
the substance of theological disagreements over the place of mercy and forgiveness in salvation; he also draws on it in a show of aggression, using pity
as a barricade in various factional struggles. The term "compassion" is reserved for suffering Protestants, like the Calvinist Anne du Bourg, executed
in 1559, or the Protestant martyrs under Henri II who made "un spectacle
digne de toute compassion" ["a spectacle worthy of every compassion"], Jurieu's term recalling the Protestant pitiful spectacle of a century before.[47] A
chapter on Protestant martyrs castigates Catholic judges for their cruelty and
contrasts it with the behavior of wise judges, who show "une grande charité
et une tres grande compassion pour les misérables qu'ils se voient obligés
d'envoyer au supplice" ["a great charity and a great compassion for the miserable people that they find themselves obliged to punish"].[48] Of Protestant
refugees, he writes: "Dieu veüille que ces misérables trouvent dans les païs
étrangers des ames attendries et pleines de compassion." ["God willing, these
poor people shall find tender and compassionate souls in foreign lands."][49]
Compassion holds together the fragmented world of the Protestant diaspora;
it binds the dispersed community together in suffering and in an imagined
response to that misery, and in recalling the terms of the Wars of Religion it
binds sufferers into a historically rich Protestant tradition, too. The Protestants of the Refuge must imagine an affective proximity even as they are
compelled to scatter far from one another.

Jurieu's sectarianism also shapes his semantic distinctions, which take
him closer to modern usage in their separation of compassion and pity. On
the one hand, "worthy of every compassion," we have the Protestant; on the
other, the Catholic is to be pitied for the idiocy of his doctrine. Here, as sometimes in today's usage, pity denotes not kindness but contempt. One of Jurieu's most significant works, the giant *Histoire du Calvinisme et celle du
Papisme mises en parallele* of 1683, was written in angry response to the Catholic Louis Maimbourg's *Histoire du Calvinisme*, and from its opening page Jurieu deploys pity as a rhetorical weapon against his opponent: "Je ne suis quasi

plus en colere, la pitié a succedé presque à toute mon indignation." ["I am almost no longer angry, pity has nearly succeeded my indignation."][50] Likewise, Jurieu describes the Jesuit Père Menestrier's reasoning as "trop pitoyable pour en rire" ["too pitiful to be laughed at"].[51] In these iterations, pity is scornfully unfurled in order to distinguish superior Protestant judgment from contemptible Catholic opinion. This usage of pity appears also as the final instance in Furetière's 1690 definition of pity: "On dit aussi d'un homme qui raisonne, qui harangue, qui escrit mal, qu'il fait pitié." ["We also say of a man who reasons, who harangues, who writes badly, that he gives cause for pity."][52] Furetière's examples seems to suggest that pity is essentially a rhetorical tool used to dismantle precisely the rhetorical skills of one's opponent; it is not the man who dances badly or sings poorly who is derided as pitiful. By 1690, then, pity can be understood as a weapon in a verbal war, and it is the ferocious sectarian dialogue of the period, forged from Pascal to Jurieu, that makes room for our modern distinction.

The Protestant reading of compassion speaks back from compassion's edge; the Protestant experience redraws compassion's bitterly structural divides. Protestant writers make stronger distinctions (between *caritas* and compassion, or pity and compassion) than their Catholic counterparts do because their exceptional situation in the French seventeenth century—first tolerated and then exiled, but in each case a legal exception—brings them to reflect on compassion in very different ways. If Catholic compassion is troubled by the proper focus of compassion between proximity and distance, the diaspora of the Huguenot community in the first years of the Refuge pushes Jurieu and his peers to think very differently about the relation between near and far, us and them. Jurieu is the first of these writers to regard his own community—to be *compelled* to regard his own community—as the object of compassion rather than as the instigator of it.

The early modern official pronouncements (like the Edict of Nantes) which allowed or enforced some degree of toleration also succeeded in neatly categorizing and indeed reifying difference such that it could not be surmounted. The early modern discourse of *caritas* and its compassionate derivations, too, succeeded in delineating sectarian interests even as it claimed the status of a universal bond. Caritas and compassion regulated social and religious difference; although this compassionate language gestured across social gulfs and often was able to motivate real-world attempts to do the same, it also confirmed the distance between otherwise proximate communities.

In our present time, commentators and critics reproach us for our differential compassion, for our failure to respond to events in places that do not resemble our own with the same emotion that surges up when we consider places closer to us, in whatever way we imagine that proximity. But compassion is, as these debates suggest, always and necessarily differential, always seen from its edge. Instead of retraining our compassion, we should instead take care for compassion not to be our only response to suffering.

Chapter 4

Pitiful States

Marital Miscompassion and the Historical Novel

We can live in peace with those who have different opinions, as
we see in a family . . . and apply what is said about the defects of
wives . . . they must either be corrected or tolerated.

—Michel de l'Hôpital

I'll begin with a scene from an aristocratic marriage. A man recently returned
from a journey discovers his wife distraught, and, we are told, "touché de l'état
où il la voyait; il s'attendrit pour elle" (71) ["touched by the state he found her
in, felt compassion for her"] (201).[1] She has told the household that she is in
pain, and her domestics tell him she is sick; he goes to her and tries to distract
her from this unspecified bodily distress. "Croyant faire quelque diversion à
ses douleurs" ["believing that he might thereby divert her mind from her
pain"], he tells her about the death of another nobleman, the prince de Navarre. But as the reader knows, the woman is weeping because she is pregnant
by that particular man, whose battle death has just been reported to her. She
weeps all the harder when her husband, not knowing that she knew the man
in such a way nor that she already knows of his death, (re)tells her that the
prince is now dead.

At this point the tale—the *Histoire de la Comtesse de Tende*, by Marie-
Madeleine Pioche de la Vergne, comtesse de Lafayette—briefly proffers a very
muted sort of black humor: for the husband of the weeping woman, the comtesse de Tende, to imagine that, whatever her trouble, she might be diverted
by news of battle deaths says something of the peculiarity of communication

in early modern marriage.[2] This scene of compassionate marital misunderstanding, in which compassion marks a cognitive misfire, will be repeated constantly throughout Lafayette's work.[3] I call these scenes moments of "miscompassion," a compassion that points to a misreading of the other's pain. In the three previous chapters, we saw how early modern writers framed compassion as a form of judgment; in anxious counterpoint, Lafayette's work shows how compassion's judgment can often get things radically wrong. In this chapter, drawing on Lafayette's shorter fictions as well as a novel, I inquire into the repetition of these scenes of miscompassion and ask what it means for the new genres of historical fiction to build themselves around such repetitively unpromising affective forms.

To say that men sometimes misread women is perhaps old news, but such a term is curiously fitting, since the name for Lafayette's new genre experiment is the "nouvelle historique" or historical novella: a story that is about history but that is also new. The *nouvelle* is novel without yet being what we today call a novel.[4] In the confusion of ways one can translate the titles of genres, we should not lose sight of the fact that this genre is the same old story made over afresh. In repeating these moments of marital miscompassion, Lafayette points her reader to a larger historical repetition, and her forging of the novel from the fragments of other genres draws continually on the religious wars of the late sixteenth century.[5] Lafayette's scenes of failed marital compassion, seemingly disconnected from the official historical record, nonetheless look to the late seventeenth century's relation to the religious wars and their legacy; her fiction takes shape around this affective-political compromise.

In the *nouvelle* described above, the countess writes to her husband to tell him she is pregnant by the dead Navarre, and asks him to kill her to spare her shame and his. He refuses, and later she and her preterm baby die of fever. Hearing of his wife's death, we are told, "Le comte de Tende reçut cette nouvelle sans inhumanité, et même avec quelques sentiments de pitié, mais néanmoins avec joie" (124). ["The Comte de Tende received the news without inhumanity, and even with some sentiments of pity, but none the less with joy"] (204). The unnameably brief instance of the count's humanity seems importantly distinguished from the similarly swiftly dismissed passing of pity; human response is the most straightforward reaction to the news, whereas pity must be hailed with a "même," figuring its more complex schooling of emotion.[6] The neatly formal delineation of the husband's complicated emotions, in which pity is swiftly eclipsed by a positive joy, recalls and refines the contrary emotions we saw in the genre of the *histoire tragique* of Chapter 1, where a man's hatred and pity, love and disdain fought against one another.[7] In the *histoire tragique*, contradictory emotions were simultaneous; in Lafayette's version, surely influenced by Descartes's *Passions de l'âme*, conflicting emotions mark a movement from one response to the other: emotion is in itself a narrative form. This reworking of earlier topoi of the wars will be repeated in moments of marital drama seen elsewhere in Lafayette's work.

There has been much important and often contentious work on the social history of marriage, but Lafayette's strange spatialization of intimacy calls for another way of thinking about the place of marriage in the early novel.[8] Lafayette makes of marriage something more akin to what Stanley Cavell, in an ebullient reading of the Hollywood comedy of remarriage, has called "a mode of association."[9] In a very different vein, the anthropologist Elizabeth Povinelli has explored how we might imagine "a set of systematic relations between forms of love and forms of liberal governance," asking how the subject-in-love's "relay with another subject" takes place in a context of larger social dynamics which it figures or builds.[10] Putting Cavell and Povinelli in relay with one another, we see the kind of association sketched by Lafayette's marriages, a marital association placed in relation to other larger forms of social relations that we more usually designate as political. In Chapter 1, we saw how a dystopian version of the mother-child relation figured national crisis; in this chapter, the marital bond allows for an exploration of that same crisis, now seen from almost a century's distance. In Lafayette's writing, marriage is a structural question, considering what it takes to bring together two entities in a mode of association, and the new genre of the novel builds itself around such associative modes.

What does that structural association have to do with the work of compassion itself? One striking seventeenth-century definition of the verb "compatir"—to feel compassion, but also to get on well with, to be compatible—points to the ways we might understand these modes of association. In Furetière's 1690 dictionary, "compatir" encompasses the notion that to compassionate, as the early modern English verb puts it, is to be sensitive to the pain or suffering of another: "estre sensible à la douleur, à l'affliction d'autruy, avoir pitié de luy. Un cœur vrayement Chrêtien doit *compatir* aux maux de son prochain, et les soûlager de tout son possible." ["To be sensitive to the pain, the affliction of another, to have pity on him. A truly Christian heart must *compassionate* with the sufferings of his neighbor, and soothe them as best he can."][11] But the primary meaning Furetière gives is one of coexistence or at least mutually assured nondestruction: "demeurer ensemble . . . sans se

détruire l'un l'autre. L'eau et le vin se peuvent mesler et compatir ensemble."
["To stay together without destroying one another. Water and wine can mix
and *compassionate* together."] His definition of the verb *compatir* continues:
"Vivre bien avec quelqu'un. Ces deux associez sont de même humeur, ils compatissent bien ensemble. Ce mari est complaisant, il *compatit* bien avec sa
femme, il s'accommode à toutes ses humeurs." [To live well with someone.
These two associates are of the same humor, they *compassionate* well together.
This husband is agreeable, he *compassionates* well with his wife, he accommo-
dates himself to all her moods.][12]

In these definitions, compassion and space-sharing are associated with a
private or intimate relationship, that of the husband and wife, but they also
make room for larger social compatibility, as a definition from much earlier in
the century makes clear. In Randall Cotgrave's 1611 bilingual dictionary, compassion's relation to coexistence or forbearance or toleration is very evident.
For Cotgrave, "compatir" means primarily "to suffer, indure, abide, or beare
with, one another; to agree, concurre, accord, together," bringing us closer to
the baseline task of tolerance: to put up with someone different from oneself.[13] The range of this verb yokes together domestic stories, like the one I
recounted above, and larger questions of space sharing, like that between
Catholic and Protestant in early modern France.[14] In reading Lafayette, I follow the verb's ambition in bringing together two diverse parties—marital miscompassion and the question of religious toleration—and asking them to
accord together.

La Princesse de Montpensier: The Emotional Tableau

Let me pursue that question of compatibility by turning to another scene
from Lafayette's *La Princesse de Montpensier* of 1662, usually identified as the
first of the *nouvelles historiques*.[15] Where the story I described above, *La Comtesse de Tende*, uses the war as backdrop to the marital drama, *Montpensier* sets
the private and public story in explicit relation to one another. This is a longer
and more complicated story than *Tende*, drawing together reflections on all
sorts of alliances—friendships, contracts, accords—and suggesting the precariousness of those relations in times of war. The scene takes place on a night in
August 1572, on an aristocrat's estate where the prince de Montpensier, a
Catholic, has retreated for some respite from the wars. He is looking forward
to seeing his young wife, whom he had left in company with his best friend,

the comte de Chabannes, a Protestant in childhood who had converted to Catholicism out of friendship for the prince. The prince hears a noise coming from his wife's room. Being a jealous man, he thunders on the door and eventually forces it open. Inside the room, he finds his friend the comte de Chabannes "appuyé sur la table, avec un visage où la tristesse etait peinte, et comme immobile" ["leaning motionless on the table, his face a picture of sadness"] (184).[16] The prince is also immobile with shock. Across the room is the princess his wife, half-fainting on the floor. In the original edition of the text, the narrator comments, "Jamais peut-être la fortune n'a mis trois personnes en des états si pitoyables" (95). ["Fortune has perhaps never brought together three people in such a pitiful state"] (184). (Fortune, here, must surely be a nod to the novelist's capriciously self-interested disposition of her materials; in texts of the religious wars, it is Providence and not Fortune which brings about something worthy of our pity.)[17] The three figures, poised in tableau, are still. Finally the prince begins to speak, and he asks his wife and his friend what is going on, retaining, the narrator tells us, a tone of friendliness toward the count. In response to this, there is only silence: "La Princesse n'était pas capable de répondre, et le comte de Chabannes ouvrit plusieurs fois la bouche sans pouvoir parler" (95). ["The princess was not capable of replying, and the Comte de Chabannes opened his mouth several times without being able to speak"] (184). The three remain, looking at one another, triangulated around the room: one at the door, one at the table, one on the floor.

Lafayette's narrator leans in at this moment of paralysis to point the readers toward an appropriate reaction. This is a "pitoyable" or pitiful scene, the narrator tells us in the 1662 edition; it is worthy of our readerly pity even if pity is not operative between the characters themselves. Various manuscripts and later editions of the text, however, hesitate in describing the particularity of the scene; in some versions, "états pitoyables" ["pitiful states"] is replaced by "états violents" ["violent states"].[18] In the first, the reader is directed to feel in a particular way; in the other, we are given a glimpse of the feelings of the characters. This prevarication seems symptomatic of the author's uncertainty over the correct placement of compassion in the novel: Does it fall to the sixteenth-century characters, or to the seventeenth-century readers, to exercise the proper fellow-feeling? In keeping with this prevaricatory mode, both variations share a sort of tentative certitude; the narrator's axiomatic announcement (fortune has never) also proffers an equivocal "perhaps," slipped in for security in the midst of larger gestures. The narrator claims to know the emotions of the characters, or to know what we should think about them, but reserves the right to imagine that somewhere else someone is, or was, or will be suffering more, will feel more violently, or will better deserve our pity; her intervention sustains mixed meanings of the term "état," so that the text flickers in between the interior mood and the larger political state in which the scene takes place. Already in these intimate scenes there is a small gesture to the wider world and to the difficulty of describing it.

Another pause, and then the count speaks: things are more complicated than you think, he tells the prince, and you have misread the scene; actually, I am even unhappier than you. The prince, furious, moves toward the count and toward the scene of revenge presaged by his pounding on the door. The princess, fearing the worst, tries to block her husband's passage, but she is so enfeebled by her emotion that instead she faints at his feet. Now nothing stands between the prince and the man he imagines is his rival. But the prince pauses again, looking from his wife to the count:

> Le Prince fut encore plus touché de la voir de cet évanouissement
> qu'il n'avait été de la tranquillité où il avait trouvé le comte quand il
> s'était approché de lui et, ne pouvant plus soutenir la vue de ces
> deux personnes qui lui donnaient des mouvements si tristes, il
> tourna la tête de l'autre côté, et se laissa tomber sur le lit de sa
> femme, accablé d'une douleur incroyable. (97)

> [The prince was still more touched by her fainting than he had been
> by the Comte de Chabanne's calmness when he had threatened
> him. No longer able to bear the sight of two people who caused in
> him such deep feelings of sadness, he turned his head away from
> them and fell onto his wife's bed, struck down by a pain and sorrow
> beyond belief.] (185)

The vengeance scene falls apart with a feeling of something like forbearance. Again, the manuscripts suggest that Lafayette was experimenting with a variety of ways to read this encounter. In another version, the prince's feelings are not "tristes" but rather "opposés" ("sad" rather than "opposed") suggesting more of a struggle between the "pitiful" and the "violent." Feelings sputter in and out. The verb "toucher," common to both versions, sustains a variety of different emotions and relations to the other: surprise, pity, shock. The prince's pain, likewise, is both for the others and for himself. Now, the figures around the room are unable even to look at one another, so "beyond belief" is their pain. Each leaves the room and a confrontation that had seemed to usher in a moment of cataclysmic crisis is sidestepped.[19]

The prince's departure was described by a contemporary critic, the abbé de Villars, as a display of his clemency, a particularly politically charged term more appropriate to matters of state than the heart, to tragedy rather than the novel.[20] In this period, clemency is very clearly coded as a public virtue. It applies to the subjects of a sovereign as well as to his wife. A 1694 dictionary, for example, notes that the term "ne se dit proprement que de Dieu, des Souverains & de ceux qui ont droit de vie ou de mort" [can only properly be said of God, of sovereigns and of those who have the right over life and death].[21] Furetière's more strictly secular definition in his 1690 dictionary describes clemency as a "vertu de Souverain, ou de Superieur, qui le porte à traitter doucement les vaincus, à moderer les peines des criminels" ["virtue of the sovereign or of the superior, which brings him to treat the vanquished with kindness and to moderate the punishments of criminals"], and the first example he gives of clemency is that of Auguste, familiar to French readers from Pierre Corneille's successful 1642 tragedy *Cinna ou la clémence d'Auguste*.[22] To claim the prince's gesture as one of clemency suggests that these intimate marital dramas were also read in relation to larger political conflicts, and that the new form of the *nouvelle historique* could be considered alongside tragedy, the most noble of genres. In reflecting on "états violents," Lafayette does not allow the reader to separate the question of marital status from that of the state, and she repeatedly pushes us to see that what she is writing has a larger resonance beyond the love triangle.[23]

Indeed, as the text goes on to show, the public and the particular are hard to keep apart in even the most prosaically geographical way. A few pages later we reencounter both men, now engulfed by a wider painful narrative, at which point we remember the "perhaps" of the narrator, who hesitated in naming the private sufferings of a courtly love triangle as the most violent *états* one could imagine. Here, the state of private feeling walks right into the crisis of the embattled state, where there is literally no place in which private grief can be indulged.[24] The count, we are told, had come to hide in Paris in order to abandon himself to his pain. But as any seventeenth-century reader would have known, Paris was not a good place to hide in August 1572; in the violence of what came to be called the Saint Bartholomew's Day massacre, thousands of Huguenots were slaughtered. Our unfortunate count is "enveloppé dans la ruine des Huguenots," ["engulfed in the ruin of the Huguenots"], and the people he was staying with, remembering him to have

Huguenot connections, "le massacrèrent cette même nuit qui fut si funeste à tant de gens" (99) ["murdered him on the very night that was fatal to so many others"] (186). The historian Mézeray used the same verb to describe people drawn into the massacre, recounting that "ce deluge de sang envelopa aussi quantité de Catholiques" ["this deluge of blood also engulfed many Catholics"].[25] Even in this most restrained of sentences, Lafayette brokers a relation between the individual's story and the larger, if unrecounted, national drama.[26]

Lafayette's linkage of these stories is reinforced by her use of the language of the Wars of Religion that I described in Chapter 1. The narrator goes on to recount the scene the following morning when the prince de Montpensier, who still imagines the count to be his rival, finds the count's body:

> Il fut d'abord saisi d'étonnement à ce pitoyable spectacle. Ensuite, son amitié se réveillant lui donna de la douleur; mais enfin le souvenir de l'offense qu'il croyait en avoir reçue lui donna de la joie, et il fut bien aise de se voir vengé par la fortune. (99)

> [At first, he was profoundly shaken by this piteous sight; then, as his feelings of friendship reawoke in him, they brought him pain and sorrow; but the memory of the offense he believed he had received from the Comte de Chabannes finally gave him joy, and he was glad to find that he had been avenged by the hand of fortune.] (186–87)

The prince's discovery of the body, recounted as its own miniature narrative with a careful beginning, middle, and end (at first . . . then . . . finally), repeats the terms of his previous discovery of the love triangle.[27] Again, pity lurches up against a welter of mixed emotions: shock, friendly memory, and vengeance. In this scene, though, the result of violence is unequivocally "pitoyable," and this time that term also suggests the prince's own reaction to the body, rather than prodding the reader into response. But pity leads nowhere and changes nothing; it is an emotion played only as an aside. Anne-Lise François has described the plot in *La Princesse de Clèves* as "a form of narrative action so chaste that, in retrospect, it might as well not have happened."[28] We might well say the same of Lafayette's fleeting moments of pity.

Yet in recalling the "pitoyable spectacle" trope of the religious wars, Lafayette undoes its original polemical ferocity. The original deployment of the term was certain of its power; here, Lafayette's use of it is more elegiac. This pitiful spectacle is a hinge between past and present, an undigested memory rather than a drive to the future. For the writers of the sixteenth century the pitiful spectacle marshaled a response to partisan suffering, in order to ensure that a single event be echoed throughout the future formation of a community. In the seventeenth century's pitiful spectacle, at the moment that we might retrospectively call the beginning of the novel, the topos functions differently. In recalling the sights of the wars, it offers what James Chandler, in another context, calls a "second-order affective experience" in which readerly emotion echoes more violent responses of a century earlier.[29] In a genre that was already insisting on its newness and which has been celebrated for it ever since, we find a stubborn remainder of a history beyond which the seventeenth century was unable to move.[30]

The prince, looking over the body, could well serve as a figure for the reader picking through unfolding discoveries, but it is important to acknowledge how our knowledge of the scene differs from his. Lafayette makes us constantly aware of our status as readers and of the particular perspective from which we see these emotionally significant scenes. The prince's reading of both scenes is based on a misunderstanding that neatly displaces a historical truth. As the reader knows the comte de Chabannes did indeed love the princess, but she used him only as go-between for her affair with still another man, the duc de Guise, who plays the invisible villain in this romantic drama. Chabannes was unhappily stationed outside the room of the princess while she was with Guise and broke in to tell them that the prince was on his way; Guise had left the room before the prince entered. In his haste to understand, the prince imagines the right story but with the wrong protagonists. Guise is the guilty party in the story of presumed adultery, and in an obfuscated fashion he figures as that in the second bodily discovery, too. Although Lafayette does not fully articulate what Guise was up to in that August night, her readers would have known that he was one of the prominent ultra-Catholic family faction held responsible for the murder of the Protestant leader admiral Coligny, and thereby of launching the massacre; in an aside, she reminds us that he was to move on from this body to take joyful revenge for his father's death. The absent figure of Guise represents the "historical" truth of both stories and prompts us to consider the husband's competing emotions of pity and revenge in relation to the larger promise of religious coexistence and its subsequent failure.

Even in its staging of the prince bent over his rival's body, Lafayette's text recalls one of the most infamous scenes of the massacre, celebrated and reviled in collective memory. In Mézeray's history, the Guise brothers bend over the body of their rival Coligny in the street to make sure that the cadaver is indeed their man:

> Le Duc de Guise et le Chevalier le considerent à loisir, et parce qu'il avoit le visage tout couvert de sang, le Chevalier (d'autres disent que ce fust le Duc) se baissant dessus, prit la peine de l'essuyer avec un mouchoir pour le mieux reconnestre; quelques-uns adjoustent, qu'après cela il luy mit le pied sur le ventre, avec des paroles outrageuses.[31]

> [The Duke of Guise and the Chevalier considered the body at length, and since the face was still covered in blood, the Chevalier (others say it was the Duke) bent over and took pains to wipe it with a handkerchief, so they could recognize him; some add that after that he put his foot on his stomach, with offensive words.]

The pored-over spectacle of Coligny's body swiftly became a site of spectacular memory in the history of the wars.[32] This iconic scene had already been recounted in earlier Protestant histories of the events like that of Jean de Serres; it seems probable that Mézeray drew on such accounts for his later version (where he comments "acte barbare" ["barbarian act"] in the margin), and that Lafayette in turn drew on that history of reading the wars.[33] Lafayette's tableau of the prince examining his dead friend recalls the key sight of the massacre and further binds together the domestic dispute and the larger horror of the wars. In acknowledging that Chabannes is a Protestant who was wrongly massacred, she suggests that we must think of his death in relay with those of the "so many others" who also died.

Lafayette's work is built around repeating tableaux that recall familiar scenes of the wars and that also build a series of internal repetitions in the texts. These constellations of figures, arranged so that they are deliberately placed on view and so they call attention to our own viewing, turn emotion into an arrangement in which object and subject, sufferer and spectator appear to be distinctly drawn, only for the arrangement to shift again. Inquiries into such affective arrangements have been central to readings of the eighteenth century, such as Michael Fried's reading of the (painted) tableau that supposes a spectator. In Fried's reading the tableau's theatricality insists on its relation to the beholder; we could say that Lafayette's tableaux, too, draw attention to the staged relation between character and reader and to the perspective afforded to each.[34] Some literary critics have made large claims for what such an effect in the novel can bring about. David Denby, for example, posits that the tableaux of the sentimental novel punctuate the narrative by calling attention to other modes of perception such as the spatial or visual.[35] Denby suggests that this sentimental tableau becomes a way to declare "the affirmation and celebration of the possibility of a common, communicable human experience. The relation between tableau and the Enlightenment project of fraternity is a direct one" (79). In contrast, Lafayette's tableaux lead nowhere; they show us affect's inexhaustible response but suggest that it builds precisely nothing that is common and communicable. Lafayette articulates emotion chiefly through such forlorn scenes. They both foreground emotion and forestall any concrete action that might come from it.

La Princesse de Clèves and the Unemotional Reader

Lafayette's longer novel *La Princesse de Clèves*, published to great fanfare in 1678, also takes up this habitually forestalled compassion; paradoxically, the emotional response of readers to the novel was vigorously theorized from its first appearance. Like the shorter texts, the novel takes place in the sixteenth century, this time at the court of Henri II. The novel thus narrates a period of time before France fell into the religious wars, but Henri's court is connected to them in the mind of the reader through his bride, Catherine de Médicis, who will go on to be the figure most demonized by Protestants at the time of the Saint Bartholomew's Day massacre. The novel also provides a number of hints about the coming calamity, most notably, as Louise Horowitz has shown, through the elaborate presentations of the various aristocratic lineages that were to come into cataclysmic discord during the years to come.[36] Lafayette presents her reader with a world that is now inaccessible, forever lost through war, but also familiar by dint of its elaborate court structure, surely to be understood in relation to that of the late seventeenth century.

This is a novel that with its lapidary and sometimes inscrutable statements is, as Anne-Lise François puts it, "unkind to readers who value fulfillment."[37] A beautiful young woman, heiress to a great fortune, is brought to court by her mother, who watches over her with great care. After much negotiation, the daughter is eventually married to the prince of Clèves, a man who loves her even though this is not required of such marriages. Moreover, he wants her love in return; this proves impossible, since she has as yet no idea of what love means. She remains unmoved by her husband, who deeply regrets this. But she then meets a fabled figure, the duc de Nemours, and throughout a series of carefully managed scenes discovers what it means to care for someone, who, events suggest, is also *inclined* toward her, as the French term puts it. Almost every intimacy is refused by the princess. Eventually, in what was from its earliest readership the most controversial scene of the novel for ethical reasons internal and external (it featured unseemly behavior but was also often accused of being plagiarized from Villedieu's *Les désordres de l'amour*), the princess confesses her feelings for an unnamed other to her husband. Painful complications ensue: eventually the husband becomes ill with grief and dies. Now, the reader feels, a different novel is beginning, and after a decent interval of mourning we imagine the union of the two lovers. But this does not happen. After much anxious reflection, the princess retreats to the country, rejects Nemours's attempts to intrude on her retreat, and eventually moves into a convent. Some years later, we are told in brief lines at the end of the novel, Nemours's love diminishes. The princess never returns to court, and in the abrupt ending of the novel we learn that "sa vie, qui fut assez courte, laissa des exemples de vertu inimitables" (478) ["her life, which was quite short, left inimitable examples of virtue"] (156).[38]

There is a certain narrative about the development of the novel in France which places *La Princesse de Clèves* at its starting point.[39] If, as Lauren Berlant puts it, a genre is an aesthetic structure of affective expectation—an expectation about how we will feel as readers but also about the feelings we expect to encounter in a text—then Lafayette's fabled beginning of the French novel creates a distinctly muted affective expectation, quite unlike the lachrymose novels of the sympathetic eighteenth century whose advent her work is often imagined to signal.[40] Within Lafayette's work itself fellow-feeling makes an appearance only to falter and collapse. My focus in this chapter is on diegetic compassion, the emotion shown—in problematic ways—by the fictional characters themselves. But Lafayette shared with her readers a hesitation about precisely where to locate fellow-feeling in and around narrative texts. We have already seen how the manuscript versions of *Montpensier* hedged the assignment of emotion to reader or to character. That uncertainty about the proper placement of compassion is also evident in the earliest seventeenth-century reception of Lafayette's novel.

We know a great deal about the reception of *La Princesse de Clèves* because of another new genre, the newspaper.[41] The periodical *Le Mercure galant*, begun in 1672, had begun to step up its circulation in 1678, the year the novel was published.[42] Its proprietor Donneau de Visé had cannily staged the arrival of the book by issuing a teaser text which featured a similar marital confession, and he followed its publication with a series of "Questions galantes" about the novel, in answer to which many people wrote in to discuss the ethical implications of the scene, some using elaborate pseudonyms. Many of these letters detail the emotional responses to the novel.[43]

These responses suggest real caution about what it means to respond compassionately to a text and what becomes of us if we do so. A provincial reader named "L'insensible de Beauvais" ["The unemotional man from Beauvais"] wrote to the paper to report the compassionate responses of his party, who "plaignirent toutes le Malheur de cette Femme" ["all pitied the unhappiness of this woman"]; even the "insensible" man himself is touched.[44] Other critics hinted that such compassion might change the sexual behavior of Frenchwomen. The writer Valincour, whose largely critical *Lettres à madame la marquise de XXX sur le sujet de La Princesse de Clèves* were published in the same year as the novel, reports that one woman reader, in what is surely another courtly insinuation, says she is "pénétrée de celuy-cy" ["penetrated by this one"]. The marquise even suggests that women will be more receptive to extramarital liaisons after having shared the princess's story: "Je suis asseûré qu'il se trouvera plus d'une femme, qui après l'avoir leûë, se sentira le cœur plus tendre qu'elle ne l'avoit auparavant." ["I am assured that there will be more than one woman who, after having read it, will feel more tenderhearted than she had before."][45] In these jokey formulations, compassion certainly leads to action, but perhaps not of the right kind.

In one striking phrasing, Valincour suggests that readers do indeed respond compassionately to the princess, but that it is the weakness ("foiblesse") of that central character that makes us feel for her: "C'est par là que le lecteur . . . a, pour ainsi dire, de la compassion et de la pitié de toutes les démarches embarassantes où il la voit engagée." ["That is how the reader has, so to speak, compassion and pity for all the awkward maneuvers he sees her engaged upon."][46] Nicholas Paige has argued that Valincour's use of compassion and pity should be distinguished from Aristotelian understandings of the terms because it takes as object the awkward princess rather than a tragic hero, so that pity in the sense of contempt comes to the fore.[47] Valincour seems to acknowledge that difference from the Aristotelian model with his "pour ainsi dire," and his usage points to a hesitation about vulnerability on two accounts. On the first account, Valincour is clearly uncertain about the princess's weakness, which makes her a troubling kind of character for those raised on more edifying genres such as tragedy; but more importantly, he worries about the potential vulnerability of the reader who might be overly infected by compassion. Valincour's text points us to a very seventeenth-century unease about readerly compassion: If we are full of pity for the princess, are we thereby also pitiful, that is worthy of contempt? The term "pitoyable" falters in this period between the two meanings, as we saw in sectarian diatribes of the previous chapter. Valincour's rigorous assessment of a series of potential objects of compassion seeks to regulate and properly apportion readerly pity lest the reader himself—and I use the gendered pronoun deliberately— become pitiful.

The regulation and judgment of masculine emotion is central to Valincour's work. Turning to the narrative digression in which the prince de Clèves recounts the sad story of Sancerre (to which I will return later), Valincour says of this character that he is "bien propre à donner de la compassion; & il ne se peut rien de plus naturel. Sa douleur a quelque chose de nouveau, & de si touchant, qu'on ne peut s'empescher d'y prendre part" (160) ["very right that he gives grounds for compassion, and nothing could be more natural. His pain has something new about it, and so touching, that one cannot stop oneself from becoming involved"]. This well-regulated compassion is allowed to the reader; the pain it observes is new, and so also is the proper application of the reader's carefully apportioned emotion. Here compassion is justified through two seemingly oppositional rhetorics: it is both natural and modern, at once the oldest and the newest story. With such lofty legitimization, this is indeed a character who is worthy of compassion. And yet Valincour's account of Sancerre also suggests that to be a man worthy of compassion might also mean one is a figure who invites derision; he wonders if Sancerre, "aprés avoir commencé à se plaindre en amant, & en amant veritablement affligé, . . . ne finit point un peu en comédien" ["having started his complaints as a lover, and a truly afflicted lover, doesn't finish up something more like a comic figure"]. Likewise, responses to women's suffering must be regulated. Valincour reports that a male friend says of the princesse's last conversation with her mother, "Elle est fort tendre & fort touchante . . . j'ay bien veû des personnes qui ont pleuré en la lisant" (152). ["It is really tender and touching . . . I saw people who wept while reading it."] But the friend reports that he remained unmoved. Valincour's text moves through a series of such reports, charily noting the tenderness that could be felt for certain characters but insisting nonetheless that we should mind the gap that keeps their emotion safely distant from ours. Yet in refusing to let himself be swayed by compassion, Valincour is closer to the princess than he might like to admit, for the novel itself is centrally concerned with the muted observation of compassion that leads to no change.

La Princesse de Clèves and the Fleeting Bond

We might be accustomed to seeing Lafayette's novel as a beginning, but it is at least as much an ending; even as the new form of the novel might be said to break away from its past, we still find in it traces of the galloping multivolume romances such as Honoré d'Urfé's *Astrée* (1607–27) or Madeleine de Scudéry's *Clélie, histoire romaine* (1654–61). In romances, intimacy is seemingly thwarted by all sorts of catastrophes and interdictions but can also be pursued relatively easily through disguises and other such adventures. Even in *La Princesse de Clèves*, an infinitely more sober form of narrative, there are traces of that earlier genre. Figures like the princess's love object Nemours sometimes seem to imagine themselves to be in just such a forgiving and playful narrative. In one extraordinary scene, Nemours spies on the princess alone in her summer house and then begins to climb in a window to talk to her before considering that this might not be the right thing to do, and thus gets literally stuck on the edge between two genres, the one where the hero can climb in windows to meet his beloved and the other where such a thing is unthinkable. (I will return to this scene later.) Indeed, contemporary critics of the novel teasingly discussed whether Nemours's escapade in the forest is the ultimate sign that the text draws on the romance tradition, since only a hero of romance could spend a night wandering outside without coming down with a heavy and unromantic cold.[48] But in fact Nemours's inability to understand the new and more austere rules of the game, his propensity to get stuck while doing what comes naturally to a hero of romance, points to quite how far Lafayette is moving from those older prose narratives.

Lafayette's move from the romance tradition to the new genre takes particular aim at the courtly culture of pity. The opening pages of *La Princesse de Clèves* establish that the behavior of the court still follows the tropes of a highly ritualized courtly love familiar to readers of romances, according to which the married woman is asked to take pity on the supplications of her lover. Two years after Lafayette's novel, Richelet's 1680 definition of the adjective "pitoiable" gave one meaning as "qui excite à la pitié par des paroles tendres et passionnées" ["which excites pity through tender and passionate words"], specifying that this usage was common in the work of Vincent Voiture, the epitome of the mannered poet of the early seventeenth century.[49] But by 1678, Lafayette's twists on *galant* courtly culture point to an important departure from this trope.

Even if they hadn't read Voiture, readers of Lafayette's novel might have been familiar with the tropes of courtly pity from an encounter with a novel published some three years before: *Les désordres de l'amour*, written by Marie-Catherine Desjardins under her pen name Madame de Villedieu.[50] In this series of interlocking historical novellas, courtly gallantry is set up according to an elaborately coded discourse of compassion. In one scene suggesting how the courtly norms of compassion imagined some action issuing forth from the emotion, a gallant asks a woman to be moved by his lovesick misery into a response, "Le malheur où on m'a precipité, ne peut-il attirer quelques effets de votre compassion?" (112). ["Might the unhappiness into which I have been pushed attract some effects of your compassion?"] Villedieu, herself a woman wronged by courtly antics, is interested in the ways in which the proper and pleasing deployment of a woman's compassion marks her social success.[51] When the duc de Guise woos the duplicitous Madame de Sauve, he does so "avec une douleur qui auroit dû toucher Madame de Sauve" (13) ["with a pain that should have touched Madame de Sauve"], and we are given to understand that Sauve's inability to respond compassionately is a mark of her misplaced motives; some pages later, Sauve's pity is so ill-directed that on a hunting party she refuses to play along with the aristocratic pleasure in tracking down the stag: "Elle disoit que cet animal lui faisoit pitié dans ses abois, et se retira sous quelques arbres" (16). ["She said that she pitied the animal in his death throes, and retreated under some trees."] Later the duke tells her scornfully that she is not "un personnage digne de compassion" [a person worthy of compassion], telling her "vous faites mal vos applications" (38). To misapply pity—to direct it to a wounded animal rather than a wounded aristocrat—signals the woman's failure at court. Villedieu, an author from a humble background attempting to make her way in society, tracks the courtly economy of pity so that her readers might better know its rules; in contrast, the aristocratic Lafayette writes a novel that critiques that affective economy.

Lafayette's *La Princesse de Clèves* presents us with a series of scenes in which the men at court seem to follow the code of compassion seen in Villedieu's account. When Lafayette's chevalier de Guise, for example, returns from a journey to find that the young Mademoiselle de Chartres is on the verge of marrying (and thus of becoming the princesse de Clèves), he takes pains to make her aware of his sorrow according to a particular social script:

Il lui fit connaître à son retour, qu'elle était cause de l'extrême tristesse qui paraissait sur son visage, et il avait tant de mérite et tant
d'agréments qu'il était difficile de le rendre malheureux sans en avoir
quelque pitié. Aussi ne se pouvait-elle défendre d'en avoir; mais
cette pitié ne la conduisait pas à d'autres sentiments. (348)

[He let her know on his return that she was the cause of the extreme
sadness that was visible on his face, and his merit and charm were so
great that it was difficult to make him unhappy without feeling
some pity for him. Accordingly, she could not help pitying him, but
this sentiment gave rise to no others.] (21)

Mlle de Chartres pities her admirer, but that pity does not tip her into any
more shared understanding as Guise might hope. In not allowing pity to push
her to respond, the princess flouts the courtly norm of compassion as sketched
out in Villedieu, in which compassion leads to "effets" or action.

In Lafayette's text, the affective response of pity is immediately readable,
but it is never clear what will ensue from that emotion. When Nemours is
injured at a jousting, the princess's interest in him means her emotion is immediately evident: "Il vit d'abord Mme de Clèves, il connut sur son visage la
pitié qu'elle avait de lui, et il la regarda d'une sorte qui pût lui faire juger combien il en était touché" (393). ["The first thing he saw was Mme de Clèves. He
recognized in her face the pity she felt for him and looked at her in such a way
that she could easily see how touched he was by her response"] (68).[52] In another scene toward the end of the novel, a weeping Nemours gets to his knees
in front of the princess, and she in turn has tears in her eyes on seeing his
sadness:

M. de Nemours se jeta à ses pieds, et s'abandonna à tous les divers
mouvements dont il était agité; il lui fit voir, et par ses paroles et par
ses pleurs, la plus vive et la plus tendre passion dont un cœur ait
jamais été touché. Celui de Mme de Clèves n'était pas insensible, et
regardant ce prince avec des yeux un peu grossis par les larmes.
(473)

[M. de Nemours threw himself at her feet and surrendered himself
utterly to the feelings that shook his soul. In his words and tears she
saw revealed the most ardent and tender passion that has ever

touched a human heart. Mme de Clèves's own heart was not insensible; she gazed at Nemours, her eyes brimming with tears.] (150)

That final sentence is staged such that the reader expects the following clause to indicate some form of union. But the princess tells Nemours only that an invincible obstacle separates them, and the moment is lost. Though readers then and now may imagine that compassion will lead to other forms of shared passions (think how Valincour's Marquise, who described women being penetrated by novels, would have imagined the ending), Lafayette presents another scenario, one in which women can acknowledge men's pain with pity and then turn their head away. Lafayette's compassion, like her fiction itself, is built around gaps and distance and acknowledges their necessary existence rather than seeking to overcome them.

But if the princess shuns extramarital pity, what of the place of marital fellow-feeling? In the first part of the novel Clèves demonstrates the sort of ability to "compatir" with his wife described in Furetière's dictionary, having "naturellement beaucoup de douceur et de complaisance pour sa femme" (384) ["an inclination to treat his wife with kindness and indulgence"] (58), and she is able to respond in kind, if only out of her need for support; as she mourns her mother and fears Nemours's power over her, she shows him more "amitié et plus de tendresse" (367) ["more friendship and affection"] (41) than ever before. Yet the unfortunate Monsieur de Clèves also becomes the figure for still another sort of husband, who refuses to be infected by compassion. In one of the digressions that punctuate the novel and suggest how individuals might be understood in relation to a larger history, Clèves tells his wife a story about his friend Sancerre, who, mourning his secret mistress, discovers that she was also the mistress of another and that his emotion for her was misplaced. This secret mistress, Madame de Tournon, has already shown us that at court it is difficult to ensure that affects attach to worthy recipients. The princess tells her husband that when young women like Tournon die, "c'est toujours une chose digne de pitié" (367) ["it is always a cause for pity"] (41), and in response to his wife's miscompassion Clèves sets out the story of Sancerre to demonstrate that the duplicitous Tournon is not worthy of such grief. In recounting this story and in denouncing the duplicity involved, Clèves reports to his wife in an importantly proleptic moment that he had told Sancerre,

la sincérité me touche d'une telle sorte, que je crois que si ma
maîtresse et même ma femme m'avouait que quelqu'un lui plût, j'en

serais affligé sans en être aigri. Je quitterais le personage d'amant ou
de mari, pour la conseiller et pour la plaindre. (372)

[Sincerity moves me so profoundly that, if my mistress, or even my
wife, confessed to me that she was attracted to another man, I believe I should feel distress but not bitterness. I should abandon the
role of lover or husband in order to offer her my advice and my
compassion.] (46)

Clèves's vision of marital exchange is a model of Stoic judgment, in which the
coolheaded man can choose to apply pity without himself becoming an object
of it. This is a sketch of an optimistically enlightened sympathy that rationally
vacates the pains of subjectivity in order to counsel the other; the blush of his
wife as she listens to him indicates she is unable to control her emotions in
such a fashion.[53] This considered application of compassion appears to set
him apart from the husbands in Lafayette's *nouvelles historiques*; unlike them
Clèves will not, or so he announces, let pity drift into self-pity. Clèves proposes a sort of cool sympathy not unlike that of Sancerre himself, who was
able to acknowledge that he pities even his rival Estouteville.[54]

Of course, shortly thereafter Clèves is faced with just such a situation as
that presented in the digression. The princess, beginning by saying that the
confession she will make is such as has never been made by a wife to her husband, tells him that she has feelings for another man. Stressing that she speaks
only out of friendship and respect for her husband, she falls to her knees pleading, "Conduisez-moi, ayez pitié de moi, et aimez-moi encore, si vous pouvez"
(419). ["Be my guide, have pity on me, and continue to love me if you can"]
(95). This position was apparently deeply shocking to contemporary readers,
reversing the tradition that would have the pitiless woman spurning her kneeling admirer, and suggesting that the woman on her knees did not respect the
boundaries and conventions of courtly love.[55] In that tradition, it is the lover,
on his knees and supplicating, who seeks to conquer the distance between him
and his married object of desire, but here the distance is within the marriage
itself, and both parties share the burden of inhabiting conflicting roles, being
all at once the pitier and the pitied. In asking for guidance the princess asks the
prince to be the husband he had declared himself to be. Meanwhile,

M. de Clèves était demeuré pendant tout ce discours, la tête ap-
puyée sur ses mains, hors de lui-même, et il n'avait pas songé à faire

relever sa femme. Quand elle eut cessé de parler, qu'il jeta les yeux
sur elle, qu'il la vit à ses genoux le visage couvert de larmes, et d'une
beauté si admirable, il pensa mourir de douleur, et l'embrassant en
la relevant:

—Ayez pitié de moi vous-même, Madame,
lui dit-il, j'en suis digne. (419)

[Throughout this speech, M. de Clèves sat with his head in his
hands. He was quite beside himself: it had not even occurred to him
to raise his wife to her feet. When she stopped speaking, when he
cast his eyes upon her and saw her at his feet, her face covered in
tears, wonderfully beautiful, he thought he would die of grief. Raising her up and embracing her, he said:
    "Have pity on me yourself, Madame, for I deserve it."] (95)

This scene is an important reworking of the meetings between husbands and
wives I described in Lafayette's other texts. Unlike in those *nouvelles*, here the
crisis and vulnerability of the married couple is also the moment of their
greatest intimacy and greatest mutual knowledge. The repetition of the line
"Ayez pitié de moi" makes for an antiphonic marital kyrie that is the truest
moment of reciprocity in the novel, even as it is unable to sustain any more
lasting form of understanding. In one reading, the repetition of "Ayez pitié de
moi" sacramentalizes the social horrors of the situation and brokers a possibility of accord, albeit an unusual one. (One of Valincour's rare instances of
compassion comes in response to this scene: "Avez-vous pû vous empescher de
pleurer?" [Were you able to stop yourself from crying?]) Let me emphasize the
rarity of this moment of compassionate reciprocity: this is one of the only
moments of mutual compassion or affective parity I have seen in any of the
examples explored in this book.

   We can compare it with a scene from Villedieu's 1675 *Les désordres de
l'amour*, from which Lafayette took the central scene of the wife's *aveu* to her
husband.[56] Lafayette's lifting of the scene was widely criticized at the time, by
Valincour among others, and her borrowing from and refinement of Villedieu's texts has been widely discussed since then. But the scene in itself is already a borrowing from Lafayette's earlier texts. Though critics since Valincour
have focused on this scene of an extraordinary confession, on which Lafayette
clearly draws to describe the conversation between the prince and princesse de
Clèves, Villedieu's scene begins when the husband finds his young wife in

tears and asks her to tell him honestly what is wrong, declaring himself "moins un époux sévère que le plus intime de vos amis" (70) ["less a severe spouse than the most intimate of your friends"]. Here we find ourselves in a scene already familiar to the reader of Lafayette's earlier *nouvelles historiques*, and the mixed-emotion response of the husband to the aveu is also familiar: "Le marquis son époux étoit si surpris et si touché de ce qu'il entendoit qu'il n'avoit pas la force de l'interrompre. Mais enfin, ce premier trouble étant un peu dissipé, et la tendresse qu'il avoit pour elle triomphant d'un mouvement de jalousie qui le sollicitoit au mépris ou à la vengeance . . ." (73). ["The marquis her husband was so surprised and so touched by what he heard that he did not have the force to interrupt. But finally, this first trouble being somewhat dissipated, and the tenderness that he had for her triumphing over a movement of jealousy which called for scorn or revenge . . ."] Villedieu, it would seem, took from Lafayette the swiftly narrated emotions of the husband (although they move in the other direction), before Lafayette took from her, in turn, the notion of the unusual marital avowal. This multiple movement of cross-readings allows the only moment of sustained pity in Lafayette's novel, almost as if, in borrowing from Villedieu, she briefly harkened back to a more reciprocally touching economy of pity.[57]

Yet in Lafayette's text Clèves's addendum to the exchange "j'en suis digne" also raises the troubling question of compassion's judgment. In seventeenth-century aristocratic marriage, a man in love with his wife is essentially ridiculous, since he misroutes an emotion which should be reserved for courtly and therefore extramarital engagements. When Clèves, already rendered "indigne" (unworthy or undignified) by his love, ignores courtly decorum and insists on his worthiness, his status as "digne," he draws further attention to this vulnerability and enables the reader to judge him as someone unworthy of our emotion. Valincour's critique confirms that for some seventeenth-century readers compassion was squeezed out by scorn; he reports that one reader asked "quelle compassion pour un homme qui meurt, parce qu'il veut mourir; qui meurt comme un sot, sans vouloir estre éclairci; qui s'afflige, et qui se desespere, sans sçavoir de quoy" (75–76) ["what compassion is possible for a man who dies because he wants to die, who dies like a fool, without wanting illumination, and who is in despair without knowing why"]. Lafayette's decorous prose manages to sustain both possibilities, the heartening and the sourly comic, and suggests that a trace of scorn might inflect even the noblest forms of fellow-feeling. The novel erodes fellow-feeling from within.

Even this doubtful moment of mutual pity is lost after the scene of the *aveu.* Leaving for Spain, the prince asks his wife to let him know who is the object of her affection:

> ayez quelque compassion de l'état où vous m'avez mis, et songez que quoi que vous m'ayez dit, vous me cachez un nom qui me donne une curiosité, avec laquelle je ne saurais vivre. (425)

> [please have some compassion, too, for the state you have put me in, and remember that, despite everything you have told me, you are hiding a name that arouses in me a curiosity I cannot live with.] (101)

The prince's formerly natural compassion, a concern for the other, has lapsed into curiosity, here only a care for the self; he does not respond to his wife's affliction but seeks only to know its cause. He has abandoned emotion for the detective work of an anxious rationality. Eventually, worn out by worry, Monsieur de Clèves is dying, and the tearful princess comes to see him. At first he tries to hide his anger from her, but then

> les soins qu'elle lui rendait, et son affliction qui lui paraissaient quelquefois véritable, et qu'il regardait aussi quelquefois comme des marques de dissimulation et de perfidie, lui causaient des sentiments si opposés et si douleureux qu'il ne les put renfermer en lui-même. (458)

> [the care she lavished on him, together with her distress, which at times appeared to him to be genuine but which at others he interpreted as evidence of hypocrisy and treachery, gave rise in him to feelings so contradictory and painful that he was unable to contain them.] (136)

Like the husband in Lafayette's earlier texts, M. de Clèves loses his pity in a welter of contradictory emotions, and the moment of mutual agreement, brokered by pity, is lost in resentment and fear of treachery. Unlike in the other texts, the husband who feels the contradictory emotions is the one who dies; the princess then backs away from Nemours and from the remarriage plot that seems initially to be promised, and retreats to a space of solitude beyond the reach of suitor or reader.

In Lafayette's text emotion's manifestations demand us to venture a reading; they make analogies visible. When M. de Clèves initially tells his wife that he would respond calmly to a wife's confession of extramarital emotion, "Ces paroles firent rougir Mme de Clèves, et elle y trouva un certain rapport avec l'état où elle était" (372). ["These words made Mme de Clèves blush. She saw in them a certain connection with her own position"] (46). Lafayette's text also points to "a certain connection" between marital miscompassion and the drama of the religious wars. Of course, *La Princesse de Clèves* is not a text about the wars in the ways that Lafayette's shorter texts set during them are. But the novel's retreat from a worshipful and compassionate mutual knowledge certainly builds on Lafayette's earlier series of meditations on marital pity in times of martial crisis. The novel unsettles the easier figuration of the *nouvelles*, where war and marriage might be understood more straightforwardly in relation to each other: as backdrop, as figure, and so on. In the novel that historical discord is so obfuscated as to not yet have taken place. Despite its careful relation to historical record, *La Princesse de Clèves* is not a novel that clings to an account of what did or did not happen. Instead, the novel broods over the significance of things (speeches or couplings) which have not happened and whose not-happening hangs heavily on both character and reader. The violence of the religious wars is no mere "background" story as it was in the *nouvelles*. Instead, in leaving it to the reader to observe the gaps between the time that is represented and the time of reading, Lafayette asks us to think instead of all that has come between 1559 and 1678. The novel's persistent imagining of a peace found only in a space apart, rather than of any kind of commonality or exchange, must be read in what Povinelli calls a "mode of association" with the late seventeenth century's idealization of accords and toleration, its celebration of a century of new beginnings, but also of that story's difficult passage into the real.

The novel's abrupt ending, with its flouting of the marriage plot, has in the last thirty years often been read largely in relation to a liberal feminist narrative about choices and conventions in relation to the princess's own trajectory.[58] This crucial work has had the effect of turning the novel into a step on one particular liberal narrative of progress, that of the self-determining move toward a room of one's own. Yet Lafayette's miscompassion also places her work in relation to another liberal narrative, that of religious toleration.[59] The problematic ending of the novel offers a sort of formal toleration, understood in early modern terms not as an ideal but as a compromise. It shows us the princess's right to disagree with the prevailing norm but suggests that to disagree she has to remove herself to a refuge of emotional dissent. The princess retreats because it is the only way for the larger community to acknowledge her otherness from it and to allow for that difference.[60] The princess's painful choice to retreat to a shielded space instead of engaging in the public worship demanded by the court—here, the public worship of courtliness itself—can be placed alongside the ways in which the crises in governance of the seventeenth century wrestled with the politicization of space; that is, the way in which France imagined itself able or unable to encompass different communities within one national border.[61] Both this novel and Lafayette's larger project of historical fiction point to the internal rupturing of that national project.[62]

If today we think of tolerance, like compassion, as a positive political virtue, it was also a form of regulation, of reification of difference. For many early modern Christians, toleration marked a kind of loss because it accepted that sectarian breakdown was irrecuperable. It marked not religious freedom but rather forbearance. Likewise, seventeenth-century compassion was not a generous response but rather a form of regulation that noted a transient affiliation with the other, who must be kept at arm's length. The gap of forbearance was essential to the difficult compromises of seventeenth-century religious settlements. Such gaps are also central to the form of prose fiction developed by Lafayette, as any reader both frustrated by the novel's ending and admiring of its restraint could say. Her careful experiments with the repeated motif of failed compassion offer us fleeting moments of pity that punctuate the plot without quite managing to change its direction. Lafayette builds her tableau-novel around gaps and around the subdued knowledge of their unfillability, asking us to be compassionate rather than curious; it is from those gaps that the new (if backward-glancing) form of the novel takes shape. The affective structures of her writing take root in the compromised territory of toleration.

What sort of politics of pity does Lafayette operate? It is certainly not one that imagines pity as a conduit to change. Perhaps we could call the relation it builds between sufferer and spectator something like an attentive form of bystanding, without imagining that term to designate a moral lack but rather asking it to take a particular kind of ethical stance. Lafayette's pity observes and regulates its objects rather than responding to them, urging an attentive and active regard without responding to suffering in the way that sufferers seem to solicit. It is itself a "mode of association" that proffers "a certain connection"; the moments of pity between characters allow for the recognition of a paradoxically fleeting bond, but one which cannot translate into a lasting identity.

In the first half of this book, I set out the structures of early modern compassion, showing that in this period affective response to the suffering of another was always dependent on, and indeed grew out of, a set of rigorously defined limits. In Lafayette's miscompassionate aesthetic, in contrast, we see how literary form responds to and reshapes compassion's edge. Where theologians and theorists wielded compassion as a categorizing device, Lafayette is able to imagine compassion's limits differently: no more optimistically, perhaps, but finding space for a peculiarly poised aesthetic and ethical stance within its strictures.

Chapter 5

Affective Absolutism and the Problem of Religious Difference

Absolutism struggled with religious difference. Where the Edict of Nantes had allowed Protestants at least a limited freedom of worship, the seventeenth century gradually eroded such rights, and in 1685 Protestantism was outlawed in France. The political history of toleration's failure has often been told; this chapter takes up instead the centrality of absolutism's affective rhetoric to the question of religious difference in early modern France. Catholic accounts of attempts to convert Protestants, and Protestant responses to such attempts, formed a cross-confessional emotional dialog underpinned by an elaborate rhetoric figuring the king as Compassionater-in-Chief. This chapter explores these varied compassionate rhetorics and their fallout in and around the Revocation of the Edict of Nantes in 1685.

In pursuing revocational rhetoric, I address a range of very different textual and political positions: first, the ritualistic language of pity and compassion that structured relations between the absolutist king and his suffering subjects; then Catholic texts praising the Revocation as a compassionate act; and in response to that, the myriad ways in which Protestants as targets of absolutist affect reimagined compassion's address. Rejecting the rhetoric of Catholic compassion, Protestant responses to Catholic impositions came to voice a new language of political emotion which still resonates today. The seemingly secular language of international humanitarianism found its first articulations in battles over religious difference.

Yet this chapter does not sketch out a political teleology of emotional progress. In drawing out the cross-confessional and transnational revoicings of compassion's call, I want to insist on the rhetorical murkiness of

compassion uncovered by the events of 1685. In supplement to Catholic and
Protestant polemics, I conclude with the richly affective language of Jean Racine's strange play *Esther*, first performed for the king four years after the Revocation and centrally concerned with supplication and religious difference.
Esther stages a crisis of compassion's voice that warns us of the precariousness
of articulating emotion under affective absolutism.

Since the revocational texts I describe here return repeatedly to the Wars
of Religion described in Chapter 1, let me give a brief overview of the French
situation since last we left the Edict of Nantes.[1] Despite a firm Protestant belief that the nature of the edict made it perpetual and unchangeable, an initial
apparent toleration quickly turned to resentment and to persecution. The
Cardinal minister Richelieu saw his efforts to centralize the state and to quash
noble rebellion threatened by the continuing resistance of the Protestant communities, and he ushered in a new series of attacks culminating in the 1629
siege of La Rochelle, formerly designated a Protestant safe city. After the 1629
treaty of Alès, Protestant power was significantly eroded and obliged to con-
form to what Christian Jouhaud terms a "theater of submission." This chapter
suggests both the varied forms of that theater and the ways in which Protestants eventually imagined themselves in relation to a different audience.[2]

By midcentury, things initially looked better. When Louis XIV attained
his majority in 1652 he announced that Protestants should enjoy the full privileges of the Edict of Nantes.[3] Despite such announcements, attempts to bring
Protestants back to the Catholic fold intensified. From 1661 the severity of
actions against Protestants increased, and so did the number of enticements to
conversion. There was state financial support for Protestants who renounced
their faith, a policy excoriated by Protestant writers.[4] From 1669 Protestants
were no longer allowed to emigrate. Over the course of the 1680s Protestants
were barred from public office and the professions; they were forced to move
their schools out of urban areas; mixed marriages between Catholics and Protestants were forbidden; and, causing uproar, the age at which children were
deemed able to choose conversion was lowered from fourteen to seven. The
figure of the child ripe for conversion was central to the affective drama of
revocational rhetoric on both sides. After 1680, Protestant midwives were forbidden to practice, lest they seize newborns and baptize them into heresy.[5] By
this point, almost none of Nantes's original protections remained in place.

By 1681, with soldiers billeted in Protestant homes, the persecution entered a phase of active violence, culminating in the attacks of the infamous
troops known as *dragonnades*. From 1685, soldiers were directed to conduct

mass conversions in the provinces, and on October 15 the official signing of
the Revocation gave Protestant pastors fifteen days to leave the country but
constrained the remaining Protestants to stay and to convert.[6] Some of Louis's
supporters voiced qualms about the Revocation. In December 1689 the lieu-
tenant general Vauban lodged a series of objections which probably never
reached the king, suggesting among other things that conversion lay out of
the domain of governance, since it drew on an individual and interior sentiment and could not be regulated.[7]

Kingly Compassion and Clemency

In believing individual emotion to lie out of the realm of government, Vauban
set himself apart from most Catholic political thought, in which individual
emotion was central to larger actions. The Jesuit Nicolas Caussin, confessor to
Louis XIII, wrote: "Il n'y a rien de plus souverain pour le gouvernement des
esprits que la douceur et la compassion." ["There is nothing more sovereign
for the government of minds than sweetness and compassion."] Caussin's treatise on the passions, *La cour sainte*, follows many early modern accounts of
compassion in insisting on the emotion's strategic interest for those in positions of power.[8] A prince who is compassionate, says Caussin,

> trouve des corps de garde dans les plus grandes solitudes, de l'as-
> seurance dans les perils, de la protection dans les combats . . .
> Quand il dort, un million d'yeux veillent pour luy . . . et s'il n'estoit
> au throne, tous ses sujets luy voudroient faire des degrés de leurs
> corps pour y monter.[9]

> [finds bodyguards in the greatest solitude, safety in danger, protec-
> tion in combat . . . When he sleeps, a million eyes watch over
> him . . . and if he were not on the throne, all his subjects would
> form steps from their bodies for him to ascend there.]

Writers bound to praise kingliness in general or their king in particular tend,
like Caussin, to bind private and public virtues together and to imagine public clemency stemming untrammeled from individual emotion, with no distinction marked between compassion and clemency. But more skeptical sorts
such as the Jansenist moralist Jacques Esprit distinguished between the public

and private emotions. In *La fausseté des vertus humaines* Esprit suggested that although public clemency is praised by all, individual "douceur" (kindness or sweetness) is infinitely harder, since it involves battling against a personal emotion or interest:

> Les Rois ne sont sensibles à la pluspart des crimes que par leur de-voir, & que leur clemence n'ayant point à combattre leurs senti-mens, ils ne font aucun effort sur eux-mêmes pour pardonner; au lieu que la douceur a affaire aux boüillans mouvemens de la colere, qui s'élevent dans un homme vivement offensé dans son honneur, ou injustement choqué dans ses interêts.[10]

> [Kings are aware of most crimes only through their duty, so their clemency does not have to battle their sentiments and they must make no effort in themselves to grant pardon; whereas sweetness deals with the boiling movements of anger, which rise up in a man vividly offended in his honor, or unfairly shocked in his interests.]

The distinction that Esprit makes between public clemency and individual emotion was murky from the time of the Roman Republic, when the concept of clemency was first carved out. David Konstan argues that even as Caesar made clemency a policy, its complicated terminology was not yet fixed.[11] Early modern discussions of the distinction between a rational application of mercy in the case of public need and a private response often draw on Seneca's *De clementia*, which distinguished between *clementia* as rational decision and a *misericordia* or pity which affects only the weak-minded and women.[12] Seventeenth-century vocabularies of kingship often mingled these terms: pity, compassion, clemency, mercy, *douceur*.[13] These varied terms all hid a capacity for aggression.

The choice between such terms was often strategic. For Restoration En-gland, for example, struggling with the legacy of civil war, the terms switch depending on writer or audience; as Andrew Shifflett describes it, the terms clemency, pardon, mercy, indemnity, and so on are "allied or contrasted as needed by the writer."[14] After the Great Fire of London in 1666, for example, Charles II made an official published declaration announcing his "princely compassion and very tender care."[15] Yet addressing the Lords on the subject of the indemnity bill in 1660, the king took care to spread a different affective language. His announcement carefully distinguished the subject who feels, against those who are concerned by that emotion: "This Mercy and Indulgence is the best way to bring them to a true repentance, and to make them more severe to themselves, when they find We are not so to them. It will make them good Subjects to me, and good Friends and Neighbors to you; and We have then all Our end, and you shall find this the securest expedient to prevent future mischief."[16] Charles's careful deployment of pronouns took place within the very particular political context of Restoration England. The restored king's public emotion took a distinctly parliamentary tone, needing to balance the monarchical person with the newly significant body of Parliament, whose interests also needed to be weighed. In the English parliamentary system, compassion could no longer be the sole preserve of the king.[17]

The King and I: Supplication Scripts

In contrast, Charles's cousin Louis XIV, enjoying the privileges of the absolutist political model, appeared as the sole representative and ultimate arbiter of political compassion, even at times displacing God as the giver of mercy. The king was compassionater as judge, and his construction as Chief Compassionater can be traced in the bundles of pleading letters addressed to him by his imprisoned subjects. These letters voice emotion in the first person, speaking through a careful formula of supplication.

It was of course standard for begging letters from or on behalf of prisoners to ask for royal compassion. A prisoner's letter of 1650 asking for his belongings to be returned to the family begins, for instance, "Plaise à S[on].A[ltesse].R[oyale]., avoir compassion du sieur de Marchin."[18] These formulaic letters were nonetheless crafted with a care for the problematics of address under absolutism. To whom could the needy subject address himself, and under what rhetorical terms? In a reading of supplication as both a social and a literary scenario, Leah Whittington describes the precariousness of operating such a "force from below," and its potential for bringing about not resolution but "emotional friction."[19] The early modern subject's ability to deploy these registers of pity could mark not only his success as a writer but also his ability to survive.[20]

Under absolutism, the supplicatory mode was mobile in scale at one end, able to speak of anything from the singularity of a sufferer to the largest questions of populations, but it was always relentlessly focused on the monarch.

Letters written to Louis XIV speak of compassion not merely as a formula but
rather as a compelling singular characteristic of the king. In an example of
that formula, in a letter written in 1661 by Louis's imprisoned financial *surintendant* Nicolas Fouquet, the prisoner begins:

> S'il est vrai que la personne la plus affligée doit être la plus digne de
> compassion, je viens, avec confiance, me jetter aux pieds de Votre
> Majesté, bien assuré d'obtenir les effets de sa miséricorde, puisque je
> suis certain qu'aucun de ses sujets ne peut avoir une douleur qui soit
> comparable à la mienne.[21]

> [If it is true that the most afflicted person must be the most worthy
> of compassion, I fling myself confidently at the feet of Your Majesty,
> well assured that I will receive his mercy, since I am certain that
> none of his subjects can have a pain comparable to mine.]

The begging letter is a performance of a deeply intimate bond between sovereign and subject. Fouquet's plea for compassion choreographs king and subject into a special affective coupling. He who is most needy of compassion is
matched by the king, who is cast as the best giver of it, and both compassionater and sufferer are singularized as superlative, as if to use that symmetry to
paper over the wide gulf between their asymmetric positions. The rhetorical
positioning also, crucially, draws on a bodily posture: Fouquet will be at the
king's feet, performing a traditional gesture of supplication. His voice depends
on this present-tense bodily staging, which lends an immediacy to the imagined interaction.

As Fouquet continues his letter, the affective bond with the king is under-
scored by a repeated series of rhetorical set pieces:

> J'ai plusieurs afflictions ensemble, SIRE, dont chacune séparément
> est capable de faire des malheureux avec excès. Mais j'en ai une
> grande et si sensible, au-delà des autres, que je suis peu touché du
> reste et ne puis seulement me résoudre à en plaindre.
>   Je laisserai à d'autres, SIRE, à représenter à Votre Majesté, la
> perte de leurs charges, de leurs emplois et de leurs biens, la ruine de
> leurs famille [*sic*], l'accablement de leur créanciers et la mendicité à
> laquelle ils sont réduits. Je leur laisserai regretter l'éloignement de
> leurs proches, la privation de toute société civile avec leurs femmes

et enfans, frères et parens, amis et domestiques; je ne ferai point à Votre Majesté, SIRE, le récit d'une dure et ennuyeuse prison, pendant une longue et fâcheuse maladie, avec toutes les incommodités qui peuvent ajouter de la peine et du chagrin à la perte de la liberté.

[I have several afflictions together, sire, of which each one separately is capable of causing excessive grief. But I have one so great and so sensitive, beyond all others, that I am little concerned with the rest and can only resolve myself to bewail it.

I will leave to others, sire, to represent to Your Majesty the loss of their offices, their jobs and their goods, the ruin of their family, the blows of their creditors and the beggary to which they are reduced. I will let them mourn the distance of those closest to them, the privation of all civil society with their wives and children, brothers and relations, friends and domestics; I will not tell Your Majesty, sire, the tale of a hard and dull imprisonment, during a long and distressing illness, with all the discomforts that can add pain and disappointment to the loss of liberty.]

Fouquet uses the rhetorical figure of preterition to emphasize what he seems to dismiss, running his reader through a multitude of sufferings which might well be experienced by a multitude of other prisoners and their multiply evoked families who call on Louis's compassion. But only Fouquet himself, the singular sufferer, suffers the greater pain of being cut off from Louis:

Mais mes souffrances sont supportables; je n'en dis mot; je me tais et cherche seulement à soulager celles qui me pressent. SIRE, c'est la douleur d'avoir déplu à Votre Majesté, dans le temps que je m'efforçois de la mieux servir, qui fait toute ma peine. C'est le regret d'être demeuré l'objet de son aversion et de sa colère, moi qui n'ai jamais eu d'autre dessein que de lui plaire. (65–66)

[But my sufferings are bearable; I say nothing of them: I keep silent and look only to relieve those which press upon me. Sire, it is the pain of having displeased Your Majesty, during the time when I sought to serve him best, that is all my affliction. It is the regret to be the object of his aversion and his anger, I who have never had any other aim but to please him.]

Fouquet's focus narrows to encompass only the emotionally fraught binding of king and subject, in which the anger of the king is countered by the subject's desire only to please. In Fouquet's rendering of his position past and present, it is the subject's proper affective disposition, at least as much as his actions, that make him worthy in the eyes of the king.

Over a series of pages Fouquet sets out the proper affective positioning of the dutiful subject: "Votre Majesté . . . voudra-t-elle bien se mettre en mémoire avec quelle promptitude et quelle joie j'ai toujours exécuté ses commandements!" (67). [May Your Majesty . . . recall with what promptitude and what joy I always executed his commandments."] A good subject has the proper emotions, properly displayed and properly recognized. But where the subject's interior emotions must be revealed and shown, the king is known only through his actions, and his interior feeling cannot be deciphered; his clemency is all that counts, whether that clemency be motivated by interest or emotion alone. Hedging his bets, Fouquet asks for Louis to respond "par son propre intérêt et par une compassion généreuse" (69) ["through his own interest and through a generous compassion"]; either motivation will do. Supplication aspires here to be a call-and-response; the formulaic rhetoric suggests that the hoped-for response will be merely a matter of form, too. Fouquet's pitch to the king casts the roles of sovereign and subject as affectively fraught positions of mutual dependence. In this staging of compassion, the outside world—those others who might undergo similar material deprivations—is cast off so that only the singular subject remains in relation to the singular monarch.

Louis did not, of course, respond as Fouquet might have hoped; the former *surintendant* was imprisoned in Pignerol in 1664, where he was to die in 1681. Though Fouquet and his supporters asked for pity on the prisoner, Louis's response refused to follow the lead of such language.[22] Perhaps, once Fouquet was exiled, Louis would have been able to comfort himself with passion theorist Jean-François Senault's observation, in 1641, "Il faut que le Prince se ressouvienne que les suplices sont des remedes, et que la mort méme qu'il ordonne est une espece de misericorde qu'il fait aux coupables." ["The Prince must remember that punishments are remedies, and the very death he orders is a kind of mercy he gives to the guilty."][23]

1685: Pity/Piety/Paradiastole

The language of the chief compassionater glimpsed in the Fouquet affair was still central at the time of the Revocation. But in addressing the theological well-being of the nation, Catholic writing adds piety to the cluster of compassional terms—pity, *douceur*, clemency, and so on—familiar from earlier texts. The terms "pity" and "piety" were only beginning to be pried apart in the seventeenth century, and revocational rhetoric marks their last dance together.[24] It was not new to imagine religious difference through an emotional prism. The great Protestant theologian Moïse Amyraut, for example, had written of his "tendresse" for the Jews, even while insisting on the necessity of excluding them.[25] Under Louis, though, it was not distant historicizing regard that was imagined to be tender but rather an active and often violently wrought conversion. The standard praise of the Revocation typically cast forced conversions as an act of generosity. In renaming violence as compassion, Louis's affective absolutism heightened the stakes of compassionate rhetoric.

The historian Peter Burke describes the Revocation as a high point of representational fervor in what he calls the "fabrication" of Louis XIV, a frenzy of inscriptions, statues, and speeches all in praise of the king's action against the Protestants.[26] Piety is a key term of that fabrication, encompassing a larger population than the singular pity solicited by Fouquet. Piety addresses itself to the whole nation, and both print culture and public events made the king's piety and zeal known. This "fabrication" of Louis XIV as figure of piety depended on the fabrication of concomitant objects of pity: the Protestants. Revocational pity was hierarchical, operating in a single direction. The display of tenderness to those on the other side of a sectarian divide did not indicate sympathy for Protestant doctrine or lives. The rhetoric of kingly compassion was provisional: in order for there to be fellow-feeling, Protestants had to first accept to be Catholic fellows. This was a compassion foisted upon Protestants, making them pitiful in the modern sense of the word.

The rhetoric of the Revocation depended on the juxtapositional coupling of contrary affects, force and kindness. We could contrast this with the declaration made by the 1573 Edict of Boulogne, the year after the Saint Bartholomew's Day massacre, which called for governance "plustost par doulceur et voie amiable que par force" ["through sweetness and amiable ways rather than through force"], seeking to cancel out force through kindness.[27] Breaking away from this sixteenth-century affective aim in which one mode replaces the other, the revocational formula doubles down on affect, seeking to stage both force and kindness at once. Over 1685 and 1686, the newspaper *Mercure galant* reported frequently on the Revocation and responses to it, praising Louis's clement piety and portraying the repeated scenes of destruction as occasions for Catholic kindness. At the destruction of the Protestant temple of Aubusson, the paper reported, the Catholic governor gave out refreshments to those pulling the temple down, and the marquis de Saint Germain spoke to the crowd with "caresses," apparently bringing about the conversions of many.[28] Over 1685, the paper avidly reported the multiple conversions throughout the country, noting of one occasion that those who resisted conversion were spoken to "avec tant de force et de douceur" ["with so much force and sweetness"] that they fell into line and sang a mass together.[29] This pairing—force *and* sweetness—is central to the seventeenth-century tradition of passion theory and its concern for the proper management of subjects' passions. Senault's *De l'usage des passions* (1641), dedicated to Richelieu, had insisted that "douceur" must be accompanied by severity.[30] The Revocation follows this to the letter: a 1687 text describes the king's success in having acted "par la seule force de [ses] Edits et par les douceurs d'une bonté paternelle" ["through the sole force of his Edicts and through the sweetness of a paternal goodness"]. The conjunction "and" becomes the very location of Louis's affective absolutism.[31]

Revocational rhetoric did not only pair two contrasting attitudes; it also frequently asked its readers to imagine one emotion as another. A 1686 poem in a special issue of the *Mercure galant* in honor of the Revocation urged Huguenots to think of violence as a sort of clemency, rhyming *violence* and *clémence* menacingly.[32] This paradiastole (the rewriting of one thing as another) is the rhetorical trope we saw in the work of the moralists in Chapter 2, central to the discourse of political virtue in this period.[33] In revocational writing paradiastole forms a sort of rhetorical conversion, perhaps the only conversion that affective absolutism could securely compel. Revocational texts routinely converted Catholic violence to compassion and transmuted Protestant fear into gratitude. This is nonconsensual compassion.

Yet even the *Mercure*'s volume of paradiastolic praise leaves some room for doubt that Huguenots might be convinced by such a conversion. A satirical poem featuring Calvin in the underworld describes Calvin's horror at the tears of a Catholic who wept out of emotion for him: "Jamais insulte ne m'a esté si sensible que la compassion de ce Devot." ["Never have I felt an insult as much as I have the compassion of this devout man."][34] Calvin's revulsion at finding himself an instance of nonconsensual compassion is, of course, designed to make the Catholic readership laugh. But it also leaves a residue of doubt: Could all Protestants really be imagined as grateful recipients of Louis's piety?

One text from 1687 illustrates the rhetorical violence of revocational paradiastole in rather surprising ways, showing how the Protestant voice was appropriated and ventriloquized as part of the new affective government. The *Triomphe de la religion sous Louis le Grand* is a little booklet dedicated to the king, stemming from an event held at the Jesuit Collège de Louis le Grand, recently renamed in honor of the king.[35] The event featured a live explanation of various figures and emblems; in the text the images are explained first in Latin by the Jesuit Gabriel-François Le Jay and then translated into French. This rhetorically complex text casts the Protestant conversion as a private sentimental choice instead of a strategic decision or forced move.

The text announces the triumph of religion, but as the emblems suggest, that triumph is brought about by a proprietary blend of emotions ushered in by the king. For the seventeenth-century French, "triomphe" does not yet explicitly suggest an emotion in itself. Where the OED gives sixteenth-century English usages of "triumph" signifying joy or elation, French dictionaries of the period cling to the Triumph as Roman processional, what Cotgrave calls "a pompous, and publike shew."[36] But that public display of victory is made possible by a particular emotional exchange in which public necessity compels a rearrangement of private feeling. The emblems vehicle two very distinct kinds of emotion. On the one hand, we see the violence-as-tenderness of the Catholic forces which sought to convert the Protestants, here embodied by the king; on the other hand, the grateful recipients of such a forceful tenderness. An image of dogs shepherding their lost sheep, for example, is framed by two mastiffs between the motto "Vis Amica," *vis* meaning either force or violence.[37] This pairing of force and gratitude—the emotional pas de deux of absolutism—animates the whole text. The *Triomphe* sets out the terms of the new revocational emotional economy.

In its most significant deployment of emotional rhetoric, the *Triomphe* appropriates the voice of the Protestant as victim of the Revocation and makes that voice speak in the Revocation's praise. Paradiastole joins forces with prosopopoeia, the figure in which a dead being or inanimate object is animated. Perhaps the French translator of the original text, Fontenelle, was chosen because of his deft deployment of that figure in his *Dialogues des morts* published a few years earlier. This appropriation of voice is heard through two speaking stones, a diamond and a coral, who figure grateful Protestant children. The *Triomphe* makes Protestants speak up in the first person to thank Louis XIV for the policies that targeted them, and sets them to describe the Revocation as a form of kindness.

This prosopopoeic praise recalls the singularity figured in Fouquet's articulation of affective absolutism. In that supplication scenario, the lone sufferer petitioned the singular king for relief. Here, a lone Protestant voice is orchestrated post-event to speak of their gratitude to that king. Gratitude was important to the rhetoric of the Revocation. Sample letters from similarly grateful new converts featured in the issue of the *Mercure galant* of October 1685, mingled with more worldly announcements about which readers had correctly guessed the previous month's printed enigma. Where supplication asks for a potential future kindness, Protestant gratitude acknowledges and publicizes a kindness that has already taken place. Both modes observe and enforce a hierarchy from different points on a timeline.

Under the title "Adamas," the Greek for diamond, the *Triomphe* offers us a diamond poised on an anvil, "Un Diamant que l'on taille et que l'on polit" ["A diamond that is cut and polished"], with a tag first in Italian and then in French, both voiced in the first person: "ben mi fa, chi mi ferisce," "qui me frappe me fait du bien" ["he who hits me does me good"]. This declaration is followed by a longer account of the diamond's preferences:

> Je ne tiens pas de moy cét éclat que je jette,
> Par qui des feux du ciel l'éclat est imité;
> Je n'éstois né qu'une pierre imparfaite,
> Et jamais l'œil sur moy ne se fust arresté.
> Ce brillant vif et pur dont on est enchanté,
> Combien faut-il que je l'achete?
> De ce que j'ay souffert, vient toute ma beauté. (101)

> [This dazzle I give off doesn't come from me
> This dazzle that imitates the flames of the sky;
> I was born an imperfect stone
> And nobody gave me a second look.
> This lively and pure sparkle which charms the world
> How much have I had to pay for it?
> All my beauty comes from what I have suffered.]

The Greek *adamas* signifies fortitude. Since Pliny, diamonds had been praised for an extraordinary strength that was not just material but also somehow morally significant. Yet here our diamond's tale speaks of its weakness and imperfection, and the strength and value of the diamond is bestowed on it only by the figure of the king. The diamond's masochistic embrace of violence makes him a very particular sort of diamond: a *French* diamond. The 1680s French diamond signaled the work of human skill and artifice in perfecting nature. The stones that dazzled the French court were all Indian, brought back by the Huguenot traveler and merchant Jean-Baptiste Tavernier, but the raw stones were radically recut in France to show off "ce brillant vif et pur"; Louis employed two official stonecutters to facet the stones to display them in the new French style.[38] Likewise the Protestant raw original requires an intervention, shrugging off its own sparkle paradoxically at just the moment that it speaks up in the first person: in the *Triomphe*, even subjectivity is always dependent on another's action.

The remaking of the diamond also remakes an image that had long been central to Protestant history, a *devise* that comes back in many texts, such as the title page of Théodore de Bèze's 1580 history of the reformed Churches. It shows a diamond-shaped anvil so sturdily resistant that the persecuting hammer has broken, declaring, "Plus à me frapper on s'amuse, Tant plus de marteaux on y use." ["The more they amuse themselves in hitting me, the more hammers they wear out."][39] This time, the *Triomphe* triumphantly declares, the Catholic hammer has vanquished the Protestant resistance, and the diamond has learned to like it. In the diamond's sparkle, Protestant suffering is redeemed for the glory of the French court.

The other voice of the *Triomphe* comes from another stone that was not native to France but celebrated at its court: a coral, often in seventeenth-century France to be found in settings with diamonds, as the coral itself will explain. The coral illustrates the happy situation of those Protestant children removed from their parents to be brought up Catholic. The coral's *devise* gives us a third person generalized statement which is almost an accounting tally, setting up a painful play on different registers of value: "De la main qui l'arrache, il reçoit tout son prix" (71). ["From the hand that tears him away, he receives all his value."] Then the verse moves to the first person voice as the coral speaks up and recounts a miniaturized autobiography:

Si cette Onde où je fus formé
Dans son liquide sein m'eust toujours enfermé,

Je n'étois qu'une vile et méprisable Plante:
Maintenant que plus fortuné
Parmi les Diamants je voy que l'on me vante;
Je dois ce nouveau prix à la main bienfaisante
Qui m'arrache des lieux où je suis né.

[If this wave where I was formed
Had always hidden me in its liquid breast
I was only a vile and despicable plant
Now, more fortunate
Among Diamonds I see they set me
I owe this new value to the kindly hand
Which tore me from the place where I was born.]

As in the case of the diamond, the coral's conversion narrative overhauls the notion of value; the object itself is worth nothing until an emotional operation is brought about by the intervention of the "main bienfaisante." This is no invisible hand that regulates the triumphant economy but rather the precise and strategic gesture of a very identifiable monarch, who prompts the Protestant to raise his voice in happy Frenchness.

The affect theorist Sara Ahmed describes the move from negative to positive feelings as "affective conversion," using the commonly understood figure of religious conversion to illuminate affective instances in contemporary culture.[40] Yet Ahmed's figure can also be usefully returned to the scene of early modern conversions themselves, for affect was central to early modern understandings of sectarian difference. Revocational rhetoric made affective conversion key to the conversion from Protestant to Catholic, from birth family to national unit. In imagining an affectively homogeneous nation, it casts out from its borders those who might feel differently.

The Protestant Response

How did Protestants respond to these increasingly elaborate emotional gestures and redirect the language of compassion? In the earlier examples, the affective relation between sovereign and subject constructs a singularly intimate dance of subject and object, compassionater and object of compassion. For Fouquet as for the diamond or coral, the only community figured narrows

to the emotional transaction between subject and king, the "main bienfaisante" that guides all. In contrast, Protestant responses to the Revocation
crowdsource pity: they figure crowd reactions (both Protestant and Catholic)
to the spectacle of Protestant suffering, and they also gesture to an unseen
audience, an international public who will compassionate with Huguenot distress. Pity's political community widens.

The most significant contemporary Protestant account of the Revocation
is the monumental work of Élie Benoist, the *Histoire de l'édit de Nantes*. A
minister before the Revocation, in exile Benoist settled with the Huguenot
community in Delft. In 1687, after the death of Abraham Tessereau who had
gathered the initial documents, he took over the project of this multivolume
history covering events throughout the seventeenth century as well as the Revocation itself. The five volumes were published in Delft from 1693 to 1695
and very swiftly translated into English, since accounts of Protestant suffering
had wide international appeal. Part of Benoist's mission was to persuade the
international community to assist in restoring the original terms of Nantes.[41]
Benoist's account of Protestant history drew on the resonant terms of Aristotelian dramatic theory to present Huguenot suffering as a tragic spectacle. The
siege of La Rochelle, he writes, gave "la pitié et de la terreur à toutes les autres
villes Reformées" ["pity and terror to all the other Reformed towns"].[42] As we
saw in Chapter 2, the Aristotelian language of pity and terror was a source for
many different approaches to ethical or aesthetic questions; Benoist's use of
these terms looks not to a schooling for the self, as in dramatic theory, but to
an affective charge for the dispersed Huguenot community and for all those
who might respond compassionately to it.

In drawing on the familiarly Aristotelian language, Benoist sought a political catharsis. In his thorough account of Protestant travails, we are presented on the one hand with the pitilessness of Catholic forces, and on the
other with the huge potential pity of the readership for Benoist's work, Protestant and otherwise. He begins his project with a memorializing account of
Protestant sufferers, hoping that their sufferings will bear fruit "dans la pitié
de ceux qui liront l'Histoire" ["in the pity of those who will read this History"].[43] Yet if the Protestants of France were urged that their misery might be
redeemed in the eventual readership of Benoist's huge work, the work itself is
stitched through with examples of appeals for compassion that go unnoticed.
Protestant officials "tâcherent de faire pitié par le tableau de leurs malheurs"
(3.661) ["sought to cause pity through the tableau of their griefs"], just as Benoist does with his project, describing the Huguenots imprisoned as "une vuë

qui ne pouvoit manquer de toucher les ames encore sensibles à quelque pitié"
(3.965) ["a sight that could not fail to touch souls still capable of some pity"].
That "encore," still, is crucial; Benoist writes as if from a time when pity is put
under such pressure that it has almost disappeared from the range of human
response to suffering.

Sometimes Benoist details a limited and transitory Catholic compassion,
but with no lasting political effects. Echoing the partisan spectacles of the religious wars, he describes a scene in 1681 of Protestants trying to flee who
"faisoient encore plus de pitié. Plusieurs Catholiques qui eurent la curiosité de
les aller voir, ne purent s'empêcher d'être touchez de ce spectacle" (4.488–89)
["gave rise to even more pity. Several Catholics who had the curiosity to go
and see them, could not stop themselves being touched by this spectacle"].
Even in the year of the Revocation itself, Benoist acknowledges that "il y eut
neanmoins des Catholiques pitoyables, et des Dragons même qui ne furent
pas inaccessibles à la compassion" (3.909) ["there were nonetheless some
Catholics who showed pity, and even some soldiers who were not inaccessible
to compassion"]. These, however, are isolated exceptions. For the most part
Benoist describes pity only to note that it is no longer available to most Catholic forces, whose scorning of misery marks out their inhumanity and whose
only compassion is in itself a form of cruelty designed to make the victim
suffer more. In 1683, officers spit in the faces of Protestant women, laughing at
their suffering: "Ils ne s'avisoient d'avoir pitié, que quand ils voyoient
quelqu'un prêt à mourir, et tombant en defaillance. Alors par une cruelle
compassion, ils lui faisoient revenir les esprits" (3.834). ["They only thought to
have pity when they saw someone ready to die, and falling down in a faint; at
that point through a cruel compassion they would revive her."] The soldiers'
paradoxical "cruel compassion" (a term that will return in the next chapter,
when Jesuits describe Iroquois behavior) marks a world in which neither virtue nor language can hold stable. When Benoist repeatedly details women
and children spurned by the pitilessness of the forces (3.855), their lack of
compassion is not merely a lack of the proper sentiment but marks a broader
breakdown in civic order. Protestant discussions of compassion repeatedly
link the emotion to larger political virtues, here evoked only as lost ideals.
Benoist details how the leaders of the troops charged with converting Protestants had "ni justice, ni compassion, ni civilité pour personne" (3.857) ["neither justice, nor compassion, nor civility for anyone"]. And compassion is
increasingly made even more complicated by the trickster deployment of sentiment. The Catholic converters show a "feinte compassion" (3.859) ["fake

compassion"] to their targets, as do those trying to make money by finding passage for Protestants fleeing France: "Ils vendoient leur compassion, mais ils étoient sans misericorde pour ceux qui n'avoient pas de quoi les payer" (3.950). ["They sold their compassion, but they were without mercy for those who couldn't pay them."] Catholic compassion cannot be taken as the basis of Protestant life.

In contrast Benoist describes Protestant emotion as something so authentic and durable that it becomes, under these political conditions, thoroughly dangerous: the human care Protestants show for the Catholic other becomes a form of self-harm. A 1681 injunction had forbidden Protestant women to work as midwives lest they interfere with proper Catholic baptismal procedures. But for such women, Benoist recounts, sometimes professional duty and personal emotion trumped sectarian difference, with troubling consequences since they were often arrested:

> Il arriva neanmoins à quelques-unes de se laisser toucher à la pitié, quand elles voyoient des personnes de leur sexe même Catholiques dangereusement malades: mais les suites de leur compassion firent connoître à la plûpart, qu'avec des gens qui avoient renoncé à la justice et à l'humanité, il étoit fort dangereux d'être pitoyable. (4.422)

> [Sometimes they were so touched by pity, when they saw women, even Catholic ones, fall dangerously ill; but the result of their compassion made them known to the wider world, so that among people who had renounced justice and humanity it was very dangerous to show pity.]

One Protestant woman who assists a Catholic woman in childbirth is denounced to the authorities by the Catholic husband (4.422), who even covers his betrayal with what Benoist sees as a falsely generous affect, claiming that forcing the midwife to convert is a reward for her work: this is surveillance as *douceur*.

Catholic crowds and troops might have displayed a distinct lack of compassion, but Protestants still hoped for compassion from the Catholic king himself. In the first half of the seventeenth century, the Protestant community still related to the king according to the standard supplicatory model, in which the king's hoped-for compassion is imagined to respond to the suffering of his people. Protestant leaders often drew on the language of pity and

compassion when they addressed the king. A report from the Synod of Cas-
tres in 1626 urges Protestants to show "toute la Civilité possible" ["all civility
possible"] to Catholics, and in the same sentence asks the king to show "sa
Compassion Roiale" ["his royal compassion"] for the distress of his distressed
Protestant subjects who seek only to "conserver l'Afection et l'Amitié de leurs
Compatriotes et Concitoiens" ["keep the affection and friendship of their
compatriots and cocitizens"].[44] Protestants pictured kingly compassion as a
reward for the good emotional behavior of those Protestants who had managed in difficult circumstances to keep on good terms with their Catholic
neighbors. But kingly compassion was in fact contingent on a rather different
sort of behavior. A 1629 edict pardoning the Protestant noble the duc de
Rohan clearly equates compassion with conversion. In order to earn the
proper affective stance of the king, subjects need not just to be nice to their
neighbors but rather must return to the Catholic fold. The edict begins:

> L'amour que nous portons à nos sujets, et la compassion que nous
> avons des miseres que leur causent les guerres et divisions, des-
> quelles cet Estat est de si long-tems affligé; nous a tellement tou-
> chez, que . . . nous avons employé tous les moyens pour reduire en
> notre obéisssance, ceux qui pour s'en être separez avoient donné
> cause à toutes ces afflictions.[45]

> [The love we bear our subjects, and the compassion we have for the
> sufferings caused them by the wars and divisions by which this State
> has for so long been afflicted, has so touched us, that . . . we have
> employed all means to reduce in our obedience those who having
> been separated from it have caused all these afflictions.]

In these formulations, affect is always instrumental:

> nous avons voulu par un si rare exemple de clemence . . . gaigner
> plus advantageusement les cœurs de nos sujets, épargner leur sang,
> le degât de la Province, et tous les désordres et calamitez de la
> guerre, émus à cela par la seule compassion de leurs miseres, et
> amour de leur bien. (Benoist, appendix 2.93)

> [By so rare an example of clemency we have wanted . . . to win
> more advantageously the hearts of our subjects, to save their blood,

the destruction of the Province, and all the disorders and calamities
of war, moved to this solely by compassion with their suffering, and
love for their good.]

Louis XIII's self-presentation as clement and compassionate figures an emotion that is at once disinterested—it is compassion alone which makes him
act—and clearly strategic, an affective-political mix that Pierre Corneille was
to explore in his tragedy *Cinna* twelve years later.[46] The language of this edict
makes the structural anomaly of Protestantism clear: Protestants are "our subjects," but in choosing to separate themselves from the fold they have brought
about their own misery. In response to that choice comes the concomitant
choice of Louis XIII to respond with the emotion he deems appropriate.

Supplication and Conversation

In Benoist's telling, Protestant subjects continued to seek compassion from
the king under Louis XIV. One account suggests the way in which standard
scenarios of supplication and compassion were starting to erode, moving away
from a bodily choreography and looking to a new and more equal negotiation. In 1668, Benoist reports, one Pierre Du Bosc, a Protestant minister from
Normandy, was deputized to inform the king about the activities of the Catholic clergy in the provinces and their threats against Protestant temples. Du
Bosc, writes Benoist, was chosen for his fine oratory, his voice, and his appearance (4.99). This insistence on the presentability of his personal qualities suggests that Protestant advocates were in essentially ambassadorial positions;
Benoist's tomes detail innumerable legal battles about the proper interpretations of the edict and the advocates needed to fight them.[47] Du Bosc petitions
at length to have an audience with the king over one legal issue, and Benoist
notes that it was thought no other option but flinging himself at the king's
feet would work (4.102). The king being "equitable de son naturel" ["naturally
fair"], Protestants hoped he would listen to their cause directly and no longer
be turned away from it by the bad counsel of his clergy. Eventually Du Bosc
gained audience, and the king, far from expecting the Protestant to fling himself down, instead asked him to speak while standing (4.103). This invitation
shifts the traditional bodily rhetoric of supplication, and Benoist glimpses it
as a political opportunity. We have seen how Amyraut (Chapter 3) refused to
kneel, and how Fouquet promised that he would do so, but this moment of

dialog appears to point to a new political compact: in deeming the standard gesture of supplication superfluous, the king seems to grant the Protestant concern legitimacy.[48]

Benoist recounts that the king then asked Du Bosc to approach in order to hear him better; now they are not just on the same level but intimates. Through this exchange, Du Bosc hoped, writes Benoist, to awaken the king's "compassion," and he worries at first that the king seems distracted. But then the king hears Du Bosc's famous voice and through it the authenticity of his words, "un discours d'un autre caractere que les harangues pleines d'une fausse Rhetorique, dont il avoit les oreilles souvent batuës" (4.104) ["a discourse of another character than the harangues full of a false rhetoric with which his ears were so often battered"]. In Benoist's telling, Protestant speech is logos set against the slippery rhetoric of the clergy. Little by little "l'audience prit à peu près une forme de conversation, où Du Bosc eut le moyen de mêler quelque chose de touchant sur la condition generale des Reformez" (4.105) ["the audience took almost the form of a conversation, where Du Bosc was able to slip in something touching on the general condition of the Protestants"]. Compassionate supplication has given way to something closer to civility. But this moment of real communication, of conversation brokered by compassion, leads nowhere.

Although the fantasy that a Protestant might speak to the king with "free access" and be heard by him with any lasting action remains right up until the Revocation, it eventually evaporates.[49] In his hope of a reciprocal conversation between men on the same level, Benoist briefly imagines that supplicatory gestures might give rise to a different sort of affective exchange, even though his reader knows things happened otherwise. Written from exile, after the crisis of the Revocation, Benoist's text is punctuated by these wistful encounters in which history could have turned and been told differently; the strange temporality of a hope that was not to be is central to the affective power of his rare instances of compassion or conversation between sides. The reader is brought to reflect on these moments and their significance even as we know they will be lost in the course of events.

Eventually, the king's longed-for clemency is imagined not as an end in itself but as part of a link to a larger divine mercy. In 1683 a Protestant quoted by Benoist imagines "qu'on pouvoit esperer un meilleur tems, ou par la clemence du Roi aux pieds de qui on iroit se jetter, ou par quelque retour des compassions de Dieu, qui après de si longues épreuves auroit pitié de son peuple" (4.599) ["that we might hope for a better time, whether through the clemency of the king at whose feet we would fling ourselves or by some effect of the

compassion of God, who after such long trials would take pity on his people"].
Protestants came to look to a longer and larger history for their redemption.

Beyond the King: Pamphlet Literature

Affective appropriations or accusations—for example, that someone is worthy
of pity, that another is the chief compassionater, that someone else is pitiless—
were ceaselessly present in and around 1685. Writers at the time of the Revocation sought to redraft the emotional grammars of their opponents, redefining
the objects and subjects of compassion. Yet all these accounts stay largely
within a familiar structure, in which each writer changes only the direction of
emotion: from Catholic to Protestant, from Protestant to Protestant, from
king to subject, from subject to king, and so on. Like the rhetoric which battered the ears of the king, these exchanges rapidly become exhausting.

Yet out of these arduous affective and rhetorical constraints, Protestants
eventually began to find new forms through which to articulate their position. In
emergency conditions, Protestant solicitation of compassion began to rewrite the
traditional supplication script. Working on temporary art forms and new modes
of writing, Debarati Sanyal has described how in the appalling conditions of the
Calais "jungle" some refugees today are able to find "alternate subjectivations,
potential 'lines of flight' and ephemeral solidarities within these 'borderscapes.'"[50]
In the crisis of the Revocation, Protestant refugees looking away from standard
modes of supplication found similar affordances in new modes of writing and
new interrogations of language, eventually imagining new forms of political life.

In response to the structural stalemate of the Revocation, Protestants increasingly began to speak a new emotional vocabulary, with the imagined
compassionater no longer the king but rather a broader community. Letters
from the Bastille indicate how Protestant solicitation of compassion played to
a different script than that exemplified by the letter from Fouquet to Louis. A
letter from 1689 by Monsieur le duc de La Force, arrested for Protestantism, is
addressed not merely to the king but to Catholics in general. La Force was
from a prominent Protestant family, the son-in-law of the military leader
Turenne, a Protestant who had abjured his faith in 1668.[51] A forwarding letter
to a Catholic intermediary begins:

> Vous ne serez pas fâché, Monsieur, s'il vous plait, qu'on vous fasse
> part d'une lettre qui est adressé à toutes les honetes gens de votre

Religion, peut-être sera-t-on enfin touché des maux que l'on fait
souffrir à des pauvres gens, qui n'ont fait tort à personne, qui sont
dignes de la pitié de tous les Chrétiens.[52]

[You will not be angry, Monsieur, that I share with you a letter addressed to all the honest people of your Religion, perhaps they will
finally be touched by the evils these poor people are made to suffer,
they who have done no wrong to anyone, who are worthy of the
pity of all Christians.]

The letter itself does not lay claims to common doctrine but rather to a shared
humanity, in language that begins with the terms of seventeenth-century civility ("honetes gens") and proceeds to make a larger case. The opening of the
letter itself stays largely within the terms of *caritas* we saw deployed by Catholic writers in Chapter 3. The writer carves out a language of a shared humanity that nonetheless marks exclusions. Even Jews, even animals, are capable of
such fellow-feeling, he writes, binding himself to the Catholic gentlemen by
reminding them of his distance from such others:

Messieurs,
Qui pourroit maintenant voir la funeste desolation, où nous sommes
réduits en divers lieux de l'Europe, sans en être vivement touché?
Quoique nous ne professions pas avec vous une meme Religion, nous
avons avec vous une communion de nature, car nous avons été formés
avec vous d'un meme sang, et en Adam nous n'avons tous qu'un
meme père. Si vous n'avez donc pas dépouillé les sentimens de l'humanité, comme nous n'avons garde de le croire à l'égard des personnes
raisonnables qui sont parmi vous, pouvez-vous considerer les maux
qu'on nous fait souffrir, sans en ressentir de la douleur? Jésus-Christ ne
vous apprend-il pas, que le Juif même doit regarder le Samaritain
comme son prochain, et prendre part à sa souffrance, comme à celle
de son frère? Les animaux, les plus farouches, n'ont-ils pas de l'amour
pour ceux que la nature a faits avec eux d'une même espèce? Comment donc n'auriez-vous pitié de nous dans le lamentable état où vous
nous voyez réduits en divers lieux, où votre Religion est dominante?[53]

[Gentlemen: Who could now see the gloomy desolation to which
we are reduced in many places of Europe without being vividly

touched? Although we do not profess the same religion, we share with you a natural communion, for we were formed with you from one blood, and in Adam we have one father. If you have not then despoiled the sentiments of humanity, which we would find it hard to imagine of the reasonable ones among you, can you consider the ill we suffer without yourselves feeling pain? Does not Christ teach you that the Jew must regard the Samaritan as his neighbor, and take part in his suffering, as he does in that of his brother? Don't even the wildest animals show love for those that nature has made from their same species? How could you then not have pity for us in the lamentable estate to which you see us reduced in all the places where your religion is dominant?]

La Force's letter strategically elides Catholic agency against Protestants, focusing only on the ills that an unnamed actor makes "us" undergo. In redrafting what the historian David Hollinger terms "the circle of the 'we,'" he imagines a natural national bond, a blood tie that insists on human fraternity rather than a hierarchical relation to the unnamed king.[54]

Where Protestants were constantly asked by Catholics to articulate their relation to the imagined whole of the Church, La Force's letter redrafts that language to reach to the whole of humanity, making room for a language of political justice: "Est-il bien possible, Messieurs, que parmi vous on puisse de la sorte dépouiller tous les sentiments de l'équité, de la douceur, de la pitié et de l'humanité?" (223). ["Is it possible, gentlemen, that amongst you one can in such a way despoil all sentiments of equity, of kindness, of pity and humanity?"] Benoist's negative evocation of compassion had described its lack as injustice, but here fellow-feeling builds a distinctively positive political vocabulary, brokering a more horizontal imagining of social justice, in which the French "Messieurs" might relate to one another without recourse to the king. These letters were collected and printed as letters from the Bastille in 1789 by one Jean-Louis Carra, and his interest in them at that date is easy to imagine. Yet it is important to note that what he might have read as the glimmer of a new political language stems here not from a secular Enlightenment but from religious strife.

The seeking of new compassionaters was not just a domestic story. Protestant appeals for compassion also looked beyond France, shaping a transnational Protestant compassion that increasingly displaced the fiction of French cross-confessional emotion, and imagining a new language of international

humanitarianism brought about through compassion.[55] Benoist's circle of
compassionaters widens as he recounts the period of the Refuge, during
which Protestants "venoient chercher de quoi vivre dans la compassion des
étrangers" (3.957) ["came to look for their livelihoods in the compassion of
strangers"]. Key to the evolution of this internationalist language was the
cheaply printed and easily mobile medium of the pamphlet, which afforded
Protestants a new and multilingual voice. Whereas Benoist speaks with the
hindsight of a disappointed history, the pamphlets were able to speak from
the moment with instrumentalist vigor, in English, French, Dutch, or German as the occasion demanded, and often in two languages at once, as parallel texts.

After the Revocation, these new forms of Protestant political address
demonstrated that sovereignty need no longer be bound up in the body of the
French king. One 1686 English pamphlet praises "the Christian Compassion
shewed us by Forrein Princes, and more especially of his Majesty of England
who has received us into his Countries, succoured and relieved us, and recommended our distressed Condition to all his Subjects," and others still insisted
on Orange as the new source of royal care and "compassion able to gather up
"les tristes Debris du naufrage de nos Eglises" ["the sad Debris of our ship-
wrecked Churches"].[56] The English pamphlet suggests, though, that even as
they turned to new sovereign figures Protestants also looked for broader and
more diffuse forms of care, no longer bound up in one sole monarch. In discovering not only the English king but also his subjects, the English pamphlet
continues, "we have found in them not only new Masters, or the Affection of
new Friends, but of real Parents and Brethren."[57] Transnational Protestant
compassion shifted the traditional structures of sovereignty, looking to build a
new politics out of relations between ordinary people.

Protestants increasingly turned from the model of compassionater-kings
and called for compassion from different and more diffuse authorities.
Through the disposable mobility of print pamphlet culture, a more sustain-
able politics not dependent on royal whim is imagined. These appeals for
compassion were met by a responding voice: the pastoral literature of the Huguenot Refuge spawned copious print responses in Britain and the Low
Countries. This wave of pamphlet production commented on Protestant sufferings and criticized the policies of France. Sometimes that foreign commiseration was chiefly strategic with regard to its own national interests. A
pamphlet titled "The deplorable state and condition of the poor French Protestants commiserated," printed in London in 1681, features not so much

commiseration as a fervent desire to overturn the tyrannical king Lewis.[58]
Other accounts published outside France, however, sought to emphasize the
ties of a universal religious bond over the narrow interests of a nation, exhort-
ing their readers to remember "our Religion, which ought to inspire us with
sentiments of Compassion, Love and Charity for a people, who have so much
suffered for the truth of the same Religion we profess."[59]

Much of this international call-and-response of compassion insists on the
sheer fact of Protestant bodily existence, in which the Protestant deprived of
rights is living something similar to what Giorgio Agamben, in his reading of
the concentration camp, diagnoses as *vita nuda*, a biological existence de-
nuded of political status and social significance.[60] A 1667 text published like
many such pamphlets in parallel French and German, recounts the misery of
the Protestants banned from professional positions and living only "la vie,
c'est à dire, un triste soufle qu'ils tirent de leurs tristes cœurs affligez" ["life,
that is to say, a sad breath that they pull from their sad and afflicted hearts"].
Better death, the text argued, than such a "pitoyable estat" ["pitiful state"].[61]
But where Agamben's bare life marks the end zone of a particular model of
Western sovereignty, imagining bare life as helpless and speechless against sovereign power, the Protestant life is highly strategic, performing its nudity so as
to claim a new political role. It retains a "soufle," a breath or grounds for
speech, allowing for a new articulation of a Protestant voice that speaks multiple languages and can make itself heard internationally.[62] In response to that
voice comes a wholly new organization of political community. A pamphlet
published in London in 1686 described the refugees as "Fugitives ... who
have nothing left, but Tears and Miseries to bring along with them into Foreign Nations" and asserts that "tis certain the Protestants of France are the
most fit object of publick compassion, the World ever knew." The pamphlet
makes room for this object's own voice, which insists, "We have scarcely any
thing left us but our miserable Lives, and they are supported by the Charity of
our Christian Brethren."[63] The surprisingly vigorous "poor breath" of the first-
person Protestant finds its respondent outside France.

Where Benoist had briefly pictured a conversation possible between king
and subject, only to realize its painful impossibility, these new print genres
launch boldly into conversation with the world, quickly surpassing the older
forms of gestural supplication. The breath of the pamphlets raises Protestants
from their knees, and where Catholic texts like the *Triomphe* had sought to
turn them to stone, in the pamphlet they find new and strategic forms of
liveness.

A Protestant Philosophy of Language: Jurieu and Bayle

Other forms of Protestant voice questioned the endless slippages of this partisan paradiastole on somewhat different grounds, turning contentions with the Catholic affective order into philosophical debates about the nature of language itself. One such was the Protestant minister Pierre Jurieu, the leader of the Protestant diaspora during the Refuge years whose work on the notion of charity I discussed in Chapter 3.[64] Writing from exile in 1685, Jurieu addresses the Catholic clergy who had assembled in Saint-Germain-en-Laye to consider a possible reunion of religions. Jurieu begs that before the body of the Church is brought together "des particuliers de ce Corps" ["some particulars of this Body"], that is the Protestants, should be able to give their opinion. Jurieu's request illustrates the awkwardness of revocational imaginings of religious community: How is the Protestant part to imagine its relation to the whole when the whole speaks as if nothing is lacking from it?[65] War treaties, Jurieu reminds his readers, are made between two sides given equal bargaining weight, "autrement ce n'est pas traitter, c'est recevoir la loy du victorieux" (9) ["otherwise it is not parleying, but receiving the law of the victor"]. Jurieu makes clear that proceeding to a real reunion depends on a proper and transparent understanding of terms:

> Nous supposons qu'il s'agit icy dans vôtre intention d'une veritable reunion, à prendre ce terme dans sa signification de rigueur et d'exactitude. . . . Car autrement si par le terme de réünion on entend simplement un retour à l'Eglise Romane, sans qu'elle se reforme et qu'elle se relâche en rien, il est clair que c'est abuser des termes et cela ne s'appelle pas reunion. (10)

> [We suppose that you intend here a real reunion, taking this term in its rigorous and exact meaning . . . for otherwise if by the term reunion we understand simply a return to the Roman Church, without her reforming or conceding anything, it is clear that this is an abuse of terms and that this is not a reunion.]

Jurieu's search for a common language ends by asking for the compassion of his listeners in the hope that an emotional gesture might help the two sides to a common ground: "Nous vous conjurons, Messieurs, de vouloir réveiller les entrailles de vos compassions, sur des Freres que vous supposez dans l'égarement, mais qui sont pourtant vos Freres, tout égarez que vous les supposez" (88). ["We conjure you, gentlemen, to wake the bowels of your compassion, for these brothers that you suppose lost, but who are still your brothers, however lost you imagine them."] Jurieu asks that compassion should strike through the strategic vocabularies of negotiation. His employment of the familiarly biblical bowels of compassion is significant. Where the pamphlets sought to displace gesture through the figuration of voice, Jurieu displaces compassion from language back to the body, unseating the partisan jockeying for rhetorical primacy and insisting that Catholic and Protestant share the same understanding of the Christian body, and that this body must take precedent over the slipperiness of speech.

Jurieu's sometime combatant Pierre Bayle also shows a suspicion of compassionate language and distances himself from the affective charge of both Revocation writing and its Protestant responses.[66] In his most prominent text of this period, the defense of freedom of conscience *Commentaire philosophique sur ces paroles de Jésus-Christ, Contrains-les d'entrer* (1686), Bayle attacks the easy renamings of pro-Revocation writing. He charges that the word "convertisseur" ["converter"], used to describe the soldiers enforcing conversion, has undergone an etymological erosion:

> Il devait originairement signifier une âme véritablement zélée pour la vérité et pour détromper les errants; mais il ne signifie plus qu'un charlatan, qu'un fourbe, qu'un voleur, qu'un saccageur de maisons, qu'une âme sans pitié, sans humanité, sans équité.[67]

> [It originally signified a soul truly zealous for truth and for enlightening the errant; but now it signifies nothing more than a charlatan, a gull, a thief, a sacker of houses, a soul without pity, without humanity, without equity.]

Bayle links here the same trilogy of ideals—pity, humanity, equity—that we saw extolled in the letter by M. le Duc de La Force. But where partisan pitiers swapped their opponents' referents but stuck to similar terms, Bayle puts the affective terms themselves into doubt. In an essay of 1685, *Ce que c'est que la France toute catholique*, Bayle responds to Louis Gauthereau's joyfully pro-Revocation *La France toute catholique* by slicing through Catholic emotional displays: "Souffrez, Monsieur, que j'interrompe pour un petit quart d'heure vos cris de joïe." ["Let me, Monsieur, interrupt for a small quarter-hour your cries of joy."][68] Bayle has come not to destroy language but to point out in excoriating style the ways in which it has already been destroyed by the *dévot* supporters of the king. He targets in particular the rhetorical sidestep with which these supporters described the enactment of Catholic policy as "actes de civilité, et de charité" (43) ["acts of civility and charity"]. The future lexicographer charges Catholic writers with dangerous and willful imprecision: "Dites nous comment vous définissez les mots, et ce que c'est parmi-vous que violence, hostilité, rupture de paix; car vous confondez tellement ces termes, qu'on n'entend rien dans vôtre jargon." ["Tell us how you define words, and what violence, hostility, breach of peace mean to you; for you so confound these terms, that your jargon means nothing."] And, given Bayle's anxiety about the proper deployment of affective vocabulary, it is worth noting that he uses the term "pitoyable" in a way closer to its modern meaning: something that is pathetic and worthy of scorn, particularly the poor arguments of his opponents.[69] In their precise swipes at opponents, Protestant writers began to take the vocabulary of pity closer to its hierarchical modernity.

Yet Bayle's charge is not merely concerned with semantic precision. Instead he counsels not just the renaming but the removing of emotional reaction. An emotional response to accounts of suffering, such as that sought by all those petitioning the king or a general readership, gets in the way of proper judicial conduct; for Bayle, a judge should listen "froidement et sans passion" ["coldly and without passion"]. Bayle acknowledges pity and mercy as essential to civil society and religion, but not to justice, where someone

> qui regarderait les misérables sans ces emotions de commiseration
> qui attendrissent le cœur, serait bien plus propre à dérouiller les arti-
> fices du mensonge . . . car enfin un miserable dont l'équipage lugu-
> bre nous fait pitié, et nous émeut toutes les entrailles, peut avoir fait
> les crimes dont on l'accuse.[70]

> [who would look at the miserable without these emotions of com-
> miseration which make the heart tender, would be more able to
> undo the artifices of untruth . . . for a sufferer whose lugubrious
> baggage makes us pity him, and moves us to the core, can still have
> carried out all the crimes of which he is accused.]

Where other Protestant writers points to a form of justice necessarily related to pity, Bayle argues that justice must eschew such affective response. Bayle imagines a politics taking place beyond affective impulse, where judgment and pity could finally be severed. This impersonal justice and the clear language he aims for imagine another and more abstract form of refuge.

Racine's *Esther*, 1689

It was not only Protestant intellectuals who suggested that affective rhetorics might too easily be misused; beyond the back-and-forth of supplication and response, other forms of writing showed a charged relation to the compassionate rhetoric of the Revocation. One of the many effects of the Huguenot diaspora was an increased anti-papist sentiment in England, which contributed to the Protestant William of Orange's ousting of the Catholic James II in 1688. But by February 1689, hopeful Catholic observers in France were of the opinion that William might soon be expelled in turn. The exiled king James had fled to his cousin Louis XIV's court but left soon after for Ireland in an effort to reclaim his kingdom, backed by the financial and military support of Louis. In a letter of February 28, Madame de Sévigné praised the unhappy James and dawdled in romantic pity for his wife's kidney stones before imagining the enormity of the army gathered for the new assault on England; never had such a thing been seen, she wrote, except by the kings of Persia.[71]

Sévigné's reference to the king of Persia did not stem merely from romanesque imagination. The week before, both Sévigné and James had been guests at the court performances of Jean Racine's *Esther*, the story of religious difference at the court of the Persian king Assuérus. James had seen it twice, once even on the night before he left for Ireland.[72] In a letter of February 21, Sévigné praised Racine's play and depicted the courtly hubbub around it before going on to discuss the unfolding drama of James and the English situation. She was not the only one to draw the two together; in the *Mercure historique et politique*, the presence of the English king was also noted, but the correspondent doubted that such entertainment would have been able to make the exiled king forget the loss of his kingdom.[73] It does indeed seem unlikely that the contemplation of a play dealing with religious difference might distract James from his domestic concerns; still less so since in brooding on his kingdom lost for difference of faith, he might have also known that when his mother the French princess Henriette left France to marry the English king Charles I, Marie de Médecis had asked the bishop of Langres to preach about Esther as a queen who maintained her faith among a different people.[74] The figure of Esther commonly served as a point of reflection for royal women living their religious difference in difficult times. When André de Rivaudeau wrote his version *Aman* in 1556 he dedicated it to the Huguenot queen of Navarre Jeanne d'Albret, describing her as a new Esther. Esther, the steadfastly Jewish queen, had long allowed European courts to think through lived practices of religious tolerance.

Racine wrote *Esther* in response to a request from Louis's second wife, Françoise d'Aubigné, marquise de Maintenon, who had herself been brought up briefly as a Protestant but by the 1680s was often held responsible for Louis's turn towards *dévot* Catholicism. The queen wanted a biblical play for the schoolgirls in her new establishment at Saint Cyr. Modeled on Jesuit school drama, the new play also benefitted from the substantial dressing-up box of the court, recycling costumes from the court ballets popular some decades earlier.[75] Racine's text drew on his friend Lemaistre de Sacy's translation of the book of Esther that had appeared in 1688, also drawing on a language and musical setting familiar from the Psalms.[76]

The book of Esther recounts the deliverance of the Jewish people. It begins at the Persian court with a feast to celebrate king Assuérus, who summons his wife Vasthi to come and show off her great beauty to his guests. She refuses; the king sends her away and takes a new and modest wife, Esther. Racine's play begins there, with Esther and her young attendants in the king's household. The king is manipulated by the vengeful Aman, who hates the Jews and persuades the king to massacre them.[77] But the Esther story figures religious difference as a private question as well as a public one; the king does not know that his new bride is Jewish. Under the guidance of her uncle Mardochée, Esther dares to approach the king to plead for her people, though she fears that death may ensue. When Esther enters, her beauty speaks for her, and the king extends his scepter as a "marque de clémence" (4:2) ["mark of clemency"]; she appeals for his larger clemency (7:3), which is granted. As Sacy's translation has it, "Le Seigneur se ressouvint de son peuple, et il eut compassion de son heritage" (10:12). ["The Lord remembered his people, and had compassion on his inheritance."] In Sacy's framing of it, the book of Esther sets out the response to religious difference in richly emotional language.

Piety and Pity on Stage

The language of the Esther story came to Racine already imbued with compassion and clemency, but Racine's play figured a supplication for kingly clemency toward religious difference at a moment when such language was highly politically charged. In particular, Racine's version returns us to the familiar revocational pairing of pity and piety.

This is a play that takes place under the sign of Piety, who is even its narrator: "La Piété fait le Prologue." ["Piety speaks the Prologue."][78] The school of Saint Cyr was represented by piety on its founding medal,[79] and Racine tells us in the preface that it was founded to bring up "dans la piété" (945) ["in piety"] the young women gathered together from all across the kingdom, a kingdom firmly under the sign of revocational piety. Piety announces that she does her work of nurturing the girls of Saint Cyr thanks to

Un Roi qui me protège, un Roi victorieux
A commis à mes soins ce dépôt précieux.
C'est lui, qui rassembla ces Colombes timides
Éparses en cent lieux, sans secours, et sans guides. (949)

[A king, my refuge, whose foes bite the dust,
Committed to my care this precious trust.
'Tis he who from a hundred haunts has brought
These timorous doves, forlorn and all untaught. (313)

In a somewhat laborious mode, the prologue thus establishes a link between Esther's gathering of her people and the royal household's care for the girls of Saint Cyr and, more broadly, the revocational reworking of the Protestant child as the foundation for a nation newly under the sign of Piety.

What does it mean to consider Esther's affective language in relation to the revocational texts I have discussed in this chapter? A long history of scholarship on *Esther* has remained in thrall to allegorical interpretations: firstly a *lecture à clé* or key reading of *Esther*, understanding it as what John Campbell calls "a kind of top-drawer, coded commentary on events surrounding the court of France in 1689," in which Mme de Maintenon's replacement of Mme de Montespan at court is represented by the virtuous Esther replacing beautiful Vasthi.[80] This reading was established early on by court observers who insisted on the pleasure Maintenon took in regarding herself in such a way, although these observations should be received with some skepticism since any occasion to needle Maintenon was seized upon by her critics at court.[81] Secondly and more significantly, readings imagining the exiled Jews as either Jansenists or Protestants were suggested as soon as the play was performed: an anti-*dévot* manuscript of 1689 noted that "Dans la proscription des Juifs, / De nos Huguenots fugitifs / On voit la juste ressemblance" ["In the proscription of the Jews / we see the rightful resemblance / to our fugitive Huguenots"]. The manuscript asks why their king, so full of virtue as was Assuérus, cannot calm his anger against such difference and answers, "Je vais vous le dire en deux mots: / Les juifs n'eurent jamais l'affaire / Aux jésuites ni aux dévots." ["I will tell you in two words / the Jews never had to deal with the Jesuits and the *dévots*."][82] Like many texts of these years, here the satirical allegory takes pains to suggest that outside forces were responsible for the crisis of toleration, and earnestly praises the figure of the king himself.

In the same year a Protestant reedition of *Esther*, published in Neuchâtel, was still more explicit in its allegorical reading, the editors announcing in in the *Avertissement* that they had made a second edition because the play seemed so directly connected to the present state of the Reformed Church: "On y voit clairement un triste récit de la dernière persecution, les desseins sanguinaires des cruels ennemis des Réformés." ["We see clearly the sad tale of the last persecution, the bloody designs of the cruel enemies of the Reformed."] The editors acknowledge that their reading is unconventional and hope that Racine will not mind if their reading makes "une application si éloignée de sa pensée" ["an application so distant from his thoughts"].[83] The Neuchâtel editors drew on a familiar tradition of figuring Protestants as Jews. Of course, as Déborah Blocker has pointed out, the Neuchâtel editors' reading of the text flouted the contemporary norm according to which plays should praise the person who had commissioned them, and furthermore went against what we know about Racine's position on Protestantism. Blocker suggests that today's scholarly readings of *Esther* dependent on either courtly or religious allegory are equally flawed because they are overly static; this play is, she argues, a text in which Racine mediates adroitly between courtly and Jansenist language, and to attend to its movements we need to avoid falling into such allegorical paralysis.[84] The Neuchâtel editors are, though, more adroit in their acknowledgment of the movement they make than most critics today, nodding to their wrongdoing even as they do it. In appropriating *Esther*, they do not propose a static reading, although critics after them often have. In taking the words of Racine and wrenching them around to signify differently within their own community, the Neuchâtel editors take another shot in the battle of revocational readings and counterreadings worried over by Bayle; this is not paralysis but rather bitter movement. In its willful arrogation of meaning, the Protestant edition sits well alongside Racine's play and its concerns about rhetoric and change.

In writing *Esther*, Racine drew on the electric buzz around paradiastolic emotion. This is a play in which the familiar emotions of revocational writing are set to constant movement; Racine brings to the portrayal of affective absolutism a sense of affect's force, its tricky displacements, its slipperiness. Certainly, he inherits much of what he writes from biblical tradition. The scene of supplication, in which Esther asks her husband the king for compassion and clemency, was a moment of high emotional drama in earlier versions of *Esther*, too, and both the Protestant Antoine de Montchrestien's 1601 *Aman* and Pierre Du Ryer's *Esther* (1644) set up a neat series of pitiful moments: even, for Montchrestien, pity for the king who doesn't like to see his wife ill, as well as the more usual requests for clemency from king and God alike. In Du Ryer's play, Esther asks the king not for clemency but "un œil plus pitoyable" ["a more pitiful eye"] upon her as an "aimable" ["lovable"] princess, and the king responds to this emotional plea by letting her live as a gift of his love.[85]

Yet compared to these carefully parsed dialogues of pitiful and pitier, Racine's version of the play ups the emotional stakes. His text reads as an extraordinary exercise in affective range, with the characters of the play in constant thrall to the emotional switches of their sovereigns both temporal and divine. Where Racine's secular drama had constantly reworked the relation between action and speech, in *Esther* he tries out a different version of that relation, in which the glowering promise of potential action—of massacres, of hangings, of exiles—is counterpointed by a choric function where the voices of young women signal and transmit intense affective responses to all they witness, fear, or desire.[86] The action of the play revolves around the knowledge and non-knowledge (or non-claiming) of difference, but the text returns constantly to the clear labeling and partitioning of particular emotions: this is joy, this is revenge, this—please!—might finally be pity. Racine practices an affect that is known and brought about through naming.

The emotions signaled by *Esther* are explicitly named and often instrumentalist; in turn, each character or group shows who makes them feel in what way or to what end. Elise opens the play by recalling the joy and horror caused by a prophecy (I. 1); Esther speaks of her shame at being singled out

(I. 1); the king proclaims Mardochée to be his joy; the chorus of young women tremble in seeing Aman: "Mon cœur de crainte et d'horreur se resserre" (III.3.935) ["My heart with fear and horror quakes"] (354); and they call on God to terrify the enemies of the Jews, "Que de ton nom la terreur les disperse" (III.3.1011) ["May the terror of your name scatter them"]. This directive emotional vocabulary comes with a rich aesthetic past; it draws on the language of dramatic theory throughout the century, from the pity and fear of the Aristotelian tradition to the horror favored by commentators such as La Mesnardière. In the preface, Racine describes how the play educated the schoolgirls through instruction and pleasure, "les instruisent en les divertissant" (945) ["educate them while entertaining them"] (306), with the classical formula making the schoolgirls into a sort of audience. Racine's theatrical career had devoted itself to the emotional stimulation of audiences through these two Horatian modes, but here he turns his efforts—or so he says—to address the young actors themselves, who announce turn by turn the emotions most typically associated with the reactions of the theater audience.

But what of pity, that emotion that in the Aristotelian tradition is coupled with the fear of which the young women speak? If Aman the intriguer is the figure we fear, he is also the character whose pity must be questioned. Aman is the Machiavel intriguer who whispers in the ear of the king, and his own confidant in turn does the same for him, urging Aman to hide his real emotion, to dissimulate his rage and desire for revenge (III.1.831). Yet the chorus (at this point well instructed, if not entertained) is fortunately able to see clearly. They know that pity can be a disguise for an uglier emotion; on calumny, the chorus sings:

> De ce Monstre si farouche
> Craignez la feinte douceur.
> La vengeance est dans son Cœur,
> Et la pitié dans sa bouche. (III.3.977–80)

> [Recoil, when sweetness drips
> From this monster smart:
> Revenge is in her heart,
> Compassion on her lips.] (356)

This false emotion, like the false sweetness of the intriguer-priest in *Athalie*, raises an awkward question: If pity is subject to such questioning by the chorus, what are we to make of its presence elsewhere in the play? At the end of the play, Esther links the pity of God for his people and the clemency of the king:

> Que n'espérions-nous point d'un Roi si généreux?
> Dieu regarde en pitié son peuple malheureux,
> Disions-nous; un Roi règne ami de l'Innocence.
> Partout du nouveau Prince on vantait la clémence. (III.4.1078–81)

> [How much we hoped from such a generous king!
> "God looks with pity on His wretched people,"
> We said: "This King is friend of the innocent."
> Your sovereign mercy everywhere was praised.] (360)

The praise of the king's potential pity is in perfect step with the praise of Louis XIV as kindly governor of his people. But in a play that puts the performance of pity into question, it leaves an uncomfortable emotional-epistemological residue: to understand that pity can mask revenge (and that kings can be taken in by it) is to understand that pity can be just a performance.

Esther's anxiety about pity can be contrasted with the more stable portrayal of it in the play Racine wrote after *Esther*, the biblical drama *Athalie*, in which pity and unpity punctuate the text in order to affirm properly stable ethical judgments.[87] In a world in which even God's mercy has failed, the pity or pitilessness of humans for a child becomes the only marker of good. Joad reports that the child king Joas believes himself to be an orphan taken in only out of pity (I.2.184); the notoriously untender Athalie—she has, she reports, stifled any tendency to maternal "tendresse" [II.7.724] and rejected "une lâche et frivole pitié" (II.7.718) ["a mean and miserable pity"] (411)—nonetheless trembles with emotion at the sight of that same child:

> Quel prodige nouveau me trouble et m'embarrasse?
> La douceur de sa voix, son enfance, sa grâce,
> Font insensiblement à mon inimitié
> Succéder . . . Je serais sensible à la pitié? (II.7.651–54)

> [What miracle dismays, distresses me?
> The sweetness of his voice, his childish grace,
> Make my antipathy insensibly . . .
> Can it be possible I pity him?] (407)

Athalie's pity wells up as if naturally in homage to the particularity of this child; in this instance, the identification of the emotion tells us more about the compelling object of emotion than the feeler of the emotion. (This is another form of affective absolutism; the child Joas compels absolute homage.) The play performs an affective switch which allows us to identify the chosen community. If at the start of the play the Jews mourn the unmercifulness of God, at the close it is the flouted Athalie who rails at a pitiless God (V.6.1774). Over the course of the play, emotion is after much trouble eventually redirected in pleasing ways.

The rerouting of emotion in *Esther* is potentially more troubling. It is not just the enemy whose kindheartedness is strained; even the king's vaunted clemency often seems more like merely a redirection of violence. When Assuérus turns from Aman to make Mardochée his new favorite (III.7) then the play changes course merely by swapping the good object for the bad. For Assuérus as for Aman, we learn that love and revenge are closely connected. Of the king's annals, we learn, "On y conserve écrits le service et l'offense, / Monuments éternels d'amour et de vengeance" (II.1.397–98). ["There lie inscribed each golden deed and bad / Eternal monuments of love and vengeance"] (331). The business of kingship lies in this flipping back and forth between love and hate.[88] In this portrayal the king is not a virtuous originator of clemency. He functions merely as a lever that reorients affect, an affect that is repeatedly claimed to be that issued forth from the king but might just as much be wholly impersonal. The king channels emotion, and the play traces the pinball movement of that force around the political-theological realms of possibility. Racine records where the movement is stopped and the story can be allowed to end.

No scene signifies this better than the moment at which Aman bows in trembling supplication at the knees of Esther after his crime has been discovered (III.5). When the king sees this scene, he imagines Aman to be threatening rape. Yet this scene directly recalls Esther's own fainting at Assuérus's knees, an image that would have been familiar to Racine from Poussin's painting of "Esther devant Assuérus," owned by his patron the marquis de Seignelay.[89] One supplication scene, then, brings about revelation and revocation, but the other leads only to accusation and revenge. Through this gestural pairing, Racine suggests something of the contingency of supplication itself. Although the play ends with the chorus's joyous relief at God's refound good mood, it remains uncomfortably subject to the idea that the whole terrible movement might well begin again.

When Assuérus reads his annals to comfort himself after a bad dream, he imagines the text as what he calls an eternal monument. We have seen that the destruction or the building of monuments was central to the battle over the Revocation's significance. The destruction of the Protestant temple of Charenton was immortalized in innumerable victory prints of the Revocation; on the other side Benoist's monumental memorializing text declared itself to be a proof of Protestant suffering. Yet the continual flipping of vocabularies common to the years following the Revocation suggests that no text can ever be a monument, despite its author's best intentions; texts can be appropriated, reworked, and twisted to fit a quite different end, as in the example of the Neuchâtel *Esther*. Bayle's anxiety about the true meaning of terms plays out again in Racine's frenetic playing of the affective register. In delineating emotional vocabularies and their speedy repurposing, Racine's play points to the difficulties of articulating or identifying emotion under affective absolutism even as he celebrates the triumph of that political model.

In searching for a way to think beyond the subject as the bearer of an interiorized emotion, Rei Terada calls for an exploration of "not a theory of subjectivity but a theory of kinds of emotion as kinds of rhetoric."[90] The emotional vocabularies I have described here, shared out and reworked by supporters and critics of the Revocation and by a playwright contemporary with it, illustrate just that: on both the Catholic and Protestant sides, the terms of tenderness were themselves continually in revocation. Compassionate language was constantly eroded by the movements of rhetorical slippage, and the subject of compassion was all too often subject to being rewritten as something beyond pity. This semantic susceptibility points to the difficulty of counting on emotional or political progress, even as we glimpse moments, gestures, and conversations that seem to promise a more tolerant settlement. If Protestant attempts to speak otherwise—whether in the first-person voicing of the pamphlets or in philosophical attempts to set language apart from emotion—let us look with the refugees to a different future, then the emotional swings of Racine's *Esther*, with their hints that the whole pitiless horror might start up again anytime, remain a troubling seam to our understanding of that history of tolerance.

Chapter 6

Compassionate Labor in Seventeenth-Century Montreal

If all sympathy were agreeable, a hospital would be a more entertaining place than a ball.
            —David Hume, letter to Adam Smith, July 28, 1759

A sick woman sits up in bed (fig. 2), looking up past the nun who stands at the bedside and gazing instead toward the presiding figure of Christ in the top left-hand corner. Behind this eager if sickly spectator stretches a row of beds with similar patients, and patrolling the row at regular intervals are a series of nuns, spaced out neatly each from the other, as though on an assembly line of care. At the bottom left a new arrival is wheeled in to be shuttled toward one of those beds: the singularity of that arrival, a particularized body whose face we can determine, is set against the long and routinized perspective of beds and nurses, the one axis colliding with the other. This painting—thought to be an ex-voto left in thanksgiving for care—hung in the central ward of the Hôtel-Dieu hospital in the French settlement of Montreal in 1710.[1] In this chapter, I address a small corpus of texts associated with that hospital: a set of manuals sent from the nursing order's original home in France, and a journal produced in Montreal toward the end of the seventeenth century.

If the previous chapters of this book have inquired into the troubled relation between compassion and action, in this chapter compassionate action like that shown in the painting comes to the fore. The painting's somewhat clunky choreography also raises questions about the temporality of compassion, its framing as either event or routine. What did it mean, for the

Figure 2. Anonymous painter. *La salle des femmes*, ex-voto. Oil on canvas. Collection des Religieuses Hospitalières de Saint-Joseph de Montréal.

practitioners of such an emotion, to consider compassion not as the glancing product of a singular encounter (as in the model of the Good Samaritan) but rather something that had to be reproduced again and again in accordance with an institutional routine? How did the early modern nun as nurse make an emotion into a profession, a rule, something that could be performed by any of her colleagues at any time? In this painting, the stabilization through repetition represents hospital compassion as quotidian, always the same, though we know that care work depends on an exhausting tension between repetition and urgency. The compassion shown here is, as the anthropologist Lisa Stevenson writes of shift work on suicide hotlines, "invested in a certain way of being in time," in all the meanings of that term.[2] This is bureaucratic care.

Whereas in earlier chapters I've explored the compassion exercised by men, fictional and otherwise, this last chapter turns to the labor of women to address the gendered work of compassion. Unlike most of the texts I've discussed, this is material produced for and by women; it is material that has never approached the canonical status of the other texts I describe; and among my book's actors, the women I discuss here are not coincidentally the most likely to be engaged in compassionate action. Most important, whereas the compassionates who have already appeared chiefly considered compassion as a solitary exercise, even as it underwrote a very distinct group identity, here compassion is a group exercise, significantly changing the structures of emotion. And where the compassion I have described so far has often been impersonal or generalized—responding to "suffering" rather than to individualized sufferers—this model of compassion turns insistently to the known sufferer, responding to the proximate and personalized.

For many readers, this material will immediately call up a range of firmly entrenched theoretical perspectives. It's hard, of course, to write about early modern hospitals without thinking through the work of Michel Foucault on what he calls the "grand renfermement" of the poor.[3] The rule books discussed here certainly participate in the disciplinary structures that Foucault shows were central to the establishment of seventeenth-century institutions like the Hôpital Général in Paris, and a narrative drawing on his account has itself come to form a sort of rule for much work in early modern studies. In their insistence on a professionalization of emotion, they also anticipate the women's work that the sociologist Arlie Hochschild famously skewered by showing the compulsions of affective labor imposed upon female flight attendants and other workers attending to the needs of the public.[4] And although they are written for a post-Tridentine order, the convent rule books lie recognizably within the medieval monastic tradition described by Giorgio Agamben as "a form-of-life, that is a life that is linked so closely to its form that it proves to be inseparable from it."[5] So far, so familiar: the rule books set out how compassion ought to have been practiced according to the strictures of an ever more tightly defined regulation of women's work, and these constraints would have been familiar territory to the careful regulators of compassion whom I have observed throughout this book.

Yet I also want to counterpoint the more restricted story I have told so far and turn from the rule book to an account of a lived practice of compassion: the journal of Marie Morin, sometime superior of the Hôtel-Dieu convent in Montreal, written at the end of the century. Morin's account of the convent hospital offers a sort of antirule, but not the delightful disruption offered by Rabelais's fictional Abbaye de Thélème. Rather, she details the ups and downs of work, emotional and otherwise, as it was experienced by the first nuns of the hospital settlement. Morin's story about settlement unsettles the compassionate protocol we have seen at work throughout this book. Her account of work in the hospital makes space for notions of community in compassion, seemingly displacing the paradoxically solipsistic compassion I have described in earlier chapters. But before we get to Morin, we must take a tour through the early modern hospital in both France and Canada.

Hospital Histories

The names of early modern hospitals, like La Pitié, might suggest that such institutions understood themselves in relation to an emotional vocabulary.[6] Yet the focus of hospital historiography has not explored affective concerns, tending instead to follow a Foucauldian narrative about the governmental structures underlying the rise in charitable institutions.[7] After the Council of Trent, religious renewal led to a boom in religious confraternities and lay movements with a charitable focus. Vincent de Paul established the first charitable confraternity in the Lyonnais in 1617, and they spread rapidly in the following decades.[8] Since seventeenth-century charity managed mobile or marginal (rather than merely sick) populations, charitable interventions incorporated, as Miriam Ticktin puts it in a narrative of modern humanitarianism's roots in seventeenth-century charity, "both a form of help and a mode of social control."[9] Where hospitality was considered a largely private virtue, charitable institutions acted instead in the public realm.[10] Such institutions worked carefully to control affective impulses; the founding regulations of Paris's Hôpital Général specified that no one should give alms within a certain parameter of the hospital, notwithstanding "tout motif de compassion, nécessité pressante, ou autre prétexte que ce puisse être" ["any motive of compassion, pressing necessity, or any other excuse"].[11] The early modern hospital was vigilant in its regulation of feeling.

Recent scholarship has traced the important role of women in Counter-Reformation French charity, generally distinguishing between two different groups of women. On one side stood well-connected circles of aristocratic women, organized by Vincent de Paul as the Dames de la Charité, who fundraised for and supported the Augustinian nuns who ran the Hôtel-Dieu; Colin Jones describes how these women served jellies and cakes at functions but did not extend their labor beyond this.[12] On the other side were groups like the nonelite Filles de la Charité (founded in 1633 by one of the Dames, Louise de

Marillac) who did the hard work that joined the Dames to the down-and-outs.[13] The etcher Abraham Bosse's series of images of the corporal works of mercy—feeding the hungry, visiting the sick, and so on—shows aristocratic women engaged in the more picturesque end of this sort of Counter-Reformation fervor. But the work of the elite women was also understood to be set apart from that of the male masterminds, and the motivation and scope of their social interest was always gendered. Women's interventions were marked as charitable rather than political. In Vincent de Paul's account of the beginnings of his charitable endeavors, it might have been high emotion that moved him to it, but it was a woman who organized the work; on seeing a village afflicted by sickness with no one well enough to care for the sick, he writes:

> Cela me toucha sensiblement le cœur. Je ne manquais pas de les recommander au prône avec affection, et Dieu, touchant le cœur de ceux qui m'écoutaient, fit qu'ils se trouvèrent tous émus de compassion pour ces pauvres affligés. L'après-dînée il se fit assemblée chez une bonne demoiselle de la ville pour voir quel secours on leur pourrait donner.[14]

> [It touched my heart. I did not fail to speak about them with affection when I preached, and God, touching the heart of those who heard me, saw that they were all moved by compassion for those poor afflicted ones. After dinner there was a meeting in the house of a good woman of the town, to see what help could be given.]

And Louise de Marillac, the sidekick of Vincent de Paul, followed this distinction: asked whether men should direct the Hôpital Général by the Compagnie du Saint-Sacrement to lock up beggars after the banning of mendicity in 1656, she replied

> Si l'œuvre est regardée comme politique, il semble que les hommes doivent l'entreprendre; si elle est considérée comme œuvre de charité, les femmes la peuvent entreprendre en la maniere qu'elles ont entrepris les autres grands et penibles exercices de charité que Dieu a approuvés.[15]

> [If the work is seen as political, it seems that men should undertake it; if it is considered as a work of charity, women can undertake it in

the way they have undertaken other great and difficult charitable
exercises that God has approved.]

The work of such women was also inseparable from the larger regulation and
enclosure of women's religious communities across Europe, and subsequently
in the New World. The establishment of the *Filles* as a labor force sought to
exploit a loophole in Rome's increasingly severe rulings on the enclosure of
women's religious orders. As more and more orders had come to accept Rome's
rules of enclosure, which kept women within the convent, the possibility of
women's actions in the world was increasingly constrained. The Daughters of
Charity provided a way around this difficulty because they did not follow
what Laurence Brockliss and Colin Jones term "the external forms of conven-
tual organization."[16]

The burgeoning charitable communities were themselves also operating a
different kind of regulation: the management of religious difference after the
Edict of Nantes. Catholic charitable movements pushed for the rigorous application of the edict, insisting on the limits of Protestant rights. Historians
have long focused on the role of the Compagnie du Saint-Sacrement in that
reification and policing of difference: Brockliss and Jones describe the Compagnie as "a kind of activist caucus" for the cause.[17] The Compagnie was particularly concerned by the potential for Protestantism to spread among the
poor, and its organization of poor relief had a heavily sectarian ideology.[18]
Women too were active in these sectarian interventions: the Filles de Charité
sought to convert Protestant patients as a form of spiritual healing.[19] This
sectarian policing of domestic divisions was operative even or perhaps especially on the other side of the world in New France, where religious difference
was scrupulously outlawed. In this regard, compassion work in hospitals continued the exclusionary dynamic central to seventeenth-century compassion
talk.

Scholars today insist on the importance of these movements in the history of women's labor.[20] Yet to a certain extent the gendered distinction between forms of labor made by Louise de Marillac is still borne out in
scholarship which often draws a line between women's apparent emotional
sincerity and the political motivations of men. Colin Jones, for example, contrasts "nursing communities . . . often motivated by a compassionate concern" with confraternities such as the Company of the Holy Sacrament who
were "more authoritarian and hierarchical."[21] In such formulations, women's
emotion appears as something that escapes hierarchy or at least is

supplementary to it. The materials in this chapter invite such a reading, and to a large extent I follow it; but it is important to note that the gender difference they mark is also entwined with the difference of settler experience. New France unsettles the familiar French structures of compassion.

New France

Much of what we know about the first decades of life in New France comes from the Jesuits, who cataloged their missions with a particular French audience in mind, sending annual letters home to France recounting news and seeking funds; since the nineteenth century, these letters have been known as the Jesuit Relations.[22] In this material, women religious play a particular role, since the Jesuits saw the affective exemplarity of the nuns as central to the growth of New France. The introduction of the Ursulines in education and various kinds of Hospitalières for the sick was intended to bridge gaps to Amerindian women, who were essential to the French goals of establishing a sedentary civilization.[23] The head of the Canadian mission, Paul Le Jeune, insistent that charity would win conversions where words alone would not, launched an appeal for people to fund such an urgent enterprise, and Marie de Vignerot de Pont-de-Courlay, duchesse d'Aiguillon, stepped in first.[24] A young widow (and niece of Richelieu) who frequented the circles of Vincent de Paul and his Dames de Charité and who was also drawn to Carmelite spiritual practices, Aiguillon had read the Jesuit letters and was ready to respond to them. Aiguillon's compassion was celebrated as an infinitely extensible virtue, extendable in geographic range; the Quebec project would be the perfect occasion for her charitable ambitions. Her funeral oration would praise her for "cette tendresse et cette compassion qui la rendit sensible à toutes les misères connues" ["this tenderness and this compassion which made her sensitive to all known misery"]: compassion's reach to New France signaled the sort of universalizing of emotion described by the Jesuits we saw in Chapter 3.[25]

The contract for the hospital was signed on 16 August 1637 between Aiguillon and the bookseller Sébastien Cramoisy, who acted as procurer for the new foundation, gathering the goods to be sent overseas.[26] Aiguillon engaged three nuns from the Augustine order of hospitalière nuns at Dieppe, and in 1639 those women left for Canada.[27] This relation between working nuns abroad and aristocratic founders in France was central to female missionary work in Canada: when the Jesuit Le Moyne worried that women who might support distant hospitals would forget their duties in France, he was surely taking a swipe at the missionary ambitions of Aiguillon, which violated the domestic norm.[28] Aiguillon's reach made her a target of such attacks: the predictably gossipy Tallemant des Réaux notes: "Elle donne aux eglises, et ne paye pas ses dettes . . . On dit que presentement elle fait ramasser le sucre que l'on met sur le bord de ses plats de dessert."[29] ["She gives to the churches, and does not pay her debts . . . They say that she gathers up the sugar left on the edge of her dessert plates."] But reading through Tallemant's meanness we can also glimpse something of the emotional culture of *dévote* women: "Elle dit à toute chose: 'En vérité, cela fait dévotion,' et le dira en parlant d'une chose qui n'y aura aucun rapport. C'est simplement pour dire: 'Cela touche.'" ["She says of everything 'this draws us to devotion' and says it about things that have nothing to do with it, where she just means 'this is moving.'"] Tallemant's put-down is meant to erode the reputation of Aiguillon, but along the way it lets us see how central emotional response was to the culture which funded the New French missions.

The missionary zeal of the hospital's early years soon gave way to a very different energy. Disease introduced by the Europeans killed the Amerindian population in ever greater numbers, so that by the end of the seventeenth century the Amerindians to be converted represented only 4 percent of the hospital patients.[30] Increasingly the nuns dealt instead not with such patients but with the developing colonial enterprise of Nouvelle-France, which under Louis XIV saw a new economic and demographic development.[31] The new hospital work was rigorously cyclical: as each new boat came in from France, the rate of fever spiked in the settler population, and the nuns had to work to tend to a new round of sufferers.[32] Although they were halfway around the world from French disputes, the nuns were nonetheless particularly keen to convert heretic Huguenots. One recalcitrant Protestant in the Quebec hospital received a special drink prepared for him by the mother superior Marie Catherine de Saint Augustin, in which she had mixed fragments of bone from the great Jesuit martyr Jean de Brébeuf, who had been burnt alive by the Iroquois. On drinking this concoction, he became "doux comme un agneau, pria qu'on l'instruisit, embrassa la foy avec joye, et fit abjuration publiquement avec une ferveur admirable" ["as sweet as a lamb, asked for instruction, embraced the faith with joy, and made public abjuration with an admirable fervor"].[33]

A series of borderline hagiographic accounts of the Quebec hospital's heroic acts are given in the Jesuit Relations, but a number of other documents also give a more complex sense of the community's isolation and vulnerability. Annual lists calling for items to be sent from France to Quebec asked for, among many other things, sewing thread, reams of blotting paper, combs for the sick, six good kitchen knives, rosaries, and small books of devotion. These items were to be sent to Cramoisy's bookshop in Paris, where the bookseller would forward them to the mission once a year.[34] The lists sometimes detail the paintings that ornamented the hospital: six tiny devotional images painted on copper, resistant to water and able to travel easily, had been sent by Aiguillon, along with a painting of the duchess herself. In 1641, Paul Le Jeune reported that the indigenous women who saw that portrait imitated the gestures of the duchess in the painting, kneeling and praying.[35]

Amerindian Compassion

French reports often revolved around such stories of indigenous imitation. The Jesuits were keen to study Amerindian emotional behavior and to think about what such behavior meant for the future of their missions. The terminology of Counter-Reformation fellow-feeling structured their encounters and practices in the field, but the missionaries did not grant to the Amerindians the natural response of compassion central to the affective science of the metropolitan Jesuits we saw in Chapter 3. The missionaries understood the Amerindians to have a necessarily imitative relation to religious practice and accordingly envisioned potential conversion coming about through emotional apprenticeship. Seeing the nuns at work, so the argument went, would teach the Amerindians exterior practices that might in time lead to inner faith. The superior of the Quebec hospital nuns, Marie de Saint-Ignace, wrote, "Les Sauvages qui ne sçavoient que c'estoit de visiter les malades, apprennent le métier de charité." ["The Savages, who did not know what it is to visit the sick, are learning the practice of charity."][36] But in this European account, the charity of the Amerindians remains chiefly a mimicked action rather than an interior state—although many a Protestant might have said the same about French Catholic acts of mercy, and the Jansenists Nicole and Pascal would also have thought that mimicked action was a good way to begin the path to faith.

The writing of Amerindian pity in the Jesuit Relations is itself an imitative echo of the texts of the French Wars of Religion, where the proper pity and the horror of pitilessness demarcate opposing sides. The Jesuits insisted on sharp distinctions between their allies the Hurons, who, like Europeans, they saw as capable of the proper apportioning of pity, and their enemies the Iroquois, who according to Jesuit standards were not. The capacity to give and receive pity in the correct Catholic manner marked out the civilized man from the savage. Even when the Iroquois take care of their captives, they are described as showing a "cruelle misericorde" ["cruel compassion"], tending the captive's wounds so that they might later torture him all the better after his recovery.[37] The term recalls the actions of Catholic soldiers toward the Protestants in the account of Élie Benoist we saw in Chapter 5; compassion's sorting mechanism becomes especially apparent in these extreme conditions. In Jesuit accounts, this brutal game stands in parodic relation to the notion that the savages can learn charity from the Europeans.[38]

The absolute divide between French pity and Iroquois cruelty shapes a figure of the Amerindian as a nonhuman enemy: witness a French captive whose "misere, qui devoit fléchir des cœurs de tygre, les aigrissant davantage, fit, d'un sujet de compassion, un sujet de leur rage" ["pitiful lot, which was enough to melt tigers' hearts, only made theirs the more savage"], or a savage woman who stabs a child "inhumainement" ["inhumanly"] to watch his human blood flow, contrasted with French spectators, "nos François," who, "touchés de compassion, à la veuë d'un spectacle si triste, cherchoient les moyens de pouvoir delivrer cét enfant" ["touched with pity at so sad a spectacle, sought means to liberate the child"].[39] But the Jesuit accounts also allow for the possibility of Huron human kindness. If seventeenth-century compassion theory often distinguishes between the emotion felt by the weak and by the noble, the missionary Jesuit version shapes the figure of the rare noble savage who, usually because of their Christian education, feels correctly in response to the unfeeling horror of most Amerindians. In one otherwise horrifying account, an indigenous woman appears as an angel, rescuing French sufferers and tending to them with herbs. This fortuitous apparition then recounts her baptism and says she was shown kindness by the Ursulines so will repay it to the French.[40] Figures like this, which punctuate the Relations, serve as the sentimental exception that underwrites the mission's goals.

Huron humanity, however, is most often figured through victimhood, with Hurons playing the role of sentimentalized victim giving rise to a Jesuit commentary. The *Relation* from 1660 gives an account of four Hurons captured by the Iroquois: one old Huron man, burned at the stake, called out "Jesus ayez pitié de moy! Marie fortifiez-moy!" ["Jesus, take pity on me! Mary, give me strength!"][41] The priest narrating the story continues, "C'estoit la sa chanson de mort, c'estoit où se terminoient tous ses cris c'estoit de cette belle priere qu'il remplissoit l'air, au lieu que les autres le remplissent d'ordinaire de pleurs et de hurlement pitoiables" (94). ["That was his death-song, and therewith ended all his cries. With that beautiful invocation he filled the air, whereas others, as a general rule, fill it with pitiful weeping and wailing."] The old man's grandson is too young for such fortitude and is told by the Jesuit that he may cry out: when he gives "cris lamentables" (98) ["pitiful cries"] the grandfather berates the Iroquois captors, who set upon him with instruments of torture. The old man remains "insensible" to their efforts, and the Jesuit comments:

> J'en fus touché de compassion, et voulois luy persuader de se plaindre un peu pour s'espargner quelques-unes de ces inhumanitez: car c'est la coutume des Sauvages de ne point cesser leurs tourments qu'ils n'ayent fait crier le patient, comme si ce cry exprimé par la vehemence de la douleur, devenoit pour eux un cry de joye. (98)

> [I was touched with pity for him, and wished to persuade him to moan a little, that he might spare himself some of these inhuman inflictions; for it is the Savages' custom not to cease their torments until they have made the sufferer cry out; as if that cry, extorted by the intensity of the pain, became for them a cry of joy.]

The scene allows for two approved versions of pity: on the one hand, that of God for those who suffer in his name, and on the other those who, following the divine, are touched by such suffering. Pity must be redeemed by a salvatory potential to avoid falling into something "pitiful." But the Jesuit account is not only a theological one; in assessing the proper disposition of emotion available to certain peoples, it also makes affect central to the efforts of their writing sent back to France. If the Relations are often described as one of the earliest forms of anthropological fieldwork, then we should take seriously the role of seventeenth-century affective discourse in shaping that new discourse.[42]

In contrast to this false Iroquois compassion, the authentic compassion of the nurses in the Quebec settlement was praised in highly ritualized ways. They acted, according to hagiographical histories produced by the order in the early eighteenth century, "se refusant les moindres soulagements et souffrant avec joye le manquement des choses les plus necessaires, n'ayant de la compassion que pour les autres et en donnant des marques dans toutes les occasions par une excessive charité" ["refusing themselves the least relief and joyfully suffering their lack of the most necessary things, having compassion only for others and showing signs of it on all occasions through an excessive charity"].[43] In the same text, the narrator insists on the nuns' "extrème compassion" (55) ["extreme compassion"] for their charges. But this insistence on heroic and extreme compassion toward the suffering sick plays out very differently in the Montreal texts. As a later settlement, Montreal was less explicitly involved in missionary aims and more beset by the problems of a settler community, and these differences shaped the forms of its compassion.

Montreal

One of the leading figures in Montreal's settlement was Jerome LeRoyer de la Dauversière, a young lay nobleman attached to the projects of Catholic reform.[44] It was LeRoyer who drew in Jeanne Mance, a bourgeois laywoman from Langres, selected to found the hospital of the new settlement.[45] Mance set out for Montreal in 1641 and administered the Hôtel-Dieu hospital there until her death in 1673. But she needed support from home, and there LeRoyer could also help out. LeRoyer had founded an order of Hospitalière nuns under the sign of Saint Joseph at La Flèche in the west of France, where he had attended the Jesuit college. This was, strictly speaking, a congregation rather than a religious order under a permanent rule; it renewed "simple vows" every three years. Mance made several return trips to France and in 1658 recruited three Hospitalière nuns who had been trained in La Flèche: Judith Moreau de Brésoles, the pharmacist; Catherine Macé, who ran the household; and Marie Maillet, who served as bursar.[46]

It was not only French nuns who were imported to guide the new project. Throughout its first decades, the hospital in Montreal also relied on a set of French texts to keep it in compassionate order, like the biographies of women central to the Hospitalière establishments in France. A *Vie de Mademoiselle de Melun* (1687) recounted a young French woman's charitable instincts from childhood on, insisting on her compassion and tenderness.[47] Melun's biography was obviously central to the Hospitalière order, and it tells a story of the significance of hospital work. But the story told focuses chiefly on Melun's charitable and heroic singularity (103), which makes her akin to a figure of romance. The text presents a series of touching vignettes that showcase the young woman's particular style of care, telling us that she put songbirds around the beds of the sick and made them stews (431). The sentimentally inspiring scenes of rural France would have seemed very distant from the material realities of wintry Montreal.

Alongside these edifying hagiographies stood less heroic and more bureaucratic texts: the sets of rule books and manuals that entailed uniformity across the order. Roland Barthes describes a rule as "a way of stretching time out in a straight line."[48] But since the Montreal rule books had traveled halfway across the world, they were also a way of straightening space. They imposed a form of life meant for western France onto a very different landscape and historical moment; they sought to shape a particular form of emotional community. Yet because the new establishment in Montreal was not immediately subject to direct episcopal surveillance in the same way as the Quebec hospital, and wrestled with such authority throughout its first decades, it had a particularly strained relation to the concept of rules and vows.[49] This peculiarity makes its accounts of emotion, which lurch between rule and practice, of particular interest.

Rule Books

The Montreal foundation was at first regulated by a 1643 text, the *Constitutions des filles hospitalieres de sainct Joseph*. The text exhorts the community to be "douce en sa conversation, cordialement unie à ses Sœurs, tendrement charitable envers les pauvres malades" (7) ["sweet in conversation, cordially united with their sisters, tenderly charitable toward the sick"]. This emotional disposition was designed to facilitate the shared governance of the community, since after two years in the congregation all the *filles* were to have a right to vote and to govern communally.[50] The effort of democratic transparency necessitated a particular emotional management: if all the *filles* were to be equal, then particular and personalized friendships were not to interfere in the way the community ordered itself. The Constitutions note sternly that the *filles* should "[banir et rejeter] bien loin toute affection particuliere et toute brigue, comme chose qui est toujours pernicieuse, et principalement en ce point cause de la ruine des Communautez" (15) ["banish and reject all individual affection and any fallings-out, as something that is always pernicious, and the principal cause of the ruin of Communities"]. Likewise, in selecting those who enter the community, the *filles* should have in mind rather "le bien commun de la maison, qu'aucune affection particuliere" (23) ["the common good of the house, rather than any particular affection"]. Mutual assistance bound the congregation together: the language of reciprocal obligation underwrites the *Constitutions*. The rule book's properly prescribed affection did not allow for a distinction between individuals: "La Superieure aura envers ses Filles un cœur de mere, les aimant toutes universellement, sans affection ou familiarite particuliere" (53). ["The Superior will have a heart of a mother toward the Filles, loving them each universally, without particular affection or familiarity."] Universal affection required the *filles* to work hard at a distancing form of transparency: they could not go into each other's rooms and had to keep their doors open at all times. In the rule book, emotion is impersonal; it requires a refusal to know or to distinguish the object of one's charitable or communal actions.

This impersonalizing union also governed the relations between *filles* and *malades*. The *filles* were not allowed to complain about their charges unless they were seeking advice on how to "les gouverner mieux et regler leurs mœurs" (56) ["better govern and regulate their habits"]. This was lest such gossip get out and damage the reputation of the sick person: even in observing the spiritual union that bound Christian sufferers to Christ, the social status of the *malades* also had to be considered. The *malades* entered the community in a state of extreme vulnerability that had to be skillfully managed by the *filles*, who were also counseled to avoid friendliness or chat with their charges (75). The business of compassion required a fine organization of hierarchical distinctions.

The *Constitutions* also spoke to the problem posed by the painting at the opening of this chapter: the nurse's emotion had to be serially reproducible. The *filles* had to be wary lest their immediate emotion for their charges wore away with the repetition of their difficult tasks. In a chapter on the corporal works of mercy we learn:

> Les filles doivent bien prendre garde de ne se laisser endurcir leur cœur par l'habitude et l'accoutumance d'estre avec les malades, et ne laisser prendre pied au chagrin qui pouroit naistre de l'impatience et mauvaise humeur de quelqu'un d'iceux, ou de la continuation et assiduité du travail, et fonctions viles et incommodes environ eux: Mais il faut au contraire qu'elles s'efforcent par desirs souvent renouvellez de conserver un cœur humble, tendre et compatissant,

servant les pauvres avec un visage modestement doux et joyeux, en
sorte qu'on y lise le plaisir qu'elles prennent de servir JESUS-
CHRIST en ses membres. (70–71).

[The girls must take care not to let their heart be hardened by habit
and by getting used to being with the sick, and not to become disappointed by the impatience or bad mood of the patients, or by the
continuous hard work, and the vile and uncomfortable things they
must do; but on the contrary they must try through often renewed
desires to keep a humble, tender, and compassionate heart, serving
the poor with a modestly sweet and joyful face, so that one reads on
it the pleasure they take in serving Jesus Christ through these
people.]

The *filles* had to renew their internal emotions but also take care to appear
sweet and cheerful so that those who encountered them could easily read their
inner state. In the rule book, compassion must be an infinitely renewable
emotion even as it performs its exceptionality: it must be received as a singularized event by the patient even when the nurse understands it to be routine.
This professionalization of care anticipates the affective labor diagnosed by
feminist sociologists like Arlie Hochschild: it is a model of women's work in
which feelings must be managed by turning them outward to the world in a
continual display, in contrast to a very different model of feminine display—
that of interiority—operative in mystical autobiographies of this period.[51] The
rule books shape an "emotional practice" like those described by the anthropologist Monique Scheer: "habits, rituals, and everyday pastimes that aid us
in achieving a certain emotional state. This includes the striving for a desired
feeling as well as the modifying of one that is not desirable . . . they are part of
what is often referred to as 'emotional management' and the ongoing learning
and maintaining of an emotional repertoire."[52] If the *filles* were urged to think
of themselves as in the world without being of the world (6), the books that
guided them were nonetheless rigorously concerned with the world's assessment of this new congregation and with the emotional management that
entailed.

After the *filles* became an order bound by solemn vows, approved by
papal brief in 1666, a new and more complex constitution was required, and
in 1686 came the *Règles et constitutions pour les Religieuses Hospitalières de Saint
Joseph*. This wordier volume (233 pages as opposed to 109) expanded the

previous formulations and also gave the women—now referred to as *sœurs* rather than *filles*—the rule of Saint Augustine, to which they were now bound. An important prepositional shift pointed to a change in the community's relation to its law: where the earlier text was "des filles Hospitalières" or *of* the community, this version was "pour les Religieuses," or *for* them. Like the earlier *Constitutions*, this text insisted on the union of the women, although that union was now inflected by an array of differentiations. In an important new development, sisters were encouraged to correct each other's faults and to report them to the superior. The new constitution also insisted on the importance of pardon after disagreement between the sisters. But this call to union also revealed an accompanying fear: for the first time, sisters were warned, "L'amour qui est entre vous ne doit pas être charnel, mais spirituel" (31–32) ["The love between you must not be carnal, but spiritual"]. The hierarchy of the community was more explicitly set out, and where the earlier text urged union without recognizing the difficulties that it might entail, the 1686 edition evoked the possibility of discord and determined the proper response on such occasions. Although the honest acknowledgment of potential difficulty might seem to speak of a greater transparency or frankness about life in a community, the constitutional regulation of such questions also points to the increasing importance of hierarchical government in the affairs of the order.

As in the earlier text, affective relations in daily life were scrupulously monitored: sisters were urged to avoid showing more "sympathie" to those with whom it is easy to get along (77). A careful script indicated the hesitations about the new governance and communal relations ushered in by the rule: the sisters must not allow themselves to be called "madame," they must call the Mother Superior "Mère" and the novices must call the instructor "maîtresse"; everyone else must call each other "ma sœur" except for the domestic sisters, who are called by their baptismal first names (78–79).

The more practical *Coutumier* of 1688 described the affective labor of the order in greater detail.[53] A new series of rules specified the tasks and emotional disposition required of each kind of nun, in which those at the top have more need to display the appropriate emotion, with those at the bottom of the hierarchy dispensed from such highly skilled affective labor. Thus the matron needs limitless charity as well as "douceur" (162) [sweetness], courage and patience; the nurse must "avoir un Cœur plein de tendresse pour les Sœurs malades . . . compatissant charitablement a leurs infirmités" (248) ["have a heart full of tenderness for the sick sisters . . . compassionating charitably with their infirmities"]; and so on down to the *sœur domestique*, whose labor of emptying chamber pots needed no emotional specification, and who was allowed to outsource the removal of spiders to a man visiting once a week (304–8).

The new regulations created an order-wide identity that required a new regulation of relations between each of the order's houses and that demanded the sisters to think of their order above all others, building a new form of orderly fellow-feeling like that which Saint-Jure recommended to his fellow Jesuits. The union between the houses was to extend even to the tableware and linen, which was all to be marked with the same seal, an image of Saint Joseph building the cross which also adorned the frontispiece of the *Constitutions* themselves. Joseph, laboring to build an occasion for suffering, was the organizing figure for a community needing to routinize their own relation to suffering—both that of the patients and their own as laborers.[54] The rule books brought about a group identity through the management of everything from table linen to emotion. They depersonalized emotion. Yet Marie Morin's account of the life of the order suggests a somewhat different story. How did the French rules play out in New French practice?

Marie Morin

Where the Jesuit Relations sent to France urged increased funding and recruitment, aiming at a broad readership, the Hospitalière orders in New France produced "Annales," histories of the order crafted for internal reading, often functioning as almanacs or record books. One of them is the first text produced by a Canadian-born writer: Marie Morin, born in Montreal in 1649, schooled with the Ursulines, and a Hospitalière by the age of thirteen. Morin became the first Canadian-born nun; her older brother was the first Canadian-born priest.[55] Morin grew up with the young order. She was twice superior of the Hôtel-Dieu (1693–96, 1708–11) and in 1697 began to write a set of *Annales*, completed in 1725. Her text, known as the *Histoire simple et veritable*, describes an emotional community from the inside.

Morin's writing is rough and often repetitive; as she notes, carpenters and builders and others essential to the life of the hospital frequently interrupted her as she wrote.[56] But it is also vivid with the details of life in the convent: she describes the delight of fireflies caught in a bottle and illuminating the chapel at dusk. Morin tells ghost stories, marvels at the skills of the druggists, details the wonders of meals made out of little, and punctuates her accounts of what

we would consider the proper business of a hospital with the inevitable bureaucratic wrangles with episcopal authorities over the status of the order in
both France and Canada. This is a portrait of life on what Morin calls "le pavé
du Canada, c'est a dire dans la neige" (195) ["the paving stones of Canada,
that's to say the snow"]. Through all the quotidian descriptions, Morin insists
on her status as eyewitness, in one delightful moment even acknowledging
that she knows as much as she does about her order because she had made a
little hole in the wall between her cell and that of the apothecary Judith
Brésoles, so that over fifteen or sixteen years she could "la voir et l'antandre a
mon aise, a son insçu" (179) ["see and hear her comfortably, without her
knowing"].

Morin's account describes the beginnings of the Montreal community,
but it also reaches back to the French house at La Flèche, providing a form of
written continuity that shapes the community. As befits an origin myth, Morin's account of La Flèche shows that the first community displayed "actes
heroiques dans leur hospitalité" (28) ["heroic acts in their hospitality"], a language which takes a private virtue and makes it into something worthy of
public display. The early community is characterized by its solidarity: they
sought to "partager leurs peines et travaux ensemble, qui n'estois pas petis"
(28) ["share their suffering and labors together, which were not small"]. In her
account, Le Royer and Olier's first plans for Montreal take place in an atmo-
sphere of fervent reciprocity: "Les voila tous deux a s'anbrasser, et dans une
sainte jubilation" (37). ["There they were, the two of them, embracing each
other in holy jubilation."] This shared emotion is heightened by the emotional otherness of their opponents; the two acted, Morin writes, despite the
jeering of pitiless *libertins* (28).

This history of the congregation describes a particular kind of Hospitalière feeling: sociability and shared affect are what make the community,
rather than the externally imposed identity markers offered by the rule books.
In his affective anthropology of Cistercianism, Damien Boquet has described
how memories of friendship in Cistercian writing, drawing on classical models, create a new mode of spiritual friendship that builds Cistercian community and makes clear that affect is central to the order and its history.[57] Morin's
history similarly insists on friendship in order to build a sense of fellow-
feeling, although her models come from the history of Christianity rather
than Cicero. In Morin's account, the new order is built on a form of affective
friendship that makes larger social unions possible. Marie de Boullongne, the
wife of the governor of Canada, made friends with Jeanne Mance "à la mode

des saints qui s'eiment en Dieu et pour Dieu, ce qui a continué tant qu'elles ont esté ensemble, vivant en union et cordialité mutueles comme sy ells avois esté sœurs" (49–50) ["in the way of saints who love each other in and for God, which they continued as long as they were together, living in union and mutual cordiality as if they had been sisters"]; similar friendships are described between Mance and other laywomen. Describing the delighted making of friends allows Morin a way to recount the beginning of the settlement. Morin paints her order as a place of affective particularity; this is not the uniformly imposed depersonalized affect of the rule book, nor is it the impersonal but affectively charged Jesuit fellow-feeling set out by Saint-Jure. Instead, these tropes of friendship allow for a more individualized account of emotion which makes room for partiality.

In the stories Morin tells in order to bind the community together, this shared affect specifically recalls the history of Christianity, allowing her readers to see themselves as part of a holy continuum. The first journey to Montreal, she says, sees the French offering thanks in the manner of the Israelites (52). The group of five men and five women pioneers share fraternal bonds: "Ils ne s'apellois que freres et sœurs, s'estudiès a ce deferer en tout, a servir tous les autres quand ils aurois besoin d'eux, a les consoler, a servir les malades, &c" (53–54). ["They called themselves brothers and sisters, studied giving way to each other in everything, helping each other when they were needed, consoling each other, serving the sick, and so on."] In these early days of missionary Montreal, every act on behalf of the community could be described as charitable. Of the soldiers who defended the fort, Morin writes: "Plusieurs sont morts dans cet exercise de la plus parfaite charité" (67). ["Several died in this exercise of the most perfect charity."] This halcyon past is blessed in the historical memory of the order established by Morin; it sets apart the more strained time in which Morin writes from a golden age where people shared all they had:

> Aussy vivois ils en saints, tous unanimement . . . Rien ne fermèt a clef en ce tamps, ni maison, ni cofre, ni caves, &c . . . Enfin, c'estoit une image de la primitive Eglise que ce cher Montreal dans son commencement et progres, c'est a dire pandant 32 ans ou environ. (96)

> [Thus they lived as saints, all unanimously . . . Nothing was locked in those days, neither houses nor coffers nor cellars . . . It was a

picture of the early Church, this dear Montreal in its first days, that is during 32 years or so.]

The early settler community had constant opportunities for a heroic form of charity akin to that practiced by Mademoiselle de Melun in the hagiography central to the French order: "ce cher pays tant desiré qui leur fournissèt des occasions de pratiquer les vertus propres de leur estat, heroïquement et frequanment" (174) ["this dear and so desired land which provided them occasions to practice the virtues proper to their estate, heroically and frequently"]. In these accounts, as in many missionary reports, Canada is nothing but a series of repeated and never-ending occasions for heroic adventure and thus salvation, in which heroism is set outside of historical time. But this golden age was lost as the Montreal settlement shifted its emphasis from missionary work to merchandise, and as the French state became directly involved in the settlement under Louis XIV's minister Colbert, bringing waves of soldiers to enforce its existence. From this point on the hospital work became much heavier, and the nuns increasingly dealt with the contagious illness that was brought in by each new ship.

In Morin's text, we never forget that suffering bodies are the reason for the hospital's existence. Morin describes one French hospital as being "bien fourny de malades" (59) ["well provided with patients"]; the bodies are the raw material that fuels an industry of salvation. And yet the bodies that are particularized and whose pain is described at length are not those of the patients themselves but rather those of the founder, whose dysentery merits a lengthy description (111), or of the early nuns of the order (160–61); other bodies are particularized and narrativized only when they die and leave money or land to the hospital (120). Nor does Morin focus on sentimentalizing or praising the nurses' attention to the patients, perhaps out of a refusal to arrogate to herself the interior emotional states of the other nuns. The only moment at which she speaks of a "grande affection" (128) of a nun for her patients is when she describes her own feelings, and even then it is in the third person (Morin's position as third-person annalist reminds us that the emotives diagnosed by William Reddy can issue forth only from a particular sort of autonomous subject). Instead, rather than giving a sentimental account of suffering, focusing on the relation between nurse and patient (as the French biography of Mademoiselle de Melun had done), Morin turns her attention to the bodies of the order itself.

Yet the body Morin describes is not the isolated body in pain. In contrast,

Morin emphasizes a nonphysical and more generalized suffering that pulls the order together, evidenced in the relations between the sisters. It might seem strange to draw attention to the relational nature of Morin's compassion. In common parlance we imagine compassion as something that does not happen in isolation but that is responsive to another, always in relation. Yet, as we have seen in earlier chapters, early moderns often drew on the language of compassion to fence in their individual autonomy and to retreat from the pressing demands of others. Morin's text does something rather different, alerting us to a different kind of relation that granted coherence to a community: that between the sisters themselves.

Care and Caress

In the last thirty years, feminist political theorists have addressed the distinction between autonomous agency and a more relational understanding of the self, prompted in part by feminist reflections on the social. Thinkers drawn to questions of vulnerability, recognition, and gender have interrogated the philosophical centrality of the autonomous agent, a figure not unlike the male compassionates who appear in previous chapters, articulating instead a form of "relational autonomy" which stresses the primacy of community and relationships.[58] This relational autonomy emphasizes social relations and draws attention to questions of care and mutuality. Many critiques of autonomy, drawing on a reading of Carol Gilligan, have suggested that an ethics of care might provide a new understanding of moral reasoning. Gilligan proposed that we think of care for others, an area traditionally denigrated as women's work, as a form of moral concern; in her wake, feminist scholars have explored the ramifications of this new ethics in the domain of professionalized health care.[59] If its earliest proponents thought of relational autonomy as something usefully figured through child care,[60] more recent work has suggested that the relations we think through might equally be communities we choose, rather than biological family.[61] This might have resonated with Marie Morin, who chose her own community and laughed at the Amerindian assumption that the older nuns must be the biological mothers of the youngest.[62] Morin's text allows us to imagine what a practice of care, moving between written rules and lived labor, might have looked like in seventeenth-century French settler culture.

Morin's text builds a new model of coworker compassion in which fellow-feeling comes about chiefly through the sharing of labor. This is not the affective labor directed by the rule book, the proper disposition of sisterly emotion, but rather an affect that stems from the tasks women carry out together. The predominant movement of affect in the hospital is between the nursing sisters. It is the nuns, not the patients, who are described as being "digne de compasion" (210) ["worthy of compassion"].[63] Perhaps since the episcopal authorities did not officially recognize the new congregation, the need to draw a community together through emotion became even more important. Early on in the history of the hospital, Morin describes her compassion for her missionary brothers in religion who are undergoing captivity and torture in the hands of the Iroquois. She expresses the sisters' "alarmes et . . . compation de nos pauvres frères qui estois sy mal treités" (134) ["alarm and compassion for our poor brothers who were so badly treated"] and sheds "plusiers larmes de compassion et tandresse sur les prisonniers captifs et sur les mors" (138) ["several tears of compassion and tenderness for the captives and dead"].[64] Here, Morin's compassion leads her to reflect upon a religiously significant physical suffering, a martyrdom; this sort of reflection is common to many writings stemming from women's religious communities.[65] But for the most part, Morin describes a shared emotion of a very different and more reciprocal kind: the overwhelming emotion she describes is the consolation of the mutual emotion experienced between the nuns themselves. Describing the first three recruits to the order, Morin writes:

> Je n'antreprans pas de décrire isy quelle fut la joie et consolation de ces trois filles que Dieu avèt unie pour un mesme dessain sy extraordinere et genereux qu'il passèt pour folie dans l'esprit des fors esprits du siècle. Je vous le lesse a mediter, mes cheres sœurs, vous qui liré cesy, vous saves combine ces rancontres sont rares parmy les Religieuses et les effets qu'elle produisse dans le cœur de celles qui les esprouves, &c. (145)

> [I won't undertake to describe here the joy and consolation of these three girls whom God had united for one same goal, so extraordinary and generous that it looked like madness in the minds of the great minds of the time. I let you think about it, my dear sisters, you who will read this, you know how rare these meetings are between religious, and the effects that they produce in the heart of those who go through them, and so on.]

In this passage emotion is both rare and recognizable, such that its repeatable singularity forms the identity of the order. We who read in the future will know what it means to find ourselves in emotional union with others like us, and in reading we will feel emotion alongside them. Morin's description of sisterly emotion sets it as something outside of reason; the emotional madness of the nuns, which lies outside rational understanding, must be read in other ways that are not those of the world. The order's emotion is understandable only from within, in the effects it produces in the heart which feels them; it does not proffer itself to the world. Compassion operates chiefly between the sisters; sister Macé worked hard but said herself to be "la moins chargee de ces sœurs qu'elle pleignèt toujours par la compation qu'elle en avoit, cherchant les occasions de leur faire pleisir jour et nuit" (191) ["the least burdened of those sisters that she pitied always through the compassion she had for them, seeking opportunities to please them day and night"]. Where the bishops sought to impose vows to tie the congregation together, Morin shows that spontaneous sisterly emotion has already brought that about.

A particular term, unusual in seventeenth-century compassion talk, is central to Morin's sisterly fellow-feeling: "caresse." Morin writes that when the first three nuns arrived in "Kebec," where they had to wait for the Saint-Laurent to melt before proceeding to Montreal, the Augustine nuns there gave them "baucoup de caresses que le saint amour de Jesus Christ sucgere a ceux qui sont uni dans se mesme amour" (174) ["a lot of caresses that the holy love of Jesus Christ suggests to those who are united in the same love"]. This language of "caresse" to describe an attention of care between nuns runs throughout Morin's journal. Where the manuals spoke vigorously against gestures metaphorical or physical between nuns, insisting that nuns not touch each other emotionally or physically, the caresses that appear in Morin's pages give a picture of an emotion figured through touch (whether or not that touch is to be understood literally) that sustains communal life in difficult circumstances. Cotgrave's 1611 *Dictionarie* gives caresse as "a cheering, cherishing, welcomming, friendly intertainment, hugging, blandishment, kind vsage, making much of"; even the relatively chilly first dictionary of the Académie Française (1694) makes it clear that there is some degree of warmth in a caress: "Tesmoignage exterieur d'affection accompagné de quelque signe de joye" ["Exterior sign of affection accompanied by some sign of joy"].[66] The nuns' caress pushes Morin's text out of the realm of an institutionally structured and impersonal compassion and toward something we might recognize today as the fellow-feeling not of distanced compassion but of a distinguishing friendliness, dependent on the singling out of personalized particulars, "making much of" them. A different kind of group formation obtains here. Morin's emotional world is markedly warmer and more immediate than any other representation of compassion traced in this book; there is not much joy in most seventeenth-century compassion.

The same dynamic of urgent compassion bound the convent to the wider community. Like many buildings of Montreal's early settlement, the convent was beset by fires on several occasions, and when that happened the nuns were rehoused in the town with "baucoup de charité et d'affection" (76) ["much charity and affection"]. Morin repeatedly describes the convent as the place or object of urban compassion; after another fire a Monsieur Le Ber visits to make "son compliment de compastion qui etoit fort scincere" (245) ["his compliment of compassion which was very sincere"]. A "compliment" marks a short speech of praise. Does Morin mean Le Ber praised the convent for its sincere compassion, or was his speech compassionate with the convent's struggles? In any case the emotion certainly bore fruit; Morin reports he gave the convent a great deal of money to reestablish itself. However we read the compliment, the convent is shown to be poised at the heart of an emotional urban network. On the same occasion the townspeople come to mass, where they will be asked to give funds to the nuns, ready to "ecouter les propositions qu'on leur voulèt par la compassion qu'ils avois de nous" (246) ["listen to the proposals we put to them because of the compassion they had for us"]. Likewise, Morin recounts the affective union brought about by the attacks of Iroquois upon the settlement. There is great fear when the tocsin sounds, she acknowledges, but also pleasure: "C'etoit un plaisir d'estre la montees voir tout le monde courir au secours de leurs freres et exposer leur vie pour conserver la leur. Les fammes mesme, comme des amasonnes, y courois armees comme les hommes" (134–35). ["It was a pleasure to be up high and see everyone run to the aid of their brothers and to risk their life to preserve that of their brothers. Even the women, like amazons, ran armed like the men."] This form of military activity, declares Morin, is "une charité tres sublime" (135) ["a very sublime charity"]. In this writing of the disaster, a notion of community is forged through a common enemy, and the discourse of charitable heroic action stems from that distinction.

This support of the town for the convent is contrasted with a scene in which Morin tells us that the sisters who first arrived in Montreal had called on the mother house at La Flèche to send them money, and were refused: "Ce qui leur devèt estre rude que des sœurs usse sy peu de compassion d'elles dans leur pauvreté" (123). ["It must have been hard for them that the sisters had such little compassion for them in their poverty."] In a text written for an internal audience, for the nuns of Montreal, Morin makes clear that the Montreal sisters have redefined their community. If they are no longer always sisters in compassion with their mother house across the Atlantic, they have wrought a new bond with the townspeople among whom their order has grown up, and they have brought about a compassionate civic order through their work.

Out of such scenes comes a surprising language. Morin quotes one local man—you know him, she says, the man with the big nose, underlining how small a readership she addresses—a man who insists after another fire that "il estoit de l'honneur des habitans de Ville Marie de secourir ces bonnes Filles qui servois le public depuis trante six ans" (247) ["it was the honor of the inhabitants of Ville Marie to help these good sisters who had served the public for thirty-six years"]. Knowing him to be poor, the townspeople laugh, but the man urges them on to charity and the people set to work with "affection" (248). The appearance of this "public" is brief, but it suggests the building of another sociality through compassion. If hospitality was hailed as a private virtue (think of Pierre Nicole weeping over Dido's gesture of hospitality to Aeneas), the charitable labor of hospital work gestures to a public brought together through a certain affective vocabulary.

Where the painting showed individuals navigating a systematized charity, and the manuals gave each nun a rule that ensured she related to a distant authority by depersonalizing relations with her more proximate neighbors, Morin's account of compassion certainly alerts us to a warmer kind of proximate relation. It shows us a more *caressing* form of community, a community that is able to single out individuals, like the man with the big nose. It is out of this proximate, identifiable, personalized contact that the wider union in the convent or the town grows. Where Hannah Arendt worried about compassion's contagion, its abolishing of distance, Morin and her fellow nurses must embrace contagion metaphorically, if not literally, and build a different set of relations out of it. This is compassion from the ground up, an affective bricolage made possible by contact between individuals known to one another.

Morin's compassion confesses to its partiality. But it also inches compassion somewhat closer to the way we now use the term: the warmth and reciprocity of Morin's coworker compassion provides a glimmer of what we want from compassion today. Throughout most of this book, compassion's capacity as a positive political formation has appeared limited. Early modern compassion was conceptualized via exclusion and fiercely attentive to its borders and limits; it was produced by excluding a caste of uncompassionables. Morin's text seems to give us something a little more expansive, looking to build a new form of public out of compassion.

Yet that new language is perhaps brought about only in the expansiveness of emergency conditions on the frontier, conditions structured around other forms of rigorous exclusion. It is important not to fall too eagerly into the warmhearted caress of this text; Morin's compassion, be it sisterly or civic, still has an edge. The mutual understanding of her hardworking women makes a virtue of similar suffering in a territory where the experience of difference—racial, religious, geographic—was constantly threatening to overwhelm. This is settler compassion, drawing up the frontiers between a public good held compassionately in common and the unthinkable indigenous world beyond.[67] Compassion takes the form of a civic emergency pitted against that indigenous threat. Morin's text still depends upon distance, but her distance is arranged differently from that we've seen in France. It must gauge its difference from the mother house in France and also work around the settlers' attempt to distance their new community from the original community of those it has displaced. Out of that new spatialization of compassion comes something that looks very different from the metropolitan model left in France. Behind the Montreal city walls we find an immediate, neighborly, personalized emotion, but one that must give us pause even as we admire it.

In an account of Canadian government care for indigenous communities during a tuberculosis epidemic, the anthropologist Lisa Stevenson writes that attending to care even in its restrictions allows us to see "the way someone comes to matter," even if we do not always agree with the result. Thinking about the process of care critically means that we move away from judging the intention or effect of carers, so we can account for care's losses and exclusions even as we respond to (say) Morin's caress. Stevenson continues: "Since people can come to matter in all kinds of ways, it is not an oxymoron to talk about colonial forms of care . . . even though I hope to make visible the suffering those forms of care produce."[68] In placing Morin at the end of my series of more evidently restrictive compassionates, I mean to acknowledge her difference from them and the real difference she made in her community, without necessarily falling into overly comforting comparisons. To trace the varied formations of compassion's edge does not mean to reject the gestures made toward those who mattered.

Our compassionater in this chapter certainly looks very different from

those we've seen in earlier chapters, whether figured in novels, plays, or trea-
tises. She is distinguished by her gender, in the first instance; not since Mal-
herbe's largely conceptual maternal figure have we seen a woman
compassionate. She is further distinguished by the place in which she writes,
far from metropolitan France, and, relatedly, by her quotidian and embodied
involvement in compassion and by her need to provide a repeated and repeatable response to suffering. True, she writes a couple of decades later than most
of those writers, and in very different circumstances. One might be tempted,
leaning eagerly in to her writerly caress, to see in her a nascent modernity of
compassion, an emotional new world. Yet perhaps this eagerness on our part
to determine a difference or at least development that makes Morin more like
what we want to be could also be described as a kind of affective labor, a desire
to read the past and in so doing to caress both it and ourselves. If care allows
us to see how someone comes to matter, it reminds us that our own careful
readings of the past always stem from our own sense of what and who matters
in the past and in the present time.

Epilogue

Something Like Compassion

Repudietur ergo misericordia? Nequaquam.
[Must we therefore give up compassion? Not at all.]

—Augustine

Over the past six chapters, I have traced compassion's edge, looking at the limits of fellow-feeling in early modern France. In the readings that emerge from this material, compassion is mostly not a generous relation to the other; the language of compassion tends instead to point to our failure to live well together, or to let others live well. It's part of our critical tool set, of course, as readers of Foucault or the Frankfurt school, to worry that things that sustain us also constrain us, and for me that worry has intensified since I am writing as our compassion and its capacity to reach across difference has been increasingly and painfully scarce. Although I usually try not to make presentist analogies for fear that they might swiftly date, in this case I worry rather that the analogy will remain all too evident for a long while yet.

Yet I don't want to leave compassion (then or now) on the edge, as I hope some of my examples suggest: the lone Protestant who rescues a Catholic in the account of Loys de Perussiis, or the rare Catholic who weeps on seeing Protestant suffering in accounts by Élie Benoist or by d'Aubigné. In restoring the affective undertow of the history of toleration in France, I want to underline the importance of these small gestures, left behind by the direction of events but gesturing to an unrealized political history. And in the second half of the book, reading the fleeting mutuality offered in Lafayette's fiction, or more cheeringly and concretely the Protestants who managed to find compassion on foreign shores and the coworker compassion of Marie Morin, I've found that paying attention to what lies beyond compassion's edge allows us to see the flickers (if not always the firm beginnings) of forms of community that grow out of contingencies, and of the new forms of writing and media—the novel, the pamphlet, the community record—that allowed for and sustained them. If compassion as a poetics, a long-practiced response to texts, structures the response to political crisis throughout this period—think of Benoist describing the compassion and terror aroused by the siege of La Rochelle—then through patient, stretchy similitudes these old poetic strictures also evolve to make room for new voices and new kinds of texts.

In listening for those voices, over the course of this project I've been bolstered both by compassionate gestures and by scholarly voices that explore them with care, like Candace Clark, who examines the tactful networks established in waiting rooms and the socioemotional etiquette that evolves in such places, or Melissa Caldwell, who traces the uncertain compassion economies of post-Soviet Russia.[1] Augustine, dismissing what he saw as his false compassion for the plays he'd seen in Alexandria, asks, "Must we therefore give up compassion?" and answers himself, "Not at all."[2] In trying to make room for something like compassion, in the stories we tell and in the ways we think about them, this epilogue follows his lead.

In many of the texts I've discussed, compassion has a strained relation to action; sometimes it stands at a distance from suffering, refraining from spurring onlookers to intervention or to the alleviation of another's suffering, and sometimes it forestalls such action more directly. At other moments, it appears in transitory scenes that do not stabilize into any lasting compact. I began this project impatient with the reserve and transience of this kind of compassion, but I have learned to take seriously compassionate engagements that are not quantifiable in terms of a tangible effect in the world. If I started by urgently wanting action to stem from compassion, I've ended by thinking that compassion's inoperativeness pushes us to reappraise our relation to political action. This is not to dismiss compassion as much as to allow it its own limited and limiting space, and not to abandon action as much as to understand the conditions under which it might be difficult for some of us to act, taking seriously Augustine's acknowledgment in the *City of God* that we act compassionately "as far as our ability allows," and thinking through the inequitable structures revealed by that differential ability.[3] Some early modern commentators—the theologian Nicolas Coeffeteau, or the physician Marin Cureau de la Chambre—suggest briefly, tantalizingly, that compassion is related to anger. For Coeffeteau, pity is the other side of the indignation we feel when the wicked flourish; for Cureau de la Chambre, it changes us physically in ways akin to anger, the passion he is pursuing.[4] Perhaps acknowledging compassion's edge could also be a way to acknowledge our anger about what we see around us and to take seriously the idea of that anger as a form of care.

In moving away from my anxiously normative model of compassionate action, I have been helped by reading across disciplinary or historical differences: by thinking through and around the critic Heather Love's wise work on queer literary history, for example, in which Love tries to move away from the "critical compulsion to fix."[5] Love's attention to what she terms "ruined or failed sociability" (22) and her insistence on taking such sociability seriously precisely because of those failures has pushed me to take compassion's missteps seriously.[6] Thinking alongside her I've tried to think of compassion's politics as something other than instrumental and to take seriously the fleeting glimpses it gives us of exchange across difference.[7]

Early modern compassion's reflections on the relation between spectatorship and action are echoed by Jacques Rancière when he abandons the distinction between a passive spectatorship on the one hand and knowledge or action on the other. Rancière writes that we emancipate spectatorship—and compassion with it, I think—"when we challenge the opposition between viewing and acting . . . when we understand that viewing is also an action that confirms or transforms this distribution of positions. The spectator also acts, like the pupil or scholar. She observes, selects, compares, interprets. She links what she sees to a host of other things that she has seen on other stages, in other kinds of places."[8] The spectator-reader makes connections; she tries out a series of structural relations between self and something else, between one thing and another, perhaps renouncing them, perhaps trying out other forms. The reader *discerns* something, even if that something doesn't amount to much and is not immediately translatable into anything efficacious.

To think about reading and about compassion in this way distances us from the contagious identification of sentimentalism; instead, this reading looks more like the withholding structures of the Lafayette aesthetic I explored in Chapter 4, which generate a model of reading as attentive onlooking. This is not Agrippa d'Aubigné's reading, where we will be spurred to battle; it is something more like that of Pierre Nicole, who thinks tenderly if parenthetically of Dido even as he worries about compassion's weakness. In this model, reading pushes us to look with care. The forms of knowledge traced by compassion are pensive and perhaps unsatisfactory, but they keep on gesturing to "a host of other things."

Both a poetics and something like an ethics come out of that gesture. In his remarkable book on tact and contact in the age of HIV, David Caron parses our negotiations of shared bodies and shared spaces. Caron's reflections on urban awkwardness and occasional grace make me realize, among other things, that one of the many spaces that has formed my understanding of compassion's reserved regard is the London Underground: a space where I watch others and even watch out for them, but also keep the other at as much of a distance as one can do in pressured circumstances. But Caron also works through particular forms of writing and reading as a way to think about a literary ethics of tact. Of Charlotte Delbo's writing about the concentration camps, for example, he notes that "Delbo's goal is to establish enough common ground for us to stand near her while maintaining the distance necessary to ensure that we will not be able to be in her place or appropriate what is not ours."[9] Caron's Delbo marks out a territory also moved through by Roland Barthes. Katja Haustein describes how Barthes repeatedly tries out a number of terms for compassion only to settle on "délicatesse," a key early modern term for tact (and central to Barthes's reading of Sade) that Haustein describes as "a well-tempered mélange between nearness and distance, passion and reason."[10] That same delicacy is central to Hervé Guibert's *Le protocole compassionnel*, in which the tactful gestures between doctor and person with AIDS are carefully mapped. This is a text where compassionate protocol (the term refers to the possibility of an experimental drug) demands a distance inflected only by these small moments of acknowledgment. Guibert's compassion is so tactful that it is never named as such except in the title of his book. Against the contagious emotion feared by Hannah Arendt, he sets a series of gestures left unmade.[11] These models of tactful proximity allow us to respond to another's separateness and to measure the distance between us even as we look across it. This is also the mode of compassion operated by Lafayette: a way of discerning relations that brokers some shared space but also operates something like an affective rupture, marking a difference.

For example, in his 1978 essay *Qu'est-ce que la critique?* (*What Is Critique?*), Michel Foucault suggests that critique allows a way to think otherwise, to articulate a dissatisfaction with current norms.[12] A critique of government, for example, inquires into how not to be governed in a particular way rather than how not to be governed at all: how not to be governed "like that," how to differentiate and distance oneself from something in asserting that things should be "not like that, not for that, not for them."[13] Judith Butler's astute reading of this essay describes Foucault's form itself as a mode of thought, noting his very particular style of argument about critique in which he advances connections only to withdraw them:

> Whatever this is that one draws upon as one resists governmental-
> ization will be "*like* an originary freedom" and "something *akin*
> *to* the historical practice of revolt" (my emphasis). Like them, in-
> deed, but apparently not quite the same. As for Foucault's mention
> of "originary freedom," he offers and withdraws it at once. "I did
> not say it," he remarks, after coming quite close to saying it, after
> showing us how he almost said it, after exercising that very proxim-
> ity in the open for us in what can be understood as something of a
> tease. What discourse nearly seduces him here, subjugating him to
> its terms? And how does he draw from the very terms that he re-
> fuses? What art form is this in which a nearly collapsible critical dis-
> tance is performed for us?[14]

Butler discerns Foucault's procedure: first making things akin to each other but then denying that relation or putting it in abeyance, a little like Montaigne, who tries out examples to see which ones he might resemble and mulls over what he can learn from his kindredness or otherwise to others. "There is something in critique that is akin to virtue," Foucault writes; I would say that there is something in this mode of critique that is also akin to the quizzically compassionate mode I have traced in this book.[15]

Foucault's critique is a way of trying out our relation to concepts, letting us see concepts and structures in negative: *not this* way of governing, *not this* relation.[16] Through those negative structures we begin to articulate something about connections we don't have, but could have, or could have had. The medievalists Bill Burgwinkle and Jane Gilbert describe the shortcomings of thinking through actor-network theory in manuscript studies, since "it reconstructs networks only on the basis of empirically available evidence. Its mission of bringing into focus hinterland networks would be better served by paying attention also to what is *not* so verifiable."[17] They propose instead a heuristic imagining of "what we call 'dark networks', on the analogy of 'dark matter,'" a way of working that would imagine "the severed, neglected, or potential-but-unactivated connections in which texts and manuscripts significantly do not engage." (Pause and consider, compassionate reader, all that I

have left undone in this text but could or should have done.) These dark networks, they write, structure our primary materials "without leaving observ-
able traces"; they prompt us to account for even those relationships we have
rejected: "those people with whom 'we' do not trade, socialize, or intermarry."
The dark network allows us to read difference even where it is unarticulated,
to imagine capacious gestures even as we read texts that "do not engage" such
a reach. Compassion's inoperations, similarly, form a dark network structuring the affective experience of early modern difference.

Compassion is repeatedly if hesitantly comparatist: it makes something
or someone *akin to* someone or something else, even if it cannot complete on
that promise of shared terms. It forms what Butler calls a "nearly collapsible
critical distance" that draws and redraws the lines of likeness, *akinship*. In
early modern English, "kindness" is sometimes offered as a synonym for compassion; although French "douceur" sits well aside the affective moderation of
the English word, it cannot sustain the sense of kindred-sifting operated by
"kindness," which marks both a sweet civil disposition (or an act that demonstrates it) and a relation asserted between similar *kinds* of persons or entities.[18]
Those kinship bonds of kindness are too often and increasingly drawn tightly,
fenced in by constrained categories. In contrast, in placing compassion as kindred with critique I want to offer a model of kindly reading that allows us to
try out new forms of relation, to read across differences temporal or theoretical, to pay heed to even the fleeting moments of compassion such readings
proffer. Bringing this book to a close, I've offered models of reading to which
mine is akin, without always demarcating the edge from which I speak. In
citing writers from such different domains and different moments, I've tried
to reach across those differences to show the *something like* and its kindly potential for wondering about compassion; to show compassion's potential, still,
as a mode of thinking about difference.

Notes

INTRODUCTION

1. For a discussion of the drawing and the history of its naming, see Jennifer Montagu, *The Expression of the Passions*, 147–49. Montagu dates the label to Audran's 1727 edition and thinks it can be dismissed on the grounds of the drawing's violence, but notes also that part of another inscription can be made out, reading "omp," which could be "compassion" or "composition"; in my (admittedly partisan) reading it clearly reads "compassion."

2. See Huguet, *Dictionnaire de la langue française du seizième siècle*, vol. 6, s.v. "piteux." "Piteux" retains both uses in Cotgrave's 1611 *Dictionarie of the French and English Tongues*, where it means merciful as well as miserable, but by the end of the century, in Richelet's dictionary of 1680 and Furetière's of 1690, "piteux" is understood to describe a condition which occasions compassion rather than a person who feels it: "déplorable, misérable, malheureux, infortuné" ["deplorable, miserable, unhappy, unfortunate"] writes Richelet (s.v. "piteux"). "Pitoyable," on the other hand, retains both senses even at the end of the century. Furetière gives the first meaning as "estat malheureux de celuy qui excite à la pitié" ["unhappy state of he who excites pity"] and the second as "celuy qui a des sentimens de compassion pour les miseres d'autruy" ["he who has feelings of compassion for the sufferings of another"] (s.v. "pitoyable"), while the *Dictionnaire de l'Académie françoise* of 1694 puts them the other way around.

3. See Jean-Pierre Gutton, *La société et les pauvres en Europe, XVIe–XVIIIe siècles*. Early moderns also feared being hoodwinked by false suffering; see an episcopal letter describing false "miserables" seeking compassion: *Lettre d'Amolon Archevesque de Lyon*, 11.

4. An exemplary text of this sort is the Jesuit Pierre Le Moyne's *Les peintures morales* (1640); I discuss Le Moyne's other writings on compassion in Chapter 3. On the early modern passions, see Gail Kern Paster, Katherine Rowe, and Mary Floyd-Wilson, eds., *Reading the Early Modern Passions*; Victoria Kahn, Neil Saccamano, and Daniela Coli, eds., *Politics and the Passions, 1500–1850*; Susan James, *Passion and Action*.

5. On this question see David Konstan, *Pity Transformed*, 6.

6. John Staines, "Compassion in the Public Sphere of Milton and King Charles," 92.

7. Barbara H. Rosenwein, *Emotional Communities in the Early Middle Ages*.

8. William M. Reddy, *The Navigation of Feeling*, 104. See also Monique Scheer, "Are Emotions a Kind of Practice?" who notes, "The history of emotions has traditionally viewed first-person accounts as the royal road to individual feeling" (218).

9. Augustine, *City of God*, trans. David S. Wiesen, book 9.5, 167.

10. Paul Audi discusses Spinoza's unilateral declarations of compassion, i.e., a feeling without a concomitant action, in *L'empire de la compassion*, 76.

11. Elizabeth S. Belfiore, *Tragic Pleasures*, 186.

12. Henri de Campion, *Mémoires*, ed. Marc Fumaroli, 87. (Campion is describing rape as a war crime.) For an account of spectatorship that instead leads to intervention, see Kristen Monroe, *The Hand of Compassion*. In Monroe's reading of responses to the Holocaust, compassion is a generous gesture that under extraordinary conditions opens up narrowly defined communities to others.

13. Samuel Beckett, *Not I*, "Note," n.p.

14. On emotion as movement see Hélène Merlin-Kajman, "Sentir, ressentir: Émotion privée, langage public," 340. On compassion's nonaction, see also Robert Jacob's reading of Roman imperial pity: "Pietas ou la compassion: Langage de la loi et rhétorique des sentiments."

15. In this I take my cue from Alexandra Walsham's call to write the history of tolerance by "reading between the lines and even against the grain" (*Charitable Hatred*, 29).

16. I give the necessary historical background in each chapter, but the impatient reader could also consult the account given in Jean Delumeau, *Naissance et affirmation de la Réforme*.

17. Hélène Merlin-Kajman, *L'absolutisme dans les lettres*; Jacques Berchtold and Marie-Madeleine Fragonard, *La mémoire des guerres de religion*; Andrea Frisch, *Forgetting Differences: Tragedy, Historiography, and the French Wars of Religion*. For a recent reading of post-Reformation England that sets out a similar affective argument, see Steven Mullaney, *The Reformation of Emotions in the Age of Shakespeare*.

18. For an account of the significance of the passions in debates at the time of the wars, see Mark Greengrass, *Governing Passions: Peace and Reform in the French Kingdom, 1576–1585*.

19. For such an account see Joseph Lecler, *Histoire de la tolérance au siècle de la Réforme*; for a wry reading of such accounts, see Richard Rorty, "On Ethnocentrism," who notes of liberal culture that "the heroes it apotheosizes include those who have enlarged its capacity for sympathy and tolerance" (526).

20. See Pierre Bayle, *De la tolérance*, ed. Jean-Michel Gros, 13.

21. Furetière, *Dictionnaire universel*, s.v. "tolerance," "tolerer." On early modern toleration, see also William H. Huseman, "The Expression of the Idea of Toleration in French During the Sixteenth Century"; François Rigolot, "Tolérance et condescendance dans la littérature française du XVIe siècle."

22. Delumeau, *Naissance et affirmation de la Réforme*, 190.

23. Furetière, *Dictionnaire universel*, s.v. "compatir."

24. On this legal decision see Samuel Moyn, *Christian Human Rights*, 143.

25. See, for example, Benjamin Kaplan, *Divided by Faith*; Keith Cameron, Mark Greengrass, and Penny Roberts, eds., *The Adventure of Religious Pluralism in Early Modern France*; Philip Benedict, "Un roi, une loi, deux fois." In this book, I focus on the coexistence of Catholics and Protestants; the presence of Jewishness in French writing (which makes a brief appearance in Chapter 5) might allow for a different reading of toleration's affect, but that work lies beyond the scope of this book. Equally, more work needs to be done on the affective fallout from the other and shamefully underexplored restrictive measure of 1685, the regulation of the slave trade in the *Code noir*.

26. Ethan H. Shagan, *The Rule of Moderation*, 291.

27. Kirstie M. McClure, "Difference, Diversity, and the Limits of Toleration."

28. Wendy Brown, *Regulating Aversion*, 2, 15.

29. On toleration as a response to this period, see for example the account given by John Rawls in his introduction to *Political Liberalism*, where he insists that "something like the modern understanding of liberty of conscience and freedom of thought" came out of the Reformation and its violent aftermath (xxiv).

30. Marjorie Garber, "Compassion," 23. On the shared vocabularies of the period, see also Staines, "Compassion in the Public Sphere," 92. On classical vocabularies and their translations, see Konstan, *Pity Transformed*, 2–3.

31. Béatrice Delaurenti, *La contagion des émotions*, 24–25.

32. Staines, "Compassion in the Public Sphere," 101. On compassionate bowels, see especially Kristine Steenbergh, "Mollified Hearts and Enlarged Bowels."

33. On the question of terminological specificity, see Vivasvan Soni, *Mourning Happiness*, who shows how the (mis)translation of Aristotelian pity as sympathy had important effects for theories of sentimentalism in eighteenth-century England. Martha Nussbaum suggests the same is true for the history of philosophy: *Upheavals of Thought*, 301–3. Let me note that the published translations I draw on throughout the text also vary in the distinctions they draw between pity and compassion, a sign of the instability of these terms across languages and historical periods.

34. Hannah Arendt, *On Revolution*, 76.

35. Luc Boltanski, *La souffrance à distance*, translated as *Distant Suffering*. For a rehearsal of these Rousseauian-Arendtian arguments as they relate to the French political scene in the 2000s, see Myriam Revault d'Allonnes, *L'homme compassionnel*, 53–57.

36. Jean-Luc Nancy, *Being Singular Plural*, xiii.

37. For a French defense of pity that takes its lead from Nancy and Levinas in insisting on the ethics of being in relation to one another, see Emmanuel Housset's *L'intelligence de la pitié*; on Levinas and compassion, see also Audi, *L'empire de la compassion*.

38. On the Catholic valence of this language of contagion in early modern England, see Staines, "Compassion in the Public Sphere," 101.

39. The longer history of pity's philosophical rise and fall is not my concern here. For a thorough history of the question see Nussbaum, *Upheavals of Thought*, 354–400. For Nussbaum's more recent appraisal of compassion which draws on work in psychology, see *Political Emotions*, 137–60.

40. In the *Phaedo*, Plato dismisses pity for Socrates; in *Republic* 606b, Plato rejects tragedy because in encouraging pity it weakens us. For a discussion of Aristotle, see Chapter 2.

41. Seneca, "On Mercy," *Moral Essays* vol. 1, 438–39.

42. Staines, "Compassion in the Public Sphere," 98–99.

43. On the political rather than psychological nature of this bond, see Philippe Lacoue-Labarthe, "On the Sublime," 11–18.

44. Hume, *A Treatise on Human Nature*, 417. On Hume's sympathy and its significance for an understanding of social relations, see Adela Pinch, *Strange Fits of Passion*, 17–50. For an account of eighteenth-century sympathy which sets these canonical sympathizers in a broader context, see Ryan Patrick Hanley, "The Eighteenth-Century Context of Sympathy"; Michael Frazer, *The Enlightenment of Sympathy*.

45. On eighteenth-century understandings of the relations between pity and self-interest, see Pierre Force, *Self-Interest Before Adam Smith*, 25–47. On the dangers of a self-congratulatory compassion in the eighteenth century see Joseph Harris, *Inventing the Spectator: Subjectivity and the Theatrical Experience in Early Modern France*, 130.

46. Kant, *The Metaphysics of Morals*, 250. On the distinction between a willed moral duty

to the other and a more natural affective response, see also *Groundwork of the Metaphysics of Morals*, 13–14.

47. Nietzsche, *On the Genealogy of Morals*, preface, fragment 5, 19. On Nietzsche's use of the term *Mitleid*, allowing no distinction between compassion and pity, see Lawrence Blum, "Compassion," 512; on Nietzsche's variation between French and German terms in his rebuttals of pity, see Nussbaum, *Upheavals of Thought*, 303. Theodor Adorno and Max Horkheimer further describe how Sade and Nietzsche view pity as "the most compulsive form of prejudice" in *Dialectic of Enlightenment*, 101. Nietzsche built his attack on pity in part by bolstering himself with the seventeenth-century French moralist La Rochefoucauld, a model for the German philosopher in questions of substance as well as aphoristic style. Elsewhere he draws on La Rochefoucauld's maxims—to which I shall return in Chapter 2—to suggest that we should reject such emotion because of the performance of those sufferers who show a "thirst for pity." In this reading, suffering is an exercise in power which satisfies the sufferer in showing him that "he is still of sufficient importance to cause affliction in the world." Nietzsche, *Human, All Too Human*, fragment 50, 39. Nietzsche would doubtless wince to hear it, but the formulation of his argument shows more attention to suffering than can be witnessed in the moralist theory he so admires.

48. I restrict myself in this book to compassion as an imagined response to suffering and do not approach the broader imaginative reach of empathy; in tracing a particular early modern genealogy, let me be clear that I am not writing the broader history of the emotion called for by Karl F. Morrison on the first page of *"I Am You": The Hermeneutics of Empathy in Western Literature, Theology, and Art*.

49. See especially Boltanski, *Distant Suffering*.

50. This debate was launched by Peter Singer's article "Famine, Affluence, and Morality" (1972), which insisted on our obligation to respond to distant suffering. Charles Beitz's influential *Political Theory and International Relations* draws attention to the contingency of considering the state as a boundary. See also the useful summary in Mathias Risse, *On Global Justice*, 41–62.

51. The figure of the posthuman, equally, provides a compelling perspective on fellow-feeling; see Elisabeth Arnould-Bloomfield, "Posthuman Compassions." On early modern compassion and the animal, see Erica Fudge, *Brutal Reasoning*, 69–82.

52. Moyn, *Christian Human Rights*, 169; see also Moyn, *Human Rights and the Uses of History*.

53. Moyn, *Human Rights and the Uses of History*, 51.

54. Saint-Evremond, "Sur les caractères des tragédies," in *Œuvres en prose*, 331.

55. Nicolas Coeffeteau, *Tableau des passions humaines*, 335.

56. Eustache de Refuge, *Traité de la cour* (1656 edition; first published 1616), 79.

57. On the articulation of time in the theory of the passions, see Philip Fisher, *The Vehement Passions*, 71–87.

58. Lee Edelman, *No Future: Queer Theory and the Death Drive*, 72.

59. Nussbaum, *Upheavals of Thought*, 374. On the danger of linking affects to values, see Didier Fassin, *Humanitarian Reason*, 1.

60. For another take on compassion in relation to virtue ethics, see Diana Fritz Cates, *Choosing to Feel*; on compassion as "moral phenomenon" see also Blum, "Compassion."

61. Sarah McNamer, *Affective Meditation and the Invention of Medieval Compassion*.

62. Marguerite de Navarre, *La Coche*, line 101, p. 148.

63. On Bérulle, see especially Yves Krumenacker, *L'école française de spiritualité*, 125–210.

64. Bérulle, "Des souffrances de la Vierge compatissante à son Fils," in *Œuvres complètes*,

vol. 1, part 5, 385. For a very different take on compassion and the maternal bond, see Katja Haustein, "'J'ai mal à l'autre': Barthes on Pity."

65. "La compassion de la bienheureuse Vierge Marie," Bérulle, *Œuvres*, 391.

66. On Malebranche, see Susan James, *Passion and Action*, 108–23; Erec Koch, "La contagion des passions de Descartes à Malebranche"; on maternity in Malebranche, see Marie-Hélène Huet, *Monstrous Imagination*, 45–55. As Teresa Brennan suggests, Malebranche is a good starting point for a history of affect. Noting his significance, she argues that "the transmission of affect was once common knowledge" which has been lost in the establishment of another model of subjectivity: *The Transmission of Affect*, 16.

67. James, *Passion and Action*, 249–50.

68. The term comes from the *Journal des Sçavans*, November 4, 1698, cited in Wes Williams, *Monsters and Their Meanings in Early Modern Culture*. As Williams notes, "what is meant by terms such as 'compassion' and 'sympathy' in these contexts is not straightforward" (306).

69. Nicolas Malebranche, *De la recherche de la vérité* I–III, ed. Jean-Christophe Bardout, 280.

70. Malebranche, *De la recherche de la vérité*, 281.

71. Molière, *L'École des femmes. Œuvres complètes*, II.5.541–42.

72. On Malebranche's opposition to Stoicism, see Christopher Brooke, *Philosophic Pride*, 86–92. A similar appraisal of women can be found elsewhere in the period: see, for example, Nicolas Caussin, *La cour sainte*, vol. 1, 166 (first published 1624). I return to these gender distinctions in Chapter 2.

73. See the cannibal mother featured in Chapter 1, and the surprising elephant nurse of Chapter 3. On the figure of the sensitive man in today's compassion talk, see Kathleen Woodward, *Statistical Panic*, 110.

74. Heather James, "Dido's Ear: Tragedy and the Politics of Response."

75. Leah Whittington, "Shakespeare's Virgil," 101.

76. Madeleine de Scudéry, *Clélie, histoire romaine*, vol. 1, 183.

77. Eric Langley, *Ill Communications: Shakespeare's Contagious Sympathies* (in ms).

78. Thomas Hobbes, *Leviathan*, ed. Richard Tuck, 43.

79. Fellow-feeling in all its forms (a fellow-feeler, to fellow-feel) chiefly indicated a participation in the sufferings of others, though by the eighteenth century the term suggested also a wider sharing of emotion.

80. Lauren Berlant, "Introduction: Compassion (and Withholding)," 1.

81. Dacher Keltner, Jason Marsh, and Jeremy Adam Smith, eds., *The Compassionate Instinct: The Science of Human Goodness*, 5.

82. Pippa Stephens, "The World's Most Compassionate 24 Hours," BBC News, October 8, 2014, http://www.bbc.co.uk/news/business-28882749.

83. Jeremy Rifkin, *The Empathic Civilization*, 3. Steven Pinker's *The Better Angels of Our Nature* could also be put in this category, although it is less breathless and takes more care with an argument. For a critique of such work, see Paul Bloom on the limits of empathy: "The Baby in the Well," *New Yorker*, May 20, 2013, http://www.newyorker.com/magazine/2013/05/20/the-baby-in-the-well.

84. Charter for Compassion, http://charterforcompassion.org/ (accessed July 21, 2015); see also the heavily promoted book by the Dalai Lama, *How to Be Compassionate* (2011). I take seriously the impetus behind and interest in the popularity of this Buddhist perspective in Western accounts of compassion, but note that in its worst and most popularized instances the gesturing to Buddhist tradition seen in such work flirts with orientalism.

85. Paul Gilbert, *The Compassionate Mind*, 244.

86. Christopher K. Germer and Kristin D. Neff, "Self-Compassion in Clinical Practice"; for a mass-market version, see Kristin Neff, *Self-Compassion*. Today's self-compassion avoids the self-correction implicit in François de Sales's concept of kindness toward ourselves, developed in his 1609 treatise on devotion, in which we should correct our faults by way of compassion. *Introduction à la vie dévote*, 146–47.

87. Marvin Olasky, *Renewing American Compassion*, foreword by Newt Gingrich; also Olasky, *The Tragedy of American Compassion*.

88. Berlant, "Introduction: Compassion (and Withholding)," 2.

89. DNC fund-raiser speech of April 2011, reported in the *Washington Post*, April 15, 2011: http://www.washingtonpost.com/blogs/the-fix/post/president-obama-the-compassion-candidate/2011/04/14/AF7juNgD_blog.html; Allegra Stratton, "The Tory Party is 'Modern and Compassionate,'" *Guardian*, October 2, 2011, http://www.theguardian.com/politics/2011/oct/02/cameron-tory-party-modern-compassionate,. This language was already present in UK centrist politics in the 1980s: see the Social Democratic Party co-founder David Owen's *A Future That Will Work: Competitiveness and Compassion*.

90. Denis Campbell, "David Cameron's Prescription for NHS Savings: Target Pay of Nurses," *Guardian*, February 6, 2013, http://www.theguardian.com/society/2013/feb/06/david-cameron-nhs-nurses.

91. On this distinction see Fassin, *Humanitarian Reason*, 5.

92. Didier Fassin, "Compassion and Repression: The Moral Economy of Immigration Policies in France," 366. For a more journalistic account see Michel Richard, *La République compassionelle*, which attacks the rhetoric of compassion in French presidential politics of the 2000s.

93. Miriam Ticktin, *Casualties of Care: Immigration and the Politics of Humanitarianism in France*.

94. Ticktin, *Casualties of Care*, 127. In a similar vein, the sociologist Philippe Corcuff has examined the distancing effect of French state institutions in face-to-face situations that might seem to call for compassion; see, among other essays, "Ordre institutionnel, fluidité situationnelle et compassion."

95. Ticktin, *Casualties of Care*, 223. For a historical account of the development of humanitarianism in relation to discourses of compassion, see Bertrand Taithe, "'Cold Compassion in the Faces of Horrors?' Pity, Compassion and the Making of Humanitarian Protocols." These readings set national compassion in distinctly international context, an approach also taken recently by Carolyn Pedwell, who examines "empathy's uneven effects" in transnational politics, calling attention to the contingencies and differences that erode the liberal understanding of empathy as a universal: *Affective Relations*, 1; see also Sara Ahmed, *The Cultural Politics of Emotion*, 192.

96. Berlant, "Introduction: Compassion (and Withholding)," 1–13. See also Marjorie Garber, who explores the political valence of American compassion with regards to disability in a reading of a Supreme Court decision: "Compassion," 15–27; Elizabeth V. Spelman, *Fruits of Sorrow*, who reads Harriet Jacobs through Hannah Arendt's anxieties about compassion. On U.S. academic work on compassion and its attention to race, see Woodward, *Statistical Panic*, 109–33. On Bush and compassion see also Elizabeth A. Povinelli, *Economies of Abandonment*, 166.

97. Lauren Berlant, *The Female Complaint*, xii.

98. Berlant, *The Female Complaint*, 6.

99. Edelman, *No Future*, 72.

100. For a surprising perspective on compassion and inequality, see the sociologist Robert Wuthnow, who reminds us that under capitalism even good brokerage might be read as compassionate: *Acts of Compassion*, 219.

101. Berlant, "Introduction: Compassion (and Withholding)," 10.

102. For a discussion of not necessarily individualized emotion, see Rei Terada, *Feeling in Theory: Emotion After the "Death of the Subject*," 2.

103. Elspeth Probyn, "Writing Shame," 76.

104. Adela Pinch, for example, reminds us of "the vagrancy of emotions" (*Strange Fits*, 10) seen from the eighteenth century, noting that "the history of feeling and the history of the individual are not the same thing" (13). Teresa Brennan's *The Transmission of Affect* similarly insists upon the premodernness of affect's movements.

105. Norbert Elias famously made the case that in seventeenth-century France "court rationality produces a number of counter-movements even within court society itself, attempts to emancipate 'feeling', which are always at the same time attempts to emancipate the individual from social pressure" (*The Court Society*, 112–13). Elias was one of the first twentieth-century historians to turn his attention to emotion, but it was in indignant response to his model of emotion against rationality and freedom against repression that the pioneering historian of emotions Barbara Rosenwein developed her fine-grained mode of reading, memorably dismissing Elias's structure as "hydraulic" ("Worrying About Emotions in History," 834).

106. As Thomas Dixon has shown, passion, rather than emotion, was (in English) the favored word for inner turmoil until the nineteenth century. Before that point, in early modern English and French usage, emotion referred to a social disturbance rather than an interiorized feeling. Thomas Dixon, *From Passions to Emotions: The Creation of a Secular Psychological Category*. For an account of such vocabulary shifts in French, see Joan DeJean, *Ancients Against Moderns*, 79–81.

107. For the first iteration of this term in relation to early modern studies see Bruce Smith, "Premodern Sexualities." For a recent instance of playing with compassion *as* form, see the first chapter of Paul Audi's *L'empire de la compassion*, which is set out in two columns, one in the third person and one in the first, playing and disrupting with questions of emotional identification.

108. On the importance of considering the emotions rhetorically, see Terada, *Feeling in Theory*, 47; also Daniel M. Gross, *The Secret History of Emotion*. On pity and classical legal rhetoric, see Konstan, *Pity Transformed*, 29–48. Pity's literariness is brought out in a recent special issue of *PMLA*, in which pity features in many of the articles: "Emotions," special issue, *PMLA* 130.5 (October 2015), ed. Katharine Ann Jensen and Miriam L. Wallace.

109. Nussbaum, *Political Emotions*, 156.

110. Lynn Hunt, *Inventing Human Rights*, 35–69 (critiqued by Samuel Moyn in *Human Rights and the Uses of History*); see also Richard Rorty's inquiry into our ability to be moved to action by sad and sentimental stories: "Human Rights, Rationality, and Sentimentality." For a literary scholar's account of a similar process, see David Denby, *Sentimental Narrative and the Social Order in France, 1760–1820*. See also the popularizing account given by Roman Krznaric, "Does Novel-Reading Enhance Empathy?" History of Emotions Blog, July 25, 2012, http://emotionsblog.history.qmul.ac.uk/?p=1648, which draws on Harriet Beecher Stowe's *Uncle Tom's Cabin* for its case study; this text and its reception is read very differently by Lauren Berlant in *The Female Complaint*.

111. Pinker, *The Better Angels of Our Nature*, 589.

112. Suzanne Keen, *Empathy and the Novel*. On the problem of empathy in reading the material culture of the past, see Sarah Tarlow, "The Archaeology of Emotion and Affect."

113. Thomas Laqueur, "Mourning, Pity, and the Work of Narrative in the Making of 'Humanity,'" 35. In this essay Laqueur moves away from a position taken in his more often-quoted essay on humanitarian inquiry, in which he described how "the suffering bodies of others engender compassion and how that compassion comes to be understood as a moral imperative to undertake ameliorative action" ("Bodies, Details, and the Humanitarian Narrative," 176).

114. Lynn Festa, "Humanity Without Feathers," 4.

115. Lynn Festa, *Sentimental Figures of Empire in Eighteenth-Century Britain and France*, 2, 44, 51 (emphasis in the original). For a wry take on the optimistic reading of fellow-feeling see also Rachel Ablow, *The Marriage of Minds*, 1–2.

116. In a similar vein, James Chandler has recently proposed that the early American cinema stems from, or recalls, what he calls the "structuring principles" of the eighteenth-century novel of sensibility, arguing that various formal features of that genre, what he calls the eighteenth century's "techniques of vicariousness" (epistolarity, for example) are central to the "sympathetic camerawork" of early film: *An Archaeology of Sympathy*, 12.

117. On the nonliterariness of the history of emotions see Sarah McNamer, "The Literariness of Literature and the History of Emotion," 1433–42.

CHAPTER I

1. *Dictionnaire de l'Académie Françoise* (1694), s.v. "pitié."

2. "Les rues retentissoient de hauts souspirs, de lamentations, de cris & brayemens miserables, meslez dedans un bruit confus & tintamarre estrange par toute la ville brief un pitoyable spectacle." ["The streets rang with loud sighs, lamentations, yells and miserable groans, mingled in a confused noise, a strange din throughout the town: in short, a pitiful sight."] Simon Goulart, *Histoires admirables et memorables de nostre temps*, 546. On sound as a mode of violence in the writing of the wars, see Amy C. Graves-Monroe, "Soundscapes of the Wars of Religion," 63–69.

3. Of course, these writers were not the first to describe war as pitiful. On the centrality of pity in late medieval Burgundian descriptions of war, see Barbara H. Rosenwein, *Generations of Feeling*, 178.

4. Although they are described as wars of religion, it is sometimes hard to hold on clearly to theological concerns in tracking the wars, and scholars have sometimes told this story as a question of territory and household tribalism as much as theology. For an account of the wars that drafts religion in social rather than theological terms, see Mack Holt, *The French Wars of Religion*; for an account that suggests something of the religiosity of sixteenth-century Paris across all social classes, see Barbara Diefendorf, *Beneath the Cross*. On the naming of the wars, see Jacques Berchtold et Marie-Madeleine Fragonard, "La mémoire et l'écriture," 8–9; on the various genres of the war, see 23–27. On the conflicts of genres and voices, see Marie-Madeleine Fragonard, "Une mémoire individualisée."

5. On the compelled forgetting of what went before in the language of these edicts, see Andrea Frisch, *Forgetting Differences*.

6. Holt, *The French Wars of Religion*, 94.

7. On the body of Coligny and for the citation, see Denis Crouzet, *La nuit de la Sainct-Barthélemy*, 515–24. On the Saint Barthélemy massacre and its historiography more broadly, see Denis Crouzet, *Les Guerriers de Dieu*, vol. 2, 13–106; Holt, *The French Wars of Religion*, 76–97; Diefendorf, *Beneath the Cross*, 93–106; Arlette Jouanna, *La Saint-Barthélemy*; Robert M. Kingdon, *Myths about the St Bartholomew's Day Massacres*, 28–50.

8. On the naming of this group, see Edmond M. Beame, "The *Politiques* and the Historians."

9. Many scholars today mark the 1629 Peace of Alès (Alais) as a better ending point, shifting the traditional historiography of the wars and its aftermath. Holt, *The French Wars of Religion*, 153–89.

10. Susan Sontag, *Regarding the Pain of Others*. Sontag's easy assumption of the "we" with whom she speaks has often been criticized: "Sontag apparently presumes that the politics of photography consists simply in discovering a 'we' that exists, ready-made as it were, and waits only to be addressed" (James Johnson, " 'The Arithmetic of Compassion': Rethinking the Politics of Photography," 632). Johnson's reading of Sontag's *Regarding the Pain of Others* is harsher than mine. I find her attentive to the different forms of "we" worldwide, if not to their construction through spectacle. For a critique of Sontag's earlier work that insists on the importance of emotional response to photography, see Susie Linfield, *The Cruel Radiance: Photography and Political Violence*.

11. Sontag, *Regarding the Pain of Others* 90.

12. Luc Boltanski, *Distant Suffering*, 19, 21.

13. Boltanski, *Distant Suffering*, 43.

14. Of course, many printed images circulated during the wars, too. On the "primarily visual" representations of the wars, see Kathleen Long, "Child in the Water," 157.

15. Joachim Blanchon, *Sommaire discours de la guerre civile et diverse calamité de ce temps*, Aii.

16. See David Quint, *Epic and Empire*, 185–209.

17. Quintilian, *The Orator's Education Books 6–8*, trans. Donald A. Russell, book 6, chapter 1, 39.

18. Quintilian, 31.

19. On emotional shipwrecks, see Jennifer Oliver, "Au milieu d'un tel et si piteux naufrage: The Dynamics of Shipwreck in Renaissance France (1498–1616)." References to Ronsard give line numbers in Pierre de Ronsard, *Œuvres complètes*, vol 2. The *Discours* was reprinted often from 1562 to 1572, in cheap separate editions for fast circulation and then in the collected works of 1567. On the publication of the text, see Wes Williams, *Monsters and Their Meanings in Early Modern Culture*, 91. The same woeful state of affairs is bemoaned in a Catholic poem of 1572, in which France is "pitoyable, affligée": Jean Touchard, *Allégresse chrestienne de l'heureux succès des guerres de ce royaume*.

20. Wes Williams describes this as a "redirection of the insensitivity topos away from the discourse of love to that of war." *Monsters and Their Meanings*, 91.

21. Jacques Yver, *Le printemps d'Yver*, 525.

22. On the genre of the *histoire tragique*, see *Théâtre de la cruauté et récits sanglants en France (XVIe–XVIIe siècle)*, ed. Christian Biet, 38–45.

23. "Comment une demoiselle nommée Anne de Buringel, fit empoisonner son mari," Biet, *Théâtre de la cruauté*, 69.

24. On the topos of events described as tragic, see Charles Mazouer, "Ce que tragédie et tragique veulent dire."

25. On Christophe, see Biet, *Théâtre de la cruauté*, 106–8.

26. Christophe de Bordeaux, *Discours lamentable et pitoyable sur la calamite, cherté et necessité du temps present* (1586).

27. Bordeaux, *Discours lamentable*, Aii. On the trope of the friendly reader and its significance for the development of literary feeling, see Éric Méchoulan, "L'ami lecteur."

28. Histoire IX, "De la cruauté d'un frère," Biet, *Théâtre de la cruauté*, 170.

29. *Le théâtre tragique, sur lequel la Fortune représente les divers malheurs advenus aux hommes illustres*, "D'Hippasos, fils de Minyas," Biet, *Théâtre de la cruauté*, 327.

30. Pierre Boistuau and François de Belleforest, *Histoires tragiques*, "Comment un chevalier espagnol . . . ," Biet, *Théâtre de la cruauté*, 55–56.

31. Boistuau and Belleforest, *Histoires tragiques*, "Comment un chevalier espagnol . . . ," Biet, *Théâtre de la cruauté*, 57.

32. Loys de Perussiis, *Discours des guerres de la comté de Venayscin*, 404.

33. Pierre de L'Estoile, *Registre-journal du règne de Henri III: tome 5 (1585–1587)*, eds. Madeleine Lazard and Gilbert Schrenk, entry for July 9, 1587, 306.

34. The Guise camp were adept at the discourse of pity. See an account of 1563 of the death of François duc de Guise, *Le saint et Pitoyable discours*, a tearjerker which details the "pitoyable discomfort" of the mourners.

35. Jacques Pineaux, *La poésie des protestants de langue française, 1559–1590*, 199–205. Pineaux notes that the Protestant poetry of this period abandons Reform rhetoric and instead models itself on Ronsard. The volume traces the full range of Protestant lyric in this period.

36. *Complainte de la France, touchant les misères de son dernier temps*.

37. Henri Lancelot-Voisin de La Popelinière, *La vraye et entire histoire de ces derniers troubles*, end material: Sonet du Roy et de la paix.

38. Stuart Clark, *Vanities of the Eye: Vision in Early Modern European Culture*, 161. On vision in writing of the Wars of Religion, see also Graves-Monroe, "Soundscapes of the Wars of Religion," 57–60.

39. Théodore de Bèze, *Histoire ecclésiastique des Eglises reformées au royaume de France* I, i.

40. Andrea Frisch, *The Invention of the Eyewitness*, 37.

41. Frisch, *The Invention of the Eyewitness*, 50.

42. Jean de Léry, *Histoire memorable de la ville de Sancerre*, A2.

43. Léry, *Histoire memorable*, A2 recto.

44. Léry, *Histoire memorable*, 158.

45. Léry, *Histoire memorable*, 47.

46. Théodore-Agrippa d'Aubigné, *Les Tragiques*, ed. Jean-Raymond Fanlo, 231. In recent years scholars have suggested that most of the poem was in fact composed under Henri as king, chiefly in the seventeenth century; in 1603, d'Aubigné was designated official historian by the Huguenot Synod of Gap. On the dating of the text, see Frank Lestringant, *Lire 'Les Tragiques*,' 24; see also the introduction by Jean-Raymond Fanlo to his edition, vol. 1, 113–18, which makes a convincing case for understanding the *Tragiques* as an early seventeenth-century text. David Quint suggests that the publication date comes at the moment when French Protestants felt the need to begin resistance all over again: *Epic and Empire*, 190. On the Synod designation and its significance, see Kathleen Perry Long, "The Representation of Violence," 143.

47. On d'Aubigné's use of Léry, see Lestringant, *Lire 'Les Tragiques*,' 27; also Géralde Nakam, "Une source des *Tragiques*." On d'Aubigné's dedication to Ronsard and his debt to Ronsard's writings against the wars, see Lestringant, *Lire 'Les Tragiques*,' 23, 36; on the links between d'Aubigné and Ronsard in their treatment of the wars, see Edwin M. Duval, "The Place of the Present." On d'Aubigné's political theory, see Arlette Jouanna, "Le sujet, le roi et la loi."

48. See Olivier Pot, "Les tableaux des *Tragiques*"; Michel Jeanneret, "Les tableaux spirituels d'Agrippa d'Aubigné,"; Lestringant, *Lire "Les Tragiques*," 74–82; Mitchell Greenberg, "The Poetics of Trompe-l'œil." On d'Aubigné's work between media see Phillip John Usher, *Epic Arts in Renaissance France*, 160–201. On the interdependence of reading and seeing in d'Aubigné, see

Katherine Maynard, "Writing Martyrdom," 35. On the framing of spectacle in the *Tragiques*, see also John O'Brien, "Seeing the Dead."

49. On anti-Catholic insistence on Catholicism as dupery, dissembling, conjuring, see Clark, *Vanities of the Eye*, 174.

50. Goldhill, "What Is Ekphrasis For?" 2.

51. On this making of perspective see Michel Jeanneret, "Les tableaux spirituels," 237. On the question of decentered perspectives in *Les Tragiques*, see Kathleen Perry Long, "Improper Perspective."

52. All references (book and line number) to Théodore-Agrippa d'Aubigné, *Les Tragiques* ed. Jean-Raymond Fanlo (Paris: Honoré Champion, 2006). All translations are my own and made regretfully, in anticipation of Valerie Worth's forthcoming English translation of the *Tragiques*.

53. Quint, *Epic and Empire*, 194.

54. On Protestant constancy and Stoicism, see David Quint, *Montaigne and the Quality of Mercy*, 93.

55. For the repercussions of this in epic, see Quint, *Epic and Empire*, 188.

56. On what "moving" means for d'Aubigné, see Andrea Frisch, "Agrippa d'Aubigné's *Tragiques* as Testimony," 102–3.

57. Richard Regosin notes, "All through *Les Tragiques*, the eye serves to indicate the fallen state of the damned." *The Poetry of Inspiration*, 96.

58. Kathleen Perry Long suggests that the "cœur impitoyable" represents the "splitting of the witnessing subject," figuring a heartless double of d'Aubigné himself. "The Representation of Violence," 57.

59. Sarah McNamer, *Affective Meditation and the Invention of Medieval Compassion*.

60. On the importance of judicial scenes in d'Aubigné, see Gisèle Matthieu-Castellani, "La scène judiciaire dans *Les Tragiques*."

61. Michel de Montaigne, *Les Essais*, ed. Pierre Villey, vol. 3, 1046. All quotations of Montaigne refer to Villey's edition.

62. Michel de Montaigne, *The Complete Works*, trans. Donald Frame, 974. All translations of Montaigne refer to this edition. On the figure of the spectator in this passage, see Frisch, *Forgetting Differences*, 85–86.

63. Neil Kenny, *The Uses of Curiosity in Early Modern France and Germany*, 17, 158.

64. Villey, vol. 3, 1046–47; Frame, 975.

65. Villey, vol. 2, 622; Frame, 572.

66. On dating the essay, see Villey, vol. 1, 7.

67. Villey, vol. 1, 7.

68. Frame, 3.

69. Quint, *Montaigne and the Quality of Mercy*, 7.

70. Seneca, *De clementia*, II iv, 1–4, in *Moral Essays*, ed. Basore.

71. Villey, vol. 1, 7; Frame, 3.

72. On the ways in which this reading cuts against Stoic writings, see Rebecca Wilkin, *Women, Imagination and the Search for Truth in Early Modern France*, 154. On this essay see also Jean Starobinski, *Montaigne in Motion*, in which compassion appears as a defining characteristic of the *Essais*. It is literary scholars who seem to take the essay's strange open-ended form most seriously, whereas in *The Political Philosophy of Montaigne*, David Lewis Schaefer finds it to be "obscure" (39) and "mysterious" (251). For readings which make a nonhistoricist engagement with Montaigne's rhetoric, tracing instead the structures of rules and their exceptions, see

especially Lawrence D. Kritzman, *Destruction/Découverte*, 21–33; Edwin M. Duval, "Le début des 'Essais' et la fin d'un livre."

73. Quint, *Montaigne and the Quality of Mercy*, 9.

74. Peter Mack, *Reading and Rhetoric in Montaigne and Shakespeare*, 42. Steven Rendall similarly comments on the essay's relation to scholastic tradition: *Distinguo*, 15. Victoria Kahn describes Montaigne's rhetorical procedures in *Rhetoric, Prudence, and Skepticism in the Renaissance*, 116.

75. Peter Mack, *Renaissance Argument: Valla and Agricola in the Traditions of Rhetoric and Dialectic*, 204.

76. Quint and Wilkin both suggest that Montaigne's use of the term "essayer"—to be assayed by something, to be receptive—links his readily compassionate "mollesse" to the wider project of the *Essais*. On Montaigne's compassion as it reads in John Florio's translation, see also Jan Frans van Dijkhuizen, who argues persuasively that Florio intensifies Montaigne's compassionate aspect. *Pain and Compassion in Early Modern English Literature and Culture*, 216–42.

77. On this patterning of sameness and difference see both Quint and Wilkin.

78. Another way to read this would consider the essay as a meditation on chance or fortune; there is no pattern to pity, but we might draw on the language of pity and response to imagine that we can make sense of contingency. On Montaigne's handling of such questions, see John D. Lyons, who notes that "the *Essays* do not propose or adopt a method of stabilising the proliferation of contingency but instead make contemplation of that contingency an end in itself. *The Phantom of Chance*, 23.

79. I have modified Frame's translation to preserve the emphasis on reading; Frame's version reads "the rank and file of Dionysius' army showed in their countenance that, disregarding their leader and his triumph, they were softened." (5)

80. I'm grateful to Éric Méchoulan for his reading of this passage and the observation that it operates still another kind of reversal, in which the modern reader seems to read directly in the eyes of the public. *Lire avec soin: Amitié, justice et médias*, 32.

81. Kritzman notes that the essay is also the meeting place for a series of texts. *Destruction/ Découverte*, 32.

82. Quint, *Montaigne and the Quality of Mercy*, 3–41.

83. For a fine account of Henri's negotiations of these virtues, see Michel de Waele, *Réconcilier les Français*.

CHAPTER 2

1. Jean de La Taille, *Art de la tragédie*, 225.

2. Andrea Frisch shows that even the term "esmouvoir" has "still-potent martial associations"; even as La Taille seeks to distance us from the wars, we are bound up in them. *Forgetting Differences*, 147.

3. *The Art of Rhetoric*, chapter 2.8, 163. On the question of pity in the *Rhetoric*, see Stephen Halliwell, *Aristotle's Poetics*, 175–78. I limit myself in this chapter to the gradual changes wrought in early modern French versions of the formula, but it would also be possible to note at length other versions which recall Aristotle's insights: see, for example, Eustache de Refuge, *Traité de la cour* (1616), whose chapter on compassion carefully follows Aristotle in its precisions.

4. Aristotle, *Poetics*, 1453a 3–5. Debates about catharsis in early modern France lean toward one of two explanations of the process: on the one hand, what is often described as a homeopathic understanding of catharsis, in which a little pity or fear purges a larger amount of like

emotions, something seen in the work of René Rapin; alternatively, in what has been termed an instrumentalist or allopathic catharsis, pity and fear chase out or subjugate other sorts of emotions, something at work for André Dacier. On the distinction between the two models, see John D. Lyons, *Kingdom of Disorder*, 49; Racine, *Principes de la tragédie en marge de la Poétique d'Aristote*, ed. Eugène Vinaver, 58–60. On allopathic catharsis, see Elizabeth Belfiore, *Tragic Pleasures*, 260–66. Belfiore gives considerable attention to the neglect of the allopathic understanding in critical studies of Aristotle and demonstrates how the homeopathic model came to dominate the critical tradition. On catharsis in French drama of this period, see also Jean Émelina, "Corneille et la *catharsis*"; Georges Forestier, *Passions tragiques et règles classiques*, 129–40; Bradley Rubidge, "Catharsis Through Admiration"; Hélène Merlin-Kajman, *L'absolutisme dans les lettres*, 59–67; Merlin-Kajman, "Corneille, une politique de l'image scénique." On Italian models see Blair Hoxby, *What Was Tragedy?*, 62. On the standardization of the pity-fear coupling, see Joseph Harris, *Inventing the Spectator*, 175–80.

5. "De l'expérience," *Essais*, ed. Villey, vol. 3, 1091; Frame, 1019.

6. "De la vanité," *Essais*, vol. 3, 979; Frame, 909.

7. "De l'utile et de l'honneste," *Essais*, vol. 3, 791; Frame, 726.

8. Jean Starobinski, *Montaigne In Motion*, 124.

9. *Cicero on the Emotions: Tusculan Disputations 3 and 4*, 4.28, 49.

10. Pierre Charron, *Trois livres de sagesse*, in *Œuvres*, vol. 1, 90.

11. The professional example is also given by the Dutch dramatic theorist Heinsius, who describes how experience and artistry tempers our immediate response to suffering and proposes that theater school us to respond in the same way. *De tragediae constitutione*, 127.

12. René Descartes, *Les passions de l'âme*, art. 185, 232.

13. Descartes, *Les passions de l'âme*, art.186, 232–33. In recent years revisionist readings of Descartes attentive to the question of the passions and their embodiment have complicated the mind/body distinction that had dominated our understandings of what Cartesianism set out: see, for example, Erec Koch, "Cartesian Corporeality and (Aesth)Ethics"; Denis Kambouchner, *L'homme des passions: Commentaires sur Descartes*. On the complicated relation between body and mind in Descartes's conception of the passions, see especially Susan James, *Passion and Action*, 85–108.

14. Malebranche, *De la recherché de la vérité* I–III, 281 (my translations).

15. Descartes, *Les passions de l'âme*, art. 187, 233.

16. On a similar "aristocratic ethos of largess" in England, see Felicity Heal, *Hospitality in Early Modern England*, 391. On Descartes's argument here see Kambouchner, *L'homme des passions*, vol. 2, 263–64.

17. On the theatrical model see also Philippe Hamou, "Descartes, le théâtre des passions." The relationship between theater and moral discourse will be drawn out further in eighteenth-century writing.

18. Augustine, *Confessions*, book 3, section 3.

19. Art. 147, 206. On this article, see especially Victoria Kahn, "Happy Tears: Baroque Politics in Descartes's *Passions de l'âme*."

20. Henry Phillips, "Descartes and the Dramatic Experience," 418.

21. Phillips, "Descartes," 416.

22. René Descartes, *Œuvres et lettres*, ed. André Bridoux, 1183.

23. Descartes, *Œuvres et lettres*, 1184.

24. Kambouchner draws this distinction in his discussion of the passage, *L'homme des passions*, vol. 2, 264.

25. On this position, see Martha Nussbaum, *Upheavals of Thought*, 357.

26. On Descartes and self-sovereignty see Kambouchner, *L'homme des passions*, vol. 2, 268.

27. Jacques Du Bosc, *L'honneste femme*, 257–61.

28. Madeleine de Scudéry, *Clélie, histoire romaine*, vol. 1, 118.

29. "De la Conversation," *Conversations sur divers sujets*, 26.

30. La Rochefoucauld, *Réflexions ou sentences et maximes morales et réflexions diverses*, ed. Laurence Plazenet, 554. The text was first published as "Portrait de M.R.D. fait par lui-même" in *Receuil des portraits et éloges* (1659), then republished in 1663 in *La Galerie des Peintures*.

31. La Rochefoucauld, "Self-Portrait," *Maxims*, 28.

32. La Rochefoucauld, *Réflexions*, maxim 263, 167.

33. La Rochefoucauld, *Réflexions*, 135 (emphasis his). On paradiastole in La Rochefoucauld, see Michael Moriarty, *Disguised Vices*, 3; on the trope in early modern writing more broadly see Quentin Skinner, *Visions of Politics*, vol. 2, 264–85; for a shorter account of paradiastole in Quintilian, see *Visions of Politics*, vol. 2, 182–85; on paradiastole from antiquity to Hobbes, passing via Montaigne and the post-Machiavellians, see *Visions of Politics*, vol. 3, 87–141. On the moralists and emotion, see also Jon Elster, *Alchemies of the Mind*, which explores what Elster calls "the interplay between emotion and cognition" (49) by exploring literary texts, especially those of the French seventeenth century. Elster's account is chiefly interesting as a social scientist's reading of this canonical textual tradition.

34. La Rochefoucauld, *Réflexions*, 167. For La Rochefoucauld on the social status of compassion, see also maxim 463, "Il y a souvent plus d'orgeuil que de bonté à plaindre les malheurs de nos ennemis; c'est pour leur faire sentir que nous sommes au-dessus d'eux que nous leur donnons des marques de compassion" (190). ["There is often more pride than kindness in our pity for the misfortunes of our enemies, for we make a display of sympathy in order to impress them with our own superiority"] (95).

35. Richelet, s.v. "pitié." Where pity is described by Richelet as a form of compassion, the definition of compassion does not use the term pity, suggesting a newly separate identity for compassion to which I will return later in the chapter. Richelet names his source for the maxim as the *Memoires de M.D.L.R.* (1662), a text which describes the events after the death of Louis XIII, rather than the later edition of the maxims.

36. On Esprit, see Moriarty, *Disguised Vices*, 277–316: Moriarty describes the importance of Esprit for understanding the context of La Rochefoucauld. On Esprit's approach to love, see Louise K. Horowitz, *Love and Language*, 113–124. Pascal Quignard gives a searing account of Esprit's work and his circle in "Traité sur Esprit," introduction to Jacques Esprit, *La fausseté des vertus humaines*, 9–66. On the overlaps, differences and collaboration between La Rochefoucauld and Esprit, see Susan Read Baker, *Collaboration et originalité chez La Rochefoucauld*.

37. Jacques Esprit, *La fausseté des vertus humaines*, vol. 1, 366–67. All parenthetical references to this volume.

38. On Nicole, see Moriarty, *Disguised Vices*, 241–52. In recent years Nicole has been read as a precursor of Enlightenment reflections on the relationship between self-interest and a wider social good: see Pierre Force, *Self-Interest Before Adam Smith*, 76–78.

39. By 1695 there would be twelve editions; Locke translated three of the essays.

40. Nicole, "De la connaissance de soi-même," *Essais de morale*, ed. Laurent Thirouin, 323–33.

41. Nicole knew the text well: on his deathbed, he recited at least four thousand lines of the Aeneid. Béatrice Guion, *Pierre Nicole moraliste*, 427; on Nicole's insistence on learning Virgil by heart, 433. On such feats and especially the importance of Virgil, see Nicholas Hammond, *Fragmentary Voices*, 76.

42. Guion translates this as "Ces paroles de Didon dans Virgile sont pleines d'humanité, ce qui fait naître chez le lecteur une sympathie secrète à son égard" [These words of Virgil's Dido are full of humanity, which brings about a secret sympathy for her in the reader"], which seems to push Nicole's observation too far toward a modern version of identification. *La vraie beauté et son fantôme*, ed. Béatrice Guion, 109.

43. *Recueil des plus belles epigrammes des poëtes François*, trans. Germain de Lafaille, 52.

44. "Quid tibi jam restat perdere, calve? Caput." *Recueil des plus belles epigrammes*, 52.

45. In drawing on Virgil to discover this shared humanity, Nicole draws on a rich early modern tradition of thinking through Virgilian *empatheia*. On the early modern life of this literary emotion, see Leah Whittington, "Shakespeare's Virgil: Empathy and *The Tempest*."

46. On Nicole's knowledge of Augustine, see Guion, *Pierre Nicole moraliste*, 456. On Augustine's Virgil, see Sabine MacCormack, *The Shadows of Poetry: Vergil in the Mind of Augustine*.

47. "Quid enim miserius misero non miserante se ipsum et flente Didonis mortem, quae fiebat amando Aenean, non flente autem mortem suam, quae fiebat non amando te, deus." Augustine, *Confessions*, Book 1.21, trans. Hammond, 36–37. Howard Jacobson argues that such a posture is already a trope, drawing on stories from Plutarch and elsewhere: "Augustine and Dido."

48. On Dido's significance in early modern England as a figure for a gendered compassionate response, see Heather James, "Dido's Ear: Tragedy and the Politics of Response."

49. Nussbaum, *The Fragility of Goodness*, 384.

50. Paul de Man, *Blindness and Insight*, 132.

51. On this essay, see Michael Moriarty, *Fallen Nature, Fallen Selves*, 219–23.

52. Delphine Reguig-Naya argues that Nicole makes room for the chevalier Méré's language of sociability: *Le corps des idées: Pensées et poétiques du langage dans l'augustinisme de Port-Royal*, 521–67.

53. On this equivalence, see Émelina, "Corneille et la *catharsis*," 106.

54. Jean Racine, *Œuvres complètes*, vol. 1, 699; Racine, ed. Vinaver, *Principes de la tragédie en marge de La Poétique d'Aristote*, 11; *La poétique d'Aristote*, trans. Sieur de Norville. On Racine and Aristotle's *Poetics*, see Roy Knight, *Racine et la Grèce*, 195–206.

55. David Konstan, *Pity Transformed*, 58. On pity and *pietas*, see Blandine Colot, "Pietas."

56. Bernard Weinberg, *A History of Literary Criticism in the Italian Renaissance*, vol. 1, 362. On Renaissance translations of Aristotle, see also Charles B. Schmitt, *Aristotle and the Renaissance*, 64–88.

57. Weinberg, *A History of Literary Criticism*, vol. 1, 373, 407–8. On Maggi, see Kathy Eden, *Poetic and Legal Fiction in the Aristotelian Tradition*, 154.

58. Weinberg, *A History of Literary Criticism*, vol. 1, 369.

59. Weinberg, vol. 1, 435.

60. Weinberg, vol. 1, 441.

61. Weinberg, vol. 1, 506.

62. Jean Nicot, *Thrésor de la langue française*, s.v. "compassion."

63. Jean-François Féraud, *Dictionaire critique*, s.v. "compassion."

64. François Hédelin, abbé d'Aubignac, *La pratique du théâtre*, ed. Hélène Baby, 90, 73. The text refers to compassion fourteen times to pity's four. On d'Aubignac and the passions, see Harris, *Inventing the Spectator*, 50–75.

65. For an excellent account of the question, see Adrien Walfard, "Justice et passions tragiques."

66. Walfard, "Justice et passions tragiques," 269–70.

67. Walfard, "Justice et passions tragiques," 270.

68. On Ciceronian usage see Elisabeth de Fontenay, *Le silence des bêtes*, 105.

69. Gilbert Romeyer Dherbey, "Les animaux familiers," 141–42.

70. On theatrical representation as a mediator for new forms of emotional relation, see also Sylvaine Guyot and Clotilde Thouret, "Des émotions en chaîne."

71. La Mesnardière, *La poëtique*, 19.

72. On that language and its particularity, see especially Nicholas Paige, *Before Fiction*, who comments of *attendrissement* in particular that its tears "are not participatory; attendrissement is an emotion proper to the sympathetic observer, the emotion you share when you cannot share your emotions, as it were" (145).

73. On theatrical tears in this period, see especially Christian Biet, *Racine ou la passion des larmes*; on the history of teariness more generally, Anne-Vincent Buffault, *Histoire des larmes*.

74. On the *querelle*, see Larry F. Norman, *The Shock of the Ancient*.

75. McClure, "Neo-Stoicism and the Spectator in Corneille's *Horace*"; for the standard account of Corneille as Stoic see Jacques Maurens, *La tragédie sans tragique: Le néo-stoïcisme dans l'œuvre de Pierre Corneille*.

76. Pierre Corneille, *Œuvres complètes*, vol. 3, ed. Georges Couton, 145. On the significance of this admission, see Rubidge, "Catharsis Through Admiration." On Corneille's dramatic theory, see Harris, *Inventing the Spectator*, 76–104; both Rubidge and Harris stress that Corneille's interest in compassion is supplemented by a concern with admiration.

77. On this language see especially Emma Gilby, "Le 'sens commun' et le 'sentir en commun': Corneille et d'Aubignac," as well as her finely calibrated reading of Corneille's dramatic theory and the language of commiseration in *Sublime Worlds*, 35–38.

78. Corneille allows, for example, that we might feel compassion for the despair of Médée, even though in Aristotelian terms she is beyond compassion.

79. Heinsius, *De tragediae constitutione*, 203 [hominem enim hominis miseret ut hominis. Hanc humanitatis legem Philosophus vocavit. Quod et ad commiserationem veram proxime accedat] (202).

80. Corneille's broader understanding of tragic emotion illustrates Hoxby's argument that early modern tragedy depended on pathos and suffering—often figured through women— rather than the notions of the tragic hero that will be so important to nineteenth-century discussions of the tragic. Hoxby, *What Was Tragedy?*, 8–10.

81. Famously, Corneille's sympathies of kinship and friendship extend not only to his characters but even to the plays themselves: of *Nicomède*, he writes in the *Examen*, "Je ne veux point dissimuler que cette pièce est une de celles pour qui j'ai le plus d'amitié" (vol. 2, 643). ["I will not disguise the fact that this play is one of those for which I have the most friendship."] On this language of friendship for one's work, see Katherine Ibbett, "Mon ami, ce héros."

82. Saint-Evremond, "De la tragédie ancienne et moderne"(1672?), *Œuvres en prose*, vol. 4, 179.

83. Norman, *The Shock of the Ancient*, describes Rapin's text as "an eclectic amalgam of proto-Ancient and proto-Modern positions" (174), which exactly captures Rapin's loving description of the new compassion and his anxious rejection of it.

84. René Rapin, *Les réflexions sur la poétique de ce temps*, 97. On Rapin and purgation, see Ann Delehanty, *Literary Knowing in Neoclassical France*, 107–8. On Rapin and the relation between pity and action, see also Frisch, *Forgetting Differences*, 157–58.

85. Nicolas Boileau, *Œuvres complètes*, 169.

86. Konstan, *Pity Transformed*, 60.

87. *Œuvres complètes*, vol. 1, 450.

88. André Dacier, *La poétique d'Aristote*, 211.

89. Julie Ann Carlson, "Like Me: An Invitation to Domestic Tragedy," 334; on Lessing's response to Corneille's reading of pity, 340. On Lessing see also Paul Fleming, *Exemplarity and Mediocrity*, 42–75.

CHAPTER 3

1. Charles Fitz-Geffry, *Compassion Towards Captives*, 2. On Fitz-Geffrey's Anglican explorations of compassion and those of his peers see Kristine Steenbergh, "Mollified Hearts and Enlarged Bowels."

2. Terry Eagleton, *Sweet Violence*, 167; Nicolas Coeffeteau, *Tableau des passions humaines*, 350.

3. *New Jerusalem Bible*, I Corinthians 12:12.

4. This question of charity was also of interest to thinkers outside an explicitly theological tradition: on the importance of the notion to Descartes, see Vincent Carraud, "Descartes: Le droit de la charité." Drawing on Jean-Luc Marion to elucidate a theological-political theory in Descartes's work, Carraud suggests that for Descartes "charité" is an important way to think through questions of friendship and allegiance. See also Carraud, "Descartes et la Bible."

5. For an overview of writers of the Catholic Reformation (his choice of term is deliberate), see Richard Parish, *Catholic Particularity in Seventeenth-Century French Writers*. On readings of the Bible in the seventeenth century see especially Pierre Gibert, *L'invention critique de la Bible, XVe–XVIIIe siècle*, who notes that the New Testament was generally neglected in biblical exegesis but gives a useful account of Richard Simon's great exegetical labors and the significant stakes of such work at the end of the seventeenth century, in the midst of quarrels with both Jansenists and Protestants (285–90). For a useful overview of Protestant editions of the Bible, see Frédéric Delforge, "Les éditions protestantes de la Bible en langue française." See also Debra Keller Shuger, who describes how exegesis turns from philological to historical inquiries over the course of the seventeenth century (*The Renaissance Bible*, 11–54). On Jansenist approaches to the Bible, see especially Bernard Chédozeau, *Port-Royal et la Bible*, and also the overview provided by Philippe Sellier, *Port Royal et la littérature*, vol. 2, 90–135.

6. Sieur de Royaumont, *Histoire du vieux et du Nouveau Testament*, 444.

7. *Nouveau Testament de Nostre Seigneur Jesus Christ, de la traduction des docteurs de Louvain*, 182. The same verb appears in the New Testament of the *Bible de Mons*, 1667. For Protestant Bible usage, see the Geneva Bible of 1622 and later editions, which prefers "usé," as does the Amsterdam Bible of 1678.

8. Sieur de Royaumont, *Histoire du vieux et du Nouveau Testament*, 444. For a reading of the parable that draws attention to the Samaritan's wordlessness, see Luc Boltanski, *Distant Suffering*, 7–11.

9. *La cour sainte du Révérend Père Nicolas Caussin*, vol. 1, 143 (first published 1624); Jean-Baptiste Thiers, *L'avocat des pauvres*, 93. For an overview of seventeenth-century French Catholic approaches to active charity, see René Taveneaux, *Le catholicisme dans la France classique, 1610–1715*, vol. 1, 202–34.

10. See Matthew L. Jones, "Three Errors about Indifference: Pascal on the Vacuum, Sociability, and Moral Freedom"; on Jesuit science in this period, see also *The Jesuits: Cultures, Sciences and Arts, 1540–1773*, ed. John W. O'Malley.

11. Jones, "Three Errors," 107.

12. Pierre Le Moyne, *La dévotion aisée*, 251–52.

13. On the Jellyby case, see Bruce Robbins, "Telescopic Philanthrophy: Professionalism and Responsibility in *Bleak House*."

14. The major assessment of the significance of Yves de Paris is still Henri Brémond's *Histoire littéraire du sentiment religieux* of 1923, which dedicates a large portion of its volume 1, "L'humanisme dévot," to praise of Yves, hailed as "Suprême représentant de l'humanisme dévot" (vol. 1, 425). Brémond's praise of Yves is countered by the somewhat critical study of Charles Chesneau, *Le père Yves de Paris et son temps, 1590–1678*. Hélène Merlin-Kajman discusses the particularity of Yves's sociability in an analysis of his *Le gentilhomme de la cour*: see *Public et littérature en France au XVIIe siècle*, 106–8.

15. Yves de Paris, *La théologie naturelle*.

16. Yves de Paris, *Les œuvres de miséricorde*, 35. On Yves's style, see Chesneau, *Le père Yves de Paris,* vol. 2, 565–610.

17. Yves de Paris, *Les œuvres de miséricorde*, 280.

18. On Bérulle and the French school of spirituality, see Yves Krumenacker, *L'école française de spiritualité*. Henri Brémond's *Histoire littéraire du sentiment religieux* (vol. 3) had placed Saint-Jure as a follower of Bérulle, a position from which Krumenacker distances himself.

19. This book does not pursue the politics of confraternity charity, amply studied by social historians, although I return to their urban charitable concerns briefly in Chapter 6. For a brief overview of the Compagnie, see Henry Phillips, *Church and Culture*, 20–23.

20. Jean-Baptiste Saint-Jure, *L'homme religieux*, vol. 2, 76. All parenthetical references to this second volume.

21. For other elephants caring for babies in Indian travelers' tales, see M. G. Aune, "Elephants, Englishmen and India: Early Modern Travel-Writing and the Pre-Colonial Movement." Montaigne tells a creepier and less immediately moralizing story about cross-species emotion, featuring an elephant that so loved a woman of Alexandria that he would put his trunk under her collar to feel her nipples: "Apologie de Raimond Sebond," *Essais* II.12. On the compassion of elephants and its significance for understanding the emotion, see also Nussbaum, *Political Emotions*, 138, 152–54.

22. Saint-Jure, *L'homme religieux*, 162.

23. In modern Hebrew *chasid* refers to a pious person; the related word *chesed* indicated loving-kindness, either in the divine or in human relationships. My thanks to Julie Cooper for supplementing the insights of Saint-Jure.

24. Steenbergh, "Mollified Hearts and Enlarged Bowels."

25. "On dit prov. & fig. que L'habit ne fait pas le moine, pour dire, que L'on ne doit pas toujours juger des personnes par les apparences, par les dehors." *Dictionnaire de l'Académie Française*, 1694.

26. For the French text, I give references to the fragment numbers of the Sellier and Le Guern editions. For the English, I refer to Pascal, *Pensées, The Provincial Letters*, trans. W. F. Trotter (150); Trotter's translation gives "concupiscence" as "lust" but I have chosen to modify it by keeping "concupiscence."

27. Pascal, *Pensées, The Provincial Letters*, trans. W. F. Trotter, 67. On this passage's monstrosity see Wes Williams, *Monsters and Their Meanings*, 264. The bibliography on Pascal is vast: for thinking through these observations on compassion I have been most indebted to Michael Moriarty, "Grace and Religious Belief in Pascal"; on emotion and knowledge in Pascal, see Ann Delehanty, *Literary Knowing in Neoclassical France*, 41–52. We could contrast Pascal's anger for those blind to God with the gentler way in which Pascal's interlocutor responds to Pascal's own

intellectualizing in the *Entretien de Pascal avec M. de Sacy sur Épictète et Montaigne*, in which Sacy "plaignit ce philosophe," which seems to admit of a more generous compassion. Pascal, *Œuvres complètes*, vol. 2, 91.

28. This passage does not appear in the Trotter edition and is my own translation.

29. I'm grateful to Eric Langley for prompting me to see this sense of a verbal tender.

30. My translation.

31. On Amyraut, see Brian G. Armstrong, *Calvinism and the Amyraut Heresy*. For a thorough account of Amyraut's theological background and study, and especially a careful elucidation of his understanding of pluralism and tolerance, see François Laplanche, *L'Écriture, le sacré et l'histoire*, 379–522.

32. On this question see Philip Benedict, *The Faith and Fortunes of France's Huguenots, 1600–85*, 289.

33. Armstrong, *Calvinism and the Amyraut Heresy*, 116. On the *Morale chrestienne*, see also Laplanche, *L'Écriture, le sacré et l'histoire*, 475–89. On the *Paraphrases*, see Laplanche, 347–49.

34. Pierre Bayle, *Dictionnaire historique et critique*, vol. 1, s.v. Amyraut (Moïse), 186–87.

35. In an *éloge* of the Jesuit Nicolas Caussin written after his death, for example, the writers praised his charity and tears when he heard of public sufferings. "Éloge de l'auteur," published in *La cour sainte du Révérend Père Nicolas Caussin*, vol. 1. There was of course also some degree of common ground between Catholic and Protestant theologians. On Amyraut's humanism, see Armstrong, *Calvinism and the Amyraut Heresy*, 120–27; on his training in natural law, Armstrong, 275; Laplanche, *L'Écriture, le sacré et l'histoire*, 476–78.

36. Amyraut, *Sermon sur ces Paroles de Jesus Christ*, 28.

37. Amyraut, *La morale*, vol. 4, 559.

38. Amyraut, *La morale*, vol. 4, 565. In all his tussles over predestination, Amyraut had always insisted on the notion that God's revealed will shows him to be ultimately merciful to all men (Armstrong, *Calvinism and the Amyraut Heresy*, 266–67).

39. Amyraut, *La morale*, vol. 4, 565. Laplanche argues that Amyraut defines the human through his sociability, *L'Écriture, le sacré et l'histoire*, 480.

40. Amyraut, *La morale*, vol. 4, 572.

41. Amyraut, *La morale*, vol. 3, 568–69.

42. Amyraut, *La morale*, vol. 3, 569.

43. On this dispute, see John Marshall, *John Locke, Toleration and Early Enlightenment Culture*, 418–39. On Jurieu's career and political thought, see Robin J. Howells, *Pierre Jurieu: Antinomian Radical*; see also Guy Howard Dodge, *The Political Theory of the Huguenots of the Dispersion*.

44. Jurieu, *Suite de l'accomplissement des Propheties*, 59.

45. Jurieu, *Suite*, 59.

46. Jurieu, *Des droits des deux souverains en matière de religion, la conscience et le prince*, 271–72.

47. On Anne du Bourg, Jurieu, *Histoire du Calvinisme*, 150; on the martyrs, *Histoire du Calvinisme*, 408.

48. Jurieu, *Histoire du Calvinisme*, 189.

49. Jurieu, *Les derniers efforts de l'innocence affligé, ou Entretiens curieux de deux catholiques romains*, 232.

50. Jurieu, *Histoire du Calvinisme*, 1. Maimbourg's book was the focus of much Protestant outrage: Bayle's book attacking it was burnt in Paris in 1683.

51. Jurieu, *Histoire du Calvinisme*, 250; see also Jurieu, the *Religion des Jesuites ou reflexions sur les inscriptions du pere Menestrier*, 113.

52. Antoine Furetière, *Dictionnaire universel*, s.v. "pitié."

CHAPTER 4

Note to epigraph: "Vivre en repos avec ceux qui sont de diverses Opinions, comme nous voyons en une famille . . . comme l'on dit que vitia uxoris aut sunt tollenda, aut toleranda." Quoted in *Mémoires de Condé*, ed. Denis-François Secousse, vol. 2, 612.

1. The text was first published anonymously as "Histoire" in the *Nouveau Mercure* in September 1718, and subsequently although with minor changes in the *Mercure de France* of June 1724 titled "La Comtesse de Tende, nouvelle historique, par Mme de La Fayette" and dated April 1663. Page numbers given parenthetically refer to the Pléiade edition: Marie-Madeleine Pioche de la Vergne, comtesse de La Fayette, *Œuvres complètes*, ed. Camille Esmein-Sarrazin, which also gives an account of the *nouvelle's* publication and imagined composition date (1235); the English translation of all Lafayette's texts cited in this chapter comes from the translation and edition by Terence Cave, *The Princesse de Clèves / The Princesse de Montpensier / The Comtesse de Tende*. I refer to the author throughout as Lafayette in keeping with current Anglo-American scholarly practice.

2. Montaigne tells us that the best thing to do when faced with a weeping woman is to distract her: "De la diversion" (III, 4), also discussed briefly in the first chapter. I'm grateful to Tim Chesters for diverting me to that essay.

3. The comte de Tende is a better reader than other husbands depicted: he starts to understand what is happening as soon he leaves the room. In this chapter I focus on Lafayette's historical *nouvelles*, but a similar motif appears in her earlier romance *Zayde*, in which Consalve desperately tries to decipher feminine sorrow.

4. The most straightforward and brief introduction to the complexities of naming prose fiction in early modern France is that by John D. Lyons, "1678: The Emergence of the Novel." A thorough account is given by Erica Harth in *Ideology and Culture in Seventeenth-Century France*, 129–79.

5. Many scholars have focused on Lafayette's engagement with historical accounts, especially with the historians Davila and Mézeray, and on the way in which she weaves intimate stories around historical events. On the seventeenth-century novel and its use of history, see especially Faith Beasley, *Revising Memory*. On the wars in the genre of the *nouvelle*, see René Démoris, "Les guerres de religion dans la nouvelle historique entre 1660 et 1680."

6. On the absence of narratorial sympathy in this text, see Micheline Cuénin, "La terreur sans la pitié: 'La Comtesse de Tende.'"

7. Biet, *Théâtre de la cruauté*, 57; see also Chapter 1.

8. Literary scholars such as Joan DeJean, for example, describe shifts in aristocratic marriage registered in literary texts, suggesting that individual choice was gradually becoming a newly important ideal in such marriages: see *Tender Geographies: Women and the Origins of the Novel in France*, 11, 109–14. Other literary scholars have maintained that the widely studied (English, Protestant) model of companionate marriage does not hold in the French case, where the question of choice of and within marriage was rather more constrained, and where relations between men and women took place within a framework of highly codified *galanterie*: see

Elizabeth Susan Wahl, *Invisible Relations: Representations of Female Intimacy in the Age of Enlightenment*, 75–76, 88. The attention of social historians of the ancien régime has been directed largely at popular marriages and generally those of the eighteenth century: see, for example, Suzanne Desan and Jeffrey Merrick, eds., *Family, Gender and Law in Early Modern France*. On marriage in seventeenth-century Protestant communities, see Jeffrey R. Watt, *The Making of Modern Marriage: Matrimonial Control and the Rise of Sentiment in Neuchâtel, 1550–1800*, whose introduction gives an excellent bibliographic overview on early modern marriage. On the legal question of marriage read through the prism of seventeenth-century texts including *La Princesse de Clèves*, see Christian Biet's *Droit et littérature sous l'Ancien Régime*, 175–224; in an exemplary reading of the novel, Biet argues that the period Lafayette represents in the novel is the moment of a crisis in marital law in France, and that the novel renders the vacillation over the status of marriage in this period, with particular attention to the status of the widow and the youngest son. See also the useful collection edited by Françoise Lavocat, *Le marriage et la loi dans la fiction narrative avant 1800*, and especially Frank Greiner, "L'alliance des contraires: Les unions inter-confessionnelles dans quelques romans du temps de l'édit de Nantes," 201–12, which describes romances in which love serves as a form of tolerance.

9. Stanley Cavell, *Pursuits of Happiness: The Hollywood Comedy of Remarriage*, 88.

10. Elizabeth Povinelli, *The Empire of Love*, 1, 188.

11. Furetière, *Dictionnaire universel*, s.v. "compatir."

12. A similar definition is given by Richelet's dictionary and by that of the Académie in 1694.

13. Randall Cotgrave, *Dictionarie of French and English Tongues*, s.v. "compatir."

14. The title of a sixteenth-century treatise might also alert us to the similarity of these cases: Peter Martyr Vermigli, *A treatise of the cohabitacyon of the faithfull with the unfaithfull* (Strasbourg, 1555). See also the work of Philip Benedict, which shows how marriage contracts in seventeenth-century Montpellier point to patterns in interconfessional relations during those years. Philip Benedict, "Confessionalization in France? Critical Reflections and New Evidence"; see also Benedict, "Faith, Fortune and Social Structure in Seventeenth-Century Montpellier."

15. *La Princesse de Montpensier* introduced the *nouvelle*, a short-form genre which would feature the use of real historical names rather than the antique appellations beloved by the mid-century multivolume heroic romances, and which also insisted on truth or verisimilitude.

16. Page numbers for *La Princesse de Montpensier* refer to the Droz edition, which uses the original 1662 printing: Madame de Lafayette, *Histoire de la Princesse de Montpensier sous le règne de Charles IXème roi de France / Histoire de la Comtesse de Tende*, ed. Micheline Cuénin, 94. I discuss edition and manuscript variance in the next paragraph. English references to the Terence Cave translation are detailed above.

17. I'm grateful to John O'Brien for this observation. On the language of fortune and Lafayette's novels, see John D. Lyons, *The Phantom of Chance*, 104–34.

18. In this discussion I have been drawing on the 1662 edition used by Cuénin in her Droz edition, but the "violent" variant I cite here is given in the Pléiade edition, ed. Camille Esmein-Sarrazin (44), which draws on the manuscript held as BnF NAF 1563, ffos 56–87. A stable edition of *Montpensier* is hard to establish. There are four manuscript copies of the text; in 1662 three publishers shared the (anonymous, as was standard for women writers) editions, so there are minor variants even in the 1662 editions. For the notes on and variants of the text, see Esmein-Sarrazin, 1208–1216. Further complicating this situation, we know that the writer Gilles Ménage made a number of editorial interventions on this text, on both a manuscript and a printed edition, and the discrepancies between these versions are often attributed to his

intervention; Lafayette did not publically acknowledge the text as her own (Esmein-Sarrazin, 1198). On these variations and the history of the text's cataloguing, see also Cuénin, 95. Some scholars suggest the text is more that of Ménage than Lafayette; I will not enter into this question here, for the notion of Lafayette's authorship is not central to my argument.

19. The aristocrat who is so overwhelmed by feeling that he is immobilized is a common feature of texts of this period. Witness Givry in Villedieu's *Les désordres de l'amour*, who is so stricken when Mademoiselle de Guise yells at him (after he, too, has broken into her room) "qu'il demeura apuyé contre un fauteuil comme s'il eût été un terme" (203) ["he remained leaning against a chair as if he were a Term"] (a Term is a Roman statue without limbs, and the word is often used in the period to describe immobility).

20. *De la Délicatesse*, premier dialogue (1671), Lafayette, *Œuvres complètes*, 57.

21. *Dictionnaire de l'Académie Françoise*, s.v "clémence."

22. Antoine Furetière, *Dictionnaire universel*, vol. 1, s.v. "clémence."

23. In contrast, Ruth Taylor argues that the linking of war and marriage makes war seem frivolous: "War as Metaphor in *La Princesse de Montpensier*," 324.

24. On Chabannes's insistence on being read as a private individual, see Elizabeth Goldsmith, "Les lieux de l'histoire dans *La Princesse de Montpensier*," 714–15.

25. François Eudes de Mézeray, *Histoire de France depuis Faramond*, vol. 2 (1646), 1100.

26. In happier outcomes, Benjamin Kaplan notes that some Huguenots were hidden by Catholics during the massacre: *Divided by Faith*, 251.

27. On the philosophical resonances of the narrative parsing of emotion in Lafayette, see Ellen McClure, "Cartesian Modernity and the *Princesse de Clèves*."

28. Anne-Lise François, *Open Secrets*, 67.

29. James Chandler uses this phrase to describe what Hume terms an "impression of reflection." *An Archaeology of Sympathy*, 172.

30. On the first Catholic criticism of the massacre, articulated around the time of the publication of *Montpensier*, see Goldsmith, "Les lieux de l'histoire," 711.

31. Mézeray, *Histoire de France depuis Faramond*, vol. 2, 1095.

32. Denis Crouzet, *La nuit de Saint Barthélemy*, 96–98. On the death of Coligny as iconic image of the wars, including an account of Guise's inspection of the body, see also Robert M. Kingdon, *Myths About the St. Bartholomew's Day Massacres*, 28–50. On the presence of the massacre in seventeenth-century writing more generally, see René Pintard and Hubert Carrier, "Ressouvenirs de la Saint-Barthélemy au XVIIe siècle."

33. Jean de Serres, *Histoires des choses mémorables avenues en France*, 431.

34. Michael Fried, *Absorption and Theatricality: Painting and Beholder in the Age of Diderot*.

35. David Denby, *Sentimental Narrative and the Social Order in France, 1760–1820*, 75.

36. Louise K. Horowitz, "Primary Sources: *La Princesse de Clèves*."

37. François, *Open Secrets*, 68.

38. Page numbers for the French refer to Lafayette, *Œuvres complètes*; for the English, to the Terence Cave translation.

39. See, for example, Brian Nelson, *Cambridge Introduction to French Literature*, which proclaims it to be "generally regarded by literary historians as the first modern novel in French" (54), or the *Œuvres complètes* edition where Camille Esmain-Sarrazin notes its storied status as "le premier roman moderne, inaugurant une voie radicalement neuve," 1305. For an elegant refutation of this narrative, see Nicholas Paige, "Lafayette's Impossible Princess: On (Not) Making Literary History," also *Before Fiction*, 35–61.

40. Lauren Berlant, *The Female Complaint*, 4. Anne-Vincent Buffault begins her account of the history of tears and reading with *La Princesse de Clèves* with Lafayette: "Déjà, au XVIIe siècle, *La Princesse de Clèves* a fait verser des larmes aux lecteurs." *Histoire des larmes*, 21. Buffault draws on the account given by Jean-Jacques Roubine, "La stratégie des larmes au XVIIe siècle."

41. On contemporary discussions of the novel, see Beasley, *Salons, History, and the Creation of Seventeenth-Century France*, 114–34.

42. In 1678, the editions of January, March, April, May, July, and October all featured material on *La Princesse de Clèves*. On the content and circulation of the paper, see Maurice Laugaa, *Lectures de Mme de Lafayette*, 20–26.

43. This is not quite the readerly sympathy of the eighteenth century. Nicholas Paige has argued that Lafayette's readers use the text as an occasion not to describe feelings they have already had, as will Rousseau's sentimental readers a century later, but rather to detail their reaction to the princess herself. Paige, *Before Fiction*, 123. On identification and interest in the eighteenth-century novel, see April Alliston's description of the centrality of interest to vocabularies of sympathy and establishment of sympathetic communities of readership: *Virtue's Faults*, 78. On the relation between fictiveness and identification, see especially Catherine Gallagher, *Nobody's Story*, who argues that invented characters can incite anyone to feel.

44. "Réponses à la Question Galante," letter of July 1678, cited Lafayette, *Œuvres complètes*, 525–26.

45. Valincour, *Lettres à madame la marquise de XXX sur le sujet de La Princesse de Clèves*, 278–79. The subsequent joking in the text indicates that "tender heart" is in this instance a euphemism.

46. Valincour, *Lettres à madame la marquise de XXX*, 128.

47. Paige, *Before Fiction*, 52.

48. Charnes's *Conversations sur la Critique de la "Princesse de Clèves"* (1679) responds to Valincour's original accusation. I quote from Charnes in Lafayette, *Œuvres complètes*, 635; Valincour, 47). Similarly, a reader featured in the *Mercure galant*, known as the *géomètre de Guyenne* (probably Fontenelle), wrote of the scene in which Nemours overhears the *aveu* that "cela sent un peu les traits de l'*Astrée*" [it smells a bit of the *Astrée*]. Lafayette, *Œuvres complètes*, 515.

49. Richelet, *Dictionnaire*, s.v. "pitoiable."

50. All references here to Madame de Villedieu, *Les désordres de l'amour*, ed. Micheline Cuénin; all translations of Villedieu are my own.

51. On Villedieu, see especially Faith Beasley, *Salons*, 147–66.

52. Nemours is not the only one who sees her pity; his rival Guise tells her he is more to be pitied than Nemours since she does not care for him, and the narrator describes how Guise will seek to forget the princess by pursuing military glory, only to find disappointment and death.

53. Clèves's hopeful account of pity responds to another apparently transparent affect, sincerity; in a reading of the Sancerre (pronounced "sincère") story, Hélène Merlin has described how sincerity is held up as an ideal throughout Lafayette's novel. *Public et littérature en France au XVIIe siècle*, 333–39.

54. Lafayette, *Œuvres complètes*, 1376, Cave 50.

55. Bussy-Rabutin, in a letter to Mme de Sévigné: "Une femme dit rarement à son mari qu'on est amoureux d'elle, mais jamais qu'elle ait de l'amour pour un autre que pour lui; et d'autant moins qu'en se jetant à ses genoux, comme fait la princesse, elle peut faire croire à son mari qu'elle n'a gardé aucunes bornes dans l'outrage qu'elle lui a fait." ["A woman rarely tells her husband that someone is in love with her, and never that she loves someone other than him;

especially since in flinging herself at his knees, as the princess does, she might make her husband believe that she had observed no boundaries in the outrage she has inflicted on him."] Letter of June 29, 1678, cited Laugaa, *Lectures de Mme de Lafayette*, 18. See also Valincour, who notes that "au lieu de la relever, il porte *ses mains à sa teste*. Je ne sçai pas à quel dessein" ["instead of lifting her up, he lifts his hands to his head. I don't know what for"] (207).

56. On the untranslatability of "aveu," see DeJean, *Tender Geographies*, 118–21.

57. For one of the more interesting accounts comparing Villedieu and Lafayette, see Nancy K. Miller, "Tender Economies: Mme de Villedieu and the Costs of Indifference." On a very different note, Micheline Cuénin describes a twentieth-century critical supposition that in fact Villedieu took the scene of the *aveu* from an early draft of *La Princesse de Clèves*, but she gives this theory little credence. See her edition of *Les désordres de l'amour*, xvi–xvii.

58. See, for example, Nancy Miller, "Emphasis Added: Plots and Plausibilities in Women's Fiction"; Domna Stanton, "The Ideal of 'Repos' in Seventeenth-Century French Literature"; DeJean, *Tender Geographies*, 114–26.

59. Although I am not embarking here upon an intellectual history of Lafayette's links to discourses of religious toleration, let me note a path for such work indicated by Faith Beasley, who describes how Mme de la Sablière's salon (frequented by Lafayette) provided the scene for figures such as the writer François Bernier and the diamond merchant Jean-Baptiste Tavernier to share their knowledge of India and the Mughal court, in particular that court's acceptance of religious pluralism. Beasley, "Versailles Meets the Taj Mahal."

60. The marking of this space is not only figurative; Louise Horowitz has argued that the choice of the Pyrenees as the space of the princess's final retreat might have particular political significance when one considers the important Huguenot allegiances of that region. "Primary Sources," 168.

61. On efforts at religious pluralism and coexistence in the seventeenth century, see Philip Benedict, "Un roi, une loi, deux fois: Parameters for the History of Catholic-Reformed Coexistence in France, 1555–1685"; Keith P. Luria, *Sacred Boundaries: Religious Coexistence and Conflict in Early Modern France*; Keith Cameron, Mark Greengrass, and Penny Roberts., eds., *The Adventure of Religious Pluralism in Early Modern France*; Gregory Hanlon, *Confession and Community in Seventeenth-Century France*.

62. My reading forms a domestic counterpoint to Timothy Hampton's argument that in seventeenth-century France both the world of the novel and of the nation-state define themselves in relation to outside influences, closing off their territorial borders in parallel. *La Princesse de Clèves* puts an end, he posits, to the international intrigue represented by romance, and stresses the Frenchness of the novelistic form in so doing. *Literature and Nation in the Sixteeenth Century*, 137–49.

CHAPTER 5

1. I draw the bones of this account from Jean Delumeau, *Naissance et affirmation de la Réforme*, and Elisabeth Labrousse, *Essai sur la révocation de l'Édit de Nantes: Une foi, une loi, un roi?* See also Janine Garrisson, *L'Édit de Nantes*; Jean Quéniart, *La Révocation de l'édit de Nantes*; Samuel Mours, *Le protestantisme en France au XVIIe siècle*; Jean Orcibal, *Louis XIV et les protestants*.

2. Christian Jouhaud, *La main de Richelieu ou le pouvoir cardinal*, 138.

3. Delumeau, *Naissance*, 191.

4. Delumeau, *Naissance*, 194; Labrousse, *Une foi*, 65.

5. Labrousse, *Une foi*, 168.

6. On Protestant civil status in relation to emigration see Charlotte C. Wells, *Law and Citizenship in Early Modern France*, 113–20.

7. Vauban objected to the edict largely on strategic and economic grounds. His account was sent to Louvois, minister for war, who probably did not present it to the king. Vauban, *Mémoire pour le rappel des Huguenots*, 5.

8. On the sixteenth-century rhetoric of royal pardon (including tactical compassion) and its replacement by a new emphasis on *oubliance* and amnesty, see Andrea Frisch, *Forgetting Differences*, 26–62.

9. Nicolas Caussin, *La cour sainte*, vol. 1, 168.

10. Jacques Esprit, *La fausseté des vertus humaines*, vol. 1, 281.

11. Konstan, *Pity Transformed*, 98–101. M. B. Dowling suggests that, just as in later periods, Roman clemency was related to a range of similar concepts—*moderatio, indulgentia, misericordia, mansuetudo*—but that clemency alone signaled not just an attitude but also an action, an active forgiveness of wrongdoing (Dowling, *Clemency and Cruelty in the Roman World*). On these complicated lexical fields, see also Yasmina Benferhat, *Du bon usage de la douceur en politique dans l'œuvre de Tacite*.

12. See Victoria Kahn, *Wayward Contracts*, 239.

13. See Éric Méchoulan, "La douceur du politique"; on the gendering of *douceur* see Lewis Seifert, *Manning the Margins*, 113.

14. Andrew Shifflett, " 'How Many Virtues Must I Hate': Katherine Philips and the Politics of Clemency," 104.

15. Charles II, King of England, *His Majestie's Declaration* (1666).

16. Announcement of July 27, 1660, cited in Shifflett, "How Many Virtues," 124.

17. I'm indebted to my discussions with Oliver Arnold for this insight on the petitioning of parliamentary compassion, and look forward to his work on the question.

18. *Plaise à S.A.R., avoir compassion du sieur de Marchin* (1650).

19. Leah Whittington, *Renaissance Suppliants*, 118.

20. Natalie Zemon Davis has shown how sixteenth-century French suspects crafted their tales in order to beg for pardon (*Fiction in the Archives*); Andrea Frisch shows how Jean de La Taille, writing at the time of the Wars of Religion, maneuvers the genre of the remonstrance in order to redraft the relation between Parlement and king (*Forgetting Differences*, 116–19); Elizabeth Wingrove shows that eighteenth-century writing from the Bastille played out a similarly affectively fraught political bond with immediately painful consequences for specific individuals ("Philoctetes in the Bastille").

21. This letter appears in manuscript in a *Recueil factice* at the Bibliothèque Mazarine which gathers documents relating to the Fouquet trial (cote 4° 19385). The page numbers here refer to the transcription given in Jean-Louis Carra, ed., *Mémoires historiques et authentiques sur la Bastille* (1789), vol. 1, 63; I have consulted both versions and the Carra is a faithful transcription. I take the Fouquet case here not as a singular incident but as an example of a larger rhetoric, of which the archives contain many more examples.

22. See also the letter from Fouquet's wife asking for clemency on the occasion of the fête of saint Louis: "Placet que Mme la Surintendant présenta au Roi le jour de sa fête", in Carra, *Mémoires*, 62. In an "Advis sur les principaux points contenus dans les libelles exposées au public pour la justification de M. Fouquet, adressé aux auteurs," even critics of Fouquet acknowledge that it would be possible to have "quelque compassion de sa chute" ["some compassion for his

fall"], if only his justifiers could stop their ridiculous arguments. (Both these documents are in the Mazarine *Recueil*).

23. Jean-François Senault, *De l'usage des passions*, 308. In one poem of the period which defended the king in response to the pleas of Fouquet's friends and family, an allegorized Justice notes that grace and pity must cede to her: "Réponse de la Chambre de Justice à la France," in the *Recueil* and Carra, *Mémoires*, 61. Other less high-profile miscreants were luckier recipients of the king's pity. In 1693 one Henri-Antoine Colleson de Beronne was released from the Bastille because, La Reynié the supervisor of police reported, "Le Roi touché du pitoyable état de ce gentilhomme" ["The King touched by the pitiful state of this gentleman"] chose to do so. Significantly, the man in question was not charged with anything to do with Protestantism (Carra, *Mémoires*, 281).

24. In modern English and French, we distinguish between the terms "pity" and "piety." But as Blandine Colot establishes, that distinction is forged only in the seventeenth century (Italian and Spanish maintain the more complicated polysemy—think of a *pietà*). Colot traces the movement of *pietas* from a Roman sense of duty (familial or more largely political), through the Christian affective inflections of this language and then to Augustine, who drew *pietas* into more distinctly Christian territory by tying it firmly to worship. In Old French, she notes, the capacity to distinguish between pity and piety exists from the eleventh century, although the terms often appear as synonyms. For Furetière in his 1690 dictionary, this heritage is clearly signaled: "Ce mot vient du Latin *pietas*." ["This word comes from the Latin *pietas*."] Blandine Colot, "Pietas," 942–45; Furetière, *Dictionnaire universel*, s.v. "pitié."

25. François Laplanche, *L'écriture, le sacré et l'histoire*, 488.

26. Peter Burke, *The Fabrication of Louis XIV*, 102.

27. Édits de pacification, VI. Paix de la Rochelle. Édit de Boulogne, http://elec.enc.sor bonne.fr/editsdepacification/edit_06 (accessed October 7, 2015).

28. *Mercure galant*, 1685, vol. 1, January, 191.

29. *Mercure galant*, 1685, vol. 1, January, 193.

30. Senault, *De l'usage des passions*, 308.

31. Gabriel-François Le Jay, *Le Triomphe de la Religion sous Louis le Grand* (1687). I return to a reading of this text later in the chapter.

32. "Huguenots, consolez-vous, / Si l'on vous fait violence, / Un jour vous le prendrez tous /Pour un effet de clemence." ["Huguenots, console yourselves, / If violence is done to you, / One day you will all see it / As an effect of clemency."] *Mercure galant*, 1686, vol. 2, February, 47.

33. On the trope, see Quentin Skinner, "Paradiastole: Redescribing the Vices as Virtues."

34. *Mercure galant*, 1686, vol. 2, February, 23.

35. Le Jay, *Le Triomphe de la Religion*. I have written at more length about this text and the centrality of objects to absolutist discourse on the emotions in "Being Moved: Louis XIV's Triumphant Tenderness and the Protestant Object"; the images from the text can be found (open access) in that article.

36. Cotgrave, *Dictionarie*, s.v. "triomphe."

37. Le Jay, *Triomphe*, 94.

38. On Louis's diamond mania, see Joan DeJean, *The Essence of Style*, 161–76. On French diamonds, see also Marcia Pointon, *Brilliant Effects: A Cultural History of Gem Stones and Jewellery*, 44. On Tavernier and the diamonds, see also Faith Beasley, "Versailles Meets the Taj Mahal," 207–22.

39. Théodore de Bèze, *Histoire ecclésiastique des églises réformées au royaume de France*.

40. Sara Ahmed, *The Promise of Happiness*, 45.

41. Hubert Bost, "Élie Benoist et l'historiographie de l'édit de Nantes"; on Benoist's internationalism and Huguenot relations with England, see G. C. Gibbs, "The Reception of the Huguenots in England and the Dutch Republic."

42. Benoist, *Histoire de l'édit de Nantes*, vol. 2, 442. Long after the siege of La Rochelle, the town did indeed continue to figure beleaguered Protestantism to a European audience. A 1681 Protestant pamphlet purporting to be a letter from the town (but printed in London) tells of the horrors inflicted on Huguenots in order to counter what the author alleges are lies spread by Catholic spies among London tradespeople. *A Letter from Rochel in France.*

43. Benoist, *Histoire de l'édit de Nantes*, vol. 3, n.p.

44. Jean Aymon, ed. *Tous les synodes nationaux des eglises reformées de France*, vol. 1, 335.

45. Benoist, *Histoire de l'édit de Nantes*, vol. 2, appendix p. 92.

46. I have written about *Cinna* and clemency elsewhere: Katherine Ibbett, "Italy and France, or How Pierre Corneille Became an Anti-Machiavel." On that question see also Éric Méchoulan, "Revenge and Poetic Justice in Classical France."

47. On the early modern insistence on the bodily presence of the ambassador, see Timothy Hampton, *Fictions of Embassy*, 8.

48. I reread these bodily transactions with a keener eye after reading Leah Whittington on gestures of kneeling supplication: *Renaissance Suppliants*, 114–59.

49. An English-language pamphlet of 1685 speaks of imprisoned Huguenots who imagine that an encounter with the king would change everything: "If their Humble Complaints could but meet with a free access to His Majesty's Throne, he would be moved with Compassion towards them." *A Full Account of the Barbarous and Unhumane Usages of the French Protestants in France*, 1–2.

50. Debarati Sanyal, "Calais's 'Jungle': Refugees, Biopolitics, and the Arts of Resistance, 5."

51. Labrousse, *Une foi*, 34.

52. Carra, *Mémoires*, vol. 1, 213–14.

53. Carra, *Mémoires*, vol. 1, "Première Lettre aux Catholiques-Romains," 214–15.

54. David A. Hollinger, "How Wide the Circle of the 'We'?"

55. Interpellation of international opinion was of course an option open to Catholic partisans too. In 1667 a dual-language French and German Protestant account of the erosion of Nantes's original terms complained that Catholics published "chez les estrangers" how well they had treated the Protestants. *Relation succincte du pitoyable estat ou sont maintenant les eglises reformées de France en l'an 1667*, 64.

56. Jean Claude, *An account of the persecutions and oppressions of the Protestants in France*, 46; Pierre Simond, *La discipline de Jesus Christ*, A3 verso. A surprising genre of Protestant *Larmes* increasingly praised Orange as the new center of compassionate action. The pastor Jacques Pineton de Chambrun's *Les larmes* of 1688 gave a history of Protestant persecution and praised the princess for her "compassions les plus tendres" ["tenderest compassions"] which set her apart from the courtly and uncaring high society: *Les larmes de Jacques Pineton de Chambrun* (1688). On this genre see Marianne Carbonnier-Burkard, "Larmes réformées."

57. Claude, *An account of the persecutions*, 47.

58. *The deplorable state and condition of the poor French Protestants commiserated.*

59. *The History of the Persecutions of the Reformed Churches*, 4.

60. Giorgio Agamben, *Homo Sacer.*

61. *Relation succincte du pitoyable estat*, 60.

62. Sanyal's analysis of Calais, similarly, points to the limitations of Agamben's model for imagining political life: "Calais's 'Jungle.'" Sanyal's account shows how the language of

humanitarianism (whose beginnings I trace here) and of biopolitics come to "a convergence" in accounts of the camp, "both of which pivot upon figuring the refugee as 'bare life' and apolitical, a speechless victim[s]."

63. Claude, *An account of the persecutions*, 1, 46.

64. On the diaspora, the literature is vast and insistently sectarian. For a useful overview of who goes where, see Eckart Birnstiel, ed. *La diaspora des Huguenots*. On the centrality of refugee experience to religious ideas at this time, see Nicolas Terpstra, *Religious Refugees in the Early Modern World*, which gives a comparatist perspective on refugee movements and resettlements across Europe.

65. Pierre Jurieu, *Lettre de quelques protestans pacifiques*, 8.

66. The scholarship on Bayle is vast and contentious. For a useful theological introduction see Hubert Bost, *Pierre Bayle et la religion*; for the prime defense of Bayle as Protestant precursor to the Enlightenment see Elisabeth Labrousse, *Pierre Bayle: Hétérodoxie et rigorisme*, and especially on the passions and error, vol. 2, 69–102; for a less sectarian version of the same Enlightenment teleology see Jonathan Israel, "Pierre Bayle's Political Thought"; also on Bayle and the passions, see Ruth Whelan, *The Anatomy of Superstition*, 81–83; for an overview of scholarly approaches to Bayle's toleration see Jean-Michel Gros, "La tolérance et le problème théologico-politique"; on the divisions between Bayle and Jurieu, see Thomas M. Lennon, *Reading Bayle*, 81–106.

67. Pierre Bayle, *De la tolérance*, ed. Jean-Michel Gros, 52. Bayle writes the *Commentaire* in the voice of an Englishman; in his text the characteristic Protestant reach to an international community becomes also a rhetorical affordance.

68. Pierre Bayle, *Ce que c'est que la France toute catholique sous le règne de Louis le Grand*, ed. Labrousse, 2.

69. For this use of the word see Bayle, *De la tolérance*, 58, 59, and 116.

70. Bayle, *De la tolérance*, 175–76.

71. Sévigné, *Lettres 1684–1696*, 360–61.

72. On the alliance between Louis XIV and James II see Steven Pincus, *1688*, 318–22. Maintenon was one of the rare people at court sympathetic to James, and he was given a privileged position seated at Louis's right hand. See Edward Gregg, "France, Rome and the Exiled Stuarts," 18. On James's second visit, see Raymond Picard, *Nouveau corpus raciniarum*, 236.

73. February 1689, cited in Picard, *Nouveau corpus raciniarum*, 236.

74. Jean Dubu, *Racine aux miroirs*, 321.

75. On *Esther*'s performance see Jean Racine, *Œuvres complètes* ed. Georges Forestier, vol. 1, 1674–76. For a somewhat hypothetical account of the shaping and context of the play, see Jean Orcibal, *La genèse d'Esther et d'Athalie*.

76. The translation and commentary had been finished by 1684: *Œuvres complètes*, ed. Forestier, 1682. On Racine and the Bible see also Dubu, 313–26; on *Esther*, see Dubu, 327–60.

77. *La Bible: Tobie, Judith, Esther*, trans. Isaac Lemaitre de Sacy, ed. Philippe Sellier (Est 3:8).

78. The preface is numbered separately from the play; I give page numbers from Jean Racine, *Œuvres complètes*, ed. Forestier, vol. 1 (948), and for the play itself I give line references from that edition; English translations give page numbers from Jean Racine, *Complete Plays*, trans. Samuel Solomon, vol. 2, 312. Where no page number is given for the translation, the words are my own.

79. Racine, ed. Forestier, *Œuvres complètes*, 1693.

80. John Campbell, "The Politics of Esther," 26.

81. On this necessary skepticism see Racine, *Œuvres complètes*, ed. Forestier, 1684. The reading of Esther as Maintenon is also supported by accounts of Brienne le Jeune's *Mémoires*, circulated at Port Royal in 1683–84, which had already described Maintenon as a second Esther (Nicholas Hammond, *Fragmentary Voices*, 157).

82. March 1689, cited in Picard, *Nouveau corpus raciniarum* (239), who gives the attribution as "(Baron de Breteuil?) Sur la pièce de M. de Racine intitulée *Esther*, et représentée devant le Roi par les Filles de Saint-Cyr.Bibliothèque de l'Arsenal, ms 3136, page 229; ms 2777, pages 278 and 279. Attribué au duc de Nevers in ms 3290 p.426 of Arsenal." Picard goes on to cite a response text sympathetic to Protestantism.

83. *Esther, tragédie tirée de l'Ecriture Sainte*, par Mons. Racine, Seconde Edition à Neuchâtel; cited in Picard, *Nouveau corpus raciniarum*, 249.

84. Déborah Blocker, "Figures du peuple d'Israël dans l'Esther de Jean Racine," 180. For a reading of Esther that engages allegory without falling into stasis, see Susan Maslan, "Melancholy Racine: Benjamin's *Trauerspiel* and Literary Jews." Maslan argues that the allegorical slippages of this play come about through the two ways in which Jewishness figures in the text: first as a historical community separated from Racine's readership by religious difference, that is, Jews who will not become Christians or who are what Maslan terms "future ruins," and second as the community which will make Christianity possible. On Jewishness and identification with the Esther dramas, the abbé d'Aubignac had hazarded that Du Ryer's *Esther* had been a greater hit in Rouen than in Paris because of that city's considerable Jewish community. Aubignac, *La pratique du théâtre*, ed. Hélène Baby, 121.

85. Du Ryer, *Esther*, ed. Edmund J. Campion, 39; see also Antoine de Montchrestien, *Aman*, ed. George Otto Seiver, in which the pitiful language is borne out in both manuscripts.

86. On musicality and the emotions in *Esther*, see Anne Piéjus, *Le théâtre des demoiselles*, 437–507.

87. All references to Jean Racine, *Œuvres complètes*, vol. 1, ed. Georges Forestier.

88. On this reading of history, see Ann Delehanty, "Reconciling Divine and Political Authority in Racine's *Esther*." On the significance of memory in *Esther*, see also Hammond, *Fragmentary Voices*, 157–62.

89. Jean Racine, *Œuvres complètes*, vol.1, ed. Forestier, 1683.

90. Rei Terada, *Feeling in Theory*, 46.

CHAPTER 6

Note to epigraph: David Hume, letter to Adam Smith, July 28, 1759, *Correspondence of Adam Smith*, 43.

1. "Les salles des Pauvres seront ornees autant qu'il se pourra de tableaux, cartouches, et sentences de devotion propres à exciter la charité envers les Pauvres." ["The wards for the poor will be ornamented as much as possible with paintings, cartouches, and devotional texts to excite charity towards the poor."] *Le coutumier et petites regles des religieuses hospitalieres de la congregation de saint Joseph*, 37.

2. Lisa Stevenson, *Life Beside Itself*, 134.

3. Michel Foucault, *Histoire de la folie à l'âge classique*, 67–109.

4. Arlie Hochschild, *The Managed Heart: Commercialization of Human Feeling.*

5. Giorgio Agamben, *The Highest Poverty*, xi.

6. Early modern hospitals were often known as "lieux pitoyables": see Charles IX, *Edict du roy sur le faict ordre et reiglement des hospitaulx et lieux pitoyables* (Rouen 1561).

7. See especially Colin Jones, *The Charitable Imperative: Hospitals and Nursing in Ancien Régime and Revolutionary France*. Jones's work gave rise to a boom in charitable and hospital history. For an example of more recent work in this vein, see Tim McHugh, *Hospital Politics in Seventeenth-Century France*.

8. See Jean Imbert, "Les prescriptions hospitalières du concile de Trente et leur diffusion en France."

9. Miriam Ticktin, *Casualties of Care*, 69.

10. Historians and theorists of hospitality figure it as a familial or household practice. Felicity Heal shows that in early modern England, hospitality and charity diverge to form quite separate discourses, with charity becoming that which is practiced outside the home (*Hospitality in Early Modern England*). The work of Jacques Derrida on hospitality has pushed this question to a central place in critical theory, but Derrida's work has been challenged by feminist scholars attending to the role of gender in hospitality: see, for example, Tracy McNulty, *The Hostess*; also Nancy J. Holland, "'With Arms Wide Open': Of *Hospitality* and the Most Intimate Stranger"; Maurice Hamington, ed., *Feminism and Hospitality*. For a sociology of contemporary hospitality which also traces the long history of its discourse in western Europe, see Anne Gotman, *Le sens de l'hospitalité*.

11. Article 17 of the foundational edict of the Hôpital Général, 1656, cited by Claire Garnier, *Soin des corps, soin des âmes*, 29.

12. On the establishment and range of the Dames, see Barbara Diefendorf, *From Penitence to Charity*; Elizabeth Rapley, *The Dévotes*, 84–90. On the jelly, see Jones, *The Charitable Imperative*, 93.

13. On the establishment of the *filles*, see Rapley, *The Dévotes*, 79–83; on their role throughout the century, see Susan E. Dinan, *Women and Poor Relief in Seventeenth-Century France*. For an important overview of missionary work at France and abroad, see Dominique Deslandres, *Croire et faire croire*. For an account of the efforts of Vincent de Paul and the subsequent explosion of charitable institutions, see Raymond Lucien Chalumeau, "L'assistance aux pauvres malades."

14. Cited by Chalumeau, "L'assistance aux pauvres malades," 77.

15. Cited by Pierre Coste, *Le grand saint du grand siècle: Monsieur Vincent*, vol. 2, 497. On the Hôpital Général, see Rapley, *The Dévotes*, 91–92.

16. Laurence Brockliss and Colin Jones, *The Medical World of Early Modern France*, 269.

17. Brockliss and Jones, *The Medical World*, 259.

18. McHugh, *Hospital Politics*, 31–37.

19. Dinan, *Women and Poor Relief*, 108.

20. Both Diefendorf and Jones make this argument.

21. Jones, *The Charitable Imperative*, 39.

22. On the naming of the Jesuit writings as *relations* and their problematic editorial history, see Micah True, *Masters and Students*, xiv–xv.

23. On women's orders in Quebec, see Dominique Deslandres, "Femmes missionaires en Nouvelle-France." For an account of what we know of Amerindian women's lives through European women's accounts, see Natalie Zemon Davis, "Iroquois Women: European Women." On European missionary women in Canada, see Deslandres, *Croire et faire croire*, 356–389. On race and later French colonial policy, see especially Saliha Belmessous, "Assimilation and Racialism in Seventeenth and Eighteenth-Century French Colonial Policy."

24. On Le Jeune's wishes and the subsequent founding of the Quebec hospital see François Rousseau's broadly Foucauldian account of the Quebec order of Hospitalière nuns, *La croix et le scalpel: Histoire des Augustines et de l'Hôtel-Dieu de Québec. Tome 1: 1639–1892*; for a Weberian take on the same order, which describes early heroism giving way to bureaucracy see Catherine Fino, *L'hospitalite, figure sociale de la charité: Deux fondations hospitalières à Québec*.

25. A biography of one of the Quebec nuns is dedicated to Aiguillon and praises her efforts at home and abroad: "votre charite . . . penetre encore jusqu'aux pais les plus eloigniez des Infideles" ["your charity penetrates even into the most distant lands of infidels"]. Paul Ragueneau SJ, *La vie de la mere Catherine de Saint Augustin religieuse hospitaliere*, dedication. For the funeral oration see Esprit Fléchier, *Oraisons funèbres*, vol. 1, 109.

26. Rousseau, *La croix et le scalpel*, 41.

27. On these developments and on the Amerindian connections of Dieppe, see Rousseau, *La croix et le scalpel*, 34–38.

28. On this pattern of endowment, see Deslandres, *Croire et faire croire*, 361.

29. Gédéon Tallemant des Réaux, *Historiettes*, vol. 1, 311.

30. Rénald Lessard, *Se soigner au Canada*, 47; Deslandres, *Croire et faire croire*, 365.

31. Rousseau, *La croix et le scalpel*, 55–58.

32. Rousseau, *La croix et le scalpel*, 71.

33. Jeanne-Françoise Juchereau (Mère de St.-Ignace), *Les Annales de l'Hôtel-Dieu de Québec*, 148; see also Rousseau, *La croix et le scalpel*, 127.

34. See, for example, the letter from the Mother Superior of the Hospitalière nuns in Quebec dated October 20, 1667, in Thwaites, ed., *The Jesuit Relations*, vol. 51, 113–15. Such letters were printed separately from the Relations but inserted into some copies of them.

35. Laurier Lacroix, ed., *Les arts en Nouvelle-France*, 47.

36. Thwaites, *Jesuit Relations*, vol. 22, 172; all translations given are from the parallel page in this edition. I have avoided using nineteenth-century editions of early modern texts throughout this book, but Thwaites's multivolume and bilingual collections of these writings are invaluable and in themselves a historic event.

37. Thwaites, *Jesuit Relations*, vol. 49, 120.

38. For a fine reading of the tropes of Jesuit descriptions of Amerindian cruelty, see True, *Masters and Students*, 83–112; on the differential understandings of Amerindian shows of compassion, see John Robb, " 'Meaningless Violence' and the Lived Body," 94–95.

39. Thwaites, *Jesuit Relations*, vol. 47, 50; vol. 47, 230–32 (with slight modification of the translation).

40. Thwaites, *Jesuit Relations*, vol. 49, 128–30.

41. Thwaites, *Jesuit Relations*, vol. 46, 94.

42. For a serious engagement with this common judgment, see Mary Baine Campbell, "The Dreaming Body: Cartesian Psychology, Enlightenment Anthropology, and the Jesuits in Nouvelle France."

43. Juchereau, *Annales de l'Hôtel-Dieu de Québec*, 12.

44. Some one hundred and fifty miles to the south of Quebec, Montreal was settled in a commercial-religious compromise characteristic of the history of Nouvelle France. In 1635 Jean-Jacques Olier, who had founded the Paris church of Saint Sulpice, met LeRoyer; they created a Société de Notre Dame which in 1640 bought part of the island of Montreal from the commercial Compagnie des Cent Associés. For a seventeenth-century account of this process, see François Dollier de Casson, *Histoire de Montréal*.

45. On Mance see Deslandres, *Croire et faire croire*, 382. The mission was funded by the widow Madame de Bullion; on this financing see Claire Garnier, *Soin des corps, soin des âmes*, 76.

46. She also brought with her a considerable number of religious objects and paintings (Lacroix, *Les arts en Nouvelle-France*, 56). For a brief history of the Montreal hospitalières, see Micheline d'Allaire, *Les communautés religieuses de Montréal*, vol. 1, 53–68. On the strictly medical side of the operation, see Hervé Gagnon, *Soigner le corps et l'âme*, who gives an excellent bibliography on medicine in Quebec. See also Lessard, *Se soigner au Canada*. For a very sectarian history of the hospital seen from inside the order, with a collection of important documents in appendix, see Maria Mondoux RHSJ, *L'Hôtel-Dieu, premier hôpital de Montréal, 1642–1763*. For a study which puts the Montreal institution in useful comparison with hospitals in Paris and the Auvergne, see Garnier's Foucauldian account, *Soin des corps, soin des âmes*.

47. Joseph Grandet, *La Vie de Mademoiselle de Melun* (1687). (The archivist of the Hospitalière order suggested to me that this book, which they now own, could also have been present in the original collections; even if this is not the case it seems likely that the young establishment would have had similar biographies of holy women.) On the importance of biographies of holy women in charitable organizations, see Diefendorf, *From Penitence to Charity*, 20–21.

48. Roland Barthes, *How to Live Together: Novelistic Simulations of Some Everyday Spaces*, 118.

49. The Hospitalière order had clashed constantly against ecclesiastical authorities; in Angers the city's Jansenist bishop Henry Arnauld sought to impose a new constitution on the congregation and finally got his way. In 1662, after the death of LeRoyer, Arnauld drew up the constitutions in an effort to regularize the order. Not all houses responded positively, with La Flèche holding out until the end of the century. See Marie-Claude Dinet-Lecomte, *Les sœurs hospitalières en France*, 119–23; Garnier, *Soin des corps, soin des âmes*, 82.

50. This democratic transparency was nonetheless accompanied by a distinction made between the *filles*, of whom up to thirty were admitted, and up to six domestic sisters, i.e., those who performed the manual labor or other distasteful tasks of the community, including washing the male patients, and were not allowed voting rights. *Constitutions*, 9.

51. On such texts see Nicholas D. Paige, *Being Interior*.

52. Monique Scheer, "Are Emotions a Kind of Practice?" 209.

53. *Le coutumier et petites regles des religieuses hospitalières de la congregation de saint Joseph*.

54. St. Joseph replaced the previous edition's "IHS," nestling in the heart of a tulip (with thanks to Diana Sorenson for her reading of this change).

55. *Dictionary of Canadian Biography* online, vol. 2, 1701–1740, s.v. "Morin, Marie." http://www.biographi.ca/009004-119.01 f.php?&id_nbr=1002&&PHPSESSID=ychzfqkvzape (accessed November 27, 2015).

56. Marie Morin, *Histoire simple et veritable / Les Annales de l'Hôtel-Dieu de Montréal, 1659–1725*, ed. Ghislaine Legendre, 8. All page numbers refer to this edition.

57. Damien Boquet, *L'ordre de l'affect au Moyen Age*.

58. For an overview of these arguments in response to John Rawls and others, see Catriona Mackenzie and Natalie Stoljar, "Introduction: Autonomy Refigured." On these questions see also John Philip Christman and Joel Anderson, eds., *Autonomy and the Challenges of Liberalism*. For the most cogent account of recent work in relational autonomy, see Marilyn Friedman, *Autonomy, Gender, Politics*. Feminist explorations of relational autonomy were launched by Jennifer Nedelsky, "Reconceiving Autonomy: Sources, Thoughts and Possibilities." A good overview of feminist critiques of autonomy is given in Mackenzie and Stoljar, "Autonomy Refigured."

59. Carol Gilligan, *In a Different Voice: Psychological Theory and Women's Development*. On

these "care critiques," see also Mackenzie and Stoljar, "Autonomy Refigured," 9; Friedman, *Autonomy, Gender, Politics*, 83; Eva Feder Kittay and Ellen K. Feder, eds., *The Subject of Care*. For a range of European responses to such philosophy from within a health care context, see Carlo Leget, Chris Gastmans, and Marian Verkerk, eds., *Care, Compassion and Recognition*. The reception of care theory has been of particular interest in republican France. On that history, see Patricia Paperman, *Care et sentiments*; for other accounts of care theory in French, see Jacques Ricot, *Du bon usage de la compassion*, which gives an excellent review of the lexicon of care from the eighteenth century on; see also Emmanuel Petit, *L'economie du care*; Patricia Paperman and Sandra Laugier, *Le souci des autres*.

60. Jennifer Nedelsky proposes the metaphor of child rearing as a figure for understanding relationality ("Reconceiving Autonomy, 7).

61. Linda Barclay, "Autonomy and the Social Self."

62. Morin, *Histoire simple et veritable*, 137.

63. Contrast this with the account Foucault gives of the Revolutionary Comité de Mendicité and its scheme to create communal houses for those sufferers without families, so they could be surrounded by what the committee termed "des êtres naturellement compatissants" ["naturally compassionate beings"]. *Naissance de la clinique*, 39.

64. Morin's spelling is consistently irregular, but her *compation* perhaps speaks of some familiarity with Latin.

65. The desire to share in Jesuit physical suffering can also be observed in the writings of the Quebec Ursuline Marie de l'Incarnation, who on first arrival in Canada longs for physical martyrdom, before learning to content herself with different forms of sacrifice and suffering available to those bound by the rule of enclosure. See Katherine Ibbett, "Reconfiguring Martyrdom in the Colonial Context."

66. Cotgrave, *Dictionarie*, s.v. "caresse"; *Dictionnaire de l'Académie Française*, s.v. "caresse". The term appears in another seventeenth-century professional account, also given by a nonelite figure: when the builder of the Canal du Midi Pierre-Paul Riquet writes in 1669 to Colbert about his new collaborator La Feuille, he describes how La Feuille gives "tant de caresses, tant d'assurances du bon estat de mes travaux, que je le croirois mon amy, si l'on ne m'assuroit du contraire" ["so many caresses, so many assurances of the good state of my works, that I would believe him my friend, if I had not been assured of the contrary"]. Jean-Baptiste Colbert, *Lettres, instructions et memoires de Colbert*, ed. Pierre Clément, vol. 4, 324.

67. On the hospital's location behind the town's fortifications protecting Montreal from Iroquois attack, see Garnier, *Soin des corps, soin des âmes*, 273; Garnier's work also sets out the internal spatialization of the hospital, pointing to the changes brought about by increased professionalization over the decades.

68. Stevenson, *Life Beside Itself*, 3.

EPILOGUE

1. Candace Clark, *Misery and Company: Sympathy in Everyday Life*; Melissa L. Caldwell, *Living Faithfully in an Unjust World*.

2. "Repudietur ergo misericordia? Nequaquam." Augustine, *Confessions*, 3.3.

3. Augustine, *City of God*, trans. Wiesen, 167.

4. Coeffeteau, *Tableau des passions humaines*, 354. Cureau's (largely medical) observation is about the seizing of the heart that takes place in both movements of compassion and anger, but

he concludes that these movements are differently motivated and structured; nonetheless, he discusses compassion largely within the context of action to relieve suffering and sets it amid a larger discussion of hatred. *Les characteres des passions*, 311–12.

5. Heather Love, *Feeling Backward: Loss and the Politics of Queer History*, 3. I've also thought about compassion's failures alongside a sentence of Joshua Weiner and Damon Young, who write of "a togetherness in failures to properly intersect." *Queer Bonds*, 224.

6. This failed sociability, too, could be told in still another way, with reference to Kant's figure of "unsocial sociability" (*ungesillige Gesilligkeit*) in the fourth proposition of the *Idea for a Universal History with a Cosmopolitan Aim*, something which for Kant would nonetheless be a means to some form of progress. On this question see Tracy McNulty, *The Hostess*, 58.

7. On Love's relation to political action see Annamarie Jagose, who writes that she "invites us to rethink the political less in terms of efficacious actions or exercises of intentionalist agency than as a mode of experiencing without necessarily changing the world, as an affective engagement indiscernible within models that take real-world traction as politics' true measure" (*Orgasmology*, 204). The nonefficacious space of compassion can be formulated in a number of disciplinarily different ways: for the philosopher Lawrence Blum, for example, "compassion's sole significance does not lie in its role as motive to beneficence," and feeling in itself must be considered as "an important human good." "Compassion," 515.

8. Jacques Rancière, *The Emancipated Spectator*, trans. Gregory Elliott, 13.

9. David Caron, *The Nearness of Others: Searching for Tact and Contact in the Age of HIV*, 59.

10. Katja Haustein, "'J'ai mal à l'autre': Barthes on Pity," 136.

11. Hervé Guibert, *Le protocole compassionnel* (1991). On the doctor-patient relationship in this account see David Caron, *AIDS in French Culture*, 125–32.

12. Michel Foucault, *Qu'est-ce que la critique?* (my translations, although text is available in English as "What Is Critique?"). On this essay's significance for early modern texts on government, see Marc Schachter, "'Qu'est-ce que la critique?' La Boétie, Montaigne, Foucault."

13. Foucault, *Qu'est-ce que la critique?* 37.

14. Judith Butler, "What Is Critique? An Essay on Foucault's Virtue," 224.

15. Foucault, *Critique*, 35.

16. In praise of this mode of critique, Elizabeth Povinelli writes: "'Not this' makes a difference even if it does not immediately produce a propositional otherwise." *Economies of Abandonment*, 191.

17. William E. Burgwinkle and Jane Gilbert, "Dark Networks." This model imagines manuscript dark networks as akin to the truncated family relationships tracked by the anthropologists Jeanette Edwards and Marilyn Strathern, "Including Our Own."

18. *Oxford English Dictionary*, s.v. "kindness," s.v. "kind."

Bibliography

I have not modernized early modern titles for accents or orthography, where I have consulted an early edition; the same is true for quoted material in the text. I have also shortened extremely long titles of works.

PRIMARY SOURCES

Amyraut, Moïse. *La morale chrestienne.* 6 vols. Saumur: Isaac Desbordes, 1652–60.
———. *Sermon sur ces Paroles de Jesus Christ, ayes la foy de Dieu. Le Mans, 1627.* Saumur: Jean Lesnier, 1657.
Aristotle. *The Art of Rhetoric,* trans. H. C. Lawson-Tancred. Harmondsworth: Penguin, 1991.
———. *Poetics,* ed. Stephen Halliwell. Cambridge: Harvard University Press, 1995.
———. *La poétique d'Aristote,* trans. Sieur de Norville. Paris: Chez Thomas Moette, 1671.
Aubignac, François Hédelin, abbé d'. *La pratique du théâtre,* ed. Hélène Baby. Paris: Honoré Champion, 2011.
Augustine, Saint, Bishop of Hippo. *City of God,* vol. 3 (books 8–11), trans. David S. Wiesen. Cambridge: Harvard University Press, 1968.
———. *Confessions,* ed. and trans. Carolyn J.-B. Hammond. Cambridge: Harvard University Press, 2014.
Aymon, Jean, ed. *Tous les synodes nationaux des eglises reformées de France: Auxquels on a joint des mandemens roiaux, et plusieurs lettres politiques, sur ces matieres synodales, intitulées doctrine, culte, morale, discipline, cas de conscience.* 2 vols. La Haye: Charles Delo, 1710.
Bayle, Pierre. *De la tolérance: Commentaire philosophique,* ed. Jean-Michel Gros. Paris: Honoré Champion, 2006.
———. *Ce que c'est que la France toute catholique sous le règne de Louis le Grand,* ed. Élisabeth Labrousse. Paris: Vrin, 1973.
———. *Dictionnaire historique et critique.* 4 vols. 5th edition. Amsterdam: Chez P. Brunel, 1740.
Beckett, Samuel. *Not I.* London: Faber and Faber, 1973.
Benoist, Élie. *Histoire de l'édit de Nantes, contenant les choses les plus remarquables qui se sont passées en France avant et après sa publication.* 5 vols. Delft: Adrien Beman, 1693–95.
Bérulle, Pierre de. *Œuvres complètes,* vol. 1, ed. Stéphane-Marie Morgain. Paris: Éditions du Cerf, 1997.
Bèze, Théodore de. *Histoire ecclésiastique des églises réformées au royaume de France.* 3 vols. Nieuwkoop: B. de Graaf, 1974.

La Bible: Tobie, Judith, Esther, trans. Isaac Lemaître de Sacy, ed. Philippe Sellier. Paris: Robert Laffont, 1990.

Biet, Christian, ed. *Théâtre de la cruauté et récits sanglants en France (XVIe–XVIIe siècle)*. Paris: Robert Laffont, 2006.

Blanchon, Joachim. *Sommaire Discours de la guerre civile et diverse calamité de ce temps*. Paris: Denis du Pré, 1569.

Boileau, Nicolas. *Œuvres complètes*, ed. Françoise Escal. Paris: Gallimard, 1966.

Bordeaux, Christophe de. *Discours lamentable et pitoyable sur la calamite, cherté et necessité du temps present*. Rouen: M. Blondet, 1586.

Campion, Henri de. *Mémoires de Henri de Campion*, ed. Marc Fumaroli. Paris: Mercure de France, 1990.

Carra, Jean-Louis, ed. *Mémoires historiques et authentiques sur la Bastille, dans une suite de près de trois cents emprisonnements*. 3 vols. London and Paris: Buisson, 1789.

Caussin, Nicolas. *La cour sainte du Révérend Père Nicolas Caussin*. Paris: Denis Bechet, 1653.

Chambrun, Jacques Pineton de. *Les larmes de Jacques Pineton de Chambrun*. La Haye: Chez Henry van Bulderen, 1688.

Charles II, King of England. *His Majestie's Declaration. His Majesty in his princely compassion and very tender care, taking into consideration the distressed condition of many his good Subjects, whom the late dreadful and dismal fire hath made destitute of habitations*. London: John Bill and Christopher Parker, 1666.

Charles IX, King of France. *Edict du roy sur le faict ordre et reiglement des hospitaulx et lieux pitoyables*. Rouen: Martin le Mesgissier, 1561.

Charron, Pierre. *Toutes les œuvres de Pierre Charron*. Paris: Jacques Villery, 1635.

Cicero, Marcus Tullius. *Cicero on the Emotions: Tusculan Disputations 3 and 4*, trans. Margaret Graver. Chicago: University of Chicago Press, 2002.

Claude, Jean. *An account of the persecutions and oppressions of the Protestants in France*. London, 1686.

Coeffeteau, Nicolas. *Tableau des passions humaines*. Paris: Sebastien Cramoisy, 1620.

Colbert, Jean-Baptiste. *Lettres, instructions et mémoires de Colbert*, ed. Pierre Clément. 4 vols. Paris: Imprimerie Impériale, 1867.

Complainte pitoyable d'une damoyselle angloise qui a heu la teste tranchée. Lyon: Cloquelin, 1600.

Constitutions des filles hospitalieres de sainct Joseph. S.l., s.n., 1643.

Corneille, Pierre. *Œuvres complètes*, ed. Georges Couton. 3 vols. Paris: Gallimard, 1980–87.

Cotgrave, Randle. *A Dictionarie of the French and English tongues*. London: A. Islip, 1611.

Le coutumier et petites regles des religieuses hospitalieres de la congregation de saint Joseph. Angers, 1688.

Cureau de la Chambre, Marin. *Les characteres des passions*, vols. 3 and 4. Amsterdam: Chez Antoine Michel, 1662.

Dacier, André. *La poétique d'Aristote, contenant les règles les plus exactes*. Paris: C. Barbin, 1692.

D'Aubigné, Théodore-Agrippa. *Les Tragiques*, ed. Jean-Raymond Fanlo. Paris: Honoré Champion, 2006.

The Deplorable State and Condition of the Poor French Protestants Commiserated. London: Richard Janeway, 1681.

Descartes, René. *Les passions de l'âme*, ed. Geneviève Rodis-Lewis. Paris: Vrin, 1994.

———. *Œuvres et lettres*, ed. André Bridoux. Paris: Gallimard, 1953.

Le Dictionnaire de l'Académie françoise. Paris: Coignard, 1694.

Dollier de Casson, François. *Histoire de Montréal*, ed. Marcel Trudel and Marie Baboyant. Québec: Éditions Hurtubise, 1992.

Du Bosc, Jacques. *L'honneste femme*. Rouen: Chez la veuve du Bosc, 1639.

Du Ryer, Pierre. *Esther*, ed. Edmund J. Campion, introduction by Perry Gethner. Exeter: University of Exeter Press, 1982.

Esprit, Jacques. *La fausseté des vertus humaines*. 2 vols. Paris: G. Desprez, 1678.

Féraud, Jean-François. *Dictionaire critique de la langue française*, vol. 1. Marseille: Jean Mossy, 1787.

Fitz-Geffry, Charles. *Compassion Towards Captives Chiefly Toward Our Brethren and Country-Men. Preached in Plymouth in October 1636*. Oxford: Leonard Litchfield, 1637.

Fléchier, Esprit. *Oraisons funèbres composées par M. Fléchier*. 2 vols. Paris: A. Dezallier, 1691.

François de Sales, Saint. *Introduction à la vie dévote*. Paris: Seuil, 1962.

A Full Account of the Barbarous and Unhumane Usages of the French Protestants in France. N.p., n.d., after 1685.

Furetière, Antoine. *Dictionnaire universel*. 2 vols. La Haye et Rotterdam: Leers, 1690.

Goulart, Simon. *Histoires admirables et memorable de nostre temps*. Arras: Guillaume de La Rivière, 1604.

Grandet, Joseph. *La Vie de Mademoiselle de Melun*. Paris: Josse, 1687.

Heinsius, Daniel. *De tragediae constitutione: La Constitution de la tragédie dite "la Poétique d'Heinsius,"* ed. Anne Duprat. Geneva: Droz, 2001.

The History of the Persecutions of the Reformed Churches in France, Orange and Piedmont, From the Year 1655 to This Time. London: Tho. Newborough and John Nicholson, 1699.

Hobbes, Thomas. *Leviathan*, ed. Richard Tuck. Cambridge: Cambridge University Press, 1996.

Huguet, Edmond. *Dictionnaire de la langue française du seizième siècle*. 7 vols. Paris: E. Champion, puis Didier, 1925–67.

Hume, David. *A Treatise on Human Nature*, ed. Ernest Mossner. Harmondsworth: Penguin, 1969.

Juchereau, Jeanne-Françoise (Mère de St-Ignace). *Les Annales de l'Hôtel-Dieu de Québec, 1636–1716*, ed. Dom Jamet. Montreal: Presses de Garden City, 1939.

Jurieu, Pierre. *Les derniers efforts de l'innocence affligée ou Entretiens curieux de deux catholiques romains*. Amsterdam: Daniel du Fresne, 1682.

———. *Des droits des deux souverains en matière de religion, la conscience et le prince*. Rotterdam: H. de Graef, 1687.

———. *Histoire du Calvinisme et celle du Papisme mises en parallele, ou apologie pour les reformateurs, pour la Reformation, et pour les Reformez*. Rotterdam: Reinier Leers, 1683.

———. *Lettre de quelques protestans pacifiques au sujet de la réunion des religions May 1685*. N.p., 1685.

———. *Politique du Clergé de France ou Entretiens curieux de deux Catholiques Romains*. 2nd edition. Rotterdam: Abraham Arondeus, 1681.

———. *Religion des Jesuites ou reflexions sur les inscriptions du pere Menestrier*. La Haye: Chez Abraham Troyel, 1689.

———. *Suite de l'accomplissement des Propheties, ou amplification des Preuves historiques qui font voir que le Papisme est l'Antichristianisme*. Rotterdam: Abraham Acher, 1687.

Kant, Immanuel. *Groundwork of the Metaphysics of Morals*, ed. Mary Gregor and Jens Timmermann. Cambridge: Cambridge University Press, 2012.

———. *The Metaphysics of Morals*, trans. Mary Gregor. Cambridge: Cambridge University Press, 1991.

Lafayette, Marie de la Madeleine, Pioche de la Vergne, comtesse de (Madame de). *Œuvres complètes*, ed. Camille Esmein-Sarrazin. Paris: Gallimard, 2014.

————. *The Princesse de Clèves / The Princesse de Montpensier / The Comtesse de Tende*, trans. Terence Cave. Oxford: Oxford University Press, 1992.

————. *Histoire de la Princesse de Montpensier sous le règne de Charles IXème roi de France / Histoire de la Comtesse de Tende*, ed. Micheline Cuénin. Geneva: Droz, 1979.

La Mesnardière, Hippolyte-Jules Pilet de. *La poëtique*. Geneva: Slatkine Reprints, 1972.

La Popelinière, Henri Lancelot-Voisin de. *La vraye et entiere histoire de ces derniers troubles, advenus tant en France qu'en Flandres et pays circonvoisins*. Cologne: Arnould Birckman, 1571.

La Rochefoucauld, François de. *Maxims*, trans. Leonard Tancock. Harmondsworth: Penguin, 1959.

————. *Réflexions ou sentences et maximes morales et réflexions diverses*, ed. Laurence Plazenet. Paris: Honoré Champion, 2002.

La Taille, Jean de. *Art de la tragédie*, preface to *Saul le furieux: Critical Prefaces of the French Renaissance*, ed. Bernard Weinberg. Baltimore: Waverly Press, 1950.

Le Jay, Gabriel-François. *Le Triomphe de la Religion sous Louis le Grand*. Paris: Gabriel Martin, 1687.

Lemaître de Sacy, Isaac, trans. *La Bible: Tobie, Judith, Esther*, ed. Philippe Sellier. Paris: Robert Laffont, 1990.

Le Moyne, Pierre. *La dévotion aisée*. Paris: A. de Sommaville, 1652.

————. *Les peintures morales où les passions sont representees par tableaux, par characteres, et par questions nouvelles et curieuses*. 2 vols. Paris: Sébastien Cramoisy, 1640–43.

Léry, Jean de. *Histoire memorable de la ville de Sancerre, contenant les entreprinses, sieges, approches, bateries, assaux et autres efforts des assiegans*. Geneva, 1574.

L'Estoile, Pierre de. *Registre-journal du règne de Henri III: tome 5 (1585–1587)*, ed. Madeleine Lazard and Gilbert Schrenk. Geneva: Droz, 2001.

A Letter from Rochel in France. London: R. Bentley, 1681.

Lettre d'Amolon Archevesque de Lyon, qui vivoit du temps de Charles le Chauve, à Thibaud Evesque de Langres. Dans laquelle il est parlé des Paroisses, des Curez, & des Peuples qui leur sont soûmis. Paris: s.n., 1654.

Louis, prince de Condé. *Mémoires de Condé, ou recueil pour servir à l'histoire de France*, ed. Denis-François Secousse. 6 vols. London: Claude du Bosc, 1743.

Malebranche, Nicolas. *De la recherche de la vérité I–III*, ed. Jean-Christophe Bardout. Paris: Vrin, 2006.

Marchin, Jean-Gaspard-Ferdinand, comte de. *Plaise à S.A.R. avoir compassion du sieur de Marchin*. N.p., 1650.

Marguerite d'Angoulême, reine de Navarre. *La Coche*, ed. Robert Marichal. Geneva: Droz, 1971.

Mercure galant, ed. Jean Donneau de Vizé. Paris: Au Palais, 1678–1714.

Mézeray, François Eudes de. *Histoire de France depuis Faramond*. 3 vols. Paris: M. Guillemot, 1643–51.

Molière. *Œuvres complètes*, ed. Georges Forestier. 2 vols. Paris: Gallimard, 2010.

Montaigne, Michel de. *The Complete Works*, trans. Donald Frame. New York: Everyman's Library, 2003.

————. *Les Essais*, ed. Pierre Villey, revised V. Saulnier. 3 vols. Paris: Presses Universitaires de France, 2004.

Montchrestien, Antoine de. *Aman, a Critical Edition*, ed. George Otto Seiver. Philadelphia: University of Pennsylvania Press, 1939.

Morin, Marie. *Histoire simple et veritable / Les Annales de l'Hôtel-Dieu de Montréal, 1659–1725*, ed. Ghislaine Legendre. Montreal: Presses de l'Université de Montréal, 1979.

Nicole, Pierre. *Essais de morale*, ed. Laurent Thirouin. Paris: Presses Universitaires de France, 1999.

——. *La vraie beauté et son fantôme*, ed. Béatrice Guion. Paris: Honoré Champion, 1996.

Nicot, Jean. *Thrésor de la langue françoyse, tant ancienne que moderne*. Paris: David Douceur, 1606.

Nietzsche, Friedrich. *Human, All Too Human*, trans. R. J. Hollingdale. Cambridge: Cambridge University Press, 1986.

——. *On the Genealogy of Morals*, trans. Walter Kaufmann. New York: Vintage, 1969.

Norville, Sieur de, trans. *La poétique d'Aristote, trad. Sieur de Norville*. Paris: Chez Thomas Moette, 1671.

Le Nouveau Testament de Nostre Seigneur Jesus Christ, de la traduction des docteurs de Louvain. Paris: Charles Fosset, 1672.

Pascal, Blaise. *Œuvres complètes*, vol. 2, ed. Michel Le Guern. Paris: Gallimard, 2000.

——. *Pensées, opuscules et lettres*, ed. Philippe Sellier. Paris: Classiques Garnier, 2010.

——. *Pensées: The Provincial Letters*, trans. W. F. Trotter. New York: Random House, 1941.

Perussiis, Loys de. *Discours des guerres de la commte de Venayscin, et de la Provence*. Nîmes: Lacour, 1998.

Quintilian. *The Orator's Education, Books 6–8*, trans. Donald A. Russell. Cambridge: Harvard University Press, 2001.

Racine, Jean. *Complete Plays*, trans. Samuel Solomon, vol. 2. New York: Random House, 1967.

——. *Œuvres completes*, ed. Georges Forestier. Paris: Gallimard, 1999.

——. *Principes de la tragédie en marge de La Poétique d'Aristote*, ed. Eugène Vinaver, Manchester: University of Manchester Press, 1944.

Ragueneau, Paul, SJ. *La vie de la mere Catherine de Saint Augustin religieuse hospitaliere de la misericorde de Quebec en la Nouvelle France*. Paris: Chez Florentin Lambert, 1671.

Rapin, René. *Les réflexions sur la poétique de ce temps et sur les ouvrages des poètes anciens et modernes*, ed. E. T. Dubois. Geneva: Droz, 1970.

Recueil des plus belles epigrammes des poëtes François, depuis Marot jusqu'à present. Avec des notes historiques et critiques, et un traité de la vraye et de la fausse beauté dans les ouvrages d'esprit, trans. Germain de Lafaille. Paris: Nicolas Leclerc, 1698.

Refuge, Eustache de. *Traité de la cour, ou instruction des courtisans*. Amsterdam: Elzeviers, 1656.

Règles et constitutions pour les Religieuses Hospitalières de Saint Joseph. Autun: Bernard LaMothe-Tort, 1686.

Relation succincte du pitoyable estat ou sont maintenant les eglises reformées de France en l'an 1667 / Das ist ein Kurzer Bericht vom embärmlichen Zuständeder Reformirtne Kirchen. Frankfurt? 1667.

Richelet, Pierre. *Dictionnaire françois*. Geneva: Chez Jean Herman Widerhold, 1680.

Ronsard, Pierre de. *Œuvres complètes*, ed. Jean Céard, Daniel Ménager, and Michel Simonin. 2 vols. Paris: Gallimard, 1994.

Royaumount, Sieur de. *Histoire du vieux et du Nouveau Testament representée avec des figures et des explications édifiantes*. Paris: Chez Pierre le Petit, 1670.

Le saint, et pitoyable discours, comme ce bon Prince Françoys de Lorraine Duc de Guyse se disposa a recevoir le sainct Sacrement de l'Autel. Paris: Claude Blihart, 1563.

Saint-Evremond, Charles de. *Œuvres en prose*, ed. René Ternois. 4 vols. Paris: Marcel Didier, 1962–69.

Saint-Jure, Jean-Baptiste. *L'homme religieux*. 2 vols. Paris: Denys Bechet, 1663.

Scudéry, Madeleine de. *Clélie, histoire romaine*, vol. 1, ed. Chantal Morlet-Chantalat. Paris: Honoré Champion, 2001.

———. *Conversations sur divers sujets*. Paris: Claude Barbin, 1680.

Senault, Jean-François. *De l'usage des passions*, ed. Christiane Frémont. Paris: Fayard, 1987.

Seneca, Lucius Annaeus. *Moral Essays*, vol. 1, trans. John W. Basore. Cambridge: Harvard University Press, 1928.

Serres, Jean de. *Histoire des choses memorables avenues en France, depuis l'an MDXLVII jusques au commencement de l'an MDXCVII*. N.p., 1599.

Sévigné, Marie de Rabutin-Chantal. *Lettres 1684–1696*, ed. Gérard Gailly. Paris: Gallimard, 1957.

Simond, Pierre. *La Discipline de Jesus Christ*. Leiden: Jacques Hackius, 1687.

Smith, Adam. *Correspondence of Adam Smith*, ed. Ernest Campbell Mossner and Ian Simpson Ross. Oxford: Oxford University Press, 1977.

———. *The Theory of Moral Sentiments*, ed. Knud Haakonssen. Cambridge: Cambridge University Press, 2002.

Tallemant des Réaux, Gédéon. *Historiettes*, vol. 1, ed. Antoine Adam. Paris: Gallimard, 1960.

Thiers, Jean-Baptiste. *L'avocat des pauvres: qui fait voir l'obligation qu'ont les beneficiers de faire un bon usage des biens de l'Eglise et d'en assister les pauvres*. Paris: Chez la veuve de Jean du Puis, 1676.

Thwaites, Reuben Gold, ed. *The Jesuit Relations and Allied Documents: Travels and Explorations of the Jesuit Missionaries in New France 1610–1791*. 73 vols. Cleveland: Burrow Bros., 1896–1901.

Touchard, Jean. *Allégresse chrestienne de l'heureux succès des guerres de ce royaume*. Paris: M. de Roigny, 1572.

Valancier, Estienne. *Complainte de la France, touchant les misères de son dernier temps*. N.p., 1568.

Valincour, Jean-Baptiste Henri du Trousset de. *Lettres à madame la marquise de XXX sur le sujet de La Princesse de Clèves*. Tours: Université de Tours, 1972.

Vauban, Sébastien Le Prestre, marquis de. *Mémoire pour le rappel des Huguenots*, ed. Philippe Vassaux. Carrières-sous-Poissy: La Cause, 1997.

Vermigli, Peter Martyr. *A treatise of the cohabitacyon of the faithfull with the unfaithfull*. Strasbourg, 1555.

Villedieu, Marie-Catherine-Hortense de. *Les désordres de l'amour*, ed. Micheline Cuénin. Geneva: Droz, 1995.

Yver, Jacques. *Le printemps d'Yver*. Geneva: Slatkine Reprints, 1970.

Yves de Paris. *Les œuvres de miséricorde*. Paris: Chez la veuve Thierry et Denis Thierry, 1661.

———. *La théologie naturelle*. 4 vols. Paris: Nicolas Buon, 1633–37.

SECONDARY SOURCES

Ablow, Rachel. *The Marriage of Minds: Reading Sympathy in the Victorian Marriage Plot*. Stanford: Stanford University Press, 2007.

Adorno, Theodor, and Max Horkheimer. *Dialectic of Enlightenment*, trans. John Cumming. London: Verso, 1997.

Agamben, Giorgio. *The Highest Poverty. Monastic Rules and Form-of-Life*, trans. Adam Kotsko. Stanford: Stanford University Press, 2013.

———. *Homo Sacer: Sovereign Power and Bare Life*, trans. Daniel Heller-Roazen. Stanford: Stanford University Press, 1998.

Ahmed, Sara. *The Cultural Politics of Emotion*. New York: Routledge, 2004.

———. *The Promise of Happiness*. Durham: Duke University Press, 2010.

Alliston, April. *Virtue's Faults: Correspondences in Eighteenth-Century British and French Women's Fiction*. Stanford: Stanford University Press, 1996.

Arendt, Hannah. *On Revolution*. Harmondsworth: Penguin, 2006.

Armstrong, Brian G. *Calvinism and the Amyraut Heresy: Protestant Scholasticism and Humanism in Seventeenth-Century France*. Madison: University of Wisconsin Press, 1969.

Arnould-Bloomfield, Elisabeth. "Posthuman Compassions." In "Emotions," ed. Katharine Ann Jensen and Miriam L. Wallace. Special issue, *PMLA* 130.5 (October 2015): 1467–75.

Audi, Paul. *L'empire de la compassion*. Paris: Les Belles Lettres, 2011.

Aune, M. G. "Elephants, Englishmen and India: Early Modern Travel-Writing and the Pre-Colonial Movement." *Early Modern Literary Studies* 11.1 (2005): 1–35.

Baker, Susan Read. *Collaboration et originalité chez La Rochefoucauld*. Gainesville: University of Florida, 1980.

Barclay, Linda. "Autonomy and the Social Self." In *Relational Autonomy: Feminist Perspectives on Autonomy, Agency, and the Social Self*, ed. Catriona Mackenzie and Natalie Stoljar, 52–71. New York: Oxford University Press, 2000.

Barthes, Roland. *How to Live Together: Novelistic Simulations of Some Everyday Spaces*, trans. Kate Briggs. New York: Columbia University Press, 2012.

Beame, Edmond M. "The *Politiques* and the Historians." *Journal of the History of Ideas* 54.3 (1993): 355–79.

Beasley, Faith. "Versailles Meets the Taj Mahal." In *French Global: A New Approach to Literary History*, ed. Christie McDonald and Susan Rubin Suleiman, 207–22. New York: Columbia University Press, 2010.

———. *Salons, History, and the Creation of Seventeenth-Century France: Mastering Memory*. Aldershot: Ashgate, 2006.

———. *Revising Memory: Women's Fiction and Memoirs in Seventeenth-Century France*. New Brunswick: Rutgers University Press, 1990.

Beitz, Charles. *Political Theory and International Relations*. Princeton: Princeton University Press, 1999.

Belfiore, Elizabeth S. *Tragic Pleasures: Aristotle on Plot and Emotion*. Princeton: Princeton University Press, 1992.

Belmessous, Saliha. "Assimilation and Racialism in Seventeenth and Eighteenth-Century French Colonial Policy." *American Historical Review* 110.2 (2005): 322–49.

Benedict, Philip. "Confessionalization in France? Critical Reflections and New Evidence." In *Society and Culture in the Huguenot World*, ed. Raymond A. Mentzer and Andrew Spicer, 44–61. Cambridge: Cambridge University Press, 2002.

———. "Faith, Fortune and Social Structure in Seventeenth-Century Montpellier." *Past and Present* 152 (1996): 46–78.

———. *The Faith and Fortunes of France's Huguenots, 1600–85*. Aldershot: Ashgate, 2001.

———. "Un roi, une loi, deux fois: Parameters for the History of Catholic-Reformed Coexistence in France, 1555–1685." In *Tolerance and Intolerance in the European Reformation*, ed. Ole Peter Grell and Bob Scribner, 65–93. Cambridge: Cambridge University Press, 1996.

Benferhat, Yasmina. *Du bon usage de la douceur en politique dans l'œuvre de Tacite*. Paris: Les Belles Lettres, 2011.

Berchtold, Jacques, and Marie-Madeleine Fragonard, eds. *La mémoire des guerres de religion: La concurrence des genres historiques (XVIe–XVIIIe siècles)*. Geneva: Droz, 2007.

———. "La mémoire et l'écriture: Problèmes généraux." In *La mémoire des guerres de religion: La concurrence des genres historiques (XVIe–XVIIe siècles)*, ed. Jacques Berchtold and Marie-Madeleine Fragonard, 8–28. Geneva: Droz, 2007.

Berlant, Lauren. *The Female Complaint: The Unfinished Business of Sentimentality in American Culture.* Durham: Duke University Press, 2008.

———. "Introduction: Compassion (and Withholding)." In *Compassion: The Culture and Politics of an Emotion*, ed. Lauren Berlant, 1–13. New York: Routledge, 2004.

Biet, Christian. *Droit et littérature sous l'Ancien Régime.* Paris: Honoré Champion, 2002.

———. *Racine ou la passion des larmes.* Paris: Hachette, 1996.

Birnstiel, Eckart, with Chrystel Bernat. *La diaspora des Huguenots: Les réfugiés protestants de France et leur dispersion dans le monde (XVIe–XVIIIe siècles).* Paris: Honoré Champion, 2001.

Blocker, Déborah. "Figures du peuple d'Israël dans l'*Esther* de Jean Racine." In "Port Royal et le peuple d'Israël," ed. Rita Hermon-Belot and Jean Lesaulnier. Special issue, *Chroniques de Port Royal* 53 (juillet 2004): 1142–44.

Blum, Lawrence. "Compassion." In *Explaining Emotions*, ed. Amélie Oksenberg Rorty, 505–17. Berkeley: University of California Press, 1980.

Boltanski, Luc. 1993. *Distant Suffering: Morality, Media and Politics*, trans. Graham Burchell. Cambridge: Cambridge University Press, 1999.

Boquet, Damien. *L'ordre de l'affect au Moyen Age: Autour de l'anthropologie affective d'Aelred de Rievaulx.* Caen: CRAHM, 2005.

Bost, Hubert. "Élie Benoist et l'historiographie de l'édit de Nantes." In *Coexister dans l'intolérance: L'édit de Nantes (1598)*, ed. Michel Grandjean and Bernard Roussel, 371–84. Geneva: Labor et Fides, 1998.

———. *Pierre Bayle et la religion.* Paris: Presses Universitaires de France, 1994.

Brémond, Henri. *Histoire littéraire du sentiment religieux depuis la fin des guerres de religion jusqu'à nos jours.* 11 vols. Paris: Blond et Gray, 1916–36.

Brennan, Teresa. *The Transmission of Affect.* Ithaca: Cornell University Press, 2004.

Brockliss, Laurence, and Colin Jones. *The Medical World of Early Modern France.* Oxford: Oxford University Press, 1997.

Brooke, Christopher. *Philosophic Pride: Stoicism and Political Thought from Lipsius to Rousseau.* Princeton: Princeton University Press, 2012.

Brown, Wendy. *Regulating Aversion: Tolerance in the Age of Identity and Empire.* Princeton: Princeton University Press, 2006.

Buffault, Anne-Vincent. *Histoire des larmes.* Paris: Payot et Rivages, 2001.

Burgwinkle, William E., and Jane Gilbert. "Dark Networks: Pre-Histories, Post-Histories, and Imagined Geographies." In *Medieval French Literature Abroad*, ed. Simon Gaunt, William E. Burgwinkle, and Jane Gilbert, chap. 6 (unpublished manuscript).

Burke, Peter. *The Fabrication of Louis XIV.* New Haven: Yale University Press, 1992.

Butler, Judith. "What Is Critique? An Essay on Foucault's Virtue." In *The Political: Readings in Continental Philosophy*, ed. David Ingram, 212–26. London: Basil Blackwell, 2002.

Caldwell, Melissa L. *Living Faithfully in an Unjust World: Compassionate Care in Russia.* Berkeley: University of California Press, 2017.

Cameron, Keith, Mark Greengrass, and Penny Roberts, eds. *The Adventure of Religious Pluralism in Early Modern France.* Bern: Peter Lang, 2000.

Campbell, John. "The Politics of Esther." *Seventeenth-Century French Studies* 31.1 (2009): 25–35.

Campbell, Mary Baine. "The Dreaming Body: Cartesian Psychology, Enlightenment

Anthropology, and the Jesuits in Nouvelle France." In *The Anthropology of the Enlighten-ment*, ed. Larry Wolff and Marco Cipollini, 239–51. Stanford: Stanford University Press, 2007.

Carbonnier-Burkard, Marianne. "Larmes réformées." In *De L'humanisme aux Lumières, Bayle et le protestantisme: Mélanges en l'honneur d'Elisabeth Labrousse*, ed. Michelle Magdelaine, Maria-Christina Pitassi, Ruth Whelan, and Antony McKenna, 193–206. Oxford: Voltaire Foundation, 1996.

Carlson, Julie Ann. "Like Me: An Invitation to Domestic Tragedy." *South Atlantic Quarterly* 98.3 (1999): 331–53.

Caron, David. *AIDS in French Culture: Social Ills, Literary Cures*. Madison: University of Wisconsin Press, 2001.

——. *The Nearness of Others: Searching for Tact and Contact in the Age of HIV*. Minneapolis: University of Minnesota Press, 2014.

Carraud, Vincent. "Descartes et la Bible." In *Le grand siècle et la Bible*, ed. Jean-Robert Armogathe, 277–91. Paris: Beauchesne, 1989.

——. "Descartes: Le droit de la charité." In *L'interpretazione nei secoli XVI e XVII*, ed. Guido Canziani and Yves-Charles Zarka, 515–36. Milan: Francoangeli, 1993.

Cates, Diana Fritz. *Choosing to Feel: Virtue, Friendship, and Compassion for Friends*. South Bend: University of Notre Dame Press, 1997.

Cavell, Stanley. *Pursuits of Happiness: The Hollywood Comedy of Remarriage*. Cambridge: Harvard University Press, 1981.

Chalumeau, Raymond Lucien. "L'assistance aux pauvres malades au XVIIe siècle." *Dix-septième siècle* 91 (1971): 75–86.

Chandler, James. *An Archaeology of Sympathy: The Sentimental Mode in Literature and Cinema*. Chicago: University of Chicago Press, 2013.

Chédozeau, Bernard. *Port-Royal et la Bible: Un siècle d'or de la Bible en France 1650–1708*. Paris: Nolin, 2007.

Chesneau, Charles. *Le Père Yves de Paris et son temps, 1590–1678*. 2 vols. Paris: CNRS / Société d'histoire ecclésiastique de la France, 1946.

Christman, John Philip, and Joel Anderson, eds. *Autonomy and the Challenges of Liberalism: New Essays*. Cambridge: Cambridge University Press, 2005.

Clark, Candace. *Misery and Company: Sympathy in Everyday Life*. Chicago: University of Chicago, 1997.

Clark, Stuart. *Vanities of the Eye: Vision in Early Modern European Culture*. Oxford: Oxford University Press, 2007.

Colot, Blandine. "Pietas." In *Vocabulaire européen des philosophies: Dictionnaire des intraduisibles*, ed. Barbara Cassin, 942–94. Paris: Seuil, 2004.

Corcuff, Philippe. "Ordre institutionnel, fluidité situationnelle et compassion: Les interactions au guichet de deux CAF." *Recherches et Prévisions* 45 (1996): 27–35.

Coste, Pierre. *Le grand saint du grand siècle: Monsieur Vincent*. 3 vols. Paris: Desclée de Brouwer, 1934.

Crouzet, Denis. *Les guerriers de Dieu: La violence au temps des troubles de religion, vers 1525–vers 1610*. 2 vols. Seyssel: Champ Vallon, 1990.

——. *La nuit de la Saint-Barthélémy: Un rêve perdu de la Renaissance*. Paris: Fayard, 1994.

Cuénin, Micheline. "La terreur sans la pitié: 'La Comtesse de Tende.'" *Revue d'histoire littéraire de la France* 77.3/4 (1977): 478–99.

d'Allaire, Micheline. *Les communautés religieuses de Montréal. Tome 1, Les communautés religieuses et l'assistance sociale à Montréal, 1659–1900*. Montreal: Éditions du Méridien, 1997.

Davis, Natalie Zemon. *Fiction in the Archives: Pardon-Tales and Their Tellers in Sixteenth-Century France*. Stanford: Stanford University Press, 1987.

———. "Iroquois Women: European Women." In *Women, "Race," and Writing in the Early Modern Period*, ed. Margo Hendricks and Patricia Parker, 243–59. New York: Routledge, 1994.

DeJean, Joan. *Ancients Against Moderns: Culture Wars and the Making of a Fin-de-Siècle*. Chicago: University of Chicago Press, 1997.

———. *The Essence of Style: How the French Invented High Fashion, Fine Food, Chic Cafés, Style, Sophistication, and Glamour*. New York: Free Press, 2006.

———. *Tender Geographies: Women and the Origins of the Novel in France*. New York: Columbia University Press, 1991.

Delaurenti, Béatrice. *La contagion des émotions: Compassio, une énigme médiévale*. Paris: Garnier, 2016.

Delehanty, Ann. *Literary Knowing in Neoclassical France: From Poetics to Aesthetics*. Lewisburg: Bucknell University Press, 2013.

———. "Reconciling Divine and Political Authority in Racine's *Esther*." In *Culture and Authority in the Baroque*, ed. Massimo Ciavolella and Patrick Coleman, 138–58. Toronto: University of Toronto Press, 2005.

Delforge, Frédéric. "Les éditions protestantes de la Bible en langue française." In *Le grand siècle et la Bible*, ed. Jean-Robert Armogathe, 325–40. Paris: Beauchesne, 1989.

Delumeau, Jean. *Naissance et affirmation de la Réforme*. 1965. 6th edition. Paris: Presses Universitaires de France, 1991.

De Man, Paul. *Blindness and Insight: Essays in the Rhetoric of Contemporary Criticism*. New York: Oxford University Press, 1971.

Démoris, René. "Les guerres de religion dans la nouvelle historique entre 1660 et 1680." In *La mémoire des guerres de religion: La concurrence des genres historiques (XVIe–XVIIe siècles)*, ed. Jacques Berchtold et Marie-Madeleine Fragonard, 251–66. Geneva: Droz, 2007.

Denby, David. *Sentimental Narrative and the Social Order in France, 1760–1820*. Cambridge: Cambridge University Press, 1994.

Desan, Suzanne, and Jeffrey Merrick, eds. *Family, Gender and Law in Early Modern France*. University Park: Pennsylvania State University Press, 2009.

Deslandres, Dominique. *Croire et faire croire. Les missions françaises au XVIIe siècle*. Paris: Fayard, 2003.

———. "Femmes missionaires en Nouvelle-France: Les débuts des Ursulines et des Hospitalières à Québec." In *La religion de ma mère: Les femmes et la transmission de la foi*, ed. J. Delumeau, 209–24. Paris: Éditions du Cerf, 1992.

De Waele, Michel. *Réconcilier les Français: Henri IV et la fin des troubles de religion (1589–1598)*. Laval: Presses de l'Université Laval, 2010.

Dherbey, Gilbert Romeyer. "Les animaux familiers." In *L'Animal dans l'Antiquité*, ed. Barbara Cassin and Jean-Louis Labarrière, directed by Gilbert Romeyer Dherbey, 141–54. Paris: Vrin, 1997.

Diefendorf, Barbara. *Beneath the Cross: Catholics and Huguenots in Sixteenth-Century Paris*. New York: Oxford University Press, 1991.

———. *From Penitence to Charity: Pious Women and the Catholic Reformation in Paris*. New York: Oxford University Press, 2004.

Dijkhuizen, Jan Frans van. *Pain and Compassion in Early Modern English Literature and Culture.* Cambridge: D. S. Brewer, 2012.

Dinan, Susan E. *Women and Poor Relief in Seventeenth-Century France: The Early History of the Daughters of Charity.* Aldershot: Ashgate, 2006.

Dinet-Lecomte, Marie-Claude. *Les sœurs hospitalières en France aux XVIIe et XVIIIe siècles.* Paris: Honoré Champion, 2005.

Dixon, Thomas. *From Passions to Emotions: The Creation of a Secular Psychological Category.* Cambridge: Cambridge University Press, 2003.

Dodge, Guy Howard. *The Political Theory of the Huguenots of the Dispersion, with Special Reference to the Thought and Influence of Pierre Jurieu.* New York: Columbia University Press, 1947.

Dowling, Melissa Barden. *Clemency and Cruelty in the Roman World.* Ann Arbor: University of Michigan Press, 2006.

Dubu, Jean. *Racine aux miroirs.* Paris: SEDES, 1992.

Duval, Edwin M. "Le début des 'Essais' et la fin d'un livre." *Revue d'histoire littéraire de la France* 88.5 (1988): 896–907.

———. "The Place of the Present: Ronsard, Aubigné, and the 'Misères de ce Temps.'" In "Baroque Topographies: Literature/History/Philosophy," ed. Timothy Hampton. Special issue, *Yale French Studies* 80 (1991): 13–29.

Eagleton, Terry. *Sweet Violence: The Idea of the Tragic.* Oxford: Blackwell, 2003.

Edelman, Lee. *No Future: Queer Theory and the Death Drive.* Durham: Duke University Press, 2004.

Eden, Kathy. *Poetic and Legal Fiction in the Aristotelian Tradition.* Princeton: Princeton University Press, 1986.

Edwards, Jeanette, and Marilyn Strathern. "Including Our Own." In *Cultures of Relatedness: New Directions in Kinship Studies,* ed. Janet Carsten, 149–66. Cambridge: Cambridge University Press, 2000.

Elias, Norbert. *The Court Society,* trans. Edmund Jephcott. Oxford: Basil Blackwell, 1983.

Elster, Jon. *Alchemies of the Mind: Rationality and the Emotions.* Cambridge: Cambridge University Press, 1999.

Émelina, Jean. "Corneille et la *catharsis.*" *Littératures classiques* 32 (1998): 105–20.

Fassin, Didier. "Compassion and Repression: The Moral Economy of Immigration Policies in France." *Cultural Anthropology* 20.3 (2005): 362–87.

———. *Humanitarian Reason: A Moral History of the Present.* Berkeley: University of California Press, 2012.

Festa, Lynn. "Humanity Without Feathers." *Humanity: An International Journal of Human Rights, Humanitarianism, and Development* 1.1 (2010): 3–27.

———. *Sentimental Figures of Empire in Eighteenth-Century Britain and France.* Baltimore: Johns Hopkins University Press, 2006.

Fino, Catherine. *L'hospitalité, figure sociale de la charité: Deux fondations hospitalières à Québec.* Paris: Desclée de Brouwer, 2010.

Fisher, Philip. *The Vehement Passions.* Princeton: Princeton University Press, 2002.

Fleming, Paul. *Exemplarity and Mediocrity: The Art of the Average from Bourgeois Tragedy to Realism.* Stanford: Stanford University Press, 2009.

Fontenay, Elisabeth de. *Le silence des bêtes: La philosophie à l'épreuve de l'animalité.* Paris: Fayard, 1998.

Force, Pierre. *Self-Interest Before Adam Smith: A Genealogy of Economic Science.* Cambridge: Cambridge University Press, 2003.

Forestier, Georges. *Passions tragiques et règles classiques: Essai sur la tragédie française.* Paris: Presses Universitaires de France, 2003.

Foucault, Michel. *Histoire de la folie à l'âge classique.* Paris: Gallimard, 1972.

———. *Naissance de la clinique: Une archéologie du regard médical.* Paris: Presses Universitaires de France, 1963.

———. *Qu'est-ce que la critique?* Paris: Vrin, 2015.

———. "What Is Critique?" In *The Politics of Truth,* ed. Sylvère Lotringer, 23–82. New York: Semiotext[e], 1997.

Fragonard, Marie-Madeleine. "Une mémoire individualisée: Éditions et rééditions des acteurs et témoins des guerres." In *La mémoire des guerres de religion: La concurrence des genres historiques (XVIe–XVIIe siècles),* ed. Jacques Berchtold and Marie-Madeleine Fragonard, 29–85. Geneva: Droz, 2007.

François, Anne-Lise. *Open Secrets: The Literature of Uncounted Experience.* Stanford: Stanford University Press, 2008.

Frazer, Michael. *The Enlightenment of Sympathy: Justice and the Moral Sentiments in the Eighteenth Century and Today.* Oxford: Oxford University Press, 2010.

Fried, Michael. *Absorption and Theatricality: Painting and Beholder in the Age of Diderot.* Chicago: University of Chicago Press, 1980.

Friedman, Marilyn. *Autonomy, Gender, Politics: Studies in Feminist Philosophy.* New York: Oxford University Press, 2003.

Frisch, Andrea. "Agrippa d'Aubigné's *Tragiques* as Testimony." In *Memory and Community in Sixteenth-Century France,* ed. David P. LaGuardia and Cathy Yandell, 97–111. Aldershot: Ashgate, 2015.

———. *Forgetting Differences: Tragedy, Historiography, and the French Wars of Religion.* Edinburgh: Edinburgh University Press, 2015.

———. *The Invention of the Eyewitness: Witnessing and Testimony in Early Modern France.* Chapel Hill: University of North Carolina Press, 2004.

Fudge, Erica. *Brutal Reasoning: Animals, Rationality, and Humanity in Early Modern England.* Ithaca: Cornell University Press, 2006.

Gagnon, Hervé. *Soigner le corps et l'âme: Les Hospitalières de Saint-Joseph et l'Hôtel-Dieu de Montréal, XVIIe–XXe siècles.* Sherbrooke: GGC Éditions, 2002.

Gallagher, Catherine. *Nobody's Story: The Vanishing Acts of Women Writers in the Marketplace, 1670–1820.* Berkeley: University of California Press, 1994.

Garber, Marjorie. "Compassion." In *Compassion: The Culture and Politics of an Emotion,* ed. Lauren Berlant, 15–28. New York: Routledge, 2004.

Garnier, Claire. *Soin des corps, soin des âmes: Genre et pouvoirs dans les hôpitaux de France et de Nouvelle-France aux XVIIe et XVIIIe siècles.* PhD diss., Université de Montréal and Université de Clermont-Ferrand 2, 2015.

Garrisson, Janine. *L'Édit de Nantes et sa révocation: Histoire d'une intolérance.* Paris: Seuil, 1985.

Germer, Christopher K., and Kristin D. Neff, "Self-Compassion in Clinical Practice." *Journal of Clinical Psychology* 69.8 (2013): 856–67.

Gibbs, G. C. "The Reception of the Huguenots in England and the Dutch Republic, 1680–1690." In *From Persecution to Toleration: The Glorious Revolution and Religion in England,* ed. Ole Peter Grell, Jonathan Israel, and Nicholas Tyacke, 275–306. Oxford: Oxford University Press, 1991.

Gibert, Pierre. *L'invention critique de la Bible, XVe–XVIIIe siècle.* Paris: Gallimard, 2010.

Gilbert, Paul. *The Compassionate Mind: A New Approach to Life's Challenges.* London: Constable, 2009.

Gilby, Emma. "Le 'sens commun' et le 'sentir en commun': Corneille et d'Aubignac." In "Les émotions publiques et leurs langages à l'âge classique," ed. Hélène Merlin-Kajman. Special issue, *Littératures Classiques* 68 (2009): 243–54.

———. *Sublime Worlds: Early Modern French Literature*. Oxford: Legenda, 2006.

Gilligan, Carol. *In a Different Voice: Psychological Theory and Women's Development*. Cambridge: Harvard University Press, 1982.

Goldhill, Simon. "What Is Ekphrasis For?" In "Ekphrasis," ed. Shadi Bartsch and Jaś Elsner. Special issue, *Classical Philology* 102.1 (2007): 1–19.

Goldsmith, Elizabeth. "Les lieux de l'histoire dans *La Princesse de Montpensier*." *Dix-septième siècle* 181.4 (1993): 705–15.

Gotman, Anne. *Le sens de l'hospitalité: Essai sur les fondements sociaux de l'accueil de l'autre*. Paris: Presses Universitaires de France, 2001.

Graves-Monroe, Amy C. "Soundscapes of the Wars of Religion." In *Memory and Community in Sixteenth-Century France*, ed. David P. LaGuardia and Cathy Yandell, 55–69. Aldershot: Ashgate, 2015.

Greenberg, Mitchell. "The Poetics of Trompe-l'oeil: D'Aubigné's 'Tableaux Célestes.'" *Neophilologus* 63.1 (1979): 4–22.

Greengrass, Mark. *Governing Passions: Peace and Reform in the French Kingdom, 1576–1585*. Oxford: Oxford University Press, 2007.

Gregg, Edward. "France, Rome and the Exiled Stuarts." In *A Court in Exile: The Stuarts in France, 1689–1718*, ed. Edward Corp, 11–75. Cambridge: Cambridge University Press, 2004.

Greiner, Frank. "L'alliance des contraires: Les unions interconfessionnelles dans quelques romans du temps de l'édit de Nantes." In *Le marriage et la loi dans la fiction narrative avant 1800*, ed. Françoise Lavocat, 201–12. Louvain: Peeters, 2014.

Gros, Jean-Michel. "La tolérance et le problème théologico-politique." In *Pierre Bayle dans la République des Lettres: Philosophie, religion, critique*, ed. Antony McKenna and Gianni Paganini, 411–39. Paris: Honoré Champion, 2004.

Gross, Daniel M. *The Secret History of Emotion: From Aristotle's Rhetoric to Modern Brain Science*. Chicago: University of Chicago Press, 2006.

Guibert, Hervé. *Le protocole compassionnel*. Paris: Gallimard, 1991.

Guion, Béatrice. *Pierre Nicole moraliste*. Paris: Honoré Champion, 2002.

Gutton, Jean-Pierre. *La société et les pauvres en Europe, XVIe–XVIIIe siècles*. Paris: Presses Universitaires de France, 1974.

Guyot, Sylvaine, and Clotilde Thouret. "Des émotions en chaîne: Représentation théâtrale et circulation publique des affects au XVIIe siècle." In "Les émotions publiques et leurs langages à l'âge classique," ed. Hélène Merlin-Kajman. Special issue, *Littératures Classiques* 68 (2009): 225–41.

Halliwell, Stephen. *Aristotle's Poetics*. Chapel Hill: University of North Carolina Press, 1986.

Hamington, Maurice, ed. *Feminism and Hospitality: Gender in the Host/Guest Relationship*. Lexington: Plymouth, 2010.

Hammond, Nicholas. *Fragmentary Voices: Memory and Education at Port-Royal*. Tübingen: Gunter Narr, 2004.

Hamou, Philippe. "Descartes, le théâtre des passions." *Études Épistémè* 1 (2002): 1–19.

Hampton, Timothy. *Fictions of Embassy: Literature and Diplomacy in Early Modern Europe*. Ithaca: Cornell University Press, 2009.

———. *Literature and Nation in the Sixteenth Century: Inventing Renaissance France*. Ithaca: Cornell University Press, 2001.

Hanley, Ryan Patrick. "The Eighteenth-Century Context of Sympathy from Spinoza to Kant." In *Sympathy: A History*, ed. Eric Schliesser, 171–98. Oxford: Oxford University Press, 2015.

Hanlon, Gregory. *Confession and Community in Seventeenth-Century France: Catholic and Protestant Coexistence in Aquitaine*. Philadelphia: University of Pennsylvania Press, 1993.

Harris, Joseph. *Inventing the Spectator: Subjectivity and the Theatrical Experience in Early Modern France*. Oxford: Oxford University Press, 2014.

Harth, Erica. *Ideology and Culture in Seventeenth-Century France*. Ithaca: Cornell University Press, 1983.

Haustein, Katja. "'J'ai mal à l'autre': Barthes on Pity." In "What's So Great About Roland Barthes?," ed. Tom Baldwin, Lucy O'Meara, Katja Haustein. Special issue, *L'Esprit créateur* 55.4 (2015): 131–47.

Heal, Felicity. *Hospitality in Early Modern England*. Oxford: Oxford University Press, 1990.

Hochschild, Arlie. *The Managed Heart: Commercialization of Human Feeling*. Berkeley: University of California Press, 1983.

Holland, Nancy J. "'With Arms Wide Open': Of *Hospitality* and the Most Intimate Stranger." *Philosophy Today, SPEP supplement* 45(2001): 133–37.

Hollinger, David A. "How Wide the Circle of the 'We'? American Intellectuals and the Problem of the Ethnos Since World War II." *American Historical Review* 98:2 (1993): 317–37.

Holt, Mack. *The French Wars of Religion, 1562–1629*. Cambridge: Cambridge University Press, 1995.

Horowitz, Louise K. *Love and Language: A Study of the Classical French Moralist Writers*. Columbus: Ohio State University Press, 1977.

———. "Primary Sources: *La Princesse de Clèves*." *French Forum* 25 (2000): 165–75.

Housset, Emmanuel. *L'intelligence de la pitié: Phénoménologie de la communauté*. Paris: Éditions du Cerf, 2003.

Howells, Robin J. *Pierre Jurieu: Antinomian Radical*. Durham: Durham Modern Language Series, 1983.

Hoxby, Blair. *What Was Tragedy? Theory and the Early Modern Canon*. New York: Oxford University Press, 2015.

Huet, Marie-Hélène. *Monstrous Imagination*. Cambridge: Harvard University Press, 1993.

Hunt, Lynn. *Inventing Human Rights: A History*. New York: W. W. Norton, 2007.

Huseman, William H. "The Expression of the Idea of Toleration in French During the Sixteenth Century." *Sixteenth Century Journal* 15.3 (1984): 293–310.

Ibbett, Katherine. "Being Moved: Louis XIV's Triumphant Tenderness and the Protestant Object." *Exemplaria* 26.1 (2014): 16–38.

———. "Italy and France, or How Pierre Corneille Became an Anti-Machiavel." In "Italy in the Drama of Europe," ed. Albert Russell Ascoli and William West. Special issue, *Renaissance Drama* 36/37 (2010): 379–95.

———. "Mon ami, ce héros." In *Le personnel du théâtre de Pierre Corneille*, ed. Myriam Dufour-Maître, 297–308. Rouen: Presses Universitaires de Rouen, 2013.

———. "Reconfiguring Martyrdom in the Colonial Context: Marie de l'Incarnation." In *Empires of God: Religious Encounters in the Early Modern Atlantic*, ed. Linda Gregerson and Susan Juster, 175–90. Philadelphia: University of Pennsylvania Press, 2010.

Imbert, Jean. "Les prescriptions hospitalières du concile de Trente et leur diffusion en France." *Revue d'histoire de l'Église de France* 42.138 (1956): 5–28.

Israel, Jonathan. "Pierre Bayle's Political Thought." In *Pierre Bayle dans la République des Lettres: Philosophie, religion, critique*, ed. Antony McKenna and Gianni Paganini, 349–79. Paris: Honoré Champion, 2004.

Jacob, Robert. "Pietas ou la compassion: Langage de la loi et rhétorique des sentiments." In *Les sentiments et le politique*, ed. Pierre Ansart and Claudine Haroche, 23–38. Paris: Harmattan, 2007.

Jacobson, Howard. "Augustine and Dido." *Harvard Theological Review* 65.2 (1972): 296–97.

Jagose, Annamarie. *Orgasmology*. Durham: Duke University Press, 2012.

James, Heather. "Dido's Ear: Tragedy and the Politics of Response." *Shakespeare Quarterly* 52.3 (2001): 360–82.

James, Susan. *Passion and Action: The Emotions in Seventeenth-Century Philosophy*. Oxford: Oxford University Press, 1997.

Jeanneret, Michel. "Les tableaux spirituels d'Agrippa d'Aubigné." *Bibliothèque d'Humanisme et Renaissance* 35.2 (1973): 233–45.

Jensen, Katharine Ann, and Miriam L. Wallace, eds. "Emotions." Special issue, *PMLA* 130.5 (October 2015).

Johnson, James. "'The Arithmetic of Compassion': Rethinking the Politics of Photography." *British Journal of Political Science* 41.3 (2011): 621–43.

Jones, Colin. *The Charitable Imperative: Hospitals and Nursing in Ancien Régime and Revolutionary France*. London: Routledge, 1989.

Jones, Matthew L. "Three Errors About Indifference: Pascal on the Vacuum, Sociability, and Moral Freedom." *Romance Quarterly* 50.2 (2003): 99–119.

Jouanna, Arlette. *La Saint-Barthélemy: Les mystères d'un crime d'État*. Paris: Gallimard, 2007.

———. "Le sujet, le roi et la loi (*Les Tragiques*, Livres ii et iii)." *Revue d'histoire littéraire de la France* 92.4 (1992): 619–29.

Jouhaud, Christian. *La main de Richelieu ou le pouvoir cardinal*. Paris: Gallimard, 1991.

Kahn, Victoria. "Happy Tears: Baroque Politics in Descartes's *Passions de l'âme*." In *Politics and the Passions, 1500–1800*, ed. Victoria Kahn, Neil Saccamano, and Daniela Coli, 93–110. Princeton: Princeton University Press, 2006.

———. *Rhetoric, Prudence, and Skepticism in the Renaissance*. Ithaca: Cornell University Press, 1985.

———. *Wayward Contracts: The Crisis of Political Obligation in England*. Princeton: Princeton University Press, 2004.

Kahn, Victoria, Neil Saccamano, and Daniela Coli, eds. *Politics and the Passions, 1500–1850*. Princeton: Princeton University Press, 2006.

Kambouchner, Denis. *L'homme des passions: Commentaires sur Descartes*. 2 vols. Paris: Albin Michel, 1995.

Kaplan, Benjamin. *Divided by Faith: Religious Conflict and the Practice of Toleration in Early Modern Europe*. Cambridge: Harvard University Press, 2007.

Keen, Suzanne. *Empathy and the Novel*. New York: Oxford University Press, 2007.

Keltner, Dacher, Jason Marsh, and Jeremy Adam Smith, eds. *The Compassionate Instinct: The Science of Human Goodness*. New York: W. W. Norton, 2010.

Kenny, Neil. *The Uses of Curiosity in Early Modern France and Germany*. Oxford: Oxford University Press, 2004.

Kingdon, Robert M. *Myths About the St. Bartholomew's Day Massacres, 1572–1576*. Cambridge: Harvard University Press, 1988.

Kittay, Eva Feder, and Ellen K. Feder, eds. *The Subject of Care: Feminist Perspectives on Dependency*. Lanham: Rowan and Littlefield, 2002.

Knight, Roy. *Racine et la Grèce*. Paris: Boivin, 1950.

Koch, Erec. "La contagion des passions de Descartes à Malebranche." In "Les émotions publiques et leurs langages à l'âge classique," ed. Hélène Merlin-Kajman. Special issue, *Littératures classiques* 68 (2009): 177–88.

———. "Cartesian Corporeality and (Aesth)Ethics." *PMLA* 121.2 (2006): 405–20.

Konstan, David. *Pity Transformed*. London: Duckworth, 2001.

Kritzman, Lawrence D. *Destruction/Découverte: Le fonctionnement de la rhétorique dans les Essais de Montaigne*. Lexington, Ky.: French Forum, 1980.

Krumenacker, Yves. *L'école française de spiritualité: Des mystiques, des fondateurs, des courants et leurs interprètes*. Paris: Éditions du Cerf, 1999.

Labrousse, Elisabeth. *Essai sur la révocation de l'Édit de Nantes: Une foi, une loi, un roi?* Geneva: Labor et Fides / Paris: Payot, 1985.

———. *Pierre Bayle. Hétérodoxie et rigorisme*. 2 vols. The Hague: Nijhoff, 1964.

Lacoue-Labarthe, Philippe. "On the Sublime." In *Postmodernism: ICA Documents*, ed. Lisa Appignanesi, 11–18. London: Free Association Books, 1989.

Lacroix, Laurier, ed. *Les arts en Nouvelle-France*. Québec: Publications du Québec / Musée National des Beaux-Arts du Québec, 2012.

Langley, Eric. *Ill Communications: Shakespeare's Contagious Sympathies* (unpublished manuscript).

Laplanche, François. *L'Écriture, le sacré et l'histoire: Érudits et politiques protestants devant la Bible en France au XVIIe siècle*. Amsterdam: APA-Holland University Press, 1986.

Laqueur, Thomas. "Bodies, Details, and the Humanitarian Narrative." In *The New Cultural History* ed. Lynn Hunt, 176–204. Berkeley: University of California Press, 1989.

———. "Mourning, Pity, and the Work of Narrative in the Making of 'Humanity.'" In *Humanitarianism and Suffering: The Mobilization of Empathy*, ed. Richard Ashby Wilson and Richard B. Brown, 31–57. Cambridge: Cambridge University Press, 2011.

Laugaa, Maurice. *Lectures de Mme de Lafayette*. Paris: Armand Colin, 1971.

Lavocat, Françoise, ed. *Le mariage et la loi dans la fiction narrative avant 1800*. Louvain: Peeters, 2014.

Lecler, Joseph. *Histoire de la tolérance au siècle de la Réforme*. Paris: Aubier, 1955.

Leget, Carlo, Chris Gastmans, and Marian Verkerk, eds. *Care, Compassion and Recognition: An Ethical Discussion*. Louvain: Peeters, 2011.

Lennon, Thomas M. *Reading Bayle*. Toronto: University of Toronto Press, 1999.

Lessard, Rénald. *Se soigner au Canada, aux XVIIe et XVIIIe siècles*. Québec: Musée Canadien des Civilizations, 1989.

Lestringant, Frank. *Lire "Les Tragiques" d'Agrippa d'Aubigné*. Paris: Garnier, 2013.

Linfield, Susie. *The Cruel Radiance: Photography and Political Violence*. Chicago: University of Chicago Press, 2010.

Long, Kathleen Perry. "Child in the Water: The Spectacle of Violence in Théodore Agrippa d'Aubigné's *Les Tragiques*." In "Representations of Trauma in French and Francophone Literature," ed. Nicole Semek and Zahi Zalloua. Special issue, *Dalhousie French Studies* 81 (Winter 2007): 155–65.

———. "Improper Perspective: Anamorphosis in d'Aubigné's Les Tragiques." *Mediaevalia: An Interdisciplinary Journal of Medieval Studies Worldwide* 22 (1999): 103–26.

———. "The Representation of Violence in the Works of Théodore Agrippa d'Aubigné." In *Repossessions: Psychoanalysis and the Phantasms of Early Modern Culture*, ed. Timothy Murray and Alan K. Smith, 142–67. Minneapolis: University of Minnesota Press, 1998.

Love, Heather. *Feeling Backward: Loss and the Politics of Queer History*. Cambridge: Harvard University Press, 2007.

Luria, Keith P. *Sacred Boundaries: Religious Coexistence and Conflict in Early Modern France.* Washington, D.C.: Catholic University of America Press, 2005.

Lyons, John D. *Kingdom of Disorder: The Theory of Tragedy in Classical France.* West Lafayette: Purdue University Press, 1999.

———. *The Phantom of Chance: From Fortune to Randomness in Seventeenth-Century French Literature.* Edinburgh: Edinburgh University Press, 2011.

———. "1678: The Emergence of the Novel." In *A New History of French Literature*, ed. Denis Hollier, 347–54. Cambridge: Harvard University Press, 1989.

MacCormack, Sabine. *The Shadows of Poetry: Vergil in the Mind of Augustine.* Berkeley: University of California Press, 1998.

Mack, Peter. *Reading and Rhetoric in Montaigne and Shakespeare.* London: Bloomsbury, 2010.

———. *Renaissance Argument: Valla and Agricola in the Traditions of Rhetoric and Dialectic.* Leiden: Brill, 1993.

Mackenzie, Catriona, and Natalie Stoljar. "Introduction: Autonomy Refigured." In *Relational Autonomy: Feminist Perspectives on Autonomy, Agency, and the Social Self,* ed. Catriona Mackenzie and Natalie Stoljar, 3–31. New York: Oxford University Press, 2000.

Marshall, John. *John Locke, Toleration and Early Enlightenment Culture.* Cambridge: Cambridge University Press, 2006.

Maslan, Susan. "Melancholy Racine: Benjamin's *Trauerspiel* and Literary Jews." In "Walter Benjamin's Hypothetical French *Trauerspiel,*" ed. Hall Bjornstad and Katherine Ibbett. Special issue, *Yale French Studies* 124 (2013): 64–78.

Matthieu-Castellani, Gisèle. "La scène judiciaire dans *Les Tragiques.*" In "*Les Tragiques* d'Agrippa d'Aubigné: Actes de la journée d'étude Agrippa d'Aubigné," ed. Françoise Charpentier. Special issue, *Cahiers Textuels* 9 (1991): 91–102.

Maurens, Jacques. *La tragédie sans tragique: Le néo-stoïcisme dans l'œuvre de Pierre Corneille.* Paris: Armand Colin, 1966.

Maynard, Katherine. "Writing Martyrdom: Agrippa d'Aubigné's Reconstruction of Sixteenth-Century Martyrology." *Renaissance and Reformation* 30.3 (2007): 29–50.

Mazouer, Charles. "Ce que tragédie et tragique veulent dire dans les écrits théoriques du XVIe siècle." *Revue d'histoire littéraire de la France* 109 (2009): 71–84.

McClure, Ellen. "Cartesian Modernity and the *Princesse de Clèves.*" *Seventeenth-Century French Studies* 29 (2007): 73–80.

———. "Neo-Stoicism and the Spectator in Corneille's *Horace.*" *EMF: Studies in Early Modern France* 13 (2010): 144–58.

McClure, Kirstie M. "Difference, Diversity, and the Limits of Toleration." *Political Theory* 18.3 (1990): 361–91.

McHugh, Tim. *Hospital Politics in Seventeenth-Century France: The Crown, Urban Elites and the Poor.* Aldershot: Ashgate, 2007.

McNamer, Sarah. *Affective Meditation and the Invention of Medieval Compassion.* Philadelphia: University of Pennsylvania Press, 2010.

———. "The Literariness of Literature and the History of Emotion." In "Emotions," ed. Katharine Ann Jensen and Miriam L. Wallace. Special issue, *PMLA* 130.5 (October 2015): 1433–42.

McNulty, Tracy. *The Hostess: Hospitality, Femininity, and the Expropriation of Identity.* Minneapolis: University of Minnesota Press, 2006.

Méchoulan, Éric. "L'ami lecteur: Sentiment littéraire et lien social au XVIIe siècle." In *Les liens humains dans la littérature (XVIe–XVIIe siècles)*, ed. Julia Chamard-Bergeron, Philippe Desan, and Thomas Pavel, 263–76. Paris: Classiques Garnier, 2012.

———. "La douceur du politique." In *Le doux aux XVIe et XVIIe siècles: Écriture, esthétique, politique, spiritualité*, ed. Marie-Hélène Prat et Pierre Servet, 221–37. Lyon: Université Jean-Moulin 3, 2003.

———. *Lire avec soin: Amitié, justice et médias*. Lyon: ENS Éditions, 2017.

———. "Revenge and Poetic Justice in Classical France." *SubStance* 35:1 (2006): 20–51.

Merlin-Kajman, Hélène. *L'absolutisme dans les lettres et la théorie des deux corps*. Paris: Honoré Champion, 2000.

———. "Corneille, une politique de l'image scénique." In "Présences de Corneille," ed. Charles Mazouer. Special issue, *Œuvres et critiques* 30.2 (2005): 133–48.

———. *Public et littérature en France au XVIIe siècle*. Paris: Les Belles Lettres, 1994.

———. "Sentir, ressentir: Emotion privée, langage public." In "Les émotions publiques et leurs langages à l'âge classique," ed. Hélène Merlin-Kajman. Special issue, *Littératures classiques* 68 (2009): 335–54.

Miller, Nancy K. "Emphasis Added: Plots and Plausibilities in Women's Fiction." *PMLA* 96.1 (1981): 36–48.

———. "Tender Economies: Mme de Villedieu and the Costs of Indifference." *L'Esprit créateur* 23.2 (1983): 80–93.

Mondoux, Maria, RHSJ. *L'Hôtel-Dieu, premier hôpital de Montréal, 1642–1763*. Montreal: Joseph Carbonneau, 1942.

Monroe, Kristen. *The Hand of Compassion: Portraits of Moral Choice During the Holocaust*. Princeton: Princeton University Press, 2004.

Montagu, Jennifer. *The Expression of the Passions: The Origin and Influence of Charles Le Brun's Conférence sur l'expression générale et particulière*. New Haven: Yale University Press, 1994.

Moriarty, Michael. *Disguised Vices: Theories of Virtue in Early Modern French Thought*. Oxford: Oxford University Press, 2011.

———. *Fallen Nature, Fallen Selves: Early Modern French Thought II*. Oxford: Oxford University Press, 2006.

———. "Grace and Religious Belief in Pascal." In *The Cambridge Companion to Pascal*, ed. Nicholas Hammond, 144–61. Cambridge: Cambridge University Press, 2003.

Morrison, Karl F. *"I am You": The Hermeneutics of Empathy in Western Literature, Theology, and Art*. Princeton: Princeton University Press, 1988.

Mours, Samuel. *Le protestantisme en France au XVIIe siècle (1598–1685)*. Paris: Librarie Protestante, 1967.

Moyn, Samuel. *Christian Human Rights*. Philadelphia: University of Pennsylvania Press, 2015.

———. *Human Rights and the Uses of History*. New York: Verso, 2014.

Mullaney, Steven. *The Reformation of Emotions in the Age of Shakespeare*. Chicago: University of Chicago Press, 2015.

Nakam, Géralde. "Une source des *Tragiques*: *L'Histoire memorable de la ville de Sancerre* de Jean de Léry." *Bibliothèque d'humanisme et renaissance* 33.1 (1971): 177–82.

Nancy, Jean-Luc. *Being Singular Plural*, trans. Robert Richardson and Anne O'Byrne. Stanford: Stanford University Press, 2000.

Nedelsky, Jennifer. "Reconceiving Autonomy: Sources, Thoughts and Possibilities." *Yale Journal of Law and Feminism* 1: 7 (1989): 7–36.

Neff, Kristin. *Self-Compassion: The Proven Power of Being Kind to Yourself*. New York: William Morrow, 2001.

Nelson, Brian. *The Cambridge Introduction to French Literature*. Cambridge: Cambridge University Press, 2015.

Norman, Larry F. *The Shock of the Ancient: Literature and History in Early Modern France*. Chicago: University of Chicago Press, 2011.

Nussbaum, Martha. *The Fragility of Goodness: Luck and Ethics in Greek Tragedy and Philosophy*. Cambridge: Cambridge University Press, 1986.

———. *Political Emotions: Why Love Matters for Justice*. Cambridge: Harvard University Press, 2013.

———. *Upheavals of Thought: The Intelligence of Emotions*. Cambridge: Cambridge University Press, 2001.

O'Brien, John. "Seeing the Dead: The Gaze as Commemoration." *Montaigne Studies* 4 (1992): 97–110.

Olasky, Marvin. *Renewing American Compassion: A Citizen's Guide*. Foreword by Newt Gingrich. New York: Free Press, 1996.

———. *The Tragedy of American Compassion*. Washington, D.C.: Regnery Gateway, 1992.

Oliver, Jennifer. "Au milieu d'un tel et si piteux naufrage: The Dynamics of Shipwreck in Renaissance France (1498–1616)." D.Phil. thesis, University of Oxford, 2014.

O'Malley, John W., ed. *The Jesuits: Cultures, Sciences and Arts, 1540–1773*. Toronto: University of Toronto Press, 1999.

Orcibal, Jean. *La genèse d'Esther et d'Athalie*. Paris: Vrin, 1950.

———. *Louis XIV et les protestants*. Paris: Vrin, 1951.

Owen, David. *A Future That Will Work: Competitiveness and Compassion*. Harmondsworth: Penguin, 1984.

Paige, Nicholas. *Before Fiction: The Ancien Régime of the Novel*. Philadelphia: University of Pennsylvania Press, 2011.

———. *Being Interior: Autobiography and the Contradictions of Modernity in Seventeenth-Century France*. Philadelphia: University of Pennsylvania Press, 2001.

———. "Lafayette's Impossible Princess: On (Not) Making Literary History." In "Literary Criticism for the Twenty-First Century," ed. Jonathan Culler and Cathy Caruth. Special issue, *PMLA* 125.4 (2010): 1061–77.

Paperman, Patricia. *Care et sentiments*. Paris: Presses Universitaires de France, 2013.

Paperman, Patricia, and Sandra Laugier, eds. *Le souci des autres: Éthique et politique du care*. Paris: Éditions de l'EHESS, 2006.

Parish, Richard. *Catholic Particularity in Seventeenth-Century French Writers: Christianity Is Strange*. Oxford: Oxford University Press, 2011.

Paster, Gail Kern, Katherine Rowe, and Mary Floyd-Wilson, eds. *Reading the Early Modern Passions: Essays in the Cultural History of Emotion*. Philadelphia: University of Pennsylvania Press, 2004.

Pedwell, Carolyn. *Affective Relations: The Transnational Politics of Empathy*. New York: Palgrave, 2014.

Petit, Emmanuel. *L'économie du care*. Paris: Presses Universitaires de France, 2013.

Petris, Loris. "Faith and Religious Policy in Michel de l'Hôpital's Civic Evangelism." In *The Adventure of Religious Pluralism in Early Modern France*, ed. Keith Cameron, Mark Greengrass, and Penny Roberts, 129–42. Bern: Peter Lang, 2000.

Phillips, Henry. *Church and Culture in Seventeenth-Century France*. Cambridge: Cambridge University Press, 2002.

———. "Descartes and the Dramatic Experience." *French Studies* 39 (1985): 408–22.

Picard, Raymond, ed. *Nouveau corpus raciniarum: Recueil, inventaire des textes et documents du XVIIe siècle concernant Jean Racine*. Paris: Éditions du Centre National de la Recherche Scientifique, 1976.

Piéjus, Anne. *Le théâtre des demoiselles: Tragédie et musique à Saint-Cyr à la fin du grand siècle.* Paris: Société Française de Musicologie, 2000.

Pinch, Adela. *Strange Fits of Passion: Epistemologies of Emotion, Hume to Austen.* Stanford: Stanford University Press, 1997.

Pincus, Steven. *1688: The First Modern Revolution.* New Haven: Yale University Press, 2009.

Pineaux, Jacques. *La poésie des protestants de langue française, 1559–1590.* Paris: Klincksieck, 1971.

Pinker, Steven. *The Better Angels of Our Nature: Why Violence Has Declined.* New York: Penguin, 2011.

Pintard, René, and Hubert Carrier. "Ressouvenirs de la Saint-Barthélemy au XVIIe siècle." *Revue d'histoire littéraire de la France* 73.5 (1973): 819–28.

Pointon, Marcia. *Brilliant Effects: A Cultural History of Gem Stones and Jewellery.* New Haven: Yale University Press, 2009.

Pot, Olivier. "Les tableaux des *Tragiques* ou le paradoxe de l'image." In *Poétiques d'Aubigné: Actes du colloque de Genève mai 1996,* ed. Olivier Pot, 103–34. Geneva: Droz, 1999.

Povinelli, Elizabeth. *Economies of Abandonment: Social Belonging and Endurance in Late Liberalism.* Durham: Duke University Press, 2011.

———. *The Empire of Love: Toward a Theory of Intimacy, Genealogy, and Carnality.* Durham: Duke University Press, 2006.

Probyn, Elspeth. "Writing Shame." In *The Affect Theory Reader,* ed. Melissa Gregg and Gregory J. Seigworth, 71–90. Durham: Duke University Press, 2009.

Quéniart, Jean. *La Révocation de l'Édit de Nantes: Protestants et catholiques en France de 1598 à 1685.* Paris: Desclée de Brouwer, 1985.

Quignard, Pascal. "Traité sur Esprit." Introduction to Jacques Esprit, *La fausseté des vertus humaines,* 9–66. Paris: Aubier, 1996.

Quint, David. *Epic and Empire: Politics and Generic Form from Virgil to Milton.* Princeton: Princeton University Press, 1993.

———. *Montaigne and the Quality of Mercy.* Princeton: Princeton University Press, 1998.

Rancière, Jacques. *The Emancipated Spectator,* trans. Gregory Elliott. London: Verso, 2009.

Rapley, Elizabeth. *The Dévotes: Women and the Church in Seventeenth-Century France.* Kingston, Ontario: McGill-Queen's University Press, 1990.

Rawls, John. *Political Liberalism.* New York: Columbia University Press, 1992.

Reddy, William M. *The Navigation of Feeling: A Framework for the History of Emotions.* Cambridge: Cambridge University Press, 2001.

Regosin, Richard. *The Poetry of Inspiration: Agrippa d'Aubigné's Les Tragiques.* Chapel Hill: University of North Carolina Press, 1970.

Reguig-Naya, Delphine. *Le corps des idées: Pensées et poétiques du langage dans l'augustinisme de Port-Royal.* Paris: Honoré Champion, 2007.

Rendall, Steven. *Distinguo: Reading Montaigne Differently.* Oxford: Oxford University Press, 1992.

Revault d'Allonnes, Myriam. *L'homme compassionnel.* Paris: Seuil, 2008.

Richard, Michel. *La république compassionelle.* Paris: Grasset, 2006.

Ricot, Jacques. *Du bon usage de la compassion.* Paris: Presses Universitaires de France, 2013.

Rifkin, Jeremy. *The Empathic Civilization: The Race to Global Consciousness in a World in Crisis.* New York: Penguin, 2009.

Rigolot, François. "Tolérance et condescendance dans la littérature française du XVIe siècle." *Bibliothèque d'Humanisme et Renaissance* 62.1 (2000): 25–47.

Risse, Mathias. *On Global Justice.* Princeton: Princeton University Press, 2012.

Robb, John. "'Meaningless Violence' and the Lived Body: The Huron-Jesuit Collision of World Orders." In *Past Bodies: Body-Centred Research in Archaeology*, ed. Dusan Borić and John Robb, 89–99. Oxford: Oxbow Books, 2008.

Robbins, Bruce. "Telescopic Philanthrophy: Professionalism and Responsibility in *Bleak House*." In *Nation and Narration*, ed. Homi K. Bhabha, 213–30. New York: Routledge, 1990.

Rorty, Richard. "Human Rights, Rationality, and Sentimentality." In *On Human Rights: The Oxford Amnesty Lectures 1993*, ed. Stephen Shute and Susan Hurley, 111–34. New York: Basic Books, 1993.

———. "On Ethnocentrism: A Reply to Clifford Geertz." *Michigan Quarterly Review* 25 (1986): 525–34.

Rosenwein, Barbara H. *Emotional Communities in the Early Middle Ages*. Ithaca: Cornell University Press, 2006.

———. *Generations of Feeling: A History of Emotions, 600–1700*. Cambridge: Cambridge University Press, 2016.

———. "Worrying About Emotions in History." *American Historical Review* 107.3 (2002): 821–45.

Roubine, Jean-Jacques. "La stratégie des larmes au XVIIe siècle." *Littérature* 9 (1973): 56–73.

Rousseau, François. *La croix et le scalpel: Histoire des Augustines et de l'Hôtel-Dieu de Québec, 1639–1989*. 2 vols. Sillery, Québec: Septentrion, 1989–94.

Rubidge, Bradley. "Catharsis Through Admiration: Corneille, Le Moyne, and the Social Uses of Emotion." *Modern Philology* 95.3 (1998): 316–33.

Sanyal, Debarati. "Calais's 'Jungle': Refugees, Biopolitics, and the Arts of Resistance." *Representations* 139 (summer 2017): 1–33.

Schachter, Marc. "'Qu'est-ce que la critique?' La Boétie, Montaigne, Foucault." *Montaigne After Theory / Theory After Montaigne*, ed. Zahi Zalloua, 122–41. Seattle: University of Washington Press, 2009.

Schaefer, David Lewis. *The Political Philosophy of Montaigne*. Ithaca: Cornell University Press, 1990.

Scheer, Monique. "Are Emotions a Kind of Practice (and Is That What Makes Them Have a History)? A Bourdieuian Approach to Understanding Emotion." *History and Theory* 51 (2012): 193–220.

Schmitt, Charles B. *Aristotle and the Renaissance*. Cambridge: Harvard University Press, 1983.

Seifert, Lewis. *Manning the Margins: Masculinity and Writing in Seventeenth-Century France*. Ann Arbor: University of Michigan Press, 2009.

Sellier, Philippe. *Port Royal et la littérature*. 2 vols. Paris: Honoré Champion, 1999.

Shagan, Ethan H. *The Rule of Moderation: Violence, Religion and the Politics of Restraint in Early Modern England*. Cambridge: Cambridge University Press, 2011.

Shifflett, Andrew. "'How Many Virtues Must I Hate': Katherine Philips and the Politics of Clemency." *Studies in Philology* 94.1(1997): 103–35.

Shuger, Debra Keller. *The Renaissance Bible: Scholarship, Sacrifice, and Subjectivity*. Berkeley: University of California Press, 1994.

Singer, Peter. "Famine, Affluence, and Morality." *Philosophy and Public Affairs* 1.3 (1972): 229–43.

Skinner, Quentin. "Paradiastole: Redescribing the Vices as Virtues." In *Renaissance Figures of Speech*, ed. Sylvia Adamson, Gavin Alexander, and Katrin Ettenhuber, 149–66. Cambridge: Cambridge University Press, 2007.

———. *Visions of Politics*. 3 vols. Cambridge: Cambridge University Press, 2002.

Smith, Bruce R. "Premodern Sexualities." *PMLA* 115 (2000): 318–29.

Soni, Vivasvan. *Mourning Happiness: Narrative and the Politics of Modernity.* Ithaca: Cornell University Press, 2010.

Sontag, Susan. *Regarding the Pain of Others.* London: Hamish Hamilton, 2003.

Spelman, Elizabeth V. *Fruits of Sorrow: Framing Our Attention to Suffering.* Boston: Beacon Press, 1997.

Staines, John. "Compassion in the Public Sphere of Milton and King Charles." In *Reading the Early Modern Passions: Essays in the Cultural History of Emotion*, ed. Gail Kern Paster, Katherine Rowe, and Mary Floyd-Wilson, 89–110. Philadelphia: University of Pennsylvania Press, 2004.

Stanton, Domna. "The Ideal of 'Repos' in Seventeenth-Century French Literature." *L'esprit créateur* 15 (1975): 79–104.

Starobinski, Jean. *Montaigne in Motion*, trans. Arthur Goldhammer. Chicago: University of Chicago Press, 1985.

Steenbergh, Kristine. "Mollified Hearts and Enlarged Bowels: Practicing Compassion in Reformation England." In *Compassion in Early Modern Europe: A Cultural History*, ed. Katherine Ibbett and Kristine Steenbergh. Unpublished manuscript.

Stevenson, Lisa. *Life Beside Itself: Imagining Care in the Canadian Arctic.* Berkeley: University of California Press, 2014.

Taithe, Bertrand. "'Cold Compassion in the Faces of Horrors?' Pity, Compassion and the Making of Humanitarian Protocols." In *Medicine, Emotion and Disease, 1700–1950*, ed. Fay Bound Alberti, 79–99. New York: Palgrave, 2006.

Tarlow, Sarah. "The Archaeology of Emotion and Affect." *Annual Review of Anthropology* 41 (2012): 169–85.

Taylor, Ruth. "War as Metaphor in *La Princesse de Montpensier*." *Forum for Modern Language Studies* 20.4 (1984): 323–32.

Taveneaux, René. *Le catholicisme dans la France classique, 1610–1715.* 2 vols. Paris: S.E.D.E.S., 1980.

Terada, Rei. *Feeling in Theory: Emotion After the "Death of the Subject."* Cambridge: Harvard University Press, 2003.

Terpstra, Nicolas. *Religious Refugees in the Early Modern World: An Alternative History of the Reformation.* Cambridge: Cambridge University Press, 2015.

Ticktin, Miriam. *Casualties of Care: Immigration and the Politics of Humanitarianism in France.* Berkeley: University of California Press, 2011.

True, Micah. *Masters and Students: Jesuit Mission Ethnography in Seventeenth-Century New France.* Kingston, Ontario: McGill-Queen's University Press, 2015.

Usher, Phillip John. *Epic Arts in Renaissance France.* Oxford: Oxford University Press, 2014.

Vinaver, Eugène, ed. *Racine: Principes de la tragédie en marge de la Poétique d'Aristote.* Manchester: University of Manchester Press, 1944.

Wahl, Elizabeth Susan. *Invisible Relations: Representations of Female Intimacy in the Age of Enlightenment.* Stanford: Stanford University Press, 1999.

Walfard, Adrien. "Justice et passions tragiques: Lectures d'Aristote aux XVIe et XVIIe siècles." *Poétique* 155 (2008): 259–81.

Walsham, Alexandra. *Charitable Hatred: Tolerance and Intolerance in England, 1500–1700.* Manchester: Manchester University Press, 2006.

Watt, Jeffrey R. *The Making of Modern Marriage: Matrimonial Control and the Rise of Sentiment in Neuchâtel, 1550–1800.* Ithaca: Cornell University Press, 1992.

Weinberg, Bernard. *A History of Literary Criticism in the Italian Renaissance.* 2 vols. Chicago: University of Chicago Press, 1961.

Weiner, Joshua J., and Damon Young. "Introduction: Queer Bonds." In "Queer Bonds," ed. Joshua J. Weiner and Damon Young. Special issue, *GLQ: A Journal of Lesbian and Gay Studies* 17: 2–3 (2011): 223–41.

Wells, Charlotte C. *Law and Citizenship in Early Modern France.* Baltimore: Johns Hopkins University Press, 1995.

Whelan, Ruth. The *Anatomy of Superstition: A Study of the Historical Theory and Practice of Pierre Bayle.* Oxford: SVEC, 1989.

Whittington, Leah. *Renaissance Suppliants: Poetry, Antiquity, Reconciliation.* Oxford: Oxford University Press, 2016.

———. "Shakespeare's Virgil: Empathy and *The Tempest.*" In *Shakespeare and Renaissance Ethics,* ed. John Cox and Patrick Gray, 98–120. Cambridge: Cambridge University Press, 2014.

Wilkin, Rebecca. *Women, Imagination and the Search for Truth in Early Modern France.* Aldershot: Ashgate, 2008.

Williams, Wes. *Monsters and Their Meanings in Early Modern Culture: Mighty Magic.* Oxford: Oxford University Press, 2011.

Wingrove, Elizabeth. "Philoctetes in the Bastille." *Cultural Critique* 74 (2010): 65–80.

Woodward, Kathleen. *Statistical Panic: Cultural Politics and Poetics of the Emotions.* Durham: Duke University Press, 2009.

Wuthnow, Robert. *Acts of Compassion: Caring for Others and Helping Ourselves.* Princeton: Princeton University Press, 1991.

Index

Acknowledgments

At various points during this project, people have asked me what the difference is between friendship and compassion, or kindness and compassion. The easiest answer is that this section is about friendship and kindness, and the rest of the book about compassion. I hope the ways in which these qualities are (mostly) different have become apparent throughout the preceding pages.

This project first troubled me in the form of a question Elizabeth Honig asked me years ago: Is there a difference between charity and compassion? I began to think that through, tentatively, at the University of Michigan, where conversations with wonderful colleagues fostered the earliest formulations of this book; my thanks to Ross Chambers, George Hoffmann, Mika Lavaque-Manty, Peggy McCracken, and Elizabeth Wingrove. I hope it's obvious to David Caron that I went on thinking with him even after I left. In the same years, Rebecca Wilkin made a hugely helpful intervention in a draft of an application to Michigan's Institute for the Humanities, where I eventually ended up finishing my first book but also made some forays into this one. From that year I owe much to Danny Herwitz, Elizabeth Ben-Yishai, Tirtza Even, Andrew Herscher, Scott Spector, Johannes von Moltke, and Yan Haiping. Around that time the late and sorely missed Amy Wygant published the first iteration of the project (I changed my mind about a lot of it, later, but it was a good start). Some of Chapter 2 is derived from that article, published as "Pity, Compassion, Commiseration: Theories of Theatrical Relatedness," *Seventeenth-Century French Studies* 30.2 (2008): 196–208, available online at http://www.tandfonline.com/doi/abs/10.1179/175226908X372350. My thanks to the current editor of the journal, Richard Scholar, and to Taylor and Francis for granting permission for the reuse of this material. A very few pages in Chapter 5 also draw on material published in "Being Moved: Louis XIV's Triumphant Tenderness and the Revocation of Nantes," *Exemplaria* 26.1 (2014): 16–38, available in open access under a Creative Commons license

(thanks to the generosity of UCL) at http://www.tandfonline.com/doi/full/10
.1179/1041257313Z.00000000041.

Coming to London brought me a whole new set of interlocutors. Thanks,
I *think*, to John O'Brien, who asked a question that made it take twice as long
to finish the book. My colleagues at UCL have helped generously in ways
both intellectual and practical—I'm grateful to all of them for showing me the
ropes as a bemused returnee, and for shouldering various burdens during my
periods of leave. The students I have taught at UCL have also pushed my
thinking about historical emotion in all kinds of ways; let me signal especially
Rupinder Kaur's remarkable work on joy. In the final stages of writing I was
bolstered by the many colleagues across the university working on and with
refugees; my thanks to Elena Fiddian-Qasmiyeh for her energizing leadership
on this front. By the time this book appears I will be getting to grips with a
new job in Oxford, and I look forward to the new conversations there, too.

But the book came into being chiefly thanks to the generosity of the Radcliffe Institute for Advanced Studies at Harvard University, where I found the
time both to be excited about it and to sit down and write. I'm enormously
grateful to all the staff of the institute, to Judy Vichniac, and especially to my
fellow fellows. Particular thanks go to Hectór Carrillo, Glenn Cohen, Lydia
Diamond, Bryna Goodman, Lynn Hudson, Tsitsi Jaji, David Levine, Margot
Livesey, Rajesh Parameswaran, Renée Poznanski, Jane Rhodes, Doug Rogers,
Hilary Schor, Henry Turner, and Rebecca Walkowitz, all of whom read and
responded generously to talks or drafts, or came out for dinner so I could
think about something else instead, and to Feryal Ozel, whose account of
black holes gave me the title for the book. Patricia Owens and Daisy Hay and
their families have become an ever-continuing Radcliffe in my life, which is
all the better for it. Lastly, great gratitude to my research assistant Gökcan
Demirkazik, who was a wonder, and to Sharon Bromberg-Lim for introduc-
ing us.

Over the many years the book has been percolating, I've been lucky to
think it through in a lot of places with generous inviters and interlocutors. My
thanks to colleagues at Michigan State, Brown, Lille, King's College London,
Oxford, Indiana, Virginia, the University of Illinois at Chicago, Harvard's
seminar on Women and Culture in the Early Modern World, Melbourne,
Adelaide, the Avignon festival, the University of Amsterdam, and at UC
Berkeley, and to the wonderful graduate students at Rutgers and Tsinghua
University, as well as colleagues at various conferences. I can't remember all
the questions, but I know that the book was shaped by them. At a conference

in Rouen a Frenchman told me I was wrong, and eventually I came to see that he was mostly right, so I'm grateful to him although I don't remember his name; stemming from that same conference, my thanks go also to Myriam Dufour-Maître for publishing an essay on Corneille and friendship which provided another forum to think through related ideas in their earliest stages. I was happy to discuss Chapter 6 with so very many smart people at Kristine Steenbergh's compassion conference at VU Amsterdam, and even happier to continue working with Kristine afterward: she is the model of the best sort of compassionate practice, personally and professionally. And it was a joy to work some of this out as a guest of the Australian Research Council's Centre for the History of the Emotions; at Melbourne Stephanie Trigg, Grace Moore, and Charles Zika were wonderful hosts, Tom Ford reminded me about Mr T, who has stayed with me ever since, and Damian Whitty got me to think about compassionate distance in new ways. In Perth, Susan Broomhall asked for a short piece on fellow-feeling (now in her volume *Early Modern Emotions* with Routledge) which helped me think about some of the cross-national patterns of my interests. All these talks and subsequent conversations shaped (and delayed) the final product. I'm grateful to all who invited me, and especially to those whose questions or references or wrinkled brows helped me clarify some of my arguments. Throughout all these travels, my parents and extended family have inquired about my progress and whereabouts with a forbearance for which I thank them.

For other sorts of help ranging from library advice to larger provocations, my thanks go to Penelope Anderson, Oliver Arnold, Hall Bjornstad, Déborah Blocker, Chris Braider, Chris Brooke, Terence Cave, Tim Chesters, Tom Conley, Julie Cooper, Emma Gilby, Claire Goldstein, Sylvaine Guyot, Tim Hampton, Pete Hobbs, Chloe Hogg, Katja Haustein, Ann Jefferson, Victoria Kahn, John Lyons, Susan Maslan, Jann Matlock, Andrew McGettigan, Karen Newman, Jenny Oliver, Nicholas Paige, Jeff Peters, Josephine Quinn, Julie Robert, Debarati Sanyal, Richard Scholar, Lewis Seifert, John Staines, Lisa Stevenson, Kate Tunstall, Sonia Velazquez, Alain Viala, and Wes Williams. I'm grateful, too, to librarians at the British Library, the Bibliothèque nationale de France, the Mazarine, the Taylorian, Worcester College Library, and in Montreal at the BAnQ, the Bibliothèque de la Compagnie de Jésus, the Osler Library of the History of Medicine, and especially the archives of the Religieuses hospitalières de Saint Joseph.

I'm particularly grateful to the generous friends who read chapters or proposals at various stages, including incoherent ones: Jane Gilbert, Eric Langley,

Ellen McClure, Isabelle Moreau, Michael Moriarty, Jane Newman, Jeff Peters, Jonathan Sheehan, and Leah Whittington. Leah's *Renaissance Suppliants* came out just in time for me to rethink some of Chapter 5 in its wake, and I look forward to it making many more waves. Some extraordinarily generous people read the whole manuscript, sometimes even more than once: huge thanks to Andrea Frisch for her urging of listlessness and for her good cheer along the way, to Marc Schachter for a very thorough reading of the first draft, and to Éric Méchoulan. My thanks, too, to the two readers for the press who helped me bolster my arguments and pushed me to some new ones. Finally, huge thanks to the people at Penn, especially Jerry Singerman for taking me on and for nurturing the field of early modern studies with such care, Hannah Blake for scooping up my questions patiently, and Noreen O'Connor-Abel for seeing the process through so ably.

I had a lot of fun writing this largely gloomy book, and that stems partly from the many wonderful conversations noted above. But most of it is due to Éric, whose curiosity and care have made me see so many things in new ways. My thanks and love to him, always.